TRADE AND FINANCE IN PORTUGUESE INDIA

XCHR Studies Series No. 5

1. João de Barros: Portuguese Humanist and Historian of Asia
   C.R. Boxer
2. Coastal Western India : Studies from the Portuguese Records
   M.N. Pearson
3. The Black Legend of Portuguese India
   Diogo do Couto, His Contemporaries and the Soldado Pratico: A Contribution to the Study of Political Corruption in the Empires of Early Modern Europe.
   George Davison Winius
4. Health and Hygiene in Colonial Goa, 1510-1961.
   Fatima da Silva Gracias
5. Trade and Finance in Portuguese India: A Study of the Portuguese Country Trade 1770-1840
   Celsa Pinto

ABOUT THE AUTHOR

DR. CELSA PINTO was born in Karachi, Pakistan, where she did most of her schooling, preparing for the Senior Cambridge Examination. She was awarded the M.A. degree (First Class) by the University of Bombay (1975) and the Ph. D. degree by the Goa University (1992). She was recipient of the Calouste Gulbenkian Foundation Scholarship that enabled her to conduct archival research in Europe in 1991. She has published research papers to her credit and has participated in historical conferences and seminars. She is currently teaching at S. P. Chowgule College, Goa.

XCHR Studies Series No. 5

TRADE AND FINANCE IN PORTUGUESE INDIA

A study of the Portuguese Country Trade 1770-1840

CELSA PINTO
S.P. Chowgule College
Goa

Foreword by
TEOTONIO R. de SOUZA
Director
Xavier Centre of Historical Research
Goa

CONCEPT PUBLISHING COMPANY, NEW DELHI-110059

ISBN 81-7022-507-8

First Published 1994

Published and Printed by
Ashok Kumar Mittal
Concept Publishing Company
A/15-16, Commercial Block, Mohan Garden
New Delhi-110059 (India)

Lasertypeset by
Printing Express
H-13, Bali Nagar
New Delhi-110015

To my mother

HELENA GOMES PINTO

FOREWORD

It is a matter of legitimate pride for the young Institute like the Xavier Centre of Historical Research to have yet another publication in its *XCHR Studies Series* (No.5) from its own young scholar. In the past the Xavier Centre of Historical Research had to depend exclusively on outside scholars to sustain this series of its publications. We wish that the soundness of research manifested in Dr. Celsa Pinto's *Trade and Finance in Portuguese India : A Study of the Portuguese Country Trade, 1770-1840* will be sustained by future contributions to this series.

The findings of Dr. Celsa Pinto are based on very extensive and scattered archival evidence. This feature with the quantified presentation of the data and a critical bibliographical essay, has definitely made this a source-book for many who may pursue studies in this area of Indo-Portuguese or trade history of this part of the subcontinent. This young scholar has provided an exemplary ability and courage to seek and utilise the data in support of her arguments questioning some prevailing stereotypes in the history of the Portuguese presence in Asia, or rather about the Asian presence and contribution to the Portuguese *Estado da India* during the period covered by the study.

2nd August, 1993
Xavier Centre of Historical Research

Teotonio R. de Souza
Director

PREFACE

Studies on Indian maritime history have come a long way since the times when Indian developments were viewed as extensions of European activity in the Indian Ocean region. We welcome this liberation from Euro-centredness. Though we still have studies devoted to the experience of European companies in India and often assume that this kind of history is genuine and unbiased Indian history, most scholars of to-day have begun to scrupulously keep away from any narrow approach and the viewing of events from an all-Europe standpoint.

Indo-Portuguese historiography is still plagued with biases. It has miles to go in its march towards perfection. One such bias exhibits itself in the fact that studies abound on the official sixteenth century Lisbon trade. Since the seventeenth century the *Carreira da India* was no longer a profitable enterprise worthy of note. Most Indo-Portuguese historiographers tend to either totally ignore or are ignorant of the existence of the privately-operated trade of the *Estado* from the seventeenth to the nineteenth centuries which drew its sustenance from the interport trade of Asia. Although several existing studies examine the intra-Asian commerce especially in the sixteenth century they do so to the extent to which it was beneficial to Lisbon. Little or no interest is shown in the benefits that this trade had for the *Estado da India* and its natives.

It has also been the tendency to examine the maritime history of India with the arrival of the Portuguese in the Indian Ocean waters, to describe their subsequent activities in the region and at times to examine the Indian response to such activities. A more meaningful approach would be to consider Indian activities as fundamental during the so-called 'European presence' and to proceed towards analysing the European response to such activities and developments.

Luxury items occupy the centre-stage in most studies on the commercial system of Portuguese Asia. Slaves, ivory, bullion and spices are still in the focus of attention of most historians. Trade in essentials such as rice, coconuts and timber is dismissed as the 'trade in the trifling'. If consumer items figure in recent studies they pass off as incidentals

In the present study an attempt is made to escape from the clutches of the aforesaid biases and stereotypes.

It is a study of the involvement of Portuguese India in the interport trade of Asia or in the so-called 'country trade', in the late eighteenth - early nineteenth centuries. The country trade during this period became increasingly private.

There is some obscurity about the origin of the expression 'country trade'. Applied first to the coastal trade of India and its nearby ports, it came to be referred later to the trade by Indians and Europeans based in India with Asian and African ports in the Eastern seas, especially from the end of the seventeenth century until the advent of steam ships in the middle of the nineteenth century. The country trade was carried on in Asian waters generally by employing Asian vessels. It did not include the overland trade maintained across the Hindukush which linked India with markets across the Black Sea, the Levant and across the Mediterranean Sea with Western Europe. It also excluded the traffic via the Cape of Good Hope.

The concept of 'country trade' was popularised by the renowned historian Holden Furber, whose works *Rival Empires of Trade in the Orient, 1500-1800,* (Minnesota/Oxford, 1976) and *Bombay Presidency in the Mid-Eighteenth Century* (Bombay, 1965) have been a source of inspiration to me. In fact these works have provided me valuable insights into the role of the private Portuguese in the eighteenth century country trade.

In my choice of subject I was influenced by two other factors: A glance at the existing bibliographies enabled me to come to a realisation of the imbalances in the existing Indo-Portuguese historiography. Little or no work is done on Portuguese India in the twilight of its existence. Sixteenth century 'Golden Goa' has been a favoured theme. History should receive a wholesome treatment. Confining to 'glories' and ignoring the 'tragedies' contributes to presenting a lopsided picture of the situation. Tragedies too are significant. They are the outcome of mistakes. We should not repeat these mistakes and provide fuel to 'history repeats itself' syndrome. The present study examines the commerce of Portuguese India in the throes of survival. It is hoped that it fills one of the gaps in the study of the commercial system of the *Estado da India.* Secondly, there is a vast corpus of documentation on Portuguese India in the eighteenth and nineteenth centuries in the Historical Archives of Goa, untapped and crying for attention. It was felt that indigenous records in the form of the Mhamai House Papers available at the Xavier Centre of Historical Research, Goa would supplement archival information and help me to present a precise picture of the trends in trade and the mercantile situation in the *Estado da India* in the late eighteenth-early nineteenth centuries.

I have used a partially statistical approach in this study. I do not claim absolute accuracy for the data I have built upon considering the vagaries of the customs houses and the evidence of undervaluation. I am, moreover, fully aware of the importance of the human factor in history. The statistical and personal testimonies check and recheck one another's excesses. As I am examining a field of study that is relatively unresearched, the method employed has been inclined towards description. Synthesis and analysis of Portuguese, English and French sources have been combined to produce a study throwing fresh light on commercial activities in Portuguese Asia.

This work is comprised of nine chapters. Chapter 1 provides a geographical backdrop against which the story of the Portuguese trading activities in the East unfolds itself. A preview of the Portuguese country trade in the late eighteenth-early nineteenth centuries is provided in this introductory chapter. Chapter 2 focuses on the social structuring and identity of the merchants of the *Estado*, their business operations and the extent of their mercantile network. The role of the State in the context of the intra-Asian trade is examined in Chapter 3. Its customs policies and relationship with the merchants have been identified. In addition to the response of the State, that of the Crown too needed examination. Chapter 4 focuses on this relatively important theme. Chapters 5 and 6 describe the 'Big Trade' in opium, slaves, ivory and bullion while Chapters 7 and 8 concentrate on the 'Small Trade', namely the trade in tobacco, textiles, spices, timber and victuals. 'Big Trade' refers to trade in items of high value and what could be termed as 'luxuries'. 'Small Trade' on the other hand examines the trade in low-value and bulk commodities, basically a trade in essentials. It is necessary to qualify at this stage that tobacco, spices, timber and coarse textiles were no longer luxury items during the period under study. They came to be listed as consumer goods required to meet the daily needs of the people. The concluding chapter is in the nature of a 'summing up' of issues examined in earlier chapters. It could serve as a pointer to future studies arising from this work.

Those who wish to persue the subject further may find the *References and Notes, Bibliographical Essay* and *Bibliography* useful as sources of archival material. Maps, Tables, Appendices, graphs in this work lend support to the narrative and analysis on occasions.

It is a hypothesis of this work that contrary to existing notions, the trade of the *Estado da India* in the late eighteenth-early nineteenth centuries was thriving. This might not have been argued to the extent that one would have liked. This is due to the constraints of available evidence. Still it is hoped that this exposition will contribute to a more general appreciation of Portuguese commercial effort in Asia in the eighteenth and nineteenth centuries. Hopefully, it will raise questions and stimulate critical minds into exploring and developing a variety of possible answers Indo-Portuguese studies have to offer.

ACKNOWLEDGMENTS

In preparing this work, I have received assistance from many quarters. I am indebted to Calouste Gulbenkian Foundation for the award of a scholarship which enabled me to undertake archival research in Portugal and England. For permission to examine various manuscripts and books, I am much obliged to the authorities and the staff of Historical Archives of Goa, Xavier Centre of Historical Research (Goa), Rare Books Section of Central Library (Goa), Goa University Library, Bombay Archives, Bombay University Library, Poona University Library, Gokhale Institute of Economics and Politics (Poona), Arquivo Histórico Ultramarino (Lisbon), Biblioteca Nacional de Lisboa, Biblioteca do Palãcio de Ajuda, (Lisbon), India Office Library and School of Oriental and African Studies both in London. In all these repositories I have met with much kindness and utmost cooperation. Profound thanks are also due to Augusta and Remedios Rebello for their computing and word-processing assistance. They were unfailing and unflinching in their attention to my every need. They have earned a commendation that cannot be adequately expressed here. I am grateful to Prof. C. N. Nagarcenkar, Mr. Celso Rodrigues, Miss Milena Furtado and Anik Chand for valuable assistance rendered. My greatest debts, however, are owed, first of all, to Dr. Teotonio R. de Souza, Director of the Xavier Centre of Historical Research, Goa. It is to him that I owe my initiation into studies on the Indian Ocean. It is his critical ability and perseverence in guiding me step by step that made me overcome any initial lack of confidence I might have displayed in undertaking a study on Indo-Portuguese commercial activities. I am grateful to him for accepting this book for publication in the XCHR Series. My mother has been a shining example of determination, dedication and courage in my life. In recognition of this debt, I dedicate this work to her.

CELSA PINTO

CONTENTS

LIST OF FIGURES

FIGURES

LIST OF TABLES

LIST OF APPENDICES

ABBREVIATIONS

AG	*Alfandega de Goa*
AHU	*Arquivo Histórico*
ANTT	*Arquivo Nacional de Torre do Tombo*
ARLB	Abstracts of Revenue Letters from Bombay
BA	Bombay Archives
Bandos	*Collecção de Bandos e Outras Differentes Providencias QueServem de Leis, Regulamentos Para o Governo Economico e Judicial Das Provincias Denominadas das Novas Conquistas* by Felippe Nery Xavier, Panjim, 1840-50
BD	Bombay Despatches
BNL	*Biblioteca Nacional de Lisboa*
BPA	*Biblioteca do Palácio de Ajuda*
BUL	Bombay University Library
CD	Commercial Department
CR	*Correspondencia para o Reino*
Cumbarjua	*Fábrica de Cumbarjua*
Damão	*Alfandega de Damão*
Dio	*Alfandega de Dio*
DUP	*Documentação Ultramarina Portuguesa, Centro de Estudos Históricos Ultramarinos,* Lisboa, 1960-67.
GD	General Department
HAG	Historical Archives of Goa
IDJ	*Instrucções com que El Rei D. Joze mandou passar ao Estado da India no Anno 1770,* (ed.) Claudio Lagrange Monteiro de Barbuda, Nova Goa, 1841.
IESHR	The Indian Economic and Social History Review
IOL	India Office Library, London.
Macau	*Correspondencia de Macau*
MHE	*Memória Histórico - Económica das Alfandegas do Estado da India Portugueza* by Francisco Xavier Ernesto Fernandes, Lisbon, 1899.

MHP	Mhamai House Papers
MI	*Maços de India*
Moçambique	*Correspondencia de Moçambique*
MR	*Monções do Reino*
MREIC	Miscellaneous Records : External and Internal Commerce
PD	Political Department
PDCF	*Petições Despachadas no Concelho da Fazenda*
Portarias	*Portarias do Governo*
PRA	*Provisões Regias das Alfandegas*
Provisões	*Provisões da Fazenda*
RD	Revenue Department
RGD	*Registos Gerais de Dio*
RGF	*Registos Gerais de Fazenda*
RLB	Revenue Letters from Bombay
SOAS	School of Oriental and African Studies, London.
SRBG	Selections from Records of the Bombay Government
XCHR	Xavier Centre of Historical Research, Goa.

GLOSSARY

This glossary has been provided for the convenience of the readers of this book. It has no claims to being an exhaustive authoritative linguistic guide. Many terms used in the text do not find a place in this glossary. Their meanings are provided as and when they occur in the text.

aldeia	village
alfandega	customs house
alvara	ordinance valid for a period of one year without confirmation
arrematação das rendas	farming out of monopoly rights to collect non-agricultural revenues
bania	member of the Gujarati Hindu or Jain merchant community
cabotagem	coastal trade, country trade
cafila	convoy of ships
cambolins	traditional coverlet against rain
canarim	a native Christian of Goa
capitão-mor	captain-major
Carreira	the round trip of the Portuguese India-men
cartaz	a safe-conduct pass issued to a non-Portuguese ship
Casa da India	India House at Lisbon
Casa da Supplicação	a tribunal in Lisbon
casado	a married settler
castiço	one born of Portuguese parents
chettyar	member of the Coromandel merchant community
colecta	a tax on food
Conselho da Fazenda	Royal Treasury Council at Goa
Dezembargador	A high court magistrate
Estanco Real de Tabaco	Royal Tobacco Monopoly
feitor	factor, a person in charge of a trading station or agency in an Asian port

feitoria	trading station or an agency in an Asian port
fidalgo	nobleman or a gentleman
foro	quit-rent
indiatico	Portuguese born in India
Kling	Tamil-speaking Hindu merchant
mesa	board, council
mestiço	Eurasian, half-caste or of mixed blood
nao	a large ship
navio	ship
Ouvidor	Judge with appellate jurisdiction
Ouvidor-geral	superior Crown magistrate in a High Court
palmares	palm orchards
pataxo	pinnace, vessel of 2-400 tons
pauta	shipping list, price list
Procurador	legal representative, person with powers of attorney
Procurador de Coroa e Fazenda	Royal attorney
Provincia de Norte	Portuguese territories in North-Western India (Daman and Diu)
provisão	legislative provision
quintas	country houses
recebedor	province tax collector
regimento	standing order
reinol	European-based Portuguese
renda	revenue from farmed taxes
Senado de Camara	Municipal council
soldado	soldier, an unmarried man
sura	toddy
urraca	spirit distilled from palms
Vedor de Fazenda	Royal Treasurer at Goa
vereador	Municipal Councillor
Wako	Japanese term for pirates on the China coast in the sixteenth century

CURRENCY, WEIGHTS AND MEASURES

Information derived from available records and references for the conversion of currency, weights and measures used in this study is summarised below. For the sake of uniformity, the terms used below and in the text are in their original form whether Portuguese, British or indigenous as found in the sources.

Currency :

xerafim (pl. *xerafins)*	= 5 *tangas* = 300 *reis* of Goa (singl. *real*) = 160-200 *reis/reis fortes* of Portugal = 1 *pardau*
cruzado	= 1.33 *xerafins* = 400 *reis* of Goa
bazaruco	= 0.07 *tangas*
rupia (in circulation in Daman)	= 2.26 *xerafins* = 678 *reis* of Goa = 361.8 *reis of* Portugal
pataca	= 4.4 *xerafins*
meia dobla	= 36 *xerafins*
tael (pl. taeis)	= 10 *mazes* (singl. *maz*; Eng. version maces) = 100 *conderins* = 1.33 *xerafins* = 1 *cruzado* (approximate equivalence)

Canton Spanish dollar ($)	= 4s. 2d. (intrinsic value) = 3s. 11d. (exchange value) = 0.72 *tael*
rupee (in use in Bombay Presidency)	= 16 annas = 192 pies = 2.1 *xerafins* = 630 *reis* of Goa
Sultani pagoda	= Rs. 432-433
Bahadur pagoda	= Rs. 434-435
Ikkeri pagoda	= Rs. 434-435
Porto Novo pagoda	= Rs. 3.25
gold mohur	= Rs. 15

Weights and Measures

pico (Eng. version : picul)	= 133.33 lbs = 100 *cates* (Eng. version : catties)
quintal (pl. *quintais*; Eng. version : quintal)	= 4 *arrobas* = 128 *arrateis* (singl. *arratel*; Eng. version lbs.) = 2048 *onças* (Eng. version : ounces)
candil (khandi; pl. *candis;* Eng. version : candy)	= 20 *maons* (Eng. version : *maunds*) = 16 *arrobas* (approximate equivalence) = 3 *quintais* and 4 *arrobas* (approximate equivalence) = 480-540 *arrateis*
maon (for solids)	= 24-27 *arrateis* (*maon* =

	32 *arrateis* in case of potatoes, jaggery, butter and tamarind)
	= 40 *seiras* (Eng. version : seers)
fardo (Eng. version : bale)	= 2.5-3 *maons*
	= 25-35 *corjas*
cumbo (Eng. version : coomb)	= 20 *candis*
	= 400 *curos*
corja	= 20 pieces
marco (Eng. version : mark)	= 0.5 *arratel*
	= 8 *onças*
	= 1152 *carats*
	= 64 *oitavas*
	= 4608 *graons*
graon	= 6:5 to an English grain troy
palmo (Eng. version : span)	= 4 *polegados*
covado (Eng. version : cubit)	= 3 *palmos*
	= 64 cm
pipa (Eng. version : barrel)	= 25-26 *almudes*
canada	= 3 English pints
quartilho	= 0.25 *canada*
maon (for liquids)	= 45 *quartilhos*
Bengal factory maund	= 82 lb. 2 oz.
Bengal bazar maund	= 74 lb. 10 oz.
Bombay ordinary (kuccha) maund	= 28 lb.
Bombay pucca maund	= 30 lb.

Surat maund	= 40 lb.
Bombay candy	= 560 lb.
Surat candy	= 740-746 lb.
Tellicherry candy	= 600 lb.
Calicut candy	= 560 lb.
Mangalore candy	= 560 lb.
Mahe candy	= 560 lb.
Madras candy	= 500 lb.
Cochin candy	= 500 lb.
Cannanore candy	= 500 lb.

1

SETTING THE SCENE

The disintegration of the Portuguese eastern empire and the decline of the *Carreira* did not necessarily mean the end of all trading operations in the East. A sound Portuguese trading system was in existence even in the eighteenth and nineteenth centuries. There is much documentary evidence to indicate this. Natives and Portuguese settlers in the *Estado da India* in their private entrepreneurial capacities were engaged in a flourishing trade. It is a truism that much of this trade was surreptitiously operated enabling them to amass fortunes with little being diverted into the State treasury. But the State too profitted from the lucrative interport trade of Asia. The available evidence testifies to a revival of Portuguese Indian commerce with Lisbon, Brazil, Macao and other distant lands bringing ample returns and adding substantially to the coffers of the *Estado*.

It is essential to place the study of the aforesaid trading system in its proper perspective. The trading outlets and the geographical extent need to be identified. Also necessary is an outline of the general nature of the commerce, its patterns and dimensions, its niches and networks, which would implicitly and explicitly help to provide a backdrop to the discussion and analysis that follows.

Geostrategic Outlines

The *Estado da India* in the period under review came to include a limited geographic area than it initially embraced. In the sixteenth and seventeenth centuries it had a wider connotation and included Portuguese trading stations and forts that stretched from East Africa to the Far East. But thanks mainly to the arrival of the Dutch in the Indian Ocean, by the late eighteenth century, it was reduced to just Goa, Daman and Diu.[1]

The *Estado*, ensconced in the western littoral of India, extending from the Gulf of Cambay to the Konkan, lay between the latitudes 14°47' and 20°46' N and the lines of longitude 67°25' and 74° 23'.[2] It was ideally placed to control the crucial north-western sector of the Arabian Sea. Its location brought it into close proximity with the economically rich cotton, textile and indigo-producing regions of the Deccan and Gujarat, the pepper lands of Malabar and the rice-producing areas of Kanara. The *Estado* was not a contiguous physical unit, but its three enclaves lay far apart from one other, Goa on the Konkan, Daman in Gujarat, and Diu to the south of the Kathiawar peninsula. Though physically separated by long distances, the three formed a single region, its unity stemming from factors related to historical experience, its common pattern of ecological and climatic environment and its political and economic homogeneity.

The Ports

It must be stressed at the outset that with the exception of Mormugão which came closest to what could be described as a natural harbour, the shores of Portuguese India were generally unsuitable for shipping.

Most of the ports were exposed to the full force of the heavy rainbearing currents of the south-west monsoon from June to August, making them inaccessible and therefore rendering commerce virtually non-existent. The torrential flow of rivers brought silt and sediment which were deposited at points where the rivers entered into the sea, giving rise to sandbanks. This implied that bigger vessels of over 300 tons burthern could not be admitted into these rivers or dock close to ports or berthing places which were located on the banks of these rivers.

Nevertheless, the *Estado*-based maritime trade had to develop. It learnt to accommodate to these difficulties one way or the other. In fact the ports of the *Estado* especially Goa, did rise up to the challenges posed by nature and emerged as emporia, at which ships from the various corners of the Indian Ocean and beyond, converged.

Goa which extended from latitude 14°53'30" to 15°48' and longitude 73°45'40" to 74°24', since times immemorial earned the reputation as a great commercial centre and a transit port of considerable significance, central to the active western littoral of India.[3]

The harbour of Goa was formed by the promontories of the two peninsulas namely Salcette and Bardez. It was divided by the projection from the island of Goa called Cabo, which left space on both sides at Aguada and Mormugão for ships to anchor. Both Goa's anchorages could

safely accommodate coastal as well as ocean-going shipping. At Aguada ships could float without any danger by day and night in five fathoms of water, from October to mid-May.[4] However the circumstances were entirely different during the south-west monsoons. The high winds, rough sea and sand brought by the river Mandovi swollen by the first rains of June caused the formation of sandbanks at the entrance of the port. This left scarcely two fathoms of water on new moon days and therefore made the Aguada anchorage virtually non-operational.[5] No vessel of substantial size could get to it.

Mormugão on the other hand proved to be a splendid anchorage for all seasons. It was accessible throughout the year. Situated at the mouth of the river Zuari, providing a water depth of about 22 to 30 ft., well-sheltered by break waters from monsoonal disturbances, the Mormugão bay provided a safe retreat to ships coming from Portugal and other parts of the world when they were shut out of the Aguada anchorage not being open till September. Thus it was one of the few all-weather ports of western coastal India.[6] It was well-defended by a fortress with a good garrison and cannon.[7]

In addition to the Aguada and the Mormugão anchorages there were landing jetties and quays located at strategic points along the coastline at Tiracol, Chapora, Betul, Talpona and Galgibaga. The Chapora port which marked the northern extremity of Bardez, had a major customs check-post and a fishing station. In the absence of dredging and piloting facilities at this port, the entry of vessels of large burthern was prevented. It however earned notoriety as a den of opium smuggling. Trade in coconuts directed to Daman and in rice, timber and tiles brought from Mangalore was conducted from here on a fairly large scale.[8]

Lying within 20°21'55" and 20°24'18" N latitude and 72°48'18" and 72°54'16"E longitude, about 500 km. north of Goa, was Daman, encompassing a total area of 72 sq. miles.[9] Its harbour was located in the Daman-Ganga river a little above the mouth and between the Ghats where the water was sufficiently deep to float vessels of 300 to 400 tons. Immediately beyond, the river shallowed and was rocky and unfit for navigation excepting for canoes. At the mouth of the river was a bar which was dry at the lowest ebb tide. Vessels could enter and leave the river only at high tides, that is, for only six hours in a day. At ebb, the stream was so rapid that no oars could stem it and it was therefore found necessary to anchor out at sea on firm ground and wait for the next favourable tide. This was however in the case of vessels of less burthern. Bigger ones could neither go in nor out of the harbour except for two days

in a month, that is on new and full moon days with the help of spring tides.[10]

The harbour was very narrow, just the breadth of the river Daman-Ganga and about a musket-shot wide. It could therefore accommodate just a few vessels at a time, but it had the advantage of being at a stone's throw from the town markets and this factor contributed significantly to its greatness. The entrance to the harbour was well-defended by a small castle-fortress having three guarded bastions.[11]

Diu derives its name from the Sanskrit word 'Dweep'. Admeasuring 15 km. from west to east and 5 km. from north to south, Diu was embedded in the Gulf of Cambay along the Gujarat coast. Its exact location was 20°46' northern parallel and 67°25' eastern meridian.[12]

From the fourteenth to the sixteenth centuries Diu was known to have one of the best sea-ports on the west coast of India. To the north, the island of Diu was separated from the Kathiawar peninsula by a narrow and swampy channel. This gave rise to the port of Diu with two bars, one in front of the fortress of Diu and the other at Bravancara. Such was the significance of this port that it served as a berthing place for large ocean-going ships bound for the great commercial emporium of Cambay in the sixteenth century, as the ecological circumstances around Cambay — the continual silting up of the Gulf of Cambay and the presence of dangerous tidal bores and currents — made navigation difficult.[13]

The Indian Ocean

The shores of the *Estado da India* were lashed by the Arabian Sea, the western sector of the Indian Ocean. Moreover the Portuguese country trading ventures were undertaken in areas beyond the Arabian Sea, in the Bay of Bengal and the China Seas. As such the climatology and wind system prevailing over the said waters played a crucial role in determining the appropriate time for sailings in and out of the Portuguese Indian ports, the routes undertaken and the operational nature of the port-towns.

Nuggets of information on the sectional changes of the wind system and currents had been accumulated through the ages, after decades of sailing by communities of mariners, pilots and merchants. Some of it was handed down verbally but much of it was embodied in manuals prepared by Arab pilots who displayed their sound knowledge of the winds and currents of the Indian Ocean.

One major factor determining the prospects of sailing was the

seasonal monsoon. The months from April to September were marked by an appreciable rise in temperature and a decrease in barometric pressure in the entire range from the Equator to the Himalayas including the *Estado* due to the northward movement of the Sun. A comparative condition of high pressure existed on the Indian Ocean. This resulted in the movement of the south-west winds from the sea to the land. During the months from June to August when the winds were at their strongest, the ports of Portuguese India and the rest of the western littoral would remain closed to shipping and maritime trade. The north-east monsoon extended from October to March. The winds blowing from the high pressure areas on the land to the low pressure areas in the seas would cause no rain except at Madras and on the Coromandel coast due to the configuration of the land.

In general the months of the north-east monsoon formed the open season for navigation and trade in the Arabian Sea. One witnessed the opening up of the *Estado* ports to ships arriving from the different corners of the Indian Ocean. The Customs House Records (*Livros das Alfandegas*) demonstrate quite distinctly maximum entries of inward and outward sailings for all months excepting June to September.

Ships visiting the *Estado* from the Bay of Bengal whether coming from the eastern coast of India or the Indonesian archipelago sailed with the north-eastern monsoon around January and arrived at the west coast before the south-west monsoon closed the ports and would return home in September or October. The pattern would be reversed if the Portuguese ships wanted to go to the eastern sector of the Indian Ocean. The time for sailing eastwards began as the south-west monsoon set in.[14]

The Hinterland

The hinterland of Portuguese India extended to include the fertile agricultural lands of the Deccan and the peninsula region rich in export produce particularly in industrial raw materials. The crop of significance grown in this region was cotton, cultivated in the rich black cotton soil found in abundance here, which was highly retentive of moisture. Gujarat, the Deccan, Bihar, the north-western sector and Tinnevelly were the chief centres of cotton production. Cotton was one of the items that featured prominently in the China trade. Sugarcane and indigo too were produced in large quantities. There is no doubt that the *Estado* drew on its rich cotton and textile-producing hinterland to foster its coastal and overseas trade.

The eastern flank of Goa was guarded by a densely forested craggy wall-like slope of the Western Ghats. Access to the hinterland was difficult, despite the comparatively low altitude of the Ghats largely due to the presence of deep gorges, two or three miles wide and about 1000 ft. deep. But Goa was not completely cut-off. The mountain girdle 30 to 45 miles behind it was pierced by numerous passes of the height ranging from 600 to 1800 metres.[15]

While in the pre-Portuguese era the port of Goa served the kingdoms of Bijapur and Vijaynagar with Arab and Persian horses, the productive hinterland was much more of service to it especially in the seventeenth century when the Dutch blockade caused hardships and increased Goa's dependence on it for supplies. Coolies and oxen caravans laden with salt, wheat, rice and textiles would make their way through the Ghats to various markets of Goa. Of significance was Goa's inland trade with Balaghat. Goa served as a feeder for Balaghat textiles highly in demand in Lisbon, Brazil, East Africa and various parts of Asia. Diamonds and other jewels which formed a precious portion of the *Carreira cargoes*, were also transported to Goa via the Ghats from Bijapur and Golkonda.[16] Goa was therefore an effective port of outlet serving a large portion of the hinterland lying beyond the Ghats.

Daman and Diu derived their strength from the Gujarat plains noted for their fertile soil and agricultural productivity and this added to the economic importance of the area. Gujarat was one of the most important centres of textile production in India, famous for its weaving and dyeing industry. Textiles produced at Surat, Ahmedabad and other towns supplemented local production in Daman and Diu and together formed the bulk of the cargoes moving out of these ports for East Africa, Brazil, Portugal and other countries. Daman and Diu thus served as markets for the supply of textiles from a cluster of weaving villages and cities in the vicinity. Daman, an agricultural lowland surrounded by hills and jungles served as an important outlet for the opium-producing regions of Central India lying beyond the Ghats. Opium was transported via the Mewjee ghat, Aumbagong ghat and the Waugyra ghat, across Pient and Dhurrumpor territories to Daman.[17] The luxuriant forests in and around Daman provided timber, one of the most important commodities of the coastal trade of the *Estado*. Thus we observe that the hinterland provided Daman and Diu with ample opportunities for trade. The feeder arrangement went a long way towards promoting the greatness of its ports as centres of commerce.

Portuguese Country Trading : Determining the Networks and Niches

Oceanic Trade

Traditional trading patterns persisted while new ones evolved in the late eighteenth and early nineteenth centuries.

Trade links between Portuguese India and the east African coast continued. Ivory, gold, ebony and slaves were despatched to India in exchange for cotton products. The textile crisis, sparked off in the 1820s, close on the heels of the massive onslaught of cheap Manchester textiles, disrupted this prosperous trade in fabrics.[18]

Moçambique also shipped cargoes consisting of rhinohorns, sea-horse teeth, fish maws and sundry items.[19]

The cargoes arriving at Moçambique from the *Estado* were composed of glass beads, bangles, victuals like rice, wheat, sugar, coconut-oil, coconuts, preserves, vinegar, butter, cheese, sweets, lentils, arecanuts, *soians de brindão*, spices, tea, sandal-wood, drugs, wax, pitch and the like.[20] One of the chief components of Goa's outward cargoes to Moçambique included guns and gun-powder used in tribal wars, to quell uprisings and to capture Africans sold in slavery.[21]

A new channel of brisk trading activity came into prominence in the late eighteenth century which involved the movement of slaves from Moçambique to Mauritius and other French colonies in the Indian Ocean via Goa.[22] This was a private channel managed mainly by the Mhamais who were then one of the leading merchants of Goa. The official records are virtually silent on this transit trade in slaves. These records however indicate that the *Estado* did have trade connections, though feeble, with Mauritius. For instance in 1812, Daman despatched cotton products and sundries valued at 2,289-3-15 *rupias* to Mauritius.[23] In an official price list (1772) iron, copper and sugar are listed as Goa's imports from Mauritius and Bourbon.[24]

Regarding the Goa-Maldives run, a look at the customs records reveals that occasional despatches were made to Maldives. In January 1835, Sada Shet sent on board the ship *Selet* 2 reams of Macao paper, 5 scarves, 2 *arrateis* of European linen and 3 Surat cut-pieces to Maldives.[25] Coir for ship-rigging continued to arrive from Maldives.

The phenomenal rise of the China trade in the late eighteenth century induced profound structural changes not only in the Asian trade but even in the Portuguese country trading system. One witnessed the rise and development of the lucrative but short-lived Portuguese opium trade between the western coast of India and Macao. Along with the flourishing textile re-exportation commerce, this branch of the Portuguese intra-Asian trade not only overshadowed all major traditional channels but even drove them into near oblivion.

Indo-Portuguese traders were also deeply engaged in the cotton trade with China and Macao. In 1787 efforts were afoot to launch a private company at Goa to conduct trade in cotton obtained at Bombay, with Macao and China. It was observed that Macao ships, which touched the west coast of India, would sail directly to Bombay without halting at Goa. Therefore the establishment of a commercial organisation would have far-reaching consequences. It would serve to activate Goa's commerce with the Far East and the rest of Asia. Accordingly the company came into existence in 1788 with 69 shareholders holding 200 shares collectively, each worth 2,000 *xerafins*.[26] Of the 69 shareholders, 58 were Hindus and the rest Christians, that is, 84.06 per cent were Hindus and 15.94 per cent were Christians demonstrating the place of prominence occupied by the Hindus in the Goan economy.

Apart from opium and cotton, the *Estado* exported a host of other products including slaves to Macao. Surprisingly the official lists of goods entering Macao annually, recorded in the *Correspondência de Macau* make no reference to slaves, while we find references to the export of slaves to Macao in the Goa customs records. This leads one to conclude that the commerce in human cargoes with Macao was clandestine in nature. Ivory, sandalwood, wax, saltpetre, spices, textiles, incense, and turtles were amongst the other commodities shipped to Macao.[27] The return voyages yielded crockery, Chinese silks, paper, sugar, leather-ware, parasols, fans, tea, rhubarb, camphor and sundries.[28]

Evidence exists on the rare commercial ties between the *Estado* and the Far Eastern nations China and Japan. From China were transported items like crockery, cabinets, trays, chests, Chinese textiles like satin, velvet, silk, damasks, *chamalotes, alatas, gurgoroens* and *retroz*.[29] Japan would ship cabinets, writing-desks, jars, shades and sundries.[30]

Since the fall of the Portuguese outposts of Sohor in 1644 and Muscat in 1650 trade of the *Estado* with the Persian Gulf was reduced to a shadow of its former self. The *Estado* was visited annually by ships voyaging from Muscat, usually not more than five in number, laden with dry fruits especially dates, raisins, almonds and nuts, Arabian glue, copper, incense, salt-fish, ink and drugs.[31] Shipping directed to Muscat from the *Estado* was more extensive. A maximum of twenty annual shipments from Goa and Daman would include bamboos, rafters, coconut products, salt, wax, arecanuts, coffee and yarn.[32]

Shipping records make no reference to a Goa-Mocha run and trade with Arabia appeared to be moribund which could be attributed to Arab piracy in the Indian Ocean.[33] However the possibility of such contacts cannot be ruled out. We find that in 1802, Captain Antonio Joze Freire, in command of the vessel *Nossa Senhora da Conceição* was expected to deliver at Lisbon, on behalf of Rodrigues de Souza Coutinho of Goa, a chest containing 2 *arrobas* of coffee from Mocha.[34] Diu however had more extensive trade relations with West Asia compared to the other Portuguese enclaves. Diu was visited by ships coming from Mocha. They would probably unload coffee and carry away tobacco.[35] Textiles from Surat, Cambay, Jumbasoor and other Indian ports too formed the bulk of the cargoes proceeding to Mocha.[36]

Trade relations with the cinnamon island Ceylon were not entirely snapped in the late eighteenth-early nineteenth centuries. Goa's outgoing shipments to Colombo were comprised of dates from Muscat, tea, Macao paper, military hats, shells and religious articles such as wooden statues and rosaries.[37] Goa's chief import was apparently cinnamon. Furniture and European wines and liquors too formed a component of Ceylon's outgoing consignments to Goa.[38] The principal traders on the Goa-Colombo channel were Devy Naik and Venkatesha Kamat.

Since the fall of Malacca, the Portuguese trade with Indonesia had virtually withered away. The customs records are near silent about this branch of the *Estado* trade. I have come across a reference to trade with Malacca in 1770. From a price list prepared at Goa in 1772 it seems likely that sugar, pitch, iron bars, copper, aloes and benzoin arrived at Goa from Batavia, Java, Aceh and Siam.[39] Private trading links, however, persisted especially with Batavia.[40]

We have scattered references to the sporadic and weak nature of trade between the *Estado* and South East Asian regions like Siam and Cochin-China. By a treaty signed with the king of Siam in 1820, The Portuguese Viceroy Conde de Rio Pardo succeeded in setting up a Portuguese trading station at Bangkok which remained in existence till 1833.[41] There is every likelihood that salt from Goa, textiles from Surat and Arabian commodities figured prominently in the *Estado*-Siam trade.[42] Coming to the channel between Goa and Cochin-China, I have come across just one reference in the trade records to powdered sugar being imported into Goa in November 1794 by Joaquim dos Santos Lima.[43]

The Goa Customs records reveal that occasionally ships plied between Timor and Goa. From statements made by Viera Godinho, the governor of the islands of Timor and Solor during the years 1784-88, it appears that there existed an indirect trade between Goa and Timor, that goods exported by Goa to Batavia reached Timor. The said governor made proposals to establish direct trade links between Goa and Timor. Goa, he felt, could offer Timor textiles, palm liquors and iron goods while Timor could reciprocate with cinnamon, nutmeg, saltpetre, mercury, wax, copper, brass, kerosene, mineral oil and tobacco.[44] Goa also shipped weaponry to Timor. In December 1789, Bezamy Esequiel dos Anjos exported 2 guns worth 20 *xerafins* each to Timor.[45] Likewise Inacio Alberto de Oliveira shipped to Timor 4 bundles of brass bangles, 180 guns and sundries in December 1793.[46]

Coastal Trade

Apart from the long distance trading across the Indian Ocean eastwards and westwards, emanating from Portuguese India, a flourishing trade along the coastline of India was a characteristic feature of the *Estado's* trading system for most part of the eighteenth and nineteenth centuries.

The eastern and western coasts were a scene of bustling activity where country craft designated as *patmarins, muchuas, escunas, sibares, manguerins, saudos, tonas, canoas,* etc. plied to and fro usually in the pre and post south-west monsoon months laden with local and foreign cargoes.

The *Estado's* trade links with the Konkan were intimate and extensive.

Closely-linked with the precipitous decline in the commercial fortunes of Surat in the eighteenth century, was the rise of Bombay from obscurity into a thriving commercial entrepôt and one of the chief centres of the British country trade. By virtue of its excellent harbour and its unique placement on the western seaboard, Bombay was able to have a complex commercial network encompassing the Red Sea, the Persian Gulf, the East African coast, the Indian littoral, South East Asia and, above all, China. Bombay was the focal point on the western coast of India for commodities from all corners of the Indian Ocean region and even from Europe and America. The locus of the western Indian Ocean vortex had shifted from Surat to Bombay.[47]

Until the seventeenth century, Goa was well-accepted as a port with a commercial system having world-wide ramifications. Trade in and from Goa would develop apace in different directions. But Bombay's rise to prominence in the vicinity of Goa seriously eroded her commerce and status. By the mid-eighteenth century Goa's entrepôt position came under severe pressure. In fact several Goa-based merchants shifted their base of operations to Bombay to better their economic prospects and those who continued to reside in Goa forged intimate business ties with English and Parsee traders domiciled in Bombay.

The total value of the *Estado's* trade with Bombay is provided in Table 1.1. However, the figures for the period 1801-17 are relating to Goa and Konkan and its combined trade with Bombay. This does not help us to get a precise picture of the value of trade of the *Estado da India* with Bombay during the said period. But we are more fortunate with respect to the years 1818-26. The average total value of exports was Rs. 2,79,370 per annum while that of imports was Rs. 3,54,725.37.

Goa's imports from Bombay were substantial and in fact surpassed exports. From Bombay, Goa brought a miscellany of products such as liquors, European and Indian textiles and clothes, crockery, cutlery, glassware, hardware, spices, Chinese silks, curios, paper, pitch, rhubarb, fans, parasols and foodstuffs such as rice, wheat, sugar, tea, cheese, butter and oils.[48] Her outward cargoes were composed of local liquors, salt, coconuts, coconut products, *solans de brindão*, local pottery, domesticated birds, cashewnuts, mangoes, arecanuts, wax, jaggery, butter, pepper, chillies, *nachenim*, tamarind and bamboos.[49] Daman would despatch tobacco, wood such as *patingas, cisso, cifro* and teak and textiles called *canequins* to Bombay.[50] In turn it received cotton, tea, sugar, saltpetre, spices, copra, foreign and Indian textiles, sandalwood, artificial corals, cutlery, chinaware, indigo and dry fruits.[51] From Bombay, Diu secured dates, pepper, sugar, oils, copra, paper, rice and tobacco.[52] It had ivory to offer.[53]

Patavar supplied Goa with textiles and took away *meyas doblas*, bills of exchange (*dinheiro em letras*), corals, etc.[54] From Rajapur arrived textiles and the return cargoes were composed of coconuts, copra, arecanuts, mangoes, paper, sugar, iron and corals.[55] As regards the Goa-Vengurla run, Goa provided chillies, cashewnuts and Lisbon liquors. Since the 1840s Goa increasingly turned to Vengurla for tobacco supplies.[56]

Coming to the *Estado's* commercial relations with Kanara, prior to the seventeenth century, by way of trade agreements and treaties, the Portuguese compelled the petty chieftains of Kanara to furnish pepper cargoes to the *Carreira da India*. The situation altered radically in the ensuing centuries when the Portuguese had not only to surrender their prized spice monopoly in Kanara but in fact were drawn into open conflict with the Nayaks of Ikkeri. Since the beginning of the eighteenth century the tide turned in favour of Goa. The latter, a grain deficit pocket of India heavily dependent on Kanara for its very sustenance was now assured of regular rice supplies by way of tributes extracted from local chiefs. A miscellany of other articles were purchased by the Portuguese namely sugar, iron, ginger, coir, saltpetre, timber for masts and ship-building operations conducted at the Goa Shipyard.[57]

TABLE 1.1 : THE *ESTADO*'S TRADE WITH BOMBAY, 1801-26

Year	Total Value of Exports (In rupees)	Total Value of Imports (In rupees)
1801-02	1564929	1511701
1802-03	2530230	2827781
1803-04	1260033	5898560
1804-05	1681640	7688139
1805-06	1414878	4031759
1806-07	2048297	3681135
1807-08	2513778	3978603
1808-09	3378822	4308071
1809-10	2898893	4272518
1810-11	2343876	4910803
1811-12	2040364	5129222
1812-13	5550757	7477790
1813-14	4039658	5577594
1814-15	3121017	4839452
1815-16	3037871	4393776
1816-17	3082372	4453254
1818-19	277033	467982
1819-20	216424	311245
1820-21	228296	372396
1821-22	183543	427069
1822-23	260596	360722
1823-24	286535	237333
1824-25	417268	348752
1825-26	365265	312304

Sources: BA : Compiled from *MREIC*, vols. 1-6, 8-25.
Note: Figures for 1801-17 relate to Goa and Konkan while those for 1817-26 relate to Goa, Daman & Diu.

Rice supplies would come especially from Mangalore and Basrur.[58] Honavar and Basrur would provide coconuts and coconut products.[59] They also supplied spices especially cinnamon.[60]

Malabar was the *Estado's* traditional source of pepper. Matters underwent a drastic change with the fall of this Portuguese citadel to the Dutch in the seventeenth century. But with the Dutch departure from the Indian Ocean scene, Goa resumed her trade connections with Malabar on a moderate scale. The principal components of Goa's import cargoes from Cochin included spices such as pepper, cloves, cinnamon and cardamom, coconuts and coconut products. Horses and country craft too were imported. Goa returned salt, gold *pagodes*, hides, tea and the like.[61] Calicut supplies included coconuts, copra, coconut oil, salt-fish, pepper and a variety of textiles.[62] Alleppey provided Goa with teakwood, dyes, oil, jaggery, cloth, coconuts, coconut products and in the main, country vessels.[63] The Mhamai House Papers refer to 376-½ *cumbos* of salt despatched to Alleppey by Suba Kamat in February 1822. Tobacco cargoes moved from Tuticorin, Tinnevelly and Cannanore to Goa. Though of an inferior kind when compared to Brazilian tobacco, nevertheless they served to cater to the needs of the tobacco-addicted populace of Goa at a time when Lisbon no longer supplied tobacco to the *Estado da India*.[64] From Tellicherry arrived cargoes of coconuts, copra, dates, tobacco, paper, sugar, paddy, pepper and textiles.[65] In turn, textiles from Diu, ginger and *solans de brindão* proceeded to Tellicherry.[66] The Goa-Mahe trading circuit finds no place in the official records, yet it figures significantly in the private business papers of the Mhamais. We have much evidence about the regular periodic despatch of pepper and rice supplies from Mahe to Goa. Likewise the Mhamai brothers would be called upon to send consignments of slaves, domesticated birds, salt, tiles, mangoes, cashewseeds and sundries to Mahe.[67]

Coromandel on the eastern seaboard was another area of Goa sailings. From the trade linkages with Madras, Goa derived textiles of Madras, Pulicat and Masulipatam, saltpetre, rice, sugar and chests.[68] In turn Goa offered salt, coconuts, sandalwood, tea, paper, glassware, crockery and dates from Muscat.[69]

As regards Bengal, the customs records indicate negligible commercial links with Goa but more extensive relations with Daman and Diu. Usually Bengal textiles, sugar and saltpetre did make their appearance in Goa via Bombay and the northern enclaves, to be re-shipped to Lisbon, Brazil and Moçambique.[70] But from a price list prepared in 1772 it appears that sugar, saltpetre, pitch, tobacco, iron, sack cloth and even opium came directly to Goa.[71] A stray reference in the records reveals that in 1794 a variety of fabrics, scarves and the like together with sugar arrived at Goa from Bengal.[72]

Import of Bengal saltpetre served a local need. Regular supplies of saltpetre were furnished to the *Real Fabrica de Polvora*. So long as the *Estado* felt the need to be in a state of readiness for war, the demand for saltpetre continued unabated.

In the late eighteenth century, Portuguese private traders like Rogerio de Faria and the Barettos made hay at Bengal, where the country trade was most active. They were regular suppliers of opium to Macao.[73] Bengal also catered to the needs of Lisbon ships for textiles, saltpetre and spices.

Of all the routes that sailed from Goa around 1600 those to Gujarat ranked above all others including that of Portugal. The annual capital involved in the Goa-Gujarat trade was well over Rs. 4,000,000 a year.[74] Tragically in the nineteenth century there seemed little or no trace of the early seventeenth century Goa-Gujarat trade which had reached such dizzy heights. The old trading links had almost broken. The Portuguese customs records point to occasional direct trading between Goa and Surat but it did not go beyond two annual shipments.[75] On the other hand trade with Cambay and Jumbasoor for mutual benefit was virtually extinct. The official records, however, demonstrate the entry of textiles from these areas at the port of Goa for onward carriage to Lisbon, Brazil and Moçambique.[76] If at all Goa had bi-lateral trade relations with Gujarat, they were restricted to Bhavnagar. Its cargoes directed to that region contained arecanuts, coconuts, timber, ivory, drugs, etc. and the return trips brought wheat, butter, oils, bed-linen, threads, cotton and pitch.[77] It is indeed unfortunate that the once-prosperous trade of Goa with Cambay in the sixteenth century and Surat in the seventeenth and eighteenth centuries declined so ignominously as to be driven into near oblivion in the nineteenth century.

Daman on the other hand had very extensive commercial dealings with Gujarat. The available evidence reveals the existence of an established trading nexus, well-supported by an active group of local and long distance traders. To Broach, Daman exported grains, iron, timber, bamboos, and sundries and in turn received piece-goods, maura, grains and threads.[78] It also provided Bhavnagar with ivory, lead, iron, timber and sugar. Its return cargoes were comprised of cotton, grains, oils, butter, chillies and pepper.[79] From Surat, Daman acquired piece-goods, textiles, indigo, pitch, iron bars, turtles, brass articles etc. and returned teakwood, *cisso, cifro* and textiles called *canequins*.[80] Cambay provided Daman with tobacco, textiles, paper, butter, etc.[81] Daman supplies to Cambay included teak, patingas, *cisso, cifro* and bamboos.[82]

Daman also had direct trade connections with Jaffrabad, Dhollera,

Jumbasoor, Amode and Goga. From Jaffrabad, it obtained *ghee*, oil and white *girgelim* and in turn, offered plenty of teakwood.[83] To Goga, Daman transported bamboos, rafters, teakwood, imported ghee, oil and thread.[84] Daman's shipments to Dhollera included a host of products like ivory, timber, teakwood, rafters, coconuts, rice, dry dates, almonds and sundries. While its imports were composed of cotton, grains, cotton piece-goods, thread, *ghee* and oil.[85] From Jumbasoor and Amode, Daman brought cotton, cotton threads and yarn, grains, *ghee*, and tobacco. In turn it remitted ivory, grains, coconuts, bamboos, wooden bangles, black *khar* and *rajaloo* wood, rafters and timber.[86]

Diu established trading contacts with Goga, Dhollera, Bhavnagar, Jumbasoor and Amode, in Gujarat. From Jumbasoor and Amode, Diu secured cotton, cotton thread, piece goods, tobacco and grains. In turn, it supplied ivory, dates, sugar and sundry other items.[87] Diu's exports to Bhavnagar were principally ivory and grains.[88] From Dhollera, Diu imported grains and returned ivory, jaggery and dry dates.[89] Diu derived principally grains and piece-goods from Goga.[90]

Table 1.2 has summarised the value of the trade of the *Estado da India* with Gujarat over the period 1817-26. As considered earlier, Goa's trade with Gujarat was negligible. So the figures in reality largely pertain to the commercial relations of Daman and Diu with Gujarat. The total value of the *Estado's* imports stood at Rs. 1,106,575 and that of exports at Rs. 1,995,735. The *Estado* trade was most extensively conducted with Amode and Jumbasoor, followed by Surat, Dhollera and Broach. The Portuguese Indian commerce was least with Bhavnagar.

Table 1.3 provides an elaborate picture of the total value of Goa's trade with each of the areas in the Indian Ocean region for the years 1823, 1826 and 1837. Goa's trade with Bombay ranks high above that with other ports.

The total value of the Goa-based country trade was 2,137,619-0-23 3/4 *xerafins* in 1823, 2,144,378-2-29 1/4 *xerafins* in 1826 and 1,573,019-2-49 *xerafins* in 1837 (See Table 1.4). This appears to be substantial considering that these were not commercially prosperous years, that is, years either in the pre or post Revolutionary War period. Moreover, the value of the trade for the year 1826, that is 2,144,378-2-29 1/4 *xerafins* was not much below Bocarro's estimate for the seventeenth century, that is, an average annual investment of 2,850,000 *xerafins*. This establishes very decisively that the country trade continued to be significant and a lucrative source of income to the *Estado* and its merchants even in the early nineteenth century despite the so-called decline and disintegration of the Portuguese eastern empire.

TABLE 1.2 :TRADE OF PORTUGUESE INDIA WITH BROACH, DHOLLERA, JUMBASOOR, AMODE, SURAT AND BHAVNAGAR, 1817-26

Year	Broach		Dhollera		Jumbasoor & Amode		Surat		Bhavnagar	
	Imports (In rupees)	Exports (In rupees)	Imports (In rupees)	Exports (In rupees)	Imports (In rupees)	Exports (In rupees)	Imports (In rupees)	Exports (In rupees)	Imports (In rupees)	Exports (In rupees)
1817-18	235	17493								
1818-19	4944	19744	3604	32344	128876	244234	12628			34765
1819-20	1174	3296	2922	17600	173624	220105	47629	74284	10998	15651
1820-21		31894		17030		184724		51082		20670
1821-22	4172	29439	1610	12515	154611	182613	72364	48027	13847	18502
1822-23	3525	18963	962	14223	79807	103581	57269	38121	1902	7201
1823-24	2066	11287	1920	38162	67271	118556			2452	26495
1824-25	3431	11196	320	17945	95545	111825	63565	50334		
1825-26	804	580	393	58499	54700	54161	35238	35064	2167	3530
Total	20351	143892	11731	208318	754434	1219799	276065	296912	43994	126814

Sources: BA : Compiled from *MREIC*, vols. 18-25.

TABLE 1.3 : THE GOA-BASED ASIATIC TRADE, 1823, 1826, 1837

Areas	Total Value (In *xerafins*)		
	1823	1826	1837
Macao	111131-4-25	168001-3-59 7/8	28342-1-12 1/2
Moçambique	62387-1-07 3/4	67721-1-29 1/2	8229-0-46 1/2
The South	140589-0-30	195744-1-00	57688-0-38
Diu	27489-1-30	45372-3-00	3544-1-30 (?)
Daman	42681-2-07 1/2	53563-4-12 1/2	25003-1-45
Muscat	7729-4-00	1620-0-15	1097-1-15
Bombay	710552-0-42 1/2	560671-0-53	837993-0-07
Rajapur	5641-3-07 1/2	48777-2-30	9969-2-30
Melondi		5994-0-42	
Balaghat	804949-2-10	823155-1-12 1/2	433558-0-42 1/2(?)
Ponda	163928-2-58 1/2	140745-1-45	153898-3-28 1/2
Madras		550-1-00	346-0-00
Malwan			2426-2-30

Sources: AHU : *MI*, Maço 224, no. 209; Maço 233, no. 235, docs. dated 18 Dec. 1827, 22 Dec. 1827, 28 Dec. 1827; HAG : *MR*, 212B, fl. 544.

TABLE 1.4 : TOTAL VALUE OF THE GOA-BASED TRADE 1823, 1826, 1837

Year	Lisbon Trade (In *xerafins*)	Asiatic Trade (In *xerafins*)	Total (In *xerafins*)
1823	88823-2-24 1/4	2137619-0-23 3/4	2226442-2-48
1826	403491-1-30 1/8	2144378-2-29 1/4	2547869-3-59 1/2
1837	31077-4-22 1/2	1573019-2-49	1604097-2-11 1/2

Sources: AHU : *MI*, Maço 224, no. 209; Maço 233, no. 235, docs. dated 18 Dec. 1827, 22 Dec. 1827, 28 Dec. 1827; HAG : *MR*, 212B, fl. 544.

The Goa-Lisbon trade, however was in doldrums, with the exception of the year 1826 when the value of its trade amounted to 403,491-1-30 1/8 *xerafins*. This was quite significant when compared to the value figures for 1823 and 1837, though poor when compared to 2,144,378-2-29 1/4 *xerafins*, the total value of the Goa-based Asiatic trade in 1826. The sudden spurt in the Goa-Lisbon trade in 1826 could be attributed to the granting of Brazilian independence as a result of which Brazil's commercial relations with both Portugal as well as Goa were snapped. For a time it appears that Portugal and Goa were mutually dependent on each other. But this could not be for long as the figures for 1837 seem to indicate. If we compare the value of the Goa-based Asiatic trade with that of the Goa-Lisbon trade for the years 1823, 1826 and 1837, we observe that the Asiatic trade in 1823 was 24.07 times, in 1826 5.31 times and in 1837 50.62 times more valuable than the Lisbon trade. The latter was no longer profitable to Portuguese India. The country trade remained the essence of the economic existence of the *Estado da India* and its inhabitants.

REFERENCES AND NOTES

1. The Goa Government exerted a shadowy control over Macao and the islands of Timor and Solor which was terminated by the Decree of 20th September 1844. Francisco Maria Bordalo, *Ensaio sobre a estatistica do Estado da India*, Lisboa, 1862, p. 7.
2. João Stuart da Fonceca Torrie, *Relatorio do Serviço de Saude do Estado da India Portuguesa, Relativo ao Anno de 1879,* Nova Goa, 1880, vol.I, p. 3; *SRBG.* vol. X, New Series, Bombay, 1855, pp. 313, 341.
3. *Ibid.*, p. 3.
4. SRBG, *op. cit,* p. 341.
5. *loc. cit.*
6. A. B. de Bragança Pereira, *Etnografia da India Portuguesa,* vol II, Nova Goa, 1923, p. 3.
7. S. N. Sen, (ed.), *Indian Travels of Thevenot and Careri,* New Delhi, 1949, p. 191.
8. T. R. de Souza and C. J. Borges, "Transport and Communications", *Goa Through the Ages,* vol. II, (ed.) Teotonio R. de Souza, New Delhi, 1989, pp. 233-235; Bragança Pereira, *op. cit.*, p. 4.
9. SRBG, *op. cit.*, p. 341.
10. XCHR : *J. N. Fonseca Papers,* doc. dated 7 July 1875, pp. 29-30.
11. Charles Fawcett, (ed.), *The Travels of Abbé Carré in India and the Near East, 1672-1674,* vol. I, Reprint, New Delhi/Madras, 1990, pp. 159, 166; Manoel Godinho, *Relação do Novo Caminho da India para Portugal,* Lisboa, 1974, p. 35.
12. SRBG, *op. cit.*, p. 313.
13. K. N. Chaudhuri, *Trade and Civilisation in the Indian Ocean : An Economic History from the Rise of Islam to 1750,* New Delhi, 1985, p. 108.
14. *Ibid.*, p. 132.
15. M. N. Pearson, "The Port City of Goa : Policy and Practice in the Sixteenth Century", *Coastal Western India . Studies from the Portuguese Records*, New Delhi, 1981, p. 73; Teotonio R. de Souza, "Rural Economic Life", *Goa Through the Ages*, vol. II, pp. 83-84; Claudio Lagrange Monteiro de Barbuda, *IDJ*, Nova Goa, 1841, pp. 14-17.
16. *Ibid.*, pp. 81-82.
17. BA : *RD,* 13/13, docs. dated 29 Sept. 1821, 5 Oct. 1821, pp. 173-179.
18. HAG : *Correspondencia de Damão,* 1071, doc. dated 4 Nov. 1820; *MR,* 219B, fl. 783.
19. HAG : *AG,* 6807, fls. 332, 355, 437; 6823, fls. 200-203, 205, 206, 218v-219; *MR.* 177A, fl. 324.

20. HAG : *Correspondencia de Damão*, 1096, docs. dated 3 Feb. 1842, 10 Feb. 1842; *AG*, 6318, fls. 157v-158v, 176v, 183, 186-186v, 204v, 206v, 209v, 226.
21. HAG : *AG*, 6325, fl. 75.
22. Celsa Pinto, "Goa-Based Overseas and Coastal Trade (18th - 19th Centuries), *Goa Through the Ages*, vol. II, (ed.) Teotonio R. de Souza, New Delhi, 1989, pp. 190-191.
23. HAG : *Provisões*, 1588, fl. 321.
24. HAG : *MR*, 148B, fl. 817v.
25. HAG : *AG*, 8128, fls. 19-19v.
26. AHU : *MI*, Maço 92, no. 101, docs. dated 23 April 1787, 5 Nov. 1787, 28 April 1788, 6 April 1789, 22 April 1790; no. 154, 22 April 1787, 10 May 1787, 17 June 1787.
27. HAG : *MR*, 149A, fl. 105; 171B, fl. 384v; *AG*, 6809, fls. 348; 6810, fl. 273; 6822, fl. 4; *Macau*, 1295-1299, 1305-1313, 1316-1320, 1322, 1324-1326, 1329-1330, 1332, 1335-1336, 1338, 1340-1342, 1345, 1356.
28. HAG : *AG*, 6809, fl. 351; 6810, fls. 174-493: *passim; MR*, 149A, fl. 129; *Macau*, 1294-1299, 1305, 1307-1308, 1312, 1317-1318, 1323-1324, 1326, 1333, 1335, 1343, 1356, 1359.
29. HAG : *MR*, 148B, fls. 738-738v.
30. HAG : *MR* 148B, fls. 761-768.
31. HAG : *MR*, 148B, fl. 752; 177A, fl. 327; *AG*, 6807, fl. 742; 6810, fls. 543, 577, 721; 6815, fls. 124-125; Pinto, *op. cit.*, p. 191.
32. HAG : *AG*, 2668, fl. 32v; 6810, fls. 571-766: *passim;* 6815, fls. 11-93: *passim;* 6816, fls. 173-655: *passim.*
33. Panduranga S. S. Pissurlencar, *Portuguese Records on Rustomji Manockji*, doc. nos. 56-57, Nova Goa, 1933.
34. HAG : *MR*, 181B, fl. 407v; Pinto, *op. cit.*, p. 191.
35. HAG : *CR*, 2408, fl. 72v; *MR*, 148B, fl. 752; *RGD*, 7950, fl. 97v.
36. HAG : *CR*, 2408, doc. dated 2 Jan. 1781.
37. HAG : *AG*, 8128, fls. 85-85v.
38. HAG : *AG*, 6823, fls. 115v-116.
39. HAG : *AG*, 6317, fl. 76; *MR*, 148B, fls. 737v-738.
40. XCHR : *MHP* (Portuguese), doc. dated 7 April 1790.
41. Miguel Vicente de Abreu, *O Governo do Vice-Rei Conde do Rio Pardo*, Nova Goa, 1869, pp. 152-153.
42. HAG : *AG*, 6816, fl. 775.
43. HAG : *AG*, 6331, fl. 674.
44. A. Teodoro de Matos, "Timor e o Comercio Portugues do Oriente no século XVIII", *VI ISIPH* Macau, 21-26 Oct. 1991, p. 14.
45. HAG : *AG*, 6807, fl. 731.
46. HAG : *AG*, 6809, fl. 731.
47. Pinto, *op. cit.*, pp. 192-193.
48. HAG : *AG*, 2668, fls. 10v-20v; *Macau*, 1311, fls. 207-207v.
49. Pinto, *op. cit.*, pp. 192-193.
50. HAG : *Damão*, 4848 fls. 4-72v: *passim.*
51. BA : *MREIC*, vol. 18, doc. dated 31 Oct. 1819; vol. 19, doc. dated 31 Oct. 1820; vol. 20, doc. dated 31 Oct. 1821; vol. 21, doc. dated 31 Oct. 1822; vol. 22, doc. dated 31 Oct. 1823; vol. 23, doc. dated 31 Oct. 1824; vol. 24, doc. dated 31 Oct. 1825; vol. 25, doc. dated 31 Oct. 1826; HAG : *Damão*, 4848, fls. 3-73v: *passim.*
52. HAG : *Dio*, 4958, fls. 3, 4, 7, 18, 30, 31, 76, 185, 186; 5665, 45, 49, 60-60v.
53. HAG : *Dio*, 4958, fl. 187.
54. HAG : *MR*, 177A, fl. 326.

55. HAG : *AG,* 2668, fl. 23v.
56. HAG : *AG,* 8130, fls, 4-5, 20v, 38v-40v, 132v-137, 212-212v, 250v, 290v.
57. Pinto, *op. cit.,* p. 193.
58. HAG : *MR,* 149B, fls. 451, 464; *AG,* 6818, fls. 221, 414, doc. dated 12 March 1847.
59. HAG : *AG,* 6333, fls. 99-156: *passim;* 6811, fls. 23, 275.
60. HAG : *AG,* 6333, fls. 4-132v: *passim;* 6823, fl. 22; 6826, fls. 22, 123-124; 8121, fl. 5; 8130, fls. 165v-177v.
61. HAG : *AG,* 8119, fl. 70.
62. HAG : *AG,* 6823, fls. 21v-210: *passim;* 6826, fls. 5-247: *passim.*
63. HAG : *AG,* 6811, fl. 318.
64. Pinto, *op. cit.,* p. 194.
65. HAG : *AG,* 6331, fl. 398; 6333, fls. 12-172: *passim*; 6818, fl. 227v; 6823, fls. 13v, 49v.
66. HAG : *AG,* 6329, fls. 104, 129, 227; 6331, fl. 386.
67. Teotonio R. de Souza, "Goa-Mahe Trade Links (Late 18th-Early 19th Centuries) : *A New* Source Material", *Studies in Maritime History,* (ed.) K. S. Mathew, Pondicherry, 1990, pp. 170-173; *MHP : passim.*
68. Pinto, *op. cit.,* p. 195.
69. *loc. cit.*
70. *loc. cit.*
71. HAG : *MR,* 148B, fl. 733.
72. HAG : *AG,* 6333, fls. 19, 128.
73. Teotonio R. de Souza, "Rogerio de Faria : An Indo-Portuguese Trader with China Links", *VI ISIPH,* Macau, 21-26 Oct. 1991, pp. 7-8.
74. Pearson, "The Port City of Goa", p. 105.
75. HAG : *AG,* 6318, fl. 236.
76. HAG : *AG,* 5166, 5167.
77. HAG : *AG,* 8118, fls. 110, 113; BA : *MREIC,* vol. 19, doc. dated 30 April 1820; vol. 20, doc. dated 30 April 1821; vol. 21, doc. dated 30 April 1822; vol. 22, doc. dated 30 April 1823; vol. 24, doc. dated 30 April 1825; vol. 25, doc. dated 30 April 1826.
78. BA : *MREIC,* vol. 18 Part I, doc. dated 30 April 1819; vol. 19, doc. dated 30 April 1820; vol. 21, doc. dated 30 April 1822; vol. 22, doc. dated 30 April 1823; vol. 24, doc. dated 30 April 1825; vol. 25, doc. dated 30 April 1826; HAG : *Damão,* 4848, fls. 12, 23, 28, 29, 41.
79. HAG : *Damão,* 4848, fls. 17, 44, 45; BA : *MREIC,* vol. 18, doc. dated 30 April 1819; vol. 19, doc. dated 30 April 1820; vol. 20 doc. dated 30 April 1821; vol. 21 doc. dated 30 April 1822; vol. 22, doc. dated 30 April 1823; vol. 24, doc. dated 30 April 1825; vol. 25, doc. dated 30 April 1826.
80. HAG : *Damão,* 4848, fls. 1, 2, 5, 8, 9, 10, 12, 15, 16, 21, 23, 28, 29, 41, 43, 46, 47v, 48v, 55v, 56, 62v, 63, 64v, 65, 66v, 67v, 69, 70.
81. HAG : *Damão,* 4848, fls. 8, 10, 14, 16, 18, 26, 49, 53, 59v, 62v, 71.
82. HAG : *Damão* 4848, fls. 5, 6, 7, 8, 10, 11, 16, 17, 23, 46, 62v, 68.
83. HAG : *Damão,* 4848, fls. 14, 18, 20.
84. BA : *MREIC,* vol. 22, doc. dated 31 Oct. 1823; vol. 25, doc. dated 31 Oct. 1826; HAG : *Damão,* 4848, fls. 4, 11, 22.
85. BA : *MREIC,* vol. 18, Part II, doc. dated 30 April 1819, vol. 19, doc. dated 30 April 1820; vol. 20, doc. dated 30 April 1821; vol. 21, doc. dated 30 April 1822; vol. 22, doc. dated 30 April 1823; vol. 24, doc. dated 30 April 1825; vol. 25, doc. dated 31 Oct. 1826; HAG : *Damão,* 4848, fls. 1, 2, 7, 9, 15, 25, 27.
86. BA : *MREIC,* vol. 18, Part II, doc. dated 8 Oct. 1819; vol. 19, doc. dated 1 March 1820; vol. 20, doc. dated 30 April 1821; vol. 21, doc. dated 30 April 1822; vol. 22, doc. dated

30 April 1823; vol. 24, doc. dated 30 April 1825; vol. 25, doc. dated 30 April 1826; HAG : *Damão*, 4848, fl. 9.

87. BA : *MREIC*, vol. 18, Part II, doc. dated 8 Oct. 1819; vol. 19, doc. dated 1 March 1820; vol. 20, doc. dated 30 April 1821; vol. 21, doc. dated 30 April 1822; vol. 22, doc. dated 30 April 1823; vol. 24, doc. dated 30 April 1825; vol. 25, doc. dated 30 April 1826.
88. BA : *MREIC*, vol. 19, docs. dated 30 April 1819, 30 April 1820; vol. 22, doc. dated 30 April 1823; vol. 24, doc. dated 30 April 1825.
89. BA : *MREIC*, vol. 22, doc. dated 30 April 1823; vol. 24, doc. dated 30 April 1825.
90. BA : *MREIC*, vol. 22, doc. dated 31 Oct. 1823; vol. 25, doc. dated 30 April 1826.

2

MERCHANTS : SOCIAL IDENTITIES AND BUSINESS STRATEGIES

A study of the Indian Ocean trade of the late eighteenth-early nineteenth centuries would hold no significance without an examination of the pivotal role played by the merchants. Their social composition, the varied economic roles played by them and the nature and scope of their far-flung mercantile network deserve attention. A careful analysis of evidence derived from private papers sheds light on the deep and varied ramifications of the *Estado's* mercantile practice, offers interesting insights into the complex web of merchant relationships of the time and provides substantial proof of the existence of an elaborate private trading system emanating from the west coast of India.

Before we examine the social stratification of the *Estado* merchants it would be relevant to consider their area-wise concentration and numerical strength.

Table 2.1 shows that out of a total of 3,384 traders operating in Portuguese India in 1848, 2,851 were found in Goa, 417 in Daman and 116 in Diu. So in terms of percentage 84.25 per cent resided in Goa, 12.32 per cent in Daman and 3.43 per cent in Diu. We also observe that of the 3,384 merchants, 1,618 were coastal traders and 1,766 were *balagateiros* who were active in the inland trade of the *Estado*. In brief, the coastal traders formed 47.81 per cent of the mercantile community of the *Estado* while the pedlars formed 52.19 *per cent*. The concentration of coastal traders with whom we are more concerned was found in the Old Conquest areas of Goa, and in Daman and Diu. The New Conquest areas of Goa concentrated solely on the inland trade especially with Balaghat. Table 2.1 also indicates that Daman had a larger percentage of coastal traders compared to that of the other two Portuguese settlements of the *Estado*. It had 329 coastal traders out of a total population of 33,159, amounting to 0.99 per cent. Goa (Old Conquest areas) had 1,243 coastal traders out of a total population of 196,027 forming 0.63 per cent while Diu had 46 coastal traders out of a total population of 7,471 amounting to 0.62 per cent. The interest in seaborne commercial activity in Daman could be due to the lucrative opium trade, mainly oriented towards the Far East, and the trade in slaves, ivory, precious metals and beads with East Africa.

TABLE 2.1: MERCHANTS OF THE *ESTADO*, 1848

Areas	Pedlars	Coasting Traders	Commercial Companies
Ilhas	26	23	1
Salcette			
Anjediva	356	1130	
Bardez	952	90	
Tiracol	2		
Ponda	64		
Astagar	11		
Embarbacem	23		
Bally			
Chondravady	32		
Cacorao	3		
Canacona			
Cabo de Rama			
Bicholim	87		
Sanquelim	52		
Pernem			
Daman	88	329	
Diu	70	46	

Sources: *SRBG*, X, New Series, Bombay, 1855, pp. 330-331; BNL : *Mapa Geral. Estatistica e Historica da India Portuguesa*, 1850.

Social Diversification and Structural Composition

The sources are silent about the existence of merchant communities and their relationships during the period under review. We have to seek the assistance of published contemporary works and population statistics to reconstruct a picture of the social world of the merchants. The mercantile society of Portuguese India was a happy blend of various strands of the Portuguese white population and the indigenous.

Private Portuguese

The Portuguese engaged in the country trade could be categorised according to three overlapping criteria, namely the purity of blood, rank, and marital status. Relating to the first criterion associated with blood, there were the *reinois*, born in Portugal and who served as chief administrators and clerics in Portuguese India. Their appointments were determined and sanctioned by the Lisbon authorities and on completing their term of office they would return to Portugal. The *reinois* were further graded as *fidalgos* and *nobres*. The Portuguese, born in Asia of pure Portuguese descent were called *castiços* or *Indiaticos*. Those born in India of mixed blood, that is, Portuguese and Indian or Portuguese and African parentage were called *mestiços* and *mulatos* respectively. The *castiços*, *mestiços* and *mulatos* were treated with contempt and looked upon with considerable suspicion by the upper Portuguese classes.[1]

Another classification, highly generic in character, based on rank, divided the *Estado*-based Portuguese population into three classes, the clergy, the nobility and the rest.

A third criterion provided for the division of the Portuguese into *soldados* and *casados*.

The term *soldado* referred commonly to unmarried Portuguese men who were transported in the celebrated *naos* of the *Carreira da India* from Lisboa for military undertakings in India. The total number of *soldados* in the *Estado* at a given time varied, being high at a time when the carracks made their appearance in India and low during non-monsoon seasons when the *soldados* were assigned the task of patrolling the Indian Ocean waters. But whatever the numbers, they were by no means enough to meet the military requirements of the *Estado da India*.[2]

The *casados* who formed the backbone of the Portuguese population in Goa, arrived in India as *soldados* and later took an Eurasian or an Indian wife and began to lead a settled life as lesser officials and land-owners.

The inability of the Crown to pay adequately must have soon made it imperative for all sections of the Portuguese in India to seek other means of augmenting their meagre resources. They gradually came to a realisation that the intra-Asian trade was much more lucrative than the *Carreira*. Sheer necessity to augment their poor income lured them into the trading world of Asia as freelance traders. Moreover, the growing indifference displayed by Portugal towards its eastern holdings, especially since the *Carreira* was no longer found to be profitable, emboldened the inhabitants of Portuguese India to fling themselves with all the zest at their disposal into the lucrative Asiatic trade. In fact, they quite shockingly demonstrated a total lack of patriotism, often inclined to place their business interests before that of the State, thus depriving the *Estado* of potential revenues. Even viceroys and governors were guilty of corrupt practices, remitting home substantial personal fortunes so as to enrich family coffers, while doing little or nothing to enhance the collections of the State treasury. Much wealth was also absorbed by the commercially astute clerics who spent it on ecclesiastical projects. Distance, poor administration and lack of interest were obviously at the core of Portugal's inability to effectively curb the illicit Portuguese private trading in the East.[3]

Indigenous Merchants

Trade was also significant to the native and ethnic Indians residing in the *Estado*, particularly to the Saraswat brahmins of Goa, the banias and Parsees of Daman and Diu, the *Canarins*, and the Muslims.

The Saraswats

The Saraswat brahmins, claiming descent from the Gaud Saraswats of northern India are believed to have been transported by the mythological Parashurama to Gomanchal, the ancient name for Goa. Their titular deities such as Shantadurga, serve as proofs of their close affinity with the brahmins of north-eastern India (Bengal).[4] Certain Muslim incursions in North India provoked the brahmin exodus. The inscriptions of the Kadamba rulers bear testimony to the arrival of the brahmins on the Konkan and Malabar coasts. But the question of their earliest appearance on the Goan scene remains unanswered and unsolved.

Almost all the foreign travellers, namely Linschoten, Pyrard, Mocquet, della Valle, Jacques de Coutre and Careri who visited Goa in the sixteenth and seventeenth centuries make pointed references to the business involvement of the Goan Hindus in their accounts and travelogues.

The Saraswat brahmins in particular served as village-kulkarnis, financiers, tax-farmers, traders in the intra-Asian trade and as diplomatic agents. Many sources of government income in Goa, Cochin and elsewhere, customs duties, taxes on cloth, tobacco and the like remained mainly in the hands of the Hindus, especially the Saraswat brahmins.

During the first decade of the seventeenth century the State *rendas* or non-agricultural revenue amounted to an average of 68,555 *xerafins* of which 91.5 per cent were administered by the Hindus and about 8.3 per cent by the Christians.[5] M. N. Pearson states that in the seventeenth century, out of 782 holders of the *rendas*, the names of 355 find a place in the records, and that 50 per cent were held by the Saraswat brahmins, 30 per cent by other Hindus and 20 per cent by Christians.[6]

In the mid-sixteenth century the Hindus faced the sharp edge of anti-Hindu evangelisation laws enacted by the authorities. Faced with the prospect of either disowning their ancestral faith or their landed properties, most of the Saraswat brahmins in all certainty opted for loss of landed privileges and rights. But such losses were bound to spur them on, to avail of every opportunity thrown their way by the *Estado*, for commercial profit. The Portuguese administrators could not help demonstrating their reliance on Hindu knowledge of local usages and Hindu business expertise and acumen. The Hindu natives undoubtedly exploited the situation to the fullest, in order to accumulate capital which they could invest in business particularly in the profitable Asiatic trade and commerce. Much of this capital was deposited on the mainland out of reach of the Portuguese Indian administrators who demonstrated a perennial hunger for funds to finance their war operations.[7]

With each ensuing century, the Saraswat brahmins of Goa grew from strength to strength. In the words of M.N. Pearson, "Possibly the Saraswats moved from a position of equality with the Christians and with other Hindus in the first half of the sixteenth century, to equality with these two combined in the first seventy years of the seventeenth century, and to complete domination by the end of the century".[8] A look at the Portuguese documentation on economic matters indicates quite distinctly that this position held by the Saraswat brahmins as the dominant native elite, exerting a virtual stranglehold over the Goan economy, particularly over the commercial arena, continued throughout the eighteenth and the nineteenth centuries. Sixty-four out of the 66 Hindu merchants on record in 1800 were Saraswat brahmins (96.96 per cent) and the rest Muslims.[9] All the merchants of Goa who entered into the Bengal Company (*Companhia de Bengala*) in 1769 were Hindus (100 per cent Hindu composition) and all of them belonged to the Saraswat brahmin community.[10] In all probability this dominance continued until the end of the Portuguese regime in India.

The greatest concentration of Hindu merchants in Goa was found to be at Cumbarjua. Out of 66 merchants listed, 28 were based at Cumbarjua which in terms of percentage amounted to 42.42 per cent. There were 12 Hindu merchants or 18.18 per cent in Panjim 10 or 15.15 per cent in Verem and the remaining 11 or 24.24 per cent were domiciled in Malar, Panelim, Raçaim, Ribandar, Mapuça, Betim, St. Luzia and Pomburpa.[11]

The Mhamai family, also known as Camotins or Kamats, belonging to the Saraswat brahmin community and based at Panjim, contained some of the outstanding merchants of the time, both in the scale of business operations and in the extent of political influence wielded.

Suba Kamat was prominent as one of the four official brokers of the Goa Customs and a provision supplier to the viceregal palace at Panjim. Capital accumulated not merely through brokerage but also through revenue-farming and by means of a loan contracted from the Administration of the *Confisco* of the suppressed Society of Jesus, was put to good use and served to lay down the foundations of a flourishing late eighteenth-early nineteenth century Agency House.[12] On his death, his business concerns were jointly managed by his sons Venkatesha, Narayana and Yeshwant. While Venkatesha and Narayana operated at Goa, Yeshwant managed the Bombay end until his death in 1815. The Mhamai brothers had in fact expanded the business activities of Suba Kamat and pursued more vigorously the avenues of overseas commerce, tax-farming, brokerage and the like.

As a State revenue-farmer, Venkatesha had charge of Mahem in Bicholim and Talvarda in Salcette.[13] He was appointed revenue-farmer of Talvarda for a period of six years from January 1778 to 1804 on condition that he would pay an annual amount of 6,105 *xerafins* to the State. Earlier the same farm was controlled by Francisco Xavier Fernandes of Cuncolim for 5,506 *xerafins*.[14] Narayana Kamat was in charge of the tax-farming operations in the county of Cuncolim-Veroda in Salcette.[15] Later Vithal Kamat of the Mhamai clan was appointed revenue-farmer of the same county. The Mhamai brothers also indulged in tobacco revenue-farming which formed one of the principal sources of revenue of the *Estado da India*. They held the tobacco snuff contract for three years upto the end of 1818.[16]

The Mhamais also functioned as provision suppliers and State Shipyard contractors. They rendered service to the State Shipyard by taking care of State and private vessels in need of wintering, refitting and provisioning before setting sail. It was this position that enabled the Mhamais to acquire the necessary leverage to expand their interests in many ways. They were able to establish and build up contacts with those engaged in the *Carreira* and *Cabotagem* in Goa and beyond. As brokers and insurers too, they had a substantial standing. While Venkatesha and Narayana Kamat continued with their father's job as official broker at the Goa Customs, they offered their brokerage and insurer's services to merchants based at Daman, Diu, Surat, Bombay, elsewhere in India and abroad. In fact, they were chief brokers and agents for the French in Goa and this provided them with opportunities to have close business ties with French officials at Mahe, Pondicherry, the Maratha court and even Mauritius.[17]

Disaster struck the Mhamai agency house with the coming of Viceroy Conde de Rio Pardo. The latter's policies designed to eliminate fraudulent practices and abuses, caught the Mhamais on the wrong foot. Improper methods of accounting and management of the tobacco revenue collection found them listed amongst the State debtors.[18]

To clear their debts to the State and to other merchants, they had to forfeit their properties. Their goods and credits were mortgaged and frozen.[19] Anta Keshav Parab Lawande, a merchant residing at Panjim, had proceeded to take charge of one of the houses of Venkatesha at the price of 1,300 *xerafins* because the latter was probably his debtor.[20] Decline had set in. There were no hopes of recovery. For some time the business continued to exist under Venkatesha and Narayana, later in the 1820s and 1830s under Suba, Bably and Jagarnath Kamat, and in the 1830s and 1840s under Vithal Kamat who was engaged in the tobacco trade with Brazil.[21]

The Dhempes too were Saraswat brahmins who had been engaged in a brisk coastal trade in coconuts, copra, spices, oil and cloth in the late eighteenth century. The business was then operated by Vitoji Sinai followed by Kushta Sinai Dhempe who probably belonged to the Calapur-based Dhempe clan.[22] But it was Giridhar Sinai Dhempe, who in the 1830s expanded the family business and diversified into overseas shipping. He pursued more vigorously the avenues of seaborne commerce. He would ship his merchandise to East Africa and the return voyages would yield gold, diamonds and ivory. His ships were also employed to transport troops and prisoners of the Portuguese government.[23]

The Banias

The banias of Daman and Diu were exceptionally enterprising, and displayed an extraordinary devotion to economic activities and a shrewd commercial sagacity. These unusual qualities helped them to emerge as one of the richest business communities on the west coast of India.

While it is true that certain bania castes claimed Vaishya status, it is important to note that the term was in a broad sense largely functional, including Hindu and probably even Jain traders who were not banias by caste but by profession.

In Daman the banias consisted of five main divisions namely Khadayata, Lad, Modh, Porvod and Shrimali. The name Khadayata owes its origin to Khadat, a place north-east of Ahmedabad, Lad to Lat the ancient name of southern Gujarat, Modh to Modhera found to the north-east of Ahmedabad, Porvod to Porvod in Marwar and Shrimali to Shrimal also located in Marwar.[24]

A traditional trading community, the banias, had come to specialise in specific forms of commercial activity. Opportunities for commercial profit and gain were not lacking. The flourishing nature of Gujarat's seaborne trade in the Indian Ocean from the sixteenth to the eighteenth centuries enabled the banias to participate extensively in the trade, not only as traders but also as brokers and bankers. Their control over the credit and supply system placed them in a position of relative advantage *vis-a-vis* the private Portuguese.

The banias of the *Estado* enjoyed a place of preponderance in the East-African trading circuit in the period under review.[25] They would despatch ships laden with rice and other provisions to Moçambique and the return cargoes included the prized ivory, slaves and gold.

The phenomenal rise of the China trade during 1770-1850 had far-reaching repercussions for the banias of Daman and Diu. The latter came to feature prominently in the Indo-Chinese opium trade, particularly in the early nineteenth century.[26]

The banias or the Gujarati vanias of Goa held a place of importance in the Goan economic set-up in the sixteenth and seventeenth centuries. One witnessed the vigorous selling of cloth and precious stones at the famed *Rua de Baneanes*. They even held *rendas*.[27] But in the eighteenth and nineteenth centuries the banias of Goa waned into insignificance, and their economic power was totally eclipsed by that of the Saraswat brahmins. There are however scattered references to their participation in the intra-Asian trade.

Portuguese India had a small but significant minority of Hindus from neighbouring states, especially the Gujaratis, Kanarese and Malabaris, who displayed their skills as craftsmen-goldsmiths, copper-smiths, carpenters and barbers. Many of them were engaged in the buying and selling of cloth, pepper and foodstuffs.[28]

The Canarins

The native Christians of Portuguese India, called *Canarins,* were also actively engaged in the Indian Ocean trade. The records reveal a number of Christian participants in the country trade, but it is difficult to distinguish between Portuguese and those of ethnic Indian origin. Nevertheless, Rogerio de Faria, based first in Calcutta and later at Daman and Bombay, Antonio Minguel Pereira of Britona, Sebastião Gracias of Serula and Ignacio Sebastião de Silva of Margão are specifically mentioned in the sources as *Canarins* deeply involved in the Portuguese country trade in the late eighteenth-early nineteenth centuries.[29]

Rogerio de Faria, a native of Chorão, Goa, referred to in Bombay circles as "Prince Merchant", was not only solidly ensconced in the Asiatic trade, but also conducted a commerce of wider proportions with Portugal, Brazil, and the Far East.[30] He possessed oceanic-bound and coastal vessels and operated a business concern with branch offices located at Calcutta, Surat, Daman and Macao. In fact, he belonged to the ranks of those country traders of Bombay who had changed the very face of Bombay and helped to elevate it to the position of the greatest port of India and the life-line of the British Empire.[31]

In the commercial world of Bombay, Rogerio de Faria enjoyed a place of considerable standing and earned the recognition not only of the Goans and Portuguese settled in Bombay, but also of the Parsees. He had intimate trading connections with Sir Jamsetji Jejeebhoy, the renowned Bombay-based Parsee businessman of the nineteenth century.

Rogerio de Faria was held in high esteem by the Bombay Presidency authorities. In April 1826, Rogerio de Faria, together with other prominent merchants at Bombay namely, Messrs. Reid, Richie, Framjee Cowasjee, Motichund Amichund and Cazare Gholan were appointed by the Bombay Government to frame a fresh tariff.[32] Moreover, by an order passed by the Tribunal of the Grand Jury of the Supreme Court of Bombay, on 30th March, 1829, Rogerio de Faria and his associates in Rogerio de Faria and Cia., were to be treated not as British subjects but as honoured natives of Goa and subjects of the Portuguese Crown.

The Journal of Abbe Cottineau de Kloguen describes the colourful personality, life-style and affluence of Rogerio de Faria. The latter's affluence stemmed from the fortunes he amassed through participation in the Indo-Chinese opium trade. In 1796 Faria, then based in Bengal, gained an official foothold into Macao where he earned the right to import opium cargoes into that settlement. In fact there had been much resistance to the free entry of opium into Macao, operated by non-residents, as it proved ruinous to local commercial interests. By virtue of his Portuguese nationality he was soon able to defuse this opposition and along with the Barettos of Bengal, began to enjoy the same commercial privileges enjoyed by the local traders.[33] Later in 1798, Faria was granted a licence to establish a branch office at Macao.[34]

Around 1803, Rogerio de Faria shifted his base of operations from Bengal to Bombay. Probably the growing control of the English East India

Company in the production and sale of opium in Bengal made matters difficult for private traders like Faria to pursue their business interests profitably.[35]

Rogerio de Faria maintained close contacts with the Portuguese authorities at Goa and abroad. The transfer of the Portuguese royal seat from Lisbon to Rio de Janeiro in the wake of the Napoleonic occupation of Portugal in 1807 enabled Faria to establish commercial contacts with Brazil. For the services he rendered to the Brazilian Government, the latter conferred on him the *Ordem de Rosa do Brazil* and the *Ordem de Immaculada Conceição.*[36] He was also appointed First Consul General for Brazil in Bombay and was decorated with the *Ordem do Christo* by the King of Portugal.[37] Such awards held no significance for him as they did not bring any pecuniary gain, but nevertheless earned him the title of 'Sir' in Bombay circles. What proved more lucrative to him was his appointment as factor at the Portuguese trading station at Surat in 1826 for a period of three years.[38] He was able to exploit to the fullest his connections with the Portuguese authorities in order to promote his business interests. He acquired property and set up a business house at Daman.[39] His ship, *Gloriozo,* later named *Don Manoel de Portugal,* was employed at Daman to conduct trade with Macao, Moçambique and other ports. Under the Portuguese protective umbrella, he was able to exert a virtual monopoly over the opium trade directed towards Macao via Daman and Diu in the early nineteenth century. In the 1820s, he joined the throng of country traders on the west coast of India, bent on shipping their opium cargoes to Lintin, disregarding the protests of Macao.

On the expiry of his tenure as Director of the *Feitoria de Surrate,* Rogerio de Faria returned to Bombay and placed his business affairs on a firmer footing with himself as the senior partner and his sons-in-law, Luis Francisco da Silva, Francisco Antonio de Carvalho and Jose Maria Pinto as junior partners of Rogerio de Faria and Cia. Faria continued to trade in opium with China via Daman and even via Bombay long after the introduction of the British transit pass system in 1831. His ships, *Margaret Crawford, Boa Esperança* and *Don Manoel de Portugal* would leave the west Indian littoral laden with opium for China and would return with Chinese tea, porcelain, silks and sundries.[40]

Rogerio de Faria's business received a crippling blow in 1835 as a result of a loan provided to the deposed and exiled Governor of Goa, Bernardo Peres da Silva, which set the ball rolling for his eventual bankruptcy in 1838. Peres da Silva had spent months in Bombay raising an expeditionary force to recapture Goa and to re-install himself as

Governor there. Rogerio de Faria raised loans to meet the expenses of such a force by issuing bills in favour of Sir Jamsetji Jejeebhoy and Motichund Amichund. When the venture ended in a fiasco, Peres da Silva decided to take charge of Daman which had remained loyal to him and recognised his authority. There was an understanding established that he would honour the bills on his taking charge at Daman in cash or by way of customs duties exemption. Apparently, he failed to keep his promises. The bureaucrats at Daman, while firmly upholding the claims of Peres da Silva to Governorship, questioned the manner in which he cleared his dues.[41]

Jejeebhoy held Faria responsible for this state of affairs. He held out the threat of business relations being severed especially by the Marwari associates of Motichund Amichund in case the matter was not settled immediately.[42] Despite repeated reminders, Rogerio de Faria failed to honour his debts, and consequently lost all credibility in the eyes of the merchants and financiers of western coastal India. Apparently, Faria lost 50 per cent of his assets to keep him out of jail.[43] Further misfortune befell him when he lost his only son who died of tetanus following an accidental fall just a few years prior to his own death in 1848.[44]

One cannot ignore the involvement of the clergy (both Portuguese and *Canarins*) in the Goa-based Asian trade.[45] They not only derived profits from the coastal trade of India, but also from the trade in human cargoes. Amongst the many instances reference must be made to the despatch of slaves to Macao in 1800 by clerics Joze Francisco de Figueiredo and Pascoal Antonio Lobo.[46]

The Parsees

The Parsees of India could trace their origin to emigrants from Persia, particularly from the Persian Gulf and Hormuz. It was to Diu that the earliest Parsee refugees arrived and took up residence for nineteen years, after which they deserted the port for better places of settlement.[47]

The Parsee economic importance on the west coast of India dates back to the late seventeenth century when Surat was the focal point of the West Asian trade. Largely due to their knack of ingratiating themselves with the Europeans and their intelligent business habits and integrity, intimate economic relations were established between the European merchants and Parsees at Surat. The Portuguese, the French, the Dutch and the English employed Parsees as their chief brokers. It was not smooth sailing for the latter. They must have met with stiff competition from the banias.[48] The Parsee merchants at Daman and Diu in the late eighteenth-early nineteenth centuries had close ties with those of Bombay, particularly Framji Cowasjee and Jamsetjee Jejeebhoy, and were deeply involved in the Indo-Chinese opium trade routed through their lands.

The Daman-based Beramji Bharde, and later his sons Bhikaji and Kavasji possessed a large interest in the Malwa opium commerce via Daman, as agents of chief opium merchants of Bombay. As major ship-owners and maritime traders, they would ply their ships to Bombay, Moçambique and China. In consequence of a diversion in the route of the opium trade to Bombay, Daman lost all its commercial importance and sank into insignificance. The opium trade of the family of Beramji ceased to exist.[49]

Another influential member of the Parsee community domiciled at Daman was Cauji Beramogi, the father of the owner of the village Catria, Maneckji Cauji. He had built his fortune in opium. Later misfortune was to befall this family as it had no male successor.[50]

The Muslims

The Muslims in the *Estado* owed their origin to the Arabs or Turks who in the tenth century invaded India and set up a colossal Muslim empire. They were either descendants of the Muslim invaders or those converted from Hindu stock.[51]

There was a heavier concentration of Muslims at Diu than in Daman and Goa. Both in Daman and Diu the Muslims belonged to the commercially active Khoja community. In Goa they were members of either the Bohra or the Meman sect. The Bohras were descendants of Hindus converted to Islam. The Memans on the other hand were divided into five classes, three of which were originally from India. The Cutchis originated from Sind or Kutch, Dhoraji Bhavnagris from Bhavnagar, and Veravals from Veraval (Kathiawar).[52]

Apparently the Muslim merchants played an insignificant economic role in the Goan economy during the period under review. A list of leading merchants of Goa makes a reference to just two Muslims.[53] The sources, however do indicate that the Muslim traders were active on the *Estado*-West Asia commercial run.[54]

Other Non-indigenous Merchant Groups

There were groups of foreign (alien) merchants residing in Portuguese India — Armenians, Jews, French, English, Chinese and Italians.

The discovery of the sea route via the Cape of Good Hope to India and the subsequent Portuguese conquest of Goa, Malacca and Hormuz had a profound effect on the migratory movements of the Jews. Spanish and Portuguese Jews began to flock to India since the sixteenth century. The presence of Jews in Goa in the sixteenth century is well-attested to by the earliest Portuguese sources. This presence continued to persist in the seventeenth and eighteenth centuries despite the steady threat of Inquisition.

At Surat too the Jews figured prominently. Tavernier, Fryer and other travellers testify to the existence of a Jewish settlement at Surat and leave us with no doubt that the Jews were not transient individuals, but permanent settlers. The Portuguese, the French, the English and the Dutch who had trading stations at Surat, made substantial use of them as factors, brokers, agents and interpreters.[55]

Moses Tobias emerged as one of the outstanding Jewish merchants of Surat in the eighteenth century. He played a prominent role in the economic and diplomatic arena of Portuguese India of his time. In 1728 Tobias was appointed Director of the *Feitoria de Surrate* and retained this position until 1745.[56] Following the death of Moses Tobias in 1769, and the winds of change blowing over Surat, the fortunes of the Jewish community declined, but Jews were still residing in Surat until well into the nineteenth century.

We have also evidence of an Armenian merchant settlement in Goa. In 1770 some Armenians were found at Panelim in Goa. In the Mhamai House Records we come across stray references to the Armenian Estevão Camille who had business connections with Warnet and other French officials based in India.[57] The Sarat family of Armenian stock consisting of Macara, Michel, Murat, Zacharias and Gaspar did business in Goa during the period of our study.[58]

Italians engaged in trade were also found in Goa during the period under review. Jeorge Midosse of Rome, son of an Italian merchant Joze Midosse, based at Rio de Janeiro, lived in Goa and died in the year 1817.[59]

The Merchant World : Methods and Practices

We proceed to examine next the business methods and procedures adopted by the merchants in their dealings with each other and the services rendered by the Agency Houses owned and managed by the merchants in the *Estado da India.*

The Agency House

The characteristic unit of the early modern Asian private trade was the Agency House. It was an institution which played a significant role in the economic history of the *Estado*. It was not a joint-stock company nor a concern run by an individual. It was a partnership which was usually a family affair backed by common family assets. This was preferred to prevent dissolution and to assure that the concern would remain in the family in perpetuity. The partnership was often loose, individual partners being allowed separate dealings on their own account. A look at the customs records reveal that in the *Estado da India* there were several such business houses in existence in the late eighteenth-early nineteenth centuries. To name a few, Govinda Sinai Navelkar & Co., Vaman Parab Sinari & Co., Shaba Sinai & Co., Kushta Pai & Co., Rama Pai & Co., Anta Sinai & Co., Venkatesha Kamat & Co., Chondru Sinai Dhume & Co., Venkatesha Bhandari & Co., House of Kamat, Cumbarjua, Ari Sinai & Co., Govind Naik & Co., Jacinto Domingos & Co., Minguel de Souza Ferreira & Co. and João Baptista Goethals & Co.

A business house was chosen to be set up by the sea-side, close to a harbour. It had to be spacious, with a large number of rooms and godowns, well-equipped and furnished with locks, tables, chairs, lamps, etc. The partners of the concern were expected to be adaptable and trustworthy, and they enjoyed absolute liberty to enter and leave the premises as and when desired.

In order to open a business house, it was necessary to first acquire the permission of the authorities at the respective port. A document having the basis and sanction of business law was then drawn up and it was subjected to the endorsement and ratification of all the partners in the business. The latter then had to take an oath expressing honesty in all business undertakings and dealings with each other. The gains and losses of the concern were equally shared.

By common consent one amongst them, probably the more capable and experienced one, was elected Director. He enjoyed absolute control over his subordinates. Attorneys, (*procuradores*) who were required to sign and endorse accounts, letters, bills of exchange and other despatches on behalf of the company, together with the advisors, (*conselheiros*) were selected from amongst the partners.

Meetings were held at regular intervals to discuss purchases and sales, fresh rates to be charged and any matter aimed at promoting the interests of the concern. At such meetings all were free to render their opinions.

As regards other personnel of the business house, accountants (*caixas*) were chosen from amongst the partners, whose functions included keeping a close watch over the accounts. At the end of the year they had to audit the accounts and draw up the profits and losses. They were assisted by clerks who served as their immediate subordinates.

The overseer (*fiel*) of the House was in charge of the keys of the godowns and the safes. He could undergo necessary expenditure in keeping with the instructions of the Director or attorney. A register recording such expenditure was maintained.

The company would also employ spies (*mexiriqueiros*) whose duties were to move about in the city to spy on the activities of rival business houses. They would even venture to board vessels secretly and later present confidential reports on their observations to the Director or the First Attorney of the Company, so that the future course of action could be chalked out and steps to meet competition could be discussed at company business meetings. The concern also employed porters, guards, and servants to attend to the menial and mundane work — part and parcel of any business house.[60]

An Agency House in the *Estado* was essentially a trading house indulging in buying and selling for others on a commission basis. In this type of organisation the merchants also acted as brokers, insurance agents, bankers, freighters, ship-owners, purveyors, and the like.

The Agency was a recognised institution in customary law. Merchants employed agents to manage their business affairs on their behalf. The agent was provided with a written certificate of agency or a letter of authority which passed off as a legal document and enabled him to act on behalf of the merchant. He was empowered to make sales and purchases on behalf of his principal, to represent him in his dealings with other merchants and to render any other type of service when called upon to do so, for a fixed rate of commission. A minimum amount of commission had to be paid, irrespective of results. The commission charges varied according to the standing of the agent. Special concessions were made on grounds of friendship. The commission ranged from 2 to 3 per cent for sales or purchases made in coastal India.[61] In case of Lisbon and Macao, the commission charges were about 5 per cent.[62] Commission charged for both buying and selling in India amounted to 5 per cent.[63]

The principal was obliged to acknowledge both profit and loss in all deals made on his behalf by the agent or correspondent.

A merchant tied himself to an agent at every port where he conducted business. This was especially so in the case of Europeans who possessed little or no knowledge of the local situation. The French, for instance, depended on the services of the Mhamai brothers, who were their chief agents and brokers at Goa.

A merchant while acting as a commission agent, would himself have agents in different ports.

Consignment Method

Merchants often consigned their goods for sale. Sale on consignment was an arrangement whereby the consignee agreed to sell goods on behalf of the consignor. The goods were despatched by the consignor, who claimed ownership of the goods, bore the expenses involved in despatching them, which included packing, shipping and insurance, plus any expense that the consignee might undergo due to the consignment sale. The risks attached to the sale were also to be borne by him. All that the consignee had to do was to sell the goods at the price fixed by the consignor, for which he was paid a commission. Merchants like Rogerio de Faria and Jamsetjee Jejeebhoy would consign their opium cargoes to Jardine Matheson & Co. and other British merchants stationed in China.[64]

Shroffage

The merchant needed help from the shroffs. Primarily the shroffs (*sarrafs*) in most cities on the west coast of India, particularly Surat, wielded control over the money market by virtue of their power to assay or test coins. It enabled them to fix the rate of the market exchange in the city. They were indispensable in fixing the value of a particular consignment. They provided credit in the city. Marine insurance too was managed by them and it would seem that while sending commodities abroad, merchants would either do so on respondentia or insure them. The *sarrafs* dealing in insurance or respondentia were essential for any and every shipment. Another branch of the *sarraf's* economic duties was the remittance of money by bills of exchange or *hundis*. Bills could also be bought and sold through the *sarrafs*. Undoubtedly the *sarrafs* charged a fee and made huge profits in such dealings.[65]

Brokerage

Merchants often served as brokers or even utilised the services of brokers. Brokerage was a recognised indigenous mercantile practice having the sanction of customary law. Brokerage was often a part of the traditional trading structure. Strictly speaking it was not devised to meet the needs of the European merchants, though Europeans were in need of them, much more than the natives. There were generally two types of brokers. Every merchant of significance would engage the services of a general broker who would assume charge of the entire range of merchant's sales and purchases. It was the general broker who put the merchant in touch with another type of broker dealing with specialised goods. Thus a general broker would control a wide-ranging network of middlemen, who undertook the task of supplying his principal a large variety of items required for export or would sell the goods imported. There were general brokers for individual merchants or groups of merchants.[66] The brokerage fee then charged ranged from 1/2 per cent to 2 per cent.[67]

A more specialised broker was the guarantee broker who served as an indispensable link between the indigenous credit sector and his European clients. The latter paid him a commission for procuring loans, the repayment of which he guaranteed.

Freighting and Ship-ownership

In the expanding trade on the west coast of India, shippers made much profits transporting cargoes belonging to various merchants. They charged a freighting fee which could be paid in advance or on the safe arrival of the consignments at the port of destination.[68] Freight charges varied with the distance covered. Venkatesha Kamat received Rs. 180 as freight charges for transporting fabrics and clothes from Surat on behalf of Feliciano Antonio Nogueira based at Lisbon on board the ship *Estrela de Madrugada.*[69] Freight charges for transportation to Macao ranged between 10 per cent and 20 per cent.[70] Sixteen boxes of incense weighing 18-½ picos were despatched by the Mhamai brothers to Macao from Goa and the freight charged was at the rate of 20 per cent.[71]

Consignments were freighted not only on private ships but also on crown ones. Freight charges on goods despatched on such ships from Diu to Moçambique were fixed at the rate of 5 *patacas* for every bundle of clothes and 2-½ patacas for each box of oil or butter.

Much interest was evinced in ship-building, especially with the rise of the China Trade. Indo-Portuguese merchants, especially those settled at Bombay and Daman needed vessels of their own which would be more profitable than shipping cargoes on vessels belonging to others. It was the rise and development of the opium trade that compelled the merchant to play a more active role as the ship-owner. It became necessary to have a special fleet of clippers, receiving ships and coastal vessels. Hence they invested their capital in the construction of their own ships at Surat, Bombay and Daman.

However, shipping was not developed to a great extent, because owning a ship blocked a substantial part of the merchant's capital. Ship-ownership was generally individual. Shared proprietorship was rare. The merchant did not own more than three ocean-going vessels however affluent he might have been. The Mhamais for instance possessed a few *pattamars.* Rogerio de Faria was the proud owner of three ships, plus coasting vessels used for transporting personal consignments and those belonging to others to Macao, China, Moçambique and various parts of India. The Loureiros, too, were ship-owners.[72]

Insurance

The system of insurance too, was a fairly well-organised one. Insurance was in fact indispensable in case of rich cargoes of opium, treasure, slaves, ivory and the like because of the great risks involved. Transport of goods over long distances had never been free from risks, even at the best of times. Piracy, treacherous seas, storms, floods, fires and periodic warfare made the movement of ships and their cargoes unsafe. Under such circumstances insurance policies were drawn up in the form of *Jakmi hundis*. The insurers undertook to indemnify total or partial loss caused by maritime perils, in consideration of a certain amount called 'premium'. The charge for insuring goods and ships depended upon the risks involved on a particular route and the nature of the goods. The rate of insurance charges ranged between 2 per cent and 35 per cent.[73] The exporters had to pay a premium of about 2-½ per cent for opium shipments despatched to China from Bombay during the 1830s.[74]

There are several references to the practice of insurance in the Mhamai correspondence.[75] For instance, Jacinto Domingos of Surat in April 1790 in a letter to the Mhamais speaks of three copies of an insurance policy involving a premium sum of Rs. 25,000 prepared for and at the request of the Mhamais. The policy was taken on the ship *Salvamento* travelling from Goa to Batavia.[76] There is also a reference made to an insurance policy done in Surat for Rs. 40,000 on a vessel *Marques de Anjeya* which left for Lisbon in 1798.[77]

Banking and Credit System

It is an economic law well-confirmed by events in history that prosperity in purely mercantile pursuits resulting in the accumulation of wealth leads by necessity to banking activities on the part of successful merchants. Indeed the merchants of the *Estado* were no exception to this rule. Their great wealth and the availability of liquid funds enabled them to exert great influence on the monetary markets of Goa, Daman and Diu and led to their functioning as bankers and financiers in a very extensive way.

Money-lending was considered as an honest calling. It was not the monopoly of a particular caste or community. A money-lender not only advanced loans to the known but even to unknown persons, when recommended by someone known to him and who would act as surety for the loan.

The Mhamais for instance served as bankers supplying loans and providing credit to both Asian and European traders as well as to the government. Montigny, the French Resident at Poona would repeatedly call upon the brothers to supply him large sums of money. In June 1785, two Frenchmen Souillac and Monneron requested the Mhamais, on behalf of Montigny, to provide a loan of Rs. 15,000 and assured them that against this loan, bills of exchange would be issued on the royal French treasury at Pondicherry.[78]

There is no doubt that the rates of interest charged by the indigenous money-lenders and bankers varied according to the standing of the borrower, the amount and period covered by the loan and the nature of the security offered. The rate of interest charged in Portuguese India varied between 9 and 10 per cent.[79] There is every possibility that some money-lenders might have resorted to usury and extortionist methods. But when the customers had no adequate security to offer no responsible banker would find it good business to lend money at reasonable rates. The indigenous bankers and money-lenders took extraordinary risks and had to safeguard themselves by charging a high rate.

An important source of credit for investment were respondentia bonds.[80] Loans were granted to shippers to help them purchase an export cargo and to charter a vessel. On the Coromandel coast around the mid-eighteenth century respondentia loans at times included a bottomry element. Money was provided to a ship-owner or a person loading cargo on a ship upon the merchandise laden. The ship was mentioned in the bond along with its destination. Money was either lent for a one-way trip or a return trip to the port of origin. The loan was cleared within a fixed number of days of the arrival of the ship at the declared destination. Beyond that date the lesser land interest applied. Owing to the demarcation of sailing seasons, the bond would specifically mention whether it was concerned with the south-west monsoon or the north-east. If the ship could not return before the shift of monsoon, the land interest was to apply. If money was advanced for both the seasons the interest was doubled, as the risks involved were greater. Sometimes the loan was given on the outward bound ship with the stipulation that on the return voyage from the port of destination to the port of origin, the risk could run on any ship the borrower would choose to conduct his passage on.[81] In all probability such was also the practice on the west coast of India during the late eighteenth-early nineteenth centuries.

On respondentia loans, the interest charged was heavy and depended on the length of the voyage and the risks attached to the places of destination. There were different rates for long-distance shipping and coastal shipping. The respondentia system was undoubtedly a popular system of short-term lending and credit.

The Portuguese credit system was a properly managed system, in which the duties and obligations of the creditor as well as the debtor were clearly specified. Any departure from the regulations laid down attracted social censure and action by the State.

Independent Trading and Speculation

Originally, most of the Agency Houses had little to do with mercantile transactions on their account. But later, especially after 1783, with the expansion of *Estado's* commerce, they were tempted to take to independent trading, operating exclusively with their own capital, besides acting as commission agents for others.[82] They also indulged in speculation. The lucrative interport trade of Asia favoured the fortunes of these houses and encouraged them to indulge in various activities of a speculative kind within and outside the sphere of commerce. An individual partner by virtue of his entrepreneurial ability was able to identify profit-making opportunities in the market and his high-risk ventures often succeeded through careful planning. For instance the opium trade avidly participated in, by the merchants of Portuguese India, was a risky business.[83] It was felt that the trade could be highly profitable but full of uncertainty. The profit from such business was a major source of capital accumulation.

Other Services Undertaken

The merchants also rendered services other than those associated with trade and commerce. The Mhamais for instance, were associated with a salvage operation of the vessel *Henrieta* cast away on the rocks of the Aguada fort. The sale of the cargo saved from *Henrieta* was sold by Vithal Shet of Anjediva under the supervision of the Mhamais. Later, the brothers were called upon by Brown and Dineur, a Mahe-based firm, to provide a statement of accounts proceeding from such a sale and to return the merchandise left unsold.[84] The Mhamais also played a major role in the salvage operation of *Novo Ceilão* in 1807. This Portuguese ship probably belonging to Joaquim Jose Figueiredo, was wrecked off Mangalore coast. The property of the wreck was saved and handed over to the said Figueiredo after he paid Philip Sheldon, the British Resident at Mangalore, the expenses incurred in the salvage operation.[85]

The merchants would also undertake to procure the services of one merchant for another. Rogerio de Faria in 1823 had procured the services of João Thomas de Aquino for James A. Maxwell. Maxwell himself mentions in a letter to Aquino that he would be liberally rewarded by the British Government for whatever services he might render.[86]

The merchants would also attend to the need for accommodation of those temporarily putting up in the Portuguese Indian cities, at the instructions or the request of other merchants. Thus Louis Monneron requested the Mhamais to lodge Viscount de Castries, commandant of the royal frigate *La Subtile* in his brother's house at Goa.[87] Likewise, in February 1789, St. Riveul informed the Mhamais that he planned to visit the Governor of Goa and issued instructions to arrange for his accommodation and food. He also wanted the brothers to make arrangements for him to visit Old Goa.[88]

Leading and politically influential merchants would be often approached for letters of recommendation or to intercede on their behalf with the authorities. Abbe Cottineau de Kloguen had approached Rogerio de Faria for such letters to be presented to authorities at Goa. In an undated letter addressed to the Mhamai brothers we gather that Rev. Francisco Pascoal de Menezes, Vicar for several years at Tellicherry, expired leaving all his belongings to his nephews. The Mhamais were approached to provide a letter of recommendation addressed to the Resident and commanding officer at the port of Tellicherry so as to facilitate the handing over of the estate of the deceased to Leonardo Jose de Menezes who had earlier come to Tellicherry armed with certificates to stake the claim of the nephews as lawful heirs, only to find that the belongings of the said deceased were sealed.[89]

Merchants were at times required to serve as attorneys and witnesses

Jaggivandas, Gouvaram Jaggivandas were among others — domiciled at Surat — who conducted business with the merchants of the *Estado*.[113] Jacinto Domingos, for instance, would supply textiles among other commodities to Goa merchants.[114]

Cochin

David Rabbi, the son of Ezekiel Rabbi, who had migrated from Haleb in Syria and had established himself as one of the wealthiest merchants of Cochin, also entered into commercial transactions with the Mhamais and other merchants of Goa.[115] He would often consign textiles, cloves and nuts to the Mhamais for sale in Goa.[116] In March 1784 he shipped to Goa 10 boxes of cloves weighing 1,000 lbs. worth Rs. 3,500, which cost him Rs. 3 1/2 per lb. wt. The Mhamais too elicited the services of David Rabbi to sell off European fabrics and to obtain tobacco.[117]

The French Connection

The French officials, whether at Mahe, or at Pondicherry, or those stationed at the Maratha court maintained business contacts with merchants on the west coast of India, especially with those in Goa. The Mhamais, J. B. Goethals and other Goan merchants figure significantly in the French business correspondence directed to the *Estado*. The services of the *Estado* merchants especially those of the Mhamais were used to procure certain commodities, to sell off their goods, to arbitrate in legal matters, to mediate with local authorities on their behalf in order to win favours and privileges, etc. The Portuguese Indian merchants too needed French assistance to promote their business prospects. But from available documents it appears that the French need was more clearly defined than the Portuguese Indian one.

Mahe

Picot was among those at Mahe who deserves to be mentioned. He held the position of commandant in Mahe till 1773. He was re-appointed at the end of 1775 and remained in this position till he was compelled to surrender Mahe to the British in 1779. It was Picot who conveyed to the Mhamais their appointment as the principal brokers of the French nation at Goa and that the old right to this position earlier enjoyed by their uncle, Kushta, had been annulled.[118] In his letters to the Mhamais, we gather that he was using their services to dispatch and receive correspondence in utmost secrecy and care, to and from St. Lubin, Montigny, Coronat and Warnet, French officials at the Maratha court.[119]

Canaple who had administered Mahe for three years till 1790 also had business dealings with the Mhamais. Since 1789 Canaple repeatedly requested for ducks, geese, sheep and chickens to be sent to Mahe to tide over difficult times —the scarcity of food supplies — caused by Tipu Sultan's embargo and his wars in Malabar.[120] He would also frequently order for cashewnuts and ivory figurines.[121] The Mhamais too commissioned the services of Canaple to procure pepper.[122]

Boyer, the Agent of the *Compagnie de Colonne* at Mahe drew upon the services of the Mhamais. Like Canaple he would place periodic orders for domesticated birds — chickens, ducks, turkey — to overcome shortages of food supplies.[123] Boyer in April 1788 tried to organise a slave sale between the Mhamais and Mr. Roselly, Captain of the royal frigate, *La Meduse*.[124]

The Mahe-based Brown and Dineur had developed productive links with the Mhamais, J. B. Goethals and other businessmen at Goa. Brown and Dineur would make regular requests to the Mhamais for workers.[125]

There were three to four *pattamars* plying to and fro with regularity between Goa and Mahe, carrying goods of either Brown and Dineur or the Mhamais. The latter usually placed orders for pepper, coconuts, copra, wild cinnamon and rice.[126] The Mhamais usually sent down paper, wines of Portugal, chocolate tins, some textiles, cork stoppers and sundries.[127] They would also despatch salt obtained from Nerul and Siridão in Goa, and large consignments of tiles.[128] In December 1805, Brown and Dineur planned to have their warehouses tiled. Since Goan tiles were better than their Malabar counterparts, they requested the Mhamais to send 50,000 tiles. In addition to this they wanted the brothers to send masons who would fix the tiles. Brown and Dineur would also order for mangoes, cashewnuts and the like.[129] There were also repeated orders placed with the Mhamais for ivory figurines and gold thread. Dineur had been commissioned to procure the latter for his Pallankottai clients.[130]

Pondicherry

The *Estado* merchants had connections with Moracin, a Pondicherry-based French official, who had made a fortune in privateering while holding high official positions as Intendant and Commissaire-General of the Marine. The Mhamais were requested to intervene to recover Moracin's money from the *Fazenda Real* as inordinate delay was causing considerable harm to Moracin's business interests. Once the money was recovered the Mhamais were instructed to leave it in the custody of de Souza of Goa, brother of Antonio de Souza based at Madras. The latter would then make necessary arrangements to route it to Pondicherry via Madras.[131]

The Maratha court

French officials at the Maratha court like Montigny and Warnet depended on the Mhamais to resolve problems afflicting them. The Mhamais were crucial to their immediate needs. As observed earlier the Mhamais often advanced large sums of money to Montigny and the same was reimbursed by the Pondicherry Administration.[132] In addition, Montigny conducted business with and acquired loans from the Mhamais in his private capacity.[133]

In 1778, Warnet found himself in a tight spot. He had been detained by the Marathas in their fortress at Mores (?) over the sale of the cargo of *Le Sartine*. Thereupon, his trusted servant, Lajeunesse was urged to arrange for help, financial or otherwise at Goa, for his release.[134] Warnet planned in detail the manner in which he would extricate himself from his present predicament. The Mhamais were involved in his plans. However, Warnet's plans could not materialise. This put him in a state of depression. His situation worsened when his merchandise perished in a shipwreck and consequently not a pie was left in his account at Goa.[135]

Mysore

De Lalee, a French general in the service of Hyder Ali, utilised the services of the Mhamais. He had his guns lying in the warehouses of Goa for a long time, for which in his letters addressed to the Mhamais, he expressed much anxiety.[136] In April 1780 the Mhamais tried to set his anxieties at rest by reassuring him that every care was being taken and that 12 cases had been withdrawn from the Arsenal and the guns were sent back after being thoroughly greased.[137] De Lalee thanked the Mhamais profusely for this service. Some years later when he learnt that the Mhamais might be able to clinch a deal to dispose off his guns, he expressed much satisfaction at this arrangement for he felt the proceeds would come in handy to pay off a debt of Rs. 2,700 he had contracted.[138]

Other close associates of the *Estado*-based merchants in coastal India were Antonio de Souza at Madras, Joaquim Luis Antonio Vaz at Poona,

Bento Roiz at Mangalore, Francisco Gonsalves de Lima and the Barettos at Calcutta, Mussa Beanj, Mussa Caca, Moqui Biary and Antonio Joaquim de Almeida at Tellicherry and Chouvancara Cunchy Paquey at Cochin/ Calicut.[139]

Overseas Network

The complex mercantile network of Portuguese India also encompassed those areas beyond the shores of India.

Macao

Apart from opium shipments proceeding directly from Daman to Macao some would arrive at Goa and would later be consigned to Macao by Goa merchants on their own account or on behalf of their principals at Bombay and other parts of western India.[140] Thus, for instance, the Mhamais would often despatch opium cargoes for Jose Francisco Pereira to Macao. In a letter dated 3rd April 1804, Jose Francisco Pereira requested the Mhamai brothers to receive 50 chests of opium despatched by Ira Punja of Bhavnagar, to load them on board the vessel leaving for Macao and to consign them to Januario Agostinho de Almeida based at Macao.[141] Opium was also despatched at the request of merchants residing at Macao. Thus Rogerio de Faria would despatch opium from Bombay or Daman on behalf and on the account of Joaquim Jose Ferreira Viegas, Albino G. de Araujo, D. Ignacio, Widow of Paiva, Antonio Pereira, Antonio G. de Silveira, D. L. Calvo and Co., Joaquim Jose de Santos and others domiciled at Macao.

Among other Macao-based traders having intimate business ties with the *Estado* merchants like the Mhamais mention must be made of Dona Luisa de Mello Sampayo. In January 1802, she informed the brothers of the despatch of granulated sugar, satin and damask piece-goods. In turn she expected them to send Surat thread and stockings manufactured at Anjediva.[142] The Mhamais also had dealings with Carlos Jose Pereira of Macao. They would consign sandal-wood, artillery equipment and glass-ware to him and the latter in turn would despatch Chinese crockery.[143]

East Africa

The *Estado* merchants had also forged business links with East African merchants. The Mhamais for instance were supplied black slaves by

Antonio Henriques Nogueira of Moçambique.[144] Another Moçambican merchant, João da Silva Guedes supplied slaves, ivory and other commodities. In turn he would dispose wheat, tea, piece-goods, pitch, sugar-candy and other items on behalf of the Mhamais.[145] Slaves brought to Goa would later reach Macao, Ceylon and even the French islands in the Indian Ocean.[146] Antonio da Cruz Almeida and Jose Pereira Machado were other traders at Moçambique well-disposed towards the Portuguese Indian mercantile community.[147]

Mauritius

Goa merchants had established close business relations with the French merchants and business firms in Mauritius too. The Monneron brothers Janvier, Pierre and Louis had appointed the Mhamais as their agents with powers of attorney to conduct business on their behalf at Goa. Likewise the Monnerons were required to render similar services in Mauritius for the Mhamai brothers, who had been particularly keen to recover a loan they had advanced to Chevalier and the interest on it, from the Mauritius-based Gattereau and Co. Apparently the latter served as agents for Chevalier. The Mhamais, in turn, were entrusted with the task of executing the will of late J. C. Rodrigues.[148] The Mhamais even supplied the Monnerons with slaves.[149]

Lisbon

The *Estado* merchants also had extensive dealings with the distant Lisbon-based merchants and financiers. Indian cotton textiles formed the bulk of the cargoes proceeding to Portugal. João Antonio de Amovim Viana, Pedro Quintella, Jose Alvarez de Silva, Jose Simoens Rebello, Christovão Jose Araujo, Christian and João Poppe, Manoel de Silva Franco, Carlos and Francisco Jose Marçal de Britto, João Horacio Houston, Francisco Xavier de Maya, Jose Caetano Monteiro, Joaquim Jose Gomes, Antonio Geraro, Antonio Jose Pires Bragança were amongst other Lisbon merchants who had close links with the Portuguese Indian merchants.[150]

Brazil

Brazil since the 1770s opened its doors officially to Indian cotton products. Portuguese Indian merchants including the Mhamais had business connections with Brazilian merchants like Simão de Rocha Loureiro, João Miz Barrozo, Antonio Jose Viegas, Rufino Peres Bauptista, Estevão Jose Araujo, Francisco Jose Colffs and Casmiro widow and Sons.[151]

The first section of this chapter has focused on the division of merchants on either caste or communal lines. Such groups were however not well-knit and well-integrated. They were not pure mercantile communities in the sense that all its members were merchants and were engaged in business activities by tradition. The banias of Daman and Diu alone came closest to this concept of a mercantile community. They made business the essence of their lives.

The subsequent sections have demonstrated a close affinity between merchants. Deep bonds of cooperation and expressions of trust underlined mercantile relationships. This cooperation stemmed from the over-riding profit-making motives which enabled the merchants to transcend the barriers of caste, creed and colour. In their quest for wealth, group communal and caste affiliations were set aside. Their business services were extended to any class of businessmen, whether English or French, European or Asian, Hindu or Muslim, if such relationships would yield profit.

The exigencies of the situation also demanded co-operation rather than conflict. It is unthinkable that any individual merchant, however powerful he may have been, could carry out single-handedly a large and risky oceanic and coastal trade, without the help of business associates. The very character of such an enterprise, the export and import, the sale and purchase and other operations, made cooperation and mutual assistance paramount.

REFERENCES AND NOTES

1. M. N. Pearson, "The Portuguese in India", *The New Cambridge History of India,* Cambridge, 1987, pp. 94-95.
2. A. R. Disney, *Twilight of the Pepper Empire. Portuguese Trade in South-West India in the Early Seventeenth Century,* Cambridge, 1978, pp. 19-20.
3. Celsa Pinto, "Goa-based Overseas and Coastal Trade", *Goa Through the Ages,* vol. II, (ed.) Teotonio R. de Souza, New Delhi, 1989, pp. 176-177.
4. A. B. de Bragança Pereira, *Etnografia da India Portuguesa,* vol. II, Nova Goa, 1923, p. 37.
5. Teotonio R. de Souza, "Xendi Tax : A Phase in the History of Luso-Hindu Relations in Goa, (1704-1841)", *Studies in Foreign Relations of India,* (ed.) Q. M. Joshi, Hyderabad, 1975, p. 32.
6. M. N. Pearson, "Indigenous Dominance in a Colonial Economy : The Goa Rendas, 1600-1670", *Mare Luso-Indicum,* Tome II, Geneve Librarie Droz II, rue Massot, 1973, p. 65.

7. Teotonio R. de Souza, "Mhamai House Records : Indigenous Sources for Indo-Portuguese Historiography", *Instituto de Investigação Tropical*, Lisboa, 1985, p. 935.
8. Pearson, *op. cit.*, p. 167.
9. See Appendix 1.
10. HAG : *MR*, 144A, fls. 93, 95v-96.
11. See Appendix 1.
12. Souza, *op. cit.*, p. 939.
13. XCHR : *MHP* (Portuguese), doc. dated 28 June 1797.
14. HAG : *RGF*, 2281, fl. 495.
15. XCHR : *MHP* (Portuguese), doc. dated 6 Aug. 1809; HAG : *RGF*, 2287, fl. 63.
16. HAG : *RGF*, 2822, fl. 495.
17. Souza, *op. cit.*, p. 940.
18. HAG : *RGF*, 2281, fl.292; 2287, fls. 351-352; Miguel Vicente de Abreu, *O Governo do Vice-Rei Conde do Rio Pardo*, doc. no. 46, Nova Goa, 1869, p.120.
19. Abreu, *op. cit.*, p. 120.
20. HAG : *RGF*, 2282, fls. 177, 253.
21. XCHk : *MHP* (Portuguese), docs. dated 22 April 1825, 9 Dec. 1826, 28 Feb. 1827, 23 March 1832, 3 May 1836, 21 Jan. 1838, 3 Jan. 1844, 21 June 1847, 25 Oct. 1847, 24 Nov. 1849.
22. XCHR : *MHP* (Portuguese), docs. dated 25 Feb. 1791, 2 March 1798.
23. Teresa Albuquerque, "Santa-Cruz" *Calapor. Profile of a Village in Goa*, Goa, 1989, p. 35.
24. Bragança Pereira, *op. cit.*, p. 49.
25. HAG : *MR*, 164F, fl. 1630; 168D, fl. 1020; Claudio Lagrange Monteiro de Barbuda, *IDJ*, Nova Goa, 1841, p. 51.
26. HAG : *MR*, 205B, fl. 684.
27. M. N. Pearson, "Banyas and Brahmins : Their Role in the Portuguese Indian Economy", *Coastal Western India*, New Delhi, 1987, p. 104.
28. Disney, *op. cit.*, p. 18.
29. XCHR : *MHP : passim.*
30. A. Cunha, *Sir Roger de Faria. Notas Genealógicas e Biográficas*, Nova Goa, 1828, pp. 10, 16.
31. *Instituto Vasco da Gama*, 1ª serie, 1872, p. 247.
32. BA : *RD*, 6/138, doc. dated 22 April 1826.
33. HAG : *Macau*, 1295, fls. 152-152v.
34. HAG : *Macau*, 1296, fl. 74.
35. Teotonio R. de Souza, "Rogerio de Faria : An Indo-Portuguese Trader with China Links", A paper presented at *VI ISIPH*, Macau, 21-26 Oct. 1991, pp. 7-8.
36. Cunha, *op. cit.*, p. 34.
37. *Instituto Vasco da Gama*, 1ª serie, 1872, p. 247.
38. HAG : *MR*, 211, fl. 326; A. F. Moniz, "A Feitoria Portuguesa de Surrate , *O Oriente Português*, vol. XV, 1ª serie, pp. 27-28.
39. HAG : *Correspondencia de Damão*, 1075, fl. 50; *Macau*, 1296, fl. 74; Moniz, *op. cit.*, p. 28.
40. Cunha, *op. cit.*, p. 5.
41. Teotonio R. de Souza, "Capital Input in Goa's Freedom Struggle : The Bombay Connection" *Indo-Portuguese History : Old Issues, New Questions*, (ed.) Teotonio R. de Souza, New Delhi, 1984, pp. 105-106, 111.
42. BUL : *J. J. Papers*, vol. 351, pp.170-172.
43. Souza, *op. cit.*, pp. 111-112.

44. *Ibid.*, p. 109.
45. HAG : *AG*, 6815, fls. 5. 8-9, 18-19, 43, 61, 67, 71, 85, 88-89, 102, 106, 114, 118, 127, 137, 164, 186, 195, 216, 222, 231, 236, 252, 261, 267, 275; 6816, fls. 159, 179, 192, 195, 197, 199-200, 203-205, 209, 211-212, 216, 224, 236, 253, 261, 268, 280, 283-284, 294, 305, 308-309, 319, 334, 359.
46. HAG : *AG*, 6810, fls. 315, 318.
47. Dosabhai Framji Karaka, *History of Parsees*, vol. I, p. 27.
48. *Ibid.*, p. 9.
49. Dosabhai Framji Karaka, *History of Parsees*, vol. II, p. 45.
50. Antonio Moniz, *Noticias e Documentos para Historia de Damão Antiga Provincia do Norte*, vol.IV, p. 75.
51. Bragança Pereira, *op. cit.*, p. 57.
52. *Ibid.*, p. 36.
53. HAG : *RGF*, 2279, fls. 673-675.
54. HAG : *AG*, 8117, fls. 243-244, 449; 8118, fls. 7, 9, 58, 134, 311, 316, 323-325, 335.
55. Walter J. Fischel, "Leading Jews in the Service of Portuguese India", Reprint, *Jewish Quarterly Review*, vol. XLVII, July 1956, pp. 38, 45, 49.
56. *Ibid.*, pp. 47, 49; A. F. Moniz, "Um Judeu Director de Feitoria Portuguesa de Surrate", *O Oriente Português*, vol. II, Nova Goa, 1905, pp. 55-58.
57. XCHR : *MHP* (Portuguese), doc. dated 4 July 1778.
58. Domingos Teles, "Alguns alemaes, holandeses e outros estrangeiros em Goa", *Colloquim*, vol. 2, no. 1, Jan-June 1979, p. 51.
59 *Ibid.*, p. 52.
60. XCHR : *MHP* (Portuguese), doc. dated 27 July 1787.
61. XCHR : *MHP* (Portuguese), docs. dated 15 Jan. 1788, 31 March 1791, 31 July 1799.
62. XCHR : *MHP* (Portuguese), docs. dated 16 Sept. 1788, 31 March 1799.
63. XCHR : *MHP* (Portuguese), doc. dated 15 May 1787.
64. BUL : *J. J. Papers*, vol. 351, pp. 333-334.
65. Ashin Das Gupta, *Indian Merchants and the Decline of Surat c. 1700-1750*, Weisbaden, 1979, pp. 85-86.
66. Das Gupta, *op. cit.*, p. 84.
67. XCHR : *MHP* (Portuguese), doc. dated 24 March 1791, 19 Jan. 1798.
68. HAG : *RGF*, 2154, fls. 47-48; 2287, fl. 343; HAG : *Dio*, 5665, *passim; MHP* (Portuguese), undated doc.
69. XCHR : *MHP* (Portuguese), doc. dated 14 Feb. 1785.
70. XCHR : *MHP* (Portuguese), doc. dated 10 Nov. 1792.
71. XCHR : *MHP* (Portuguese), doc. dated 4 Nov. 1810.
72. Their ship *Rainha dos Anjos* figured prominently in the Asiatic Trade : AHU : *MI*, Maço 47, no. 310, doc. dated Sept. 1790.
73. XCHR : *MHP* (Portuguese), docs. dated 8 Feb. 1796, 9 Jan. 1798.
74. BUL : *J. J. Papers*, vol. 358, docs. dated 5 May 1838, 19 May 1838.
75. XCHR : *MHP* (Portuguese), docs. dated 15 May 1787, 2 Oct. 1792, 15 Jan. 1825, undated doc 79. The official records too provide evidence of the practice of marine insurance in the *Estado da India* since the sixteenth century. T. R. de Souza, "Marine Insurance and Indo-Portuguese Trade History : An Aid to Maritime Historiography", *IESHR*, vol. XIV, no. 3, July-Sept. 1977. pp. 374-384.
76. XCHR : *MHP* (Portuguese), doc. dated 7 April 1790.
77. XCHR : *MHP* (Portuguese), doc. dated 31 Aug. 1798.
78. XCHR : *MHP* (French), vol. 7, fls. 13, 14-15, 16, 23, 24.
79. XCHR : *MHP* (Portuguese), doc. dated 31 July 1798; *MHP* (borrador), doc. dated 24 Jan. 1808.

80. XCHR : *MHP* (Portuguese), docs. dated 12 April 1783, 15 May 1787, 30 Dec. 1789, 10 Feb. 1792.
81. Sinappah Arasaratnam, *Merchants, Companies and Commerce on the Coromandel Coast,* 1650-1740, Delhi, 1986, pp. 278-279.
82. HAG : *AG,* 6325, fls. 91-92; 6331, fls. 535-599 : *passim;* 6807, fls. 467, 510, 579, 586-599, 778; 6809, fl. 348; 6810 fls. 273, 347; XCHR : *MHP* (Portuguese), docs. dated 23 Jan. 1786, 8 March 1786.
83. HAG : *Macau,* 1311, fls. 117-117v.
84. XCHR : *MHP* (French), vol. 5, fl. 107; *MHP* (English), vol. 1, doc. dated 15 Sept. 1793.
85. XCHR : *MHP* (English), vol. 2, docs. dated 8 Sept. 1807, 7 Oct. 1807, 22 Oct. 1807; vol. 3, undated doc.
86. BA : *RD,* 29/81, 1823.
87. XCHR : *MHP* (French), vol. 2, fl. 49.
88. XCHR : *MHP* (French), vol. 4, fl. 20.
89. XCHR : *MHP* (Portuguese), undated doc.
90. XCHR : *MHP* (Portuguese), doc. dated 30 July 1806.
91. XCHR : *MHP* (French), vol. 4, fl. 69.
92. XCHR : *MHP* (French), vol. 6, fls. 13-14v.
93. XCHR : *MHP* (Portuguese), doc. dated 29 Dec. 1795.
94. XCHR : *MHP* (Portuguese), doc. dated 21 Sept. 1796.
95. cf. 65; Irfan Habib, "System of Bills of Exchange (Hundis)". *Essays in Medieval Indian Economic History,* New Delhi, 1987, pp. 207-208, 212.
96. Amancio Gracias, *Regimen Economico-Financeira da India Portuguesa,* Nova Goa, 1909, p. 5; XCHR : *MHP* : *passim.*
97. Habib, *op. cit.,* p. 215.
98. XCHR : *MHP* (Portuguese), docs. dated 30 Nov. 1787, 13 March 1791, 25 May 1791, 13 July 1791.
99. XCHR : *MHP* (Portuguese), doc. dated 21 Jan. 1789.
100. XCHR : *MHP* (Portuguese), doc. dated 5 Aug. 1792.
101. XCHR : *MHP* (Portuguese), doc. dated Oct. 1788.
102. XCHR : *MHP* (Portuguese), docs. dated 22 Jan. 1783, 14 Jan. 1784, 25 Jan. 1790.
103. XCHR : *MHP* (Portuguese), doc. dated 30 Nov. 1787.
104. XCHR : *MHP* (Portuguese), doc. nos. 1242, 13282, 13298.
105. XCHR : *MHP* (Portuguese), doc. dated 26 Dec. 1793.
106. XCHR : *MHP* (Portuguese), docs. dated 22 Aug. 1791, 27 Aug. 1791, 28 Aug. 1791, 6 Sept. 1791.
107. XCHR : *MHP* (English), vol. 2, doc. dated 31 July 1803.
108. XCHR : *MHP* (English), vol. 2, doc. dated 19 Feb. 1812.
109. XCHR : *MHP* (Portuguese), doc. dated 30 March 1789.
110. HAG : *Correspondencia de Damão,* 1061, fl. 362.
111. XCHR : *MHP* : *passim.*
112. XCHR : *MHP* (English), vol. 1, docs. dated 22 Sept. 1792, 31 July 1794; vol. 2, docs. dated 31 Dec. 1802, 7 Jan. 1813.
113. XCHR : *MHP* (Portuguese), docs. dated 3 June 1788, 24 Feb. 1789.
114. XCHR : *MHP* (Portuguese), doc. dated 14 Aug. 1789.
115. Ashin Das Gupta, *Malabar in Asian Trade 1740-1800,* Cambridge, 1967, p. 104.
116. XCHR : *MHP* (Portuguese), docs. dated 22 Sept. 1783, 3 Jan. 1787.
117. XCHR : *MHP* (Portuguese), docs. dated 3 Jan. 1787, 21 Jan. 1789.
118. XCHR : *MHP* (Portuguese), doc. dated 5 Dec. 1777.

119. XCHR : *MHP* (Portuguese), docs. dated 11 Nov. 1777, 29 Nov. 1777, 5 Dec. 1777, 21 Jan. 1778, 13 Feb. 1778, 25 July 1778, 1 Dec. 1778, 14 Feb. 1779, 5 March 1779; Teotonio R. de Souza, "Goa-Mahe Trade Links (Late Eighteenth-Early Nineteenth Centuries) : A New Source Material", *Studies in Maritime History*, (ed.) K. S. Mathew, Pondicherry, 1990, p. 166.
120. XCHR : *MHP* (French), vol. 4, fls. 5, 22, 65, 78, 118.
121. XCHR : *MHP* (French), vol. 4, fls. 16, 65, 78.
122. XCHR : *MHP* (French), vol. 4, fl. 22.
123. XCHR : *MHP* (Portuguese), docs. dated 26 Nov. 1789, 10 Feb. 1790, 20 Aug. 1792.
124. XCHR : *MHP* (Portuguese), doc. dated 26 April 1788.
125. XCHR : *MHP* (French), vol. 6, fls. 8, 23.
126. XCHR : *MHP* (French), vol. 6, fls. 5, 63, 76, 81-81v, 87v, 118-119; *MHP* (Portuguese), doc. dated 25 Nov. 1789.
127. XCHR : *MHP* (French), vol. 6, fls. 16, 18, 55-55v, 126, 129-129v, 133, 240, 245; *MHP* (English), vol. 1, doc. dated 15 April 1798.
128. XCHR : *MHP* (French), vol. 6, fls. 93v, 94v.
129. XCHR : *MHP* (French), vol. 6, fls. 45-45v, 75, 77, 87-87v; *MHP* (Portuguese), doc. dated 20 March 1791; *MHP* (English), vol. 1, doc. dated 15 April 1793.
130. XCHR : *MHP* (French), vol. 6, fls. 104, 112v-113, 138, 140, 143.
131. XCHR : *MHP* (French), vol. 2, fls. 47-47v.
132. XCHR : *MHP* (French), vol. 7, fls. 13, 14-15, 16, 23, 24.
133. XCHR : *MHP* (French), vol. 2, fls. 86-86v.
134. XCHR : *MHP* (French), vol. 1, fls. 13-14.
135. XCHR : *MHP* (French), vol. 1, fls. 30-32v.
136. XCHR : *MHP* (French), vol. 1, fls. 49-49v; *MHP* (Portuguese), doc. dated 20 Aug. 1778.
137. XCHR : *MHP* (French), vol. 1, fl. 52.
138. XCHR : *MHP* (French), vol. 2, fl. 50.
139. XCHR : *MHP* : *passim*.
140. XCHR : *MHP* (Portuguese), docs. dated 3 April 1804, 21 Nov. 1807.
141. XCHR : *MHP* (Portuguese), doc. dated 3 April 1804.
142. XCHR : *MHP* (Portuguese), doc. dated 5 Jan. 1802.
143. XCHR : *MHP* (Portuguese), docs. dated 5 Jan. 1793, 9 Jan. 1793.
144. XCHR : *MHP* (Portuguese), doc. dated 20 Aug. 1787.
145. Teotonio R. de Souza, "Mhamai House Records : Indigenous Sources for Indo-Portuguese Historiography", pp. 945.
146. Pinto, *op. cit.*, p. 191.
147. XCHR : *MHP* : *passim*.
148. XCHR : *MHP* (French), vol. 2, fls. 40-40v.
149. XCHR : *MHP* (French), vol. 3, fls. 65-66.
150. XCHR : *MHP* : *passim*.
151. XCHR : *MHP* : *passim*.

3

THE STATE : TOWARDS A NEW PRAGMATISM

Since the dawn of the seventeenth century things had been going wrong for the Portuguese in the East largely due to Dutch intrusion in the Indian Ocean. The Portuguese had to forfeit many wealthy outposts, and the *Estado da India* shrank to a little more than a collection of moribund trading posts, a shadow of its former self.

As decades rolled by the fiscal problems of the *Estado* assumed alarming proportions. The regime, saddled with a chronically barren treasury, wallowed in debt. There was the distinct possibility that this precarious nature of the financial situation could cause the short-circuiting of the *Estado*. Its very survival and existence was at stake. The authorities at Goa were compelled to seek ways and means of boosting its fortunes, Portugal being in the grip of a deepening economic crisis. Much reliance was soon placed on the Portuguese country trade. Local private involvement in the intra-Asian trade helped to ameliorate the chronic financial problem, to stave off the imminent danger of collapse and thus keep Portugal's imperial possessions in the East going.

In view of the substantial financial benefits that could be derived from the Asian trade, the authorities were inclined to stimulate the trade as best as they could. The efforts of the State to revamp the customs administration, its policy of appeasement towards the mercantile classes and the vulnerability it displayed towards the unofficial involvement of officialdom, had their roots in a dependency syndrome revolving round the intra-Asiatic trade.

Customs Administration and Mechanisms : Structural Transformation and Rejuvenation

Customs House of Goa

The Customs House of Goa (*Alfandega de Goa*) underwent a thorough transformation since its establishment on the banks of the river Mandovi in 1479. The celebrated Marques de Pombal was largely responsible for this. His customs legislation on Goa thoroughly overhauled all the institutions and branches of the customs administrative system. In April 1771 steps were taken to get rid of all the cumbersome and vexed regulations aimed at containing clandestine trade but which contributed in no way to the economic betterment of the *Estado*. The staffing pattern was re-structured. While the post of City Captain (*Capitão de Cidade*) was abolished, the staff was reorganised and the salaries they were to receive revised.[1]

However Pombal's most significant contribution was the Standing Order (*Regimento*) of 20th January, 1774. It dealt with the arrival and departure of ships, how they should enter ports, the manner of loading and unloading cargoes, the system of invigilation to curb smuggling activities, the manner of conducting searches, warehousing and storehousing, etc. The *Regimento* sought to facilitate commerce without causing any injury to the interests of the State treasury (*Fazenda Real*) and those of the merchants, prescribing simultaneously, stiff penalties for those guilty of transgression.[2]

The *Regimento* also established import and export duties at 5 per cent and 2 per cent respectively.[3] These included perquisites. Finally, it attended to the reorganisation of the staff (*quadro*) of the Goa Customs.[4] It was hoped that these changes would streamline the customs administration. It must be stated however that the *Regimento* proved to be a disappointment. In the years immediately following the passing of the *Regimento*, a fall in the State customs revenues was witnessed. It appears that the restrictions and inconveniences faced by the merchants under it discouraged commerce at the port of Goa and led to commercial loss.[5] The *Regimento* also ignored the need to get rid of the obstacles and vexations in the path of free internal trade. These flaws and lapses were overcome when in November 1780 it was amended.[6]

There was further staff-reorganisation executed when the post of Inspector (*Juiz*) earlier abolished under the *Regimento* of 1774 was revived in April 1778. This put an end to a controversy debated for long during the sessions of the *Junta*.[7] In 1779, the salaries of the customs officials of the *Alfandega de Goa* were upgraded.[8] This caused a total expenditure of 8,500 *xerafins* that is an increase in expenditure to the tune of 2,896 *xerafins* when compared to that of 1771.[9]

Besides the Customs House of Goa there were customs houses set up in the adjacent provinces at Margão in Salcette, at Mapuça in Bardez and at Ponda, Zambaulim, Bicholim, Cansarpale, Sanquelim, Canacona and Pernem in the New Conquest areas. There were also check-posts established at Tinai, Kuvessu, Dighi, Kundal, Donkorpem, Rama-Ghat, Malgullim, Khelghat, Chorte-Pargor, Dumegod and Telghat. They were administered in accordance with an ancient traditional system of tariffs.[10]

Customs House of Salcette

The Customs House of Salcette was an ancient outfit. Little is known about its functioning before the early seventeenth century. From 1621 onwards it functioned in the Village Administration House (*Casa de Gauncaria*) in Margão. It was later transferred to a structure located near the Church of Margão.[11] This customs house had its affiliate offices at Rachol, Racaim, Goltim, Borim, Chandor, Sorla, Curtorim, Quelossim, Pana, Cortalim, Ambar, the passage of river Sal, Deussua, the passage of Veroda, Cuncolim, Assolna, and the pass of Murgurim.[12]

From 1772 to 1791 the *Alfandega de Salcete* was administered directly by the *Fazenda*, which had to bear the burden of financing its personnel. So to reduce this burden the system of farming revenues of this *alfandega* was adopted in January 1798. Revenues were farmed out to Francisco Barreto Xavier, Babu Naik and others on the specific condition that they would function in accordance with the old Standing Order (*Regimento*) of 13th August 1619.[13] This system continued until December 1800. Following the death of one of the aforesaid contractors the *alfandega* on 1st January 1801 once again came under the direct control of the *Fazenda*.[14]

Customs House of Bardez

The Bardez Customs House also practised the contract system for collection of revenues till 1801 when the *Fazenda* took charge of it as in the case of the Salcette Customs. Its staff was composed of the administrator (*administrador*), a tax-collector (*recebedor*), a scribe (*escrivão*), an assistant (*ajudante*), an auditor (*fiscal*), a janitor (*porteiro*), a factor (*feitor*), ten guards (*guardas*) and two border guards (*fieis de fronteira*).[15] The check-posts subordinate to this customs house were located at Porpangim, Chapora, Siolim and Colvale.[16]

It appears that the reorganisation of the customs houses of Salcette and Bardez, especially the abolition of the revenue-farming system in 1800-01 and the transfer of the said *alfandegas* to the direct control and supervision of the *Fazenda* did yield positive results, as seen in Table 3.1.

TABLE 3.1 : INCOME DERIVED FROM THE *ALFANDEGAS* OF GOA, BARDEZ AND SALCETTE, 1806-10

Year	Alfandega de Goa (In *xerafins*)	Alfandega de Bardez (In *xerafins*)	Alfandega de Salcete (In *xerafins*)
1806	343627-4-44 1/6	17974-0-03 1/4	25029-1-43 3/4
1807	211609-0-42 1/4	15358-0-03 3/4	24124-1-55
1808	190888-3-32 1/3	15139-0-41 1/2	25100-2-22 1/2
1809	177401-2-10	13779-4-22 1/4	18426-1-16 1/4
1810	248775-1-32	16558-3-16 3/4	22857-0-23

Source: HAG : *MR*, 191B, fls. 1299v-1300.

In the year 1594 the *Alfandega de Salcete* and the *Alfandega de Bardez* netted revenues amounting to 3,160 *xerafins* and 2,887 1/2 *xerafins* respectively.[17] But in the years from 1806 to 1810, the total amount collected by the *Alfandega de Salcete* amounted to 115,537-2-40 1/2 *xerafins*. The income of this customs house reached its highest level, that is, 25,100-2-22 1/2 *xerafins* in 1808, and its lowest level 18,426-1-16 1/4 *xerafins* in 1809. The average annual revenues of the *alfandega* amounted to 23,107-2-32 *xerafins*. The *Alfandega de Bardez* on the other hand collected 78,809-3-27 1/2 *xerafins* during the same period, averaging 15,761-4-41 *xerafins* per year. Its highest collection was 17,974-0-03 1/4 *xerafins* in 1806 and its lowest collection amounted to 13,779-4-22 1/4 *xerafins* in 1809.

When we compare the revenue collections made in 1594 with the annual average revenue collection made during 1806-10 by the *Alfandega de Salcete* we observe an increase of 19,947-2-32 *xerafins*. In the case of the *Alfandega de Bardez* there was a rise of 12,874-2-11 *xerafins*.

From Table 3.1 we also gather that during 1806-10, revenues of the Goa Customs House touched a maximum of 343,627-4-44 1/6 *xerafins* in 1806 and a minimum of 177,401-2-10 *xerafins* in 1809. The total revenues collected during the five years amounted to 1,172,302-2-40 3/4 *xerafins* and the average annual amount derived was 234,460-2-30 *xerafins*. The *alfandegas* of the New Conquest regions which continued to function under the traditional system of revenue-farming until 1840, during the same period, farmed revenues that averaged 47,665 *xerafins* per year.[18]

Centralisation and Uniformity

Until 1810 there was little development in customs legislation towards administrative expansion and improvement. In this year the Customs House of Goa and those of the New Conquest areas underwent radical changes. In June 1810, the customs houses of Bardez and Salcette were brought on par with the *Alfandega de Goa* with respect to payment of duties. Existing check-posts were abolished in order to liberalise and facilitate the free circulation of goods imported into the territories of the *Estado*. Measures were taken to prevent goods customarily making their descent from the Ghats and entering into New Conquest provinces of Bicholim, Sanquelim, Ponda and Madgudy, from being diverted.[19] These changes were approved and ratified in May 1811, the year which saw the transfer of the *Alfandega de Goa* from Old Goa (*Velha Cidade*) to Panjim (*Nova Goa*).[20] As regards the effects of the developments and changes of 1810, we observe that in 1812 the three customs houses of Goa, Salcette and Bardez yielded revenue amounting to 349$001-4-46 3/4 *reis* of Goa (?). But in 1813 the yield was 222$894-2-48 1/2 that is about 126$107 less than the previous year. In 1814 the said *alfandegas* collected revenues amounting to 185$846-0-5 3/4 *reis* of Goa (?) that is 37$048-2-42 3/4 less than the year 1813.[21] Table 3.2 also demonstrates the increasing decline in revenues of the Goa Customs House during the years 1811-15. This decline could be attributed to the equalisation of duties to be paid at the *alfandegas* of Goa, Bardez and Salcette. But there were other possibilities. It could have been the outcome of the Treaty of 1811 which led to a fall in the number of ships coming to Goa from Brazil. British occupation in the early nineteenth century must have also disrupted the *Estado*-based commerce.

TABLE 3.2 : INCOME OF THE *ALFANDEGA DE GOA*, 1810-15

Year	Revenues (In *xerafins*)
1810	277465-0-13 1/4
1811	290498-3-19
1812	244913-4-25 1/4
1813	118629-1-52
1814	161478-3-25
1815	191199-3-24

Sources: Claudio Lagrange Monteiro de Barbuda, *IDJ*, Nova Goa, 1841, p. 25.

The customs houses of the New Conquest areas continued to function under the traditional revenue farming system while such a system was discontinued in Salcette and Bardez.

It was decided to end this situation and to initiate legislation for a uniform system of customs administration. Under the existing system customs duties were paid to contractors in New Conquest regions and at the *Fazenda* in Old Conquest areas. The matter was a subject of much debate and consideration during 1812-14 as differences in opinion appeared in the *Junta*. Some members felt that uniformity would affect the State treasury especially the tobacco revenues. The issue was left unresolved during the administration of Viceroy Conde de Sarzedas, who left instructions to his successor to handle the matter tactfully. Nothing tangible emerged till 1835.[22]

A committee was appointed in 1835 to propose necessary measures for reforming the customs administration. It recommended uniformity throughout the *Estado* and the end of the system of revenue-farming. But these suggestions remained merely on paper until Governor General Barão de Candal decided to follow it up. Consequently, in July 1840 the age-old system of farming in the *alfandegas* of the New Conquest areas was terminated and they came under the jurisdiction of the *Fazenda*.[23]

The system of uniformity marked a watershed in the history of customs administration in Portuguese India. It boosted the customs revenues of the *Estado da India*. During 1806-10 the customs houses in the New Conquest provinces yielded an average amount of 47,665 *xerafins* per year. This figure climbed up to 68,000 *xerafins* in 1840.[24]

In October 1839 the *alfandegas* of Bardez and Salcette, formerly independent units, were subordinated to the *Alfandega de Goa*, and the latter was to serve as the central Customs House.[25] Moreover the posts and *alfandegas* subordinate to the *alfandegas* of Bardez and Salcette were abolished along with vexatious imposts which brought no benefit to the State but merely restricted free commercial movement.[26]

From all accounts it seems that centralisation and uniformity proved effective for better supervision and vigilance and for speedy implementation of measures. It freed the natives from the oppression and arbitrariness of the contractors and of the Dessais and other traders in the New Conquest regions. It put an end to obstacles in the way of internal commerce arising from the suppression of the *Alfandega de Ponda*. The area surrounded by rivers made it made it necessary to have many check-points where transit duties (*portagem*) were collected from all those who descended from the Ghats. At each stage, the merchant encountered hindrances. He was stopped for the payment of duties. Uniformity suppressed these hurdles, resulted in liberalisation and a sharp upward swing in internal and external commerce.[27]

Creation of New Customs Houses

During the administration of Lopes de Lima, radical reforms were introduced in customs administration. Since the customs houses were located in the interior and there were few in the coastal regions, the need was felt to create new ones along the coast. In December 1840, the *alfandegas* in the Old Conquest areas were reduced to three, those of Nova Goa, Chapora and Assolna, and two in the New Conquest regions, at Sanquelim and Sanguem. Of the five *alfandegas*, four were new ones. The *alfandegas* of Salcette and Bardez were shifted to Assolna and Chapora respectively and those of the New Conquest areas to Sanquelim and Sanguem.[28] The expenditure involved in the creation of the new *alfandegas* amounted to 27,265 *xerafins*. Later, as the Doromarg highway was frequented by bullock-carts descending from the Ghats into Bardez, the check-post at Doromarg was elevated to the status of a customs house in March 1841. This facilitated the effective imposition of duties and the collection of revenues on goods entering via Ramghat, Manguelim and other highways of the province of Bicholim as well as that which entered via the highways of Telghat. This would not only prove beneficial to the *Estado*, but also meant the convenience of merchants entering Goa via the Ghats.[29]

For administrative convenience and efficiency new check-posts were established in April 1841 at Tiracol and Neibaga in the province of Pernem, at Collem and Curssim in the province of Embarbacem, at Veluz and Valpoy in the province of Sanquelim, at Talpona and Uddem-Val in the province of Canacona, and at Col and Cavellossim in the province of Salcette.[30]

Customs House of Daman

The *Alfandega de Damão* was established as an independent organisation in the second half of the sixteenth century. Earlier it was subordinate to the *Alfandega de Dio*. The elevation of the *Alfandega de Damão* to an independent status was the outcome of a plea made by the inhabitants of Daman. Since then it functioned as an integral part of the customs administration of the *Estado* netting in revenues to the tune of 150,000 pardaus per year.[31]

Customs House of Diu

The *Alfandega de Dio* had been set up by the ruler of Cambay. It first came under the Portuguese jurisdiction during the rule of Nuno da Cunha, the then governor of Portuguese India. But it was only after the actual conquest of Diu during the rule of D. João de Castro that the *Alfandega* functioned effectively. Throughout the sixteenth and seventeenth centuries its administration was regulated in accordance with the regulations that were in existence before the coming of the Portuguese.[32]

Thus it would not be erroneous to infer that the attempts of the State to reorganise and streamline the customs mechanisms in existence, had a dual purpose. The primary purpose was to increase commercial activity so as to bring in revenue. But of no little significance was the need to promote the interests of the merchant community operating on the coast and the routes leading to the hinterland.

Customs Tariffs and Barriers

The manipulation of the fiscal policy by both the authorities and local tax-farmers with respect to taxes that came under their jurisdiction was widespread in the *Estado*. Taxes on commerce were either collected by customs officials or farmed out to rentiers on the basis of expected annual returns.

Revenue-farming

The origins of the above-mentioned dual system of taxation could be traced back to the times when Goa expanded so as to incorporate first Bardez and Salcette and later the New Conquest territories. It had to retain the system of revenue-farming in existence in these regions prior to Portuguese conquest. A tax farmer in a particular province had to pay a pre-determined sum of money to the State. He was *ipso facto* authorised by a public deed to collect taxes according to fixed terms of contract. The tax-farmers had punitive powers to collect taxes imposed on tobacco, toddy-tapping, taverns, distillation of liquor, passages like that of the river Sal, wood, timber, gambling in all the villages, the fair held at Mardol etc. declared in their respective contracts entered into during the Muslim rule.[33] The system was unpopular with the masses. The tax-collectors took undue advantage of the ignorance of the people and resorted to a policy of fiscal extortion and oppression. As considered earlier, the evil practice was done away with by 1801 in Bardez and Salcette and 1840 in the New Conquest areas. Shortage of manpower, the chronic problem afflicting the State, was the root cause for the continuance of this system in the said areas for such a long period of time since their annexation.

Taxes on Imports and Exports

Until the early 1770s the tax on exports and imports was fixed at 6 per cent and 9 per cent respectively. In addition *lagimas* or emoluments were to be paid to the Inspector (*Juiz*) and the scribes (*escrivães*) of the customs house. However in January 1774 this tax structure was drastically changed. The import duty was reduced to 5 per cent and the export duty to 2 per cent. Besides the emoluments (*lagimas*) amounting to 3 *tangas* and 10 *reis* per cent were to be paid in both cases.[34] Certain items like rice, wheat, salt and cattle were exempted from these duties at the *Alfandega de Goa*.[35]

In February 1774 wines imported from New Conquest areas via the Customs House of Goa (*Alfandega de Goa*) were subjected to a duty of 15 *xerafins* per *pipa* of 25 *almudes*. The duty on imported toddy and jaggery was fixed at 3 *tangas* per *almude*. Furthermore in June 1775, a duty on grape wine and other liquors entering Goa via Aguada was levied at the rate of 5 per cent. Emoluments (*lagimas*) too had to be paid. Toddy-tapping and liquor production formed one of the chief sources of income of the *Estado*. Therefore this legislation was probably enacted to protect the home liquor industry. The execution of the law however created problems as jaggery was solid and the law imposed duty on liquid jaggery. Hence in March 1775 it was determined that jaggery in its molten state would be measured in order to collect the tax fixed by the law.[36] As regards the export of jaggery and toddy, the customs duty charged was two *xerafins* per cent and three *tangas* and ten *reis* in the form of lagimas. Export of liquors involved a duty of 2-2-30 *xerafins* (?) per barrel of 24 *almudes* and one *xerafim* per *almude* of cashew liquor.[37]

We have detailed information on the tax system in existence in Daman. According to a report dated 2nd May 1832 prepared by the English authorities on Daman, we gather that most imports paid 5 per cent on the value of goods and 3 1/4 per cent on re-exportation. On products of Daman — piece-goods, jaggery, grain and cotton — the export duty paid was at the rate of 2 per cent. On the importation of *ghee* a duty of 6-1/2 per cent and on its re-exportation 2 per cent were charged. There were duties levied upon all sorts of timber, rafters, bamboos and the like.

If brought by land to Daman and its subordinate ports, the import duty charged was two annas per cent and on re-exportation a fee was levied at the customs house at 8-1/2 per cent. There was a customs levy imposed at 6-1/4 per cent on the importation of oranges, elephant teeth and sheep horns and on re-exportation a further customs duty of 2 per cent. In the case of cargoes arriving at the port of Daman after calling at other Portuguese ports like Moçambique, Goa and Diu, the cargo owners were expected to produce a certificate indicating that a duty of 8-1/4 per cent had been collected there. This freed them from any further customs on such goods at Daman. If it appeared by the certificate that they paid less than 8-1/4 per cent, the remainder would be collected at Daman.[38]

A British source also informs us that customs duties were collected at Diu in 1830 by a percentage of *ad valorem* on exports and imports at the rate of 3-1/2 per cent and 7-1/2 per cent respectively.[39]

Under an edict (*farman*) issued by the Mughals in the beginning of the eighteenth century, the Portuguese earned the right to export goods to the *Feitoria de Surrate* on the payment of 2-1/2 per cent *ad valorem.*[40]

Trans-shipment Duty

The *Regimento* of 20th January 1774 made little provision for trans-shipment. Matters were set right in January 1783 when a trans-shipment fee of 4 per cent on goods re-exported from Portuguese ports in Portuguese vessels was fixed.[41] In April 1818, the benefit of trans-shipment at the rate of 4 per cent was extended to goods of British origin consigned to Portuguese subjects. However in the case of goods trans-shipped by British or other foreign merchants the fee charged was 5 per cent.[42]

Depository and Warehouse Duties

The Depository (*Estabelecimento de Depozito*) at Goa received goods of every kind and quality, national and foreign coming from any part of Asia, Europe, America and Africa. It was under the administration and control of the Customs Inspector (*Juiz da Alfandega*) and other officials. Merchandise to be entered into the said Depository (*Depozito*) had to be declared before the Customs Inspector (*Juiz da Alfandega*) within twenty-four hours of the entry of the ship. The declaration had to specifically indicate the masters, importers, owners and agents, when and where the goods had been loaded, the volume, the brands and the like. The goods listed were then unloaded without delay and speedily despatched to the warehouse. Care was taken when stowing the goods, to place them in order so as to be accessible for counting and examining. The warehouse was opened only in the presence of the Customs Inspector (*Juiz da Alfandega*) the janitor and the owners or their agents. On goods of Portuguese origin a duty of one per cent was charged, but on foreign goods the duty imposed was 2 per cent, together with expenses of warehousing and customary emoluments. Since April 1818 all goods could be stored in the warehouses of the Portuguese *alfandegas* for a period of two years in the case of dry goods and six months in the case of wet goods. The two-year period was extendable for another two years after the payment of re-exportation duties.[43]

Other Duties

Since 1694 a sealing and stamp duty (*dereitos de sellagem*) was charged at the rate of 5 *reis* per item. An anchorage tax was also evolved from early times. It consisted of a duty of one *xerafim* charged on every vessel of the capacity of 300 *candis* for the upper portion (*para parte cima*) and half *xerafim* for the lower part (*para parte menor*). This duty was abolished in October 1880. A customs duty was also levied on water supply to ships at the rate of one rupee per *pipa* of water. Besides the above-mentioned taxes and levies, duties on food (*direitos de colecta*), the Aguada lighthouse duties (*direitos de pharol de Agoada*), emoluments of guards (*emolumentos de guardas*), etc. were also collected.[44]

Tax Structure Since 1840

A landmark in the annals of customs legislation enacted by the *Estado* was the *Pauta* of 1840. It was a happy blending of a variety of duties fixed, some old others new.

As regards import duties, a 5 per cent duty was imposed on goods produced and manufactured in Portugal or in Portuguese territories and carried in Portuguese vessels. Foreign goods imported in by Portuguese or foreign vessels paid 7 per cent and 10 per cent import duties respectively.[45] This was evidently a protectionist measure, but the purpose was probably defeated when foreign goods were passed off as Portuguese. No export duties were levied on goods of Portuguese origin, transported in Portuguese vessels and destined for other Portuguese ports. But in case of foreign merchandise, if shipped in Portuguese vessels, the duty charged was 1 per cent and 2 per cent if transported in foreign vessels.[46]

Other customs duties imposed were the *Lagimas de chitos* which involved a payment of 3 *tangas* and 10 *reis* per cent. The Depository duty (*Direitos de Depozito*) included a duty of 1 per cent, with additional charges for security, manual labour and departure from the port. Trans-shipment demanded the payment of 1 per cent, besides *lagimas* and additional charges mentioned above. A warehousing duty was imposed at the rate of 20 *reis* per quintal for solids and 16 *reis* per *almude* for liquids. *Direitos de trapiche* or a wharf duty was levied at the rate of 3 *reis* per bulk of cargo and a minimum of 2-1/2 *xerafins* per horse power. *Direitos do terço de Parangue* was a contribution made by commercial ships. It involved the payment of 1 *xerafim* per ship. In case of *direitos de colecta*, the payment was determined by the Goa Senate (*Senado de Goa*). Modelled on the lines of the *Real de Agua* of Lisbon, it was meant to finance war operations against rebels and to maintain a naval force for protecting coastal trade in victuals. *Direitos de pharol de Agoada* was an age old lighthouse duty. It had been discontinued for some time when the lighthouse was in a state of disuse. It involved the payment of two *tangas* per ship of the capacity of 200 *candis* and one *tanga* per ship of 100 *candis*.

Separate legislation was introduced in November 1840 by which the import and export duties were more clearly defined. On coir a duty of 30 *reis* per quintal was charged if imported in its crude or fibre form, but twine or ropes involved an import duty of 10 per cent. This was in case of coir shipped in by Portuguese vessels. The charge was doubled if carried in foreign vessels. Every effort was being made to provide protection to the local coir industry. On coconuts the duty collected was 9 *xerafins* per thousand, and copra involved a duty of 22-1/2 *xerafins* per *candil*, if brought in by foreign ships. Portuguese vessels however enjoyed the benefit of paying just 15 per cent. Tobacco involved a payment of 80 *xerafins* per *candil* of 6 *arrobas*, while cigars were charged a duty of two *tangas* per 1 lb. wt. Cotton textiles of Portuguese origin involved a payment of 20 per cent if transported by foreign ships, and 15 per cent if brought in Portuguese vessels.[47]

Gun-powder, salt, gold, silver and copper coins whether Portuguese or foreign in nature were exempted from the payment of export duties at the *alfandegas* of Nova Goa, Salcette and Bardez. On coconut oil and other like substances, the tax imposed was 20 *reis* per *almude*. Liquors of cashew and coconut were subjected to the payment of 15 *reis* per *almude*. Items needed for provisioning ships were excluded from the scope and purview of export duties.[48]

Since the 1820s the *Estado*-based trade was in doldrums. The *Pauta* of 1840 was probably introduced to boost commercial activity. The results were encouraging. Soon after it came into operation a positive change was observed. (See Table 3.3)

TABLE 3.3: INCOME OF THE *ALFANDEGA DE GOA*, 1836-56

Year	Revenues (In *xerafins*)
1836	43516-3-06 1/4
1837	59529-3-08 3/4
1838	56063-3-57 3/4
1839	75387-1-55
1840	93590-0-58 1/2
1841	105822-3-05
1842	100748-3-22 1/2
1843	118063-3-04 1/2 (?)
1844	160238-3-55 1/4
1850	136892-3-52 1/2
1851	138697-4-06 3/4
1852	145509-0-46
1853	148705-1-28 3/4
1854	115723-3-35
1855	133777-2-39 1/2
1856	153534-4-05 3/4

Sources: HAG: *MR*, 219B, fl. 554; *AG*, 9265, fls. 111v, 128, 168, 196v, 197; Barbuda, *IDJ*, p. 25.

The revenues of the *Estado* increased considerably in the 1850s, but did not return to the pre-1820s situation. During 1836-39 the average annual revenue collection of the Goa Customs House was 58,624-1-47 *xerafins* while in the period immediately following the implementation of the *Pauta* (1840-44) the average yearly collection was 115,692-3-51 *xerafins*. During 1850-56 the average annual revenue collection amounted to 138,977-1-30 *xerafins*. Thus the average annual returns for 1840-44 as compared to that of 1836-39 showed an increase of 57,068-2-04 *xerafins* or 97.35 per cent while the average returns in 1850-56 when compared to the average yearly revenue collection of 1840-44 showed an increase of 23,284-2-39 *xerafins* or 20.13 per cent

Since the economy of the *Estado* largely depended upon its external commerce, it was felt necessary to further simplify the processes and formalities at customs houses. The government was compelled to abolish various unnecessary duties bringing little income to the *Fazenda*. Therefore duties such as *lagimas de chitos*, emoluments of the chief clerk (*lagimas de escrivão maior*), crane duties (*direitos de gundaste*), emoluments of guards aboard the ship (*emolumentos de guardas em bordo*), duties on fishing licences (*impressas e bilhetes de licenca para pesca*), etc. were abolished. In Daman, the emoluments of the sub-director (*lagimas de sub-director*), clerk (*escrivão*), weigher (*pesador*) and the chief guard (*guarda - mor*) and in Diu, the emoluments of the chief guard and janitor (*lagimas de guarda - mor e do porteiro*) were nullified.[49]

Tariff of Sivapoy

There is some detailed evidence of inland customs duties charged at the *Alfandega de Salcete* where the Tariff of Sivapoy was in force. The Tariff contains 67 articles of tribute and fixed duties on specified goods as regards both importation and exportation.[50] The date of its commencement and cessation is obscure. It was however still in force in 1802.[51]

The general picture that emerges is that the taxation on merchants was not excessive. The port dues were quite moderate and probably less than those extracted at other European settlements. From available evidence we do not gain the impression of a government taxing and squeezing the trade and the merchants. In fact the policies of the State could at times be described as enlightened. The introduction of centralisation and uniformity demonstrated the interest of the State authorities in the welfare of the merchants, one of the factors that made trading a lucrative enterprise well into the nineteenth century.

One should not relegate to the background the pragmatic considerations that determined State trade strategies. Taxes were deliberately lowered with the hope of baiting merchants and shippers to *Estado* ports so as to eventually generate commercial prosperity. The hopes were not shattered. The tide of fortune turned remarkably in favour of the *Estado*. Commerce reached fresh peaks during the period under review. Increased commercial activity led to the expansion and reorganisation of the customs administration.

Merchant-State Interaction and Linkages

Documentary evidence seems to indicate that the State seldom interfered in the affairs of the merchants. The financial needs of the *Estado* determined the relationship of the local merchants and the rulers. Merchants were able to carry on uninterruptedly their economic activities with the minimum of State intervention. In fact the regulations and maritime laws in the *Estado* port towns and cities actively encouraged market operations which inevitably gave rise to large scale capital transactions and the accumulation of wealth. The vulnerability displayed at times by merchants along the west coast of India and elsewhere in Asia due to unpredictable shifts of official policy offering a threat to the very continuity of their business houses was absent in Portuguese India. Thus the peculiarities of the situation and the nature of the political apparatus in the *Estado* were conducive to giving considerable influence to the merchants.

Dependency Syndrome

The merchants had their own means of acquiring access to centres of political power. Many a rich merchant could make powerful friends in governmental circles and use such political connections to his personal advantage. The grant of official monopolies or exclusive rights to farm fiscal revenues or the management of national currencies might be given to particular merchants as a result of political intervention. Thus the economic power of the merchants led by necessity to political influence which they indeed asserted to their advantage as proved by many instances. Rogerio de Faria wielded immense influence with the *Estado* authorities on different occasions. One glaring instance is the *Hooghli* episode. In December 1819, James Matheson was refused permission by the Portuguese authorities to load his ship *Hooghli* with opium at Daman. The Portugeuse authorities had been influenced by Rogerio de Faria who worked on behalf of rival opium shippers namely William Jardine and Magniac & Co.[52]

One gets the impression from available evidence that the State went even further in its dealings with the merchants and extended State patronage. Many merchants like João Baptista Goethals and Rogerio de Faria were the recipients of political favours. One such privilege they enjoyed was the appointment as factor at the Portuguese trading station at Surat. Moses Tobias and other Jewish traders and businessmen like Isaac Tobias and Elias Cohen occupied the post of Director of the *Feitoria de Surrate* in the mid-eighteenth century. Similarly Rustamji Manockji was Administrator of passports in Surat *(Procurador do Português e corretor-mor dos cartazes)*.[53] Manockji also functioned as attorney to the Portuguese in the port of Surat to plead on behalf of the Portuguese Government politically or otherwise, before the Nawab of Surat and other authorities.

Antonio Pereira, a Goa-based merchant was appointed Administrator of the Royal Factory of Cumbarjua (*Fábrica de Cumbarjua*). Likewise

Sebastião Gracias, another local trader, held the post of Administrator of Playing Cards (*Administrador de Cartas Jogar*). Ignacio Xavier da Fonseca Unhão was *Escrivão da Administração do Estanco Real*. He figured significantly in the Goa-Moçambique trade.[54]

In fact it was a mutual dependency nexus. The available documentation lends support to the view that the State authorities readily utilised the services of the local merchants in emergencies, to tide over difficulties, as well as to meet daily needs. When the *Estado da India* was in the grip of a cholera epidemic in the 1820s, Rogerio de Faria came to the rescue of the State by supplying drugs and other necessities.[55] The Mhamai brothers, who enjoyed considerable influence in political circles, were of assistance to the State as provision suppliers. In October 1790 Venkatesha Kamat wrote to Caetano Fernandes, a local trader from Aldona, Goa, expressing the need for two *cumbos* of paddy for provisioning the Palace.[56] In 1786 various types of textiles were supplied to the Palace of the Governor General Francisco da Cunha e Menezes.[57] Besides attending to the needs of the viceregal palace, the Mhamais even supplied provisions to the *Fazenda Real*. Medicines and drugs were transported from Surat to Goa in 1786 on the account of the *Fazenda Real*, probably with the assistance of the Mhamais. They included almonds, white raisins, poppy heads and seeds, Arabian glue, opium, cloves, fennel, blue vitriol, nuts from Malacca, camphor, Persian rose water, soap, sealing-wax, sheep horns, etc.[58] Through the medium of the Mhamais, 3,160 bales of goods were distributed to convents and administrative institutions such as the Convent of St. Dominic, Convent of St. Francis, Convent of St. Augustine, Royal Hospital and *Camaras* of Bardez and Salcette.[59]

The Mhamais at times needed the assistance of some of the government officials and institutions. They borrowed money amounting to 32,000 *xerafins* from the pharmacy (*Botica*) of the Royal Hospital and this debt was later cleared in installments with interest rate of 6 per cent, over a period of 20 years from 25th November 1765 to 5th February 1785. The total amount paid back was 50,214-2-24 *xerafins*.[60] In January 1785 Governor Frederico William de Souza, wrote to the Monneron brothers at Mauritius urging them to accept the powers of attorney from the Mhamais in order to handle the Gattereau case and to pursue the matter vigorously on their behalf.[61]

Another Saraswat brahmin merchant, Purushotom Sinai Kenkre had been a sympathetic associate of the Portuguese authorities, and for services rendered was provided the title of *Barão de Calapur* in 1873.[62]

Giridhar Sinai Dhempe was often at the service of the local authorities. He employed his ships to transport troops and prisoners for the State government. In a crisis that the *Estado* was facing, he staved off a rice shortage by standing surety to the *Banco Ultramarino* for the Goa Government. His allegiance to the authorities bore fruit when in 1869 the Lisbon Government conferred on him the most prestigious State award *Cavalheiro da Ordem da Torre e Espada do valor, lealdade e merito.*[63]

Another powerful Hindu merchant Rama Kushta Sinari, nicknamed Godecar had strong links with the Lisbon government. His complaints to the King of Portugal resulted in several viceroys and ministers being recalled back to Portugal.[64] He was treacherously killed and disposed off at Daugim.

Services rendered by the merchants to the State were dictated by cold political calculations through which they ensured for themselves the atmosphere indispensable for their business activities. The commerce with far-reaching ramifications conducted by them was naturally dependent on a satisfactory degree of political stability. As long as the political situation was stable and the State authorities adopted a *laissez-faire* policy, the merchants could flourish and prosper. The State was equally calculating in its approach towards the merchants. State assistance and patronage to merchants was the outcome of the financial need of the *Estado*.

State Restraints and Constraints

It is well-known that the paramount concern of the merchants was profits. They were often engaged in smuggling activities in order to avoid payment of customs duties which were payable at one or other of the numerous customs houses at Goa, Daman and Diu. This had damaging consequences for the *Estado* as the Portuguese *alfandegas* formed a major source of State revenue. The more successful the smugglers were in evading the customs authorities, the less the State received. Smuggling had the potential of reducing the revenues of the *Estado* to such an extent as to seriously endanger its security and ultimately even threaten its existence.

Goods were smuggled up the rivers and overland through the Ghat passages into the interior of India. Smuggling activities were rife at various Portuguese ports, entry points, creeks and inlets. Many of the *quintas* and *palmares* that lined the rivers and coast formed a smoke screen concealing smuggling operations. Vagator in Bardez was one such den of opium smuggling. Smuggling was basically conducted by individual operators or by *ad hoc* alliances. There was no well-knit smugglers' organisation.

The State would come out with measures designed to curb the unholy activities of the smugglers. In 1843-44, circulars were issued to this effect.[65] The abuse continued unabated much to the dismay and chagrin of the State authorities who felt helpless in the matter. The State could not impose itself effectively on the contrabandists. What hampered the State was the unofficial involvement of officialdom in the intra-Asian trade itself. Private participation of State officials in the Indian Ocean trade was an integral basic feature of the Portuguese system. It prevailed in the sixteenth and seventeenth centuries and continued to persist in the eighteenth and nineteenth centuries. In the face of utter indifference of the Lisbon Government to book errant administrators, such unofficial involvement continued unabated. Many small craft involved in smuggling operations up-river appear to have been owned by important officials or prominent Portuguese *fidalgos* such as the factor at Surat, the *vedor da Fazenda,* the governors of Daman and even the viceroy himself.[66]

A striking example is that provided by the Loureiro family. The Mhamai documentation and other customs records mirror quite distinctly the involvement of its members in the interport trade of Asia as merchants and ship-owners. In such documentation we can come across names like Francisco Gomes Loureiro, João Gomes Loureiro, Henrique Joze Loureiro, Manoel Joze Loureiro, Domingos Alvarez Loureiro and Simão de Rocha Loureiro.[67]

Francisco Gomes Loureiro held the position of Portuguese Consul at Bombay and other Portuguese ports on the Malabar coast as well as Director of the Surat factory.[68]

João Gomes Loureiro, brother of Francisco Gomes Loureiro also occupied the same position for a term of three years and was subsequently reappointed for two more terms. A bill of lading drawn on 14th December 1812 indicates that the ship *Ulisses* under the command of Joaquim Ferreira, anchored at Surat would carry a consignment of 183 *fardos* of goods, probably textiles, belonging to João Gomes Loureiro to be entrusted to the Mhamais on its arrival at Goa.[69] Henrique Joze Loureiro occupied the same post held by his father João from 1814 to 1822.[70]

Manoel Joze Loureiro, another brother of Francisco Gomes Loureiro first served in Portuguese India in 1802 as Crown official (*Procurador da Coroa e Fazenda*) and provisionally as Chancellor of the High Court. In 1809, he received an appointment at the *Casa de Supplicação.* On his return to India in 1812 he took up the post of *Chancelor de Relação*. By the Aviso of 1813 he was appointed *Secretario do Estado*, and later Governor from September to December 1821, when he left for Rio de Janeiro under a cloud. Later, he returned to Portugal.[71] Even as early as 1797 while at Lisbon he had extensive business dealings with the Mhamais.[72] The latter would supply him regularly with Balaghat saltpetre and textiles. On 13th January, 1797 the Mhamais informed him of the shortage of Balaghat textiles due to the Maratha Wars.[73]

The Loureiro network was wide-ranging. It encompassed not only India and Portugal but even Brazil. Domingos Alvarez Loureiro and João Gomes Duarte, nephews of the Surat-based Francisco Gomes Loureiro, besides Thomas Loureiro and Simão de Rocha Loureiro were active on the Goa-Brazil channel as textile merchants.[74] Fabrics of every kind procured from various parts of India were trans-shipped to Brazil via Goa.

Other officials who figured in the official records as participants in the Asiatic trade were members of the Garcez Palha family. Candido Joze Garcez Palha had held high posts in the *Estado*'s administrative set-up. From the position of governor of Diu he rose up to the distinguished ranks of co-governor of the *Estado da India*.[75] His son Joaquim Mourão Garcez Palha likewise earned acclaim for his services first as governor of Diu and later as Chief War Captain (*Capitão-mor de guerra*). In March 1822 he was elected to the *Junta Provisional de Goa*, but due to political disturbances the *Junta* was dissolved in November 1822. There are pointed references to his involvement in the commerce of Asia. In January 1813, for instance, he despatched textiles worth 23,580 *xerafins* to Brazil.[76] In December 1816 he brought into Goa from Brazil 2,505 *patacas*, 359 *meyas doblas* and 4,250 *reis* of bullion valued at 24,972 *xerafins*.[77]

Hermenegildo da Costa Campos who held the position of Field Marshall was also one of those active on the Goa-Brazil run, voraciously fed by the intra-Asian commercial system. Bullion in the form of 30 *meyas doblas* worth 1,080 *xerafins* was imported into Goa by Hermenegildo in December 1816.[78] In all probability his sons Joze, Luis and Francisco too were involved in the Portuguese country trade. Joze da Costa Campos had been on the State Council as its voting member.[79]

The State could hardly come down heavily to contain the clandestine operations of the merchants, when its high-ranking officials were deeply involved in them. On the contrary it had to please and pacify them. This policy of appeasement revealed its vulnerability and its dependence on the intra-Asiatic trade. It was essentially a question of survival.

REFERENCES AND NOTES

1. Felippe Nery Xavier, *O Gabinette Litterario das Fontainhas*, vol. II, Nova Goa, 1847, p. 191; Francisco Xavier Ernesto Fernandes, *MHE*, Lisboa, 1899, pp. 41-42.
2. HAG : *AG*, 6813, fls. 246-356; AHU : *MI*, Maço 108, no. 124; Fernandes, *op. cit.*, pp. 42-43.
3. HAG : *AG*, 6813, fl. 334; *Cartas, patentes, alvarás*, 628, fl. 229; Xavier, *op. cit.*, p. 240.
4. HAG : *AG*, 6813, fls. 251-253; Fernandes, *op. cit.*, p. 43.
5. BNL : *Collecção Pombalina*, Cod. 460, fls. 10-78.
6. HAG : *PRA*, 8089, fl. 10bv; *Cartas, patentes, alvarás*, 628, fls. 55, 76-82, (28 Nov. 1780).
7. Fernandes, *op. cit.*, p. 44. In a bid to modernise the administrative machinery and to revive commerce, Marquis de Pombal established the *Junta da Fazenda* in 1769. Its composition was not very different from its predecessor the Public Revenue Council which included the viceroy, the chancellor of the High Court, the *vedor geral da fazenda, the provedor-mor dos contos*, the crown attorney general, the custodian of the property of the dead and the secretary general of the *fazenda*.
8. HAG : *Cartas, patentes, alvarás*, 628, fls. 84-85, (30 July 1779).
9. Xavier, *op. cit.*, p. 190.
10. Fernandes, *op. cit.*, pp. 45-46.
11. *Ibid.*, pp. 49-50.
12. *Ibid.*, p. 50.
13. HAG : *AG*, 6813, fls. 66-67, 69; *Ibid.*, p. 51, (1 Jan. 1798). 14. HAG : *AG*, 6813, fls. 67-68; Claudio Lagrange Monteiro de Barbuda, *IDJ*, Nova Goa, 1841, p. 22.
15. Fernandes, *op. cit.*, p. 51.
16. Francisco Xavier Ernesto Fernandes, *Regimen do Sal, Abkary e Alfandegas da India*, Lisboa, 1905, p. 42.
17. Barbuda, *op. cit.*, p. 22.
18. loc. cit.; HAG : *PRA*, 8089, fls. 39v-40, 43v-44, (3 June 1810).
19. HAG : *AG*, 6813, fl. 159; Barbuda, *op. cit.*, p. 22.
20. Fernandes, *MHE*, p. 52, (3 May 1811); J. M. do Carmo Nazareth, "Alfandegas Portuguezas no Oriente", *O Oriente Português*, vol. VI, 1909, p. 22.
21. AHU : *MI*, Maço 200, no. 198, doc. dated 16 Jan. 1815.
22. Fernandes, *op. cit.*, p. 53.
23. Barbuda, *op. cit.*, p. 23, (6 April 1835, 23 July 1840).
24. Barbuda, *op. cit.*, p. 22.
25. *Boletim do Governo do Estado da India*, no. 42, 19 Oct. 1839, (10 Oct. 1839); Fernandes, *op. cit.*, pp. 55-56.
26. HAG : *Portarias*, 1410, fl. 43; Fernandes, *op. cit.*, pp. 53-54.
27. Barbuda, *op. cit.*, p. 24.
28. Felippe Nery Xavier, *Bandos*, vol. I, Nova Goa, 1840, pp. 202-204, (23 Dec. 1840); Fernandes, *op. cit.*, p. 58; *Ibid.*, p. 24.
29. Xavier, *op. cit.*, p. 209, (6 March 1841).
30. Fernandes, *op. cit.*, p. 59, (15 April 1841).
31. Carmo Nazareth, op. cit., p. 21; A. F. Moniz, "A Alfandega de Damão", *O Oriente Português*, vol. XI, 1914, pp. 133-134.
32. Carmo Nazareth, *op. cit.*, pp. 18-19.
33. Barbuda, *op. cit.*, p. 42.
34. HAG : *CR*, 2411, fl. 128v; Fernandes, *op. cit.*, p. 54.

35. Fernandes, *op. cit.*, pp. 52, 54.
36. HAG : *PRA*, 8089, fls. 7-7v; *Cartas, patentes, alvarás*, 628, fls. 2-4; *AG*, 6813, fls. 8-10, (10 Feb. 1774, 30 June 1775).
37. HAG : *AG*, 6813, fl. 519.
38. BA : *PD*, 20/404, 1830, doc. dated 2 May 1832.
39. BA : *PD*, 20/404, doc. dated 10 Jan. 1831.
40. Amancio Gracias, "Caminho de ferro e porto de Mormugão", *O Oriente Português*, vol. 28, 1940, p. 66.
41. HAG : *MR*, 161A, fls. 115-115v, (8 Jan. 1783); *PRA*, 8089, fl. 51v; *Cartas, patentes, alvarás*, 628, fls. 136-142.
42. HAG : *PRA*, 8089, fls. 66-68v, (25 April 1818).
43. HAG : *PRA*, 8089, fls. 44v-50v, 68v-69, (25 April 1818); *Portarias*, 1410, fls. 42-42v.
44. Fernandes, *op. cit.*, pp. 56-57, (30 Oct. 1830).
45. HAG : *Portarias*, 1410, fls. 27v-28; *Ibid.*, p. 56.
46. HAG : *Portarias*, 1410, fls. 29v-30; Fernandes *op. cit.*, p. 56.
47. HAG : *AG*, 6822, fls. 3-6v; Xavier, *O Gabinette Litterario*, vol. I, pp. 243-244, 257.
48. HAG : *Portarias*, 1410, fls. 27-31; AG, 6822, 6v; Xavier, *op. cit.*, pp. 243-244, 257.
49. Fernandes, *op. cit.*, p. 60.
50. HAG : *RGF*, 2280, fls. 346, 353-356.
51. HAG : *RGF*, 2280, fls. 346, 353-356; *AG*, 6813, fls. 98-103.
52. Michael Greenberg, *British Trade and the Opening of China 1800-1842*, New York/ London, p. 125.
53. A. F. Moniz, "A Feitoria Portuguesa de Surrate", *O Oriente Português*, vol. XV, 1ª serie, pp. 24-25; Panduranga, S. S. Pissulencar, *Portuguese Records on Rustomji Manockji*, doc. nos. 8, 12, 13, 16, 18, 21-22, 24-27, 31, 36-40, 42-44, 46, 50, 66, Nova Goa, 1933.
54. HAG : *CR*, 1651, unpaginated, undated; AHU : *MI*, Maço 79, no. 56; Maço 110, no. 126; Maço 179, no. 179, doc. dated 22 March 1804; BNL : *Fundo Geral*, 9451, doc. dated 12 Sept. 1818.
55. HAG : *MR*, 205B, doc. dated 12 Jan. 1829.
56. XCHR : *MHP* (Portuguese), doc. dated 8 Oct. 1790.
57. XCHR : *MHP* (Portuguese), doc. dated 10 Nov. 1786.
58. XCHR : *MHP* (Portuguese), doc. dated 17 Feb. 1786.
59. XCHR : *MHP* (Portuguese), undated doc.
60. XCHR : *MHP* (Portuguese), doc. dated 5 Feb. 1786.
61. XCHR : *MHP* (French), vol. 2, fl. 34v.
62. A. Lopes Mendes, *A India Portuguesa*, vol. I, Reprint, New Delhi/Madras, 1989, p. 171.
63. Teresa Albuquerque, "*Santa Cruz*" *Calapor, Profile of a Village in Goa*, Goa, 1989, p. 35.
64. Lopes Mendes, *op. cit.*, p. 171.
65. Xavier, *op. cit.*, pp. 23-31.
66. HAG : *MR*, 161D, fl. 2008v; Anthony Disney, "Smugglers and Smuggling in the Western Half of the *Estado da India* in the Late Sixteenth and Early Seventeenth Centuries", *Indica*, vol. 26, nos. 1 & 2, March-Sept. 1989.
67. XCHR : *MHP* (Portuguese), docs. dated 17 May 1789, 13 Jan. 1797, 26 Oct. 1798, 8 Feb. 1806, 6 March 1806, 14 Dec. 1812.
68. HAG : *CR*, 2415, doc. dated 5 April 1805; *MR*, 197A, fls. 352-353; Moniz, *op. cit.*, pp. 26-27.
69. XCHR : *MHP* (Portuguese), doc. dated 14 Dec. 1812.

70. Moniz, *op. cit.*, p. 27.
71. XCHR : *MHP* (Portuguese), doc. dated 6 March 1806; A. C. Aragão Texeira de, *Descrição geral e historica das moedas cunhadas em nome dos reis, regentes e governadores de Portugal*, Porto, 1964, p. 352.
72. XCHR : *MHP* (Portuguese), doc. no. 9114.
73. XCHR : *MHP* (Portuguese), docs. dated 13 Jan. 1797, 26 Oct. 1797.
74. HAG : *AG*, 6347, fls. 134-233; XCHR : *MHP* (Portuguese), doc. dated 8 Feb. 1806.
75. Aragão, *op. cit.*, p. 358.
76. Celsa Pinto, "At the Dusk of the Second Empire : Goa-Brazil Commercial Relations, 1770-1825", *Purabhilekh-Puratatva*, vol. VIII, no. 1, Jan.-June 1990, p.64.
77. HAG : *AG*, 8125, fls. 4-33; 11318, fl. 4.
78. HAG : *AG*, 8125, fls. 4-33; 11318, fl. 4.
79. Aragão, *op. cit.*, p. 375.

4

PORTUGAL : ANIMATION ATTEMPTS

The so-called indifference and utter neglect on the part of Portugal directed towards its Asian domains has been overstated. In all fairness, it must be said that despite its pre-occupation with political and economic difficulties at home the Crown and expend time, energy and interest to stimulate commerce in its decadent East.

Since 1775, without much prompting, special efforts were made by the Portuguese authorities to review the existing system of commerce in Portuguese India and determine why the *Estado* was running annually in deficit. The Crown was first seized with the task of examining and analysing the existing customs laws and regulations to smoothen the way for the enactment of more enlightened legislation focused on the promotion of Portuguese commerce in the Indian Ocean. It was discovered that the *Regimento* of 20th January, 1774 was a major source of Goa's commercial problems. During the first two years since its promulgation, hardly any ship called at Goa either to dispose off or purchase merchandise or for watering.[1] From Table 4.1 we gather that the annual average revenue collection made by the *Alfandega de Goa* prior to the enforcement of the *Regimento* of 1774 was 251,579-2-30 *xerafins* while that made during 1775-78 was 170,490-2-09 *xerafins* that meant a drop of about 81,089-0-21 *xerafins*. One of the causes was the shift from Crown shipping to private mercantile shipping. It was discovered that private ships arriving from Lisbon would sail up and down the west coast of India from Cape Comorin to the north conducting trade, buying and selling goods at Bombay and other places but would avoid calling at Goa.[2] If and when they decided to touch Goa to sell off their merchandise, the merchants of Goa would bargain for lower rates causing them much loss. They also bypassed the port of Goa on account of the high customs duties charged there. The Portuguese merchants on board the Lisbon ships preferred to employ their capital and that belonging to their principals at

Lisbon to acquire clothes and fabrics derived from Balaghat, Porto Novo and Patavar rather than those that were available at Daman, Diu and Surat which would cost 25 per cent to 30 per cent more.[3] The competition offered by other European powers was perhaps another contributory factor. The position of superior gain of other European merchants lay in the fact that they could transport their ships to all their ports without hindrance, without having to pay excessive duties as the Portuguese did.[4]

TABLE 4.1: REVENUE COLLECTION OF THE CUSTOMS HOUSE OF GOA, 1768-78

Year	Revenues (In *xerafins*)
1768	155445-0-48
1769	211338
1770	317887
1772	292651-3-31
1773	254708-2-44 1/2
1774	277446-3-14 1/4
1775	157769-1-59
1776	225068-0-08 3/4
1777	148341-0-05 3/4
1778	150783-1-26 1/4

Source: HAG : *CR*, 2408, fls. 92v-94.

The merchants of Goa were consulted with respect to the inconveniences faced under the *Regimento* of 1774 and their suggestions were invited for change.[5] A memorandum was presented by 33 merchants, of which 31 were Hindus and the rest Christians. In this case too one observes the dominance of the Hindus in the Goan economy. Among the grievances voiced by the merchants stress was laid on the fact that no protection was offered to merchants against pirates lurking in waters around Goa and other dangers. The need for free movement as enjoyed by merchants at British ports was also expressed. In Goa merchants had to face vexatious tributes and duties. Foreign as well as Portuguese ships that touched Goa would not halt for long because of increasing expenditure and therefore found it necessary to conduct commerce as speedily as possible. Penalties imposed for smuggling and other illegal activities were too excessive to accept.[6]

A committee was instituted to trace the roots of the general malaise that plagued the commercial system of the *Estado* and to recommend remedies to cut losses and promote gains. It recommended the setting up of a trading company instituted on sound lines, the promotion of industries at Daman and Diu, the gearing up of efforts for the advancement of agriculture, absolute commercial freedom of circulation within the *Estado* and the establishment of an entrepôt at Goa to foster commerce with China and Europe. It also recommended the abolition of onerous duties at Goa, that Europe-bound ships from Macao laden with Chinese commodities on arriving at Cape Comorin should be diverted to Goa and on the return voyage they should ship cargoes from Goa to China. It was felt that these remedial measures would not only stimulate the growth and the development of the *Estado*-based commerce, boost State revenues, and lift the people out of their state of misery, but would also raise Portugal to the heights of glory, indicating to the world that it possessed advantages over other nations in the form of its commerce revolving round the ports of Goa, Daman, Diu, Macao, Moçambique and Sena.[7]

These investigations bore much fruit and paved the way for the enactment of the celebrated *Alvará Regio* of 8th January, 1783, which was widely acclaimed as a landmark in commercial legislation, aimed at promoting and activating commerce and navigation in Portuguese India.[8] It was decreed that merchandise manufactured at Goa and the other Portuguese Indian dominions or even obtained from other ports in the Indian Ocean region, if despatched from Goa in *naos da Carreira* or other Portuguese vessels to Lisbon, would not be charged more than a 4 per cent trans-shipment fee.[9]

The *Alvará Regio* of 8th January 1783 marked the culmination of a long-standing need for increased trans-shipment facilities regarded as essential to attract trade to Goa and to revitalise Portuguese commerce in Asia as a whole.[10] The immediate effect of this significant development was that the flagging economy of the *Estado* received a shot in the arm as indicated by the upswing in commercial activity and the revenues collected by the *Alfandega de Goa* in years following the initiation of the *Alvará Regio* of 1783.[11] This is indicated in Table 4.2. Fabrics called *negro* and those of other quality derived from Daman, Diu, Surat, Balaghat and other ports of coastal India were re-exported on a massive scale via the port of Goa. Ships arriving from Lisbon, Moçambique and Brazil both crown and privately-operated made a bee-line for Goa. Prior to the implementation of the *Alvará Regio* of 1783 around one to three ships touched the port of Goa per annum, but during the period 1783-88, an average of six ships visited Goa.[12]

The *Alvará Regio* of 1783 signalled an important departure from the traditional stand earlier taken by the Lisbon authorities towards its Portuguese Indian commerce. A high tariff policy was replaced by liberal measures much in keeping with the free trade doctrines of the times and this enabled the *Estado*-based trade to reach fresh peaks.

TABLE 4.2 : REVENUES OF THE *ALFANDEGA DE GOA*, 1778-87

Year	Revenues (In *xerafins*)
1778	198748-3-30
1779	242881-1-06
1780	223908-3-28
1781	234680-2-31
1782	331513-3-07
1783	433998-3-05
1784	450911-1-41
1785	360432-3-05
1786	552557-2-54
1787	422476-0-03

Source: HAG : *MR*, 171B, fl. 493.

The promulgation of the Decreto of 27th May 1789, the *Alvará Regio* of 17th August 1795, the *Alvará* of 25th November 1800, the *Alvará* of 4th February 1811 and other commercial legislation in the likeness of the celebrated *Alvará Regio* of 8th January 1783, were aimed at further reorganizing and revitalizing commerce in Asia.[13] Of significance was the lowering of the trans-shipment duty to 2 per cent to be paid by Portuguese vessels transporting Asian products to Lisbon, Brazil, Azores, Madeira islands and other ports of West Africa in February 1811.[14]

Special attention was directed towards Indian cotton textiles especially those manufactured at Daman and Diu. Such textiles were much in demand in Portugal and elsewhere in Europe. Commercial laws were therefore enacted by the Crown to facilitate their smooth entry into Europe. In November 1800, textiles manufactured at Daman and Diu, transported in Portuguese ships from Goa, were exempted from the payment of entry duties at Lisbon, Brazil and West African ports for a period of six years. Furthermore, in January 1802 no entry was permitted in the India House (*Casa da India*) to coloured fabrics whether woven, printed or painted. An exception was made in the case of textiles despatched from Daman and Diu which were not white but were embroidered or woven in colour.[15]

Concerted efforts were made to promote ship-building with the ultimate goal of generating commerce in the Indian Ocean region. Customs duties on materials essential for the construction of ships were abolished. It was meant to motivate merchants to construct ships to transport their cargoes.[16] In 1778 wood required for ship-building and repair work at the Goa Shipyard was exempted from the payment of duties.[17]

Although we have no revenue figures to indicate the extent to which the Portuguese Indian trade developed subsequent to the passing of liberal commercial legislation during 1789-1811, there is no doubt that the *Estado*-based commerce continued to thrive during 1790-1805. In the late 1790s Portugal's neutrality during the then European wars and the fact that it was at peace with France enabled its merchants to ship Indian piece-goods freely into the European continent while other traders were hampered by the British blockade. The trade in piece-goods brought the Indo-Portuguese traders and the *Fazenda Real* rich returns.[18] But matters changed from 1806 onwards. The average annual revenue return of the *Alfandega de Goa* which stood at 446,594-1-56 *xerafins* during 1784-87 dropped to 234,460-2-32 *xerafins* during 1806-10. (See Tables 3.1 and 4.2) This fall in State customs revenues can be attributed to the Indian Ocean being unsafe for commercial shipping during the Revolutionary War period when the French attacked ships of other nationalities. The presence of the British in the *Estado*, and the passing of the treaties of 1808 and 1810 were other factors contributing to dwindling State revenues.

Revitalising the Goa-Moçambique Channel

The once-flourishing traditional trading channel between Portuguese India and East Africa languished in doldrums in the late eighteenth century. The Lisbon authorities decided to give due attention to it. The basic cause of this decadence lay in the depressing situation in Portuguese East Africa itself.

From Moçambique, huge cargoes of gold, ivory, slaves and rhino horns of the value of 1,200,000 to 1,400,000 *cruzados* would move out annually oriented to India, Brazil and Lisbon. This must have netted in much revenue. Instead, Moçambique in February 1775 owed nearly 600,000 *cruzados* to Diu, 100,000 *cruzados* to Goa and 30,000 *cruzados* to Daman.[19] What was behind these liabilities of Moçambique ?

This situation stemmed from a myriad factors. The liberalisation of trade in 1769 brought about structural changes in the Moçambican economy. The Luso-Atlantic slave commerce engendered a spectacular increase in the circulation of gold and silver coins in Moçambique. This had damaging consequences leading to the massive outflow of capital in the form of hoarded precious metals and coins out of the country, across the Indian Ocean to Portuguese India and Gujarat. One observes that banias on the west coast of India took liberalisation to heart. They were quick to realise the advantages the situation in East Africa had to offer. Their sole intention in proceeding to Africa was to accumulate vast fortunes in the quickest possible time and to transfer the same back home.

Leaving behind their families in India, the banias began life in Africa in lowly occupations and from these humble beginnings inched their way up to high peaks. This could be attributed to their business acumen and to the established fact that they were skilled in the art of commerce, wringing as much profit as possible out of the helpless East Africans. The banias were a force to reckon with and their pre-eminence in the oriental African trade was clearly pronounced. The trade conducted by them covered a wide range, spreading its tentacles far and wide to Quelimane, Sena, Sofala and pcssibly even Cabaceira and Mussuri. Moçambican liabilities began to mount as the shy-lockian grip of the banias over the trading system continued to tighten.

The deteriorating economic situation in Moçambique triggered off a great deal of impotent reaction. Many expressed deep concern, while others bitterly denounced the bania policy of "underdeveloping Africa".[20] Though Portuguese Governors at Moçambique took concerted steps to curtail the harm being done, their efforts were in vain.[21]

Liberalisation not only brought banias to East Africa but also hordes of Muslim and European merchants, particularly the French, the English and the Dutch. At the isles of Ibo and Querimbo and at Cape Delgado, French vessels from Madagascar, Mauritius, Bourbon and other French colonies in the East would throng bringing goods from Europe and the Coromandel coast and returning with slaves, dog-whelk and ivory. Slaves were transported away on the payment of export duties of 20 *cruzados* per slave. The existence of such a channel was ruinous to Moçambique and its inhabitants who found themselves in the sorry situation of competing with these interlopers.[22] In fact they were unable to cope with this threat.

At the most the Moçambican merchants would bring commodities from the north in small sailing vessels to those areas visited by the French and depart with agricultural products. The low state of a once-thriving commerce of the Bay of Lourenço Marques had been attributed to the fact that this was a favourite haunt of British and Dutch merchants.[23] British ships coming from Bombay and Surat would proceed directly to the Bay ignoring the claims of Moçambique to bulk duties. The Dutch and the English also had a stranglehold over the commerce of Cape Delgado.[24]

At one stage the Austrians too challenged Portuguese authority in the region. Wilholm Bolts, lieutenant-colonel in the service of the Austrian government and Director General of the *Companhia Aziatica de Trieste* (Asian Company of Trieste) arrived in the Indian Ocean in an Austrian ship probably in 1778 and called at Lourenço Marques. He unloaded some goods and bought some land from a native ruler in the area. He established a fortified business house armed with artillery so as to be of service to Austrian vessels of the said company whenever they sailed beyond the Cape of Good Hope into the Indian Ocean waters. They could halt there for rest and commerce. Bolts accordingly began to enjoy privileges and benefits and to exhaust resources especially at Lagoa, making deep inroads into Portuguese commercial interests.[25]

Another cause for the decay and decline of Moçambique was its separation from the *Estado da India*. The Goa Government across the Indian Ocean used to exercise a tight rein over Moçambique. Abuses and disorders were kept at a minimum. One witnessed the safe and free movement of goods from Goa, Daman and Diu to the east coast of Africa and back. Bania settlement in Africa was low. In fact the commerce of the eastern littoral of Africa was totally controlled by East African Portuguese merchants and by the natives of Goa, some of whom would return back to Goa while others revealed their preference for settlement in Moçambique. Their fortunes would thus remain within the Portuguese dominions. The situation changed drastically in the period under study. Not only had the Portuguese involvement in the East African trade declined, but whatever fortunes were made in Portuguese East Africa would wend their way to Cambay and other parts of Gujarat.

Separation from the *Estado da India* brought to the fore a new breed of administrators. They neither possessed the capacity nor the merit essential for administration. It appears that soldiers sent by Portugal to Moçambique seemed to be lacking in interest in promoting the affairs of the State. They were not able to restore normalcy in an area disturbed by numerous civil wars between kaffirs, war-like by nature. They were not able to contain loot and plunder, a characteristic feature of the region.[26]

Certain expedient solutions were envisioned to set things right in Moçambique, which would in turn provide a fillip to the all-important Portuguese East African commerce. It was suggested that steps should be taken to initiate the restoration of the union of Moçambique with the *Estado da India* for in this lay the salvation of Moçambique. It was generally believed that the *Fazenda Real* of Goa would restore economic order in East Africa, as compared to distant Portugal. The nobility of Goa would administer Portuguese East Africa in the right spirit in keeping with their rank and position. It was believed that re-union with the *Estado* would in no way undermine the interests of Moçambique.[27]

Several other suggestions were made for the all round economic prosperity of Portuguese East Africa. It was felt necessary and convenient to limit the import duties to 5 per cent, to put into operation a law prohibiting the settlement of banias in the colony, to limit the number of bania business houses to six and to prohibit their business of shop - keeping. It was also felt essential to insist that none of the Portuguese and the natives of Goa should undertake the mercantile profession without demonstrating the necessary business capabilities.[28]

Recommendations were also made to strengthen and streamline the military organisation and to promote settlement in and development of each of the ports of Portuguese East Africa.[29]

The above proposals it was felt would serve to counter the problems afflicting Moçambique. Its recovery would pave the way for the resurgence of commerce between East Africa and Portuguese India. It appears that these recommendations were placed in cold storage. From subsequent documentation we see no move towards the re-establishment of the union of Goa with Moçambique, nor any attempt made to restrict the private illegal trade of the banias of west India or of the non-Portuguese Europeans along the East African littoral.

The *Alvará Regio* of 1783 had undoubtedly been a principal impetus for boosting commerce between Moçambique and Portuguese India (See Table 4.3). Prior to the implementation of this Royal Order (1780-83) Goa earned an annual average revenue of 5,716-1-21 *xerafins* from the Moçambique trade. In 1784 it climbed up to 6,491-1-56 *xerafins*. Thus the increase amounted to 775-0-35 or 13.56 per cent. In the case of Daman the average annual returns for the said period from the said trade prior to the *Alvará Regio* amounted to 9,676-3-38 *xerafins* while in 1784 Daman obtained 14,537-1-44 *xerafins*. The rise was by 4,860-3-06 *xerafins* or by 50.23 per cent. Unfortunately we have no figures for 1784 in the case of Diu in order to study the impact of the *Alvará* on the commercial revenue income of Diu. By and large the *Alvará* of 1783 did stimulate the finances of Portuguese India especially those of Daman and Diu.

Since 1784 plans were once again afoot to revitalise in a big way the flagging Portuguese trade of Asia with East Africa.[30] It was suggested that ships coming from the *Estado* and Lisbon should have the freedom to proceed directly to the ports of Africa without calling at Moçambique. To streamline customs procedures, to increase customs revenues and to facilitate mercantile business, the creation of new customs houses in

Portuguese East Africa was recommended. A special reference was made to the setting up of *alfandegas* at the islands of Querimbo, Quelimane, Sofala, Inhambane and the Cape.[31] A reduction in customs was suggested as the existing duties collected were steep amounting to 40 per cent.[32]

TABLE 4.3 : REVENUES ACQUIRED BY THE *ESTADO* FROM THE MOÇAMBIQUE TRADE, 1778-84

Year	Goa (In *xerafins*)	Daman (In *xerafins*)	Diu (In *xerafins*)
1778	69711-4-44		
1779	101631-4-02		
1780	5318-2-07 1/2	9986-2-48 1/2	87721-0-12 1/4
1781	8043-1-02	10015-3-50	74148-0-46
1782	4123-0-40	10548-3-40	75929-3-25
1783	5380-1-35 1/2	8155-4-10	
1784	6491-1-56	14537-1-44	

Source: HAG : *MR*, 167A, fls. 134, 154-159.

At the islands of Querimbo, Quelimane, Sofala, Inhambane, for goods transported from Lisbon and the *Estado* a payment of one-fourth of the duties paid at Moçambique was recommended. There was however generalised opposition to these suggestions. [33]

Taking cognisance of these suggestions a commercial plan was conceived in Janauary 1786, encompassing a wide range of measures for restoring commercial prosperity, especially the commerce between the *Estado* and Portuguese East Africa.

The plan of 1786 stressed that goods belonging to nationals, naturalised or otherwise, despatched to Goa in a Portuguese vessel, for onward carriage to Moçambique or any other port of East Africa, were to be exempted from the payment of duties at the *Alfandega de Goa* provided that the captain and one-third of the crew of the ship were of Portuguese origin and on the return journey the ship, would unload at the said port.[34]

Secondly, the plan indicated that goods coming to Goa from the north, Malabar or any other port, by land or sea, would be subject to the payment of entry duties. But if some of them were to be shipped to Moçambique or any other East African port, the same could be done without the payment of duties. The ship would carry a certificate stating the quantity and quality of the goods and whether entry duties had been paid for or not.[35]

Thirdly, for the economic benefit of Diu and Daman, the plan also proposed that all goods manufactured at these ports, to be transported to Goa for exportation to the ports of Africa, would enjoy duty exemption at the said ports. On reaching Goa they were to be deposited in the warehouses of the *Alfandega de Goa* before being re-exported to the said ports of Africa. This simple transit would be permitted without the payment of entry or exit duties. However, if the goods were destined to move elsewhere, all the fixed duties would be charged at the northern port of export as well as at Goa.[36]

Fourthly, according to the plan, ships were permitted to sail from Goa not only to Moçambique, but also directly to other ports of East Africa, without calling at the *Fortaleza de Moçambique*. Wherever there was a customs house, the duty charged would be one-fourth less than the prevailing rate at the Moçambican customs house. In ports which did not have *alfandegas*, the duty charged would be one-fourth less than that charged at Moçambique. On the return trip the ships coming directly to Goa on unloading, would have to pay half of the import duties fixed there.[37]

Fifthly, to promote and augment commerce and the manufactures of Daman and Diu, merchant ships belonging to Portuguese subjects, carrying the said manufactures from the ports of Daman or Diu could directly sail to Moçambique and other ports of East Africa and could trade freely there. If the captain and one-third of the crew were of Portuguese origin,the ship would enjoy the privilege of paying only half the export duties at the said ports. In the case of goods not manufactured at Daman or Diu, the customary duties in entirety would have to be paid at the said ports of the north and those of East Africa. The ships could directly return to the said northern ports and pay all the import duties but if they proceeded to Goa, they would be charged just half the duties fixed there.[38]

The above outlined plan for promoting the commerce of the *Estado* with Moçambique and East Africa was approved of and ratified by the *Carta Regia* of 5th March 1787 and this heralded the beginning of a better and more composite commercial system binding East Africa and Portuguese India.[39]

Moçambique profitted from the trade with Portuguese India in the years following the plan of 1786. In July 1787 a new tariff system was introduced at Moçambique. Arrack from Goa was charged 5 per cent duty while other goods coming to Moçambique from that port were subjected to 3 per cent duty. Exportation of ivory and gold at Moçambique involved a levy of 4 per cent in either case while the exportation of slaves involved the payment of 16 *cruzados* for an adult slave and 12 *cruzados* for a young one. Prior to July 1787 arrack and cashew liquors were charged a steep 10 per cent duty.[40]

The net result of these efforts was a marked rise in Moçambique's overall trade in slaves, gold, ivory and textiles and above all its trade with the *Estado* especially since 1787 (See Table 4.4). To Moçambique Diu's role in the Moçambique-*Estado* trade was more significant than that of Goa and Daman.[41] From Table 4.4 we observe that the gains made by the *Estado da India* from its participation in the trade with Moçambique during 1781-91 were much more than those of Moçambique. The value of exports of Goa, Daman and Diu surpassed that of imports.

TABLE 4.4 :TOTAL VALUE OF THE *ESTADO*-MOÇAMBIQUE TRADE, 1781-90

Year	Goa		Daman		Diu	
	Imports (In *reis*)	Exports (In *reis*)	Imports (In *reis*)	Exports (In *reis*)	Imports (In *reis*)	Exports (In reis)
1781	4147$200	37583$625	17590$925	51503$275	180555$425	258322$275
1782	5438$960	27202$800	35239$425	255444$800	310099$850	
1783	3987$600	108073$545	22063$925	20939$100	265481$550	290478$650
1784	1471$105	28361$230	118739$675	90111$635		
1785	3776$675	64889$300	48360$750	40430$250	145911$	150963$800
1786	29196$400	58562$675	50054$306	56333$925	214649$850	322611$025
1787	46624$425	105189$625	40071$150	66965$925	202545$625	203773$525
1788	2783$725	100525$915	50674$800	89879$680	206097$025	123834$180
1789	24825$900	85654$052	75895$425	218756$	82496$970	259982$500
1790	2093$650	90416$830	42956$800	147938$960	138127$200	193675$740

Source : AHU : *Moçambique*, Caixa 75, doc. no. 71.

Plan of 1799

Another milestone in the promotional efforts of the Lisbon Government was the formulation of a plan in 1799 to set up a company at Lisbon having within its purview the commerce of Moçambique, Goa, the Malabar coast, Bengal, the Coromandel coast and China. The plan envisaged the need to have a fund of 6 million *cruzados* to enable six ships — two for Moçambique, Goa and the Malabar coast, two for the Coromandel coast and Bengal and two for China — to make annual voyages.[42] The two ships destined for Moçambique, were expected to leave Lisbon in the month of February laden with goods meant to cater to the needs of Moçambique as well those of Goa, Surat and Malabar. Among other items, cutlery, glassware, European liquors and wines, weaponry, gun-powder, paper, butter, cheese, marmalade, preserves, artificial corals, scents, velvets, satin, damasks, silken and linen stockings were listed in the plan. The ships after a brief halt at Moçambique in August, where they would dispose off some of their merchandise, would then proceed to Goa with commodities obtained at Moçambique such as gold, ivory, seahorse-teeth, rhino horns, turtles and slaves.[43]

While in Goa, the ships would be required to sell off some of their goods and then sail to Daman, Diu and Surat. There they would dispose off the rest of their cargoes and exchange them for goods much in demand in Portugal, Brazil and Angola.[44] With saltpetre, pepper, Indian cotton products derived from Surat, Daman, Diu and Balaghat, Arabian glue, indigo and sundries, the ships would depart from Goa in February for Lisbon, without halting at Moçambique even for rest and relaxation.[45]

The plan of 1799 also emphasized the need to activate the East African commerce revolving round Goa, Daman and Diu. It was felt that the Moçambican-West coast of India channel was monopolised by Hindus residing in Goa, Daman and Diu and those of Surat, Cambay and other ports of Gujurat who would annually ship cargoes from Malabar and Gujarat and would extract large quantities of gold and ivory from East Africa. Neither the Portuguese nor the *Fazenda Real* of Goa gained much from this commerce. The Hindu merchants avoided payment of duties at Moçambique sailing directly to other east African ports where they did not make any payments. The plan spelt out steps to be taken to counter such practices and abuses. It stated that on cargoes transported to Moçambique, the import duty charged should not exceed 5 per cent, that the ships should enjoy the liberty to move to any port on the East African coast, that *alfandegas* should be set up at all the Portuguese African ports where the ships could call and pay 10 per cent import and export duties. It seems obvious that the Lisbon authorities were keen to encourage merchants of Portuguese India to navigate their ships to Moçambique to transport their goods and to conduct trade without restriction.

It was observed that privately-owned vessels leaving Lisbon for western coastal India preferred to move to British ports to dispose off their goods and to lade their ships with cargoes for the return voyage, because of misconceptions that Portuguese Indian ports had no merchandise of significance to offer nor commerce worth considering. Therefore the plan of 1799 stressed that such shipping should move to the *Estado* ports to supply European goods and to load their ships with Asian commodities.[46] These were attempts to activate the commerce of Portuguese India and to boost its customs revenues.

The plan also cited measures to attract to Goa goods from the Coromandel coast and Bengal. It envisaged the need to lower the existing duties on the entry and departure of goods arriving from these regions. It was suggested that the import duties should be reduced from 6 to 4 per cent and that no export duties should be charged. Moreover after paying the required duties at Goa, the goods could be diverted to Daman and Diu.[47]

The plan underscored the significance of the commerce of China to Portugal especially that conducted via Macao. One of the two ships destined for the Far East would be required to leave Lisbon in February and proceed directly to Macao. The other ship would disembark in the month of April and would call at Goa *en route* to Macao. The latter vessel would be laden with goods for consumption at Goa, Surat, Cambay and parts of Gujarat. Iron bars, copper in bars and plates, lead in powder and plates, weaponry, gold and silver wires, pitch, wines and liquors, marmalade, butter, cheese, preserves and gun-powder were to form part of the cargoes shipped from Portugal. They could be sold off in western littoral India and the proceeds could be utilised to purchase cotton, sandal-wood, pepper, opium, incense and sundries. With these commodities and the remnant capital, the ship could depart for Macao at the end of March or April.[48]

After selling off the said goods at Macao, the proceeds could be employed to purchase a host of Chinese goods like tea, candied sugar, crockery, cinnamon, rhubarb, borax, benjoin and textiles. The ship would then be expected to leave Macao in the month of January for Lisbon.[49]

The plan also emphasized measures needed to promote Portugal's trade with Bengal and the Coromandel coast.[50]

The success of this plan hinged on the cooperation and support of the merchants of the *Estado*. But all that the merchants were concerned with was the promotion of their own prosperity rather than that of the State. Their ever increasing appetite for profits funnelled capital flows into family coffers rather than into the State treasury.

Moreover, circumstances immediately after 1805 were not favourable for commerce. The western sector of the Indian Ocean was often the scene of French attacks on official and private commercial shipping. This continued till 1811. Nevertheless the trade in Indian cotton fabrics with Moçambique, Brazil and Lisbon continued to flourish. We also observe the beginnings of a clandestine trade in opium between the *Estado* and Macao. Opium shipments first made their appearance in Macao in 1804. It began as a trickle and developed into a flood. Therefore the *Estado*-Macao channel proved to be a windfall not only for the merchants but also for the State. It thrived due to the liberal commercial policies of the *Estado* and Portugal.

What might have prompted the Lisbon government to take concerted steps to promote commmerce in the East, despite its preoccupation in politico-economic affairs at home? The animating attempts were not born out of love for its subjects in the East but out of fear that its eastern empire would collapse. It was necessary for Portuguese India to survive. That was all that Portugal had in the East.

Another possiblity could be examined. Lisbon merchants were deeply interested in the interport trade of Asia. So efforts were probably made to please and pacify them. In fact by the end of the eighteenth century there was a radical shift from Crown shipping to private shipping. Lisbon merchants were keen to lay their hands on Indian textiles of Daman, Diu, Surat, Patavar, Porto Novo and Balaghat, saltpetre from Bengal, spices and sundries.[51] Much bullion was despatched from Portugal to acquire such commodities, very much in demand in Brazil, Portugal and other parts of Europe. In 1787, 546 sacks of saltpetre weighing 619 quintais and 2 arrobas were despatched from Goa to Portugal on board the ship *Nossa Senhora da Vida, Santo Antonio e Magdalena* and 822 sacks weighing 951 *quintais*, 2 *arrobas* and 8-1/2 *arrateis* were shipped by *O Senhor de Bomfim e S. Thiago Maior.*[52] In fact during 1766-73 there were regular despatches of saltpetre to Lisbon, amounting to 28,586 sacks. Such was the demand for saltpetre that of Lisbon merchant ships coming to Asia would procure the item directly at Bengal. There were often complaints of poor quality saltpetre reaching Lisbon via the *Carreira da India*. This might have prompted the Lisbon merchants to proceed directly to Bengal to acquire stocks of good quality saltpetre.

In the existing documentation we can observe a demand on the part of Lisbon merchants for Indian cotton fabrics. In 1790, 240 bales of textiles of Surat, 265 of Balaghat and one of Daman together with 1410 sacks of pepper were despatched on board the ship *Rainha dos Anjos* to Lisbon. Likewise in 1791 the ship *Princeza de Portugal* carried 429 bales of textiles of Surat, 16 of Balaghat, two of Diu along with 81 bales of coffee to Portugal.[53] The company of Colffs, Loureiros and Guimaraes figured significantly in the Lisbon trade with Asia. A host of other Lisbon-based merchants profitted from the Asiatic trade especially in Indian cotton fabrics.[54]

The Goa merchants had strong business ties with their counterparts in Lisbon and served as their agents and correspondents. Babaji Sinai Kabadi, Francisco Luis de Menezes, João Rodrigues Velho, Bhikya Naik Shaba, Ramchandra Prabhu Sinari, Manoel de Souza, Ari Sinai, Govinda Sinai, Jacinto Domingos, Joze Gomes, Matias Antonio de Fonseca, Joaquim Estanislaus de Souza, Inacio Alberto de Oliveira, Joze Custodio de Silva, Anta Naik, Alexandre Joze Monteiro, Anta Bhandari, Francisco da Silva Pomar, Pandurang Naik Sardessai, Narba Kamat, Raghunath Naik, Jacinto Soares and Vithoji Naik were amongst those who provided the fodder for the Goa-Lisbon trading nexus.[55]

The Lisbon authorities came to a realisation that the Asiatic trade could not only prove beneficial to the *Estado da India* but also for the home country. It could provide rich returns for Lisbon-based merchants and the Crown. It would increase the customs revenue of Portugal. The Asiatic trade could serve not only as a feeder for the Goa-Lisbon trade but in turn could serve as a feeder for the trade of Portugal with the rest of Europe. Portugal exported Asian products like textiles, pepper, tea and cinnamon to England, Holland, Castella, Russia, Italy, Barbaria and the United States as indicated in Table 4.5. It chiefly exported Asian commodities to France, the value of the exports totalling 1,77,080$000 *reis* while its export of Asian goods was least to the United States, amounting to 195$200 *reis*. Lisbon's export trade in Asian products was worth 4,43,448$820 *reis* out of a total export trade of 2,14,05,349$072 *reis*.[56]

TABLE 4.5 : TOTAL VALUE OF PORTUGAL'S EXPORT TRADE IN ASIAN PRODUCTS, 1802

Countries	Value (In *reis*)
England	619 $ 400
Hamburg	87650 $ 000
France	177080 $ 000
Castella	42489 $ 220
Russia	1120 $ 000
Italy	122738 $ 200
Barbaria	11556 $ 800
United States	195 $ 200

Source: BPA : *India*, 46-XIII-24, fls. 5-100 : *passim*.

The net result of the combined efforts of the State and the Crown to promote commerce in the East was a sharp rise in the State revenues. The revenues of the *Fazenda Real* rose from a deficit of 296,643-4-48 *xerafins* in 1752 to a surplus of 347,302-3-15 1/120 *xerafins* in 1793.[57] One gets glimpses of this new-found prosperity from the balance sheets of the State treasury. Thus the *Estado da India* began moving along the path of economic recovery.

But this relatively promising beginning soon turned sour. The bubble of commercial prosperity burst with events on the European continent taking a turn for the worse for the home country. The early nineteenth century saw Portugal in a state of flux. The imperial crisis having its roots in the Napoleonic attack on Portugal in 1807, culminated in the transfer of the royal court to Rio de Janeiro and the declaration of Brazilian independence in 1822. In the aftermath of the liberal revolution of 1820, Portugal was plunged into decades of intermittent strife. Portugal had scant time and energy to bother about its eastern empire.

Worse still, Portugal had to submit itself to the whims and fancies of England, then at the helm of the world economic order, in the name of traditional friendship and alliance. Portugal was confronted with the stark reality of subordinating its interests on the European continent as well as those in India to those of Britain. The latter had to come to its rescue during Napoleon's invasion of Portugal and had successfully organised the shift of the Portuguese royal court to Rio. It determined the entire course of events centred round Lisbon and gave it a commanding place in its relationship with Portugal. The price Portugal had to pay was high, imperilling its position in Europe and the East. It was caught in the web of its own making. By the Treaty of 28th January 1808, the entry of British commodities into Brazil was permitted on the payment of 24 per cent import duties.[58] Later, by the Treaty of 19th February 1810, the duties were lowered to 15 per cent. Ironically, this benefit of 15 per cent import duties was not enjoyed by Portuguese nationals. The matter was set right in October 1810.[59]

The opening up of Brazilian and other Portuguese ports in 1808, at the behest of Britain, sparked off a crisis — the onslaught of cheap Manchester products. It brought about the complete dislocation of the *Estado*-based re-exportation trade in Indian textiles to Portugal, Brazil and Moçambique. It was responsible for undercutting the market position of Indian fabrics in these regions. In 1816 this trade had accounted for 10 per cent of Portugal's trade with Asia, but by 1828 it had drastically declined to 1 per cent, and thereafter it was virtually non-existent.[60]

Similar was the fate of the Portuguese slave commerce across the Indian Ocean. England sought to check this baneful trade in human cargoes. Portugal had to enter into an agreement with England in 1847, enabling the latter to move to the extreme extent of subjecting ports, bays, creeks and rivers in the Portuguese territories, where illicit slave-trafficking was rife, to severe surveillance. This implied a severe drop in slave revenues.

During the period under review, the Daman customs house derived much of its income from the commerce with Moçambique. This income amounting to 36,555-4-57 *xerafins* in 1792 and 42,840-1-53 *xerafins* in 1798 dropped to 27,032-0-09 *xerafins* in 1825.[61] A look at the revenue figures of the *Alfandega de Goa* reveals that in 1806 the said customs house derived an income of 276,313-1-00 1/4 *xerafins*, that this amount climbed up to 401,675-2-30 *xerafins* in 1817. But since the 1820s the returns reveal a downward trend. One observes a slide in the revenues to 168,545-1-05 *xerafins* in 1820, to 99,066-3-20 *xerafins* in 1828, to 71,622-2-11 1/2 *xerafins* in 1833 and finally to 56,063-3-57 3/4 *xerafins* in 1838.[62] Thus we observe that there were limitations to the efforts of the Crown to promote prosperity in the East. It did live up to challenges posed by a decadent trade as was obvious from its late eighteenth century measures. But it was severely hampered in the face of mounting British pressure. Portugal had to succumb in the nineteenth century to British dictates and function within the frame-work of its control, protection and subserviency in the emerging capitalist world economy in which England enjoyed the status of the hegemonic core. This in turn had a profound bearing on her tottering out-posts in the throes of survival in far-off India.

REFERENCES AND NOTES

1. HAG : *MR*, 158A, fls. 58-58v.
   Ships that left Lisbon for Goa during 1771-1779 were as follows: *S. Joze* in 1770; *N. S. da Caridade e S. Francisco de Paula* in 1771; *N. S. do Monte do Carmo* in 1772; *N. S. da Caridade e S. Francisco de Paula* in 1773; *N. S. do Monte do Carmo* in 1774; *Santo Antonio and Neptuno* in 1775; *S^mo^ Sacramento e N. S. do Paraizo* in 1776; *Santo Antonio and Neptuno* in 1777; *N. S. da Conceição e Santo Antonio* in 1778; *Santo Antonio e Polifemo and N. S. do Livramento* in 1779. AHU : *MI*, Maço 8, no. 104, doc. dated 26 Sept. 1779.
2. HAG : *MR*, 152A, fls. 204-204v; 158A, fls. 55, 56.
3. HAG : *MR*, 158A, fl. 57.
4. HAG : *MR*, 161A, fls. 593-593v.
5. HAG : *CR*, 2408, fl. 83.
6. AHU : *MI*, Maço 138, no. 130, doc. dated 5 March 1783. HAG : *CR*, 2408, fls. 96-97v, 102: The merchants who signed the memorandum incorporating the opinions and recommendations relating to the existing system of commerce under the *Regimento* of 1774 were : Govind Naik, Dulba Naik Sardessai, Vithoji Kamat, Vithoji Naik, Anta Sinai, Kushta Kamat, Vithoji Sinai, Rama Kushta Sinai, João Colaço Roiz, Venkatesha Naik, Manoel Antonio de Menezes, Ramchandra Naik, Gopal Naik Karande, Vithoji Sinai Dhempe, Krishna Sinai Cabbadi, Daquea Kamat, Venkatesha Kamat, Rama Kushta Parab, Caetano Alberto, Ramchandra Kamat, Keshav Parab, Gopal Kushta Pai, Fondya Parab, Narba Kamat, Narba Naik, Vithoba Sinai, Raghunath Kamat, Godaba Govind Sinai, Shengrem (?) Naik, Kushta Pai, Venku Sinai and Soiru Naik. With the exception of three Christian traders the rest were Hindus indicating Hindu dominance.

7. HAG : *MR*, 161B, fls. 593v-594.
8. HAG : *PRA*, 8089, fls. 9-9v; *Cartas, patentes, alvarás*, 628, fls. 136-142.
9. XCHR : *MHP* (Portuguese), doc. dated 11 Feb. 1789.
10. HAG : *PRA*, 8089, fls. 9-9v.
11. See Appendix 4.
12. cf. 1; See Appendix 4.
13. HAG : *PRA*, 8089, fls. 22v-23v, 28-28v, 30-30v.
14. HAG : *PRA*, 8089, fl. 51v.
15. HAG : *PRA*, 8089, fls. 31-31v.
16. HAG : *PRA*, 8089, fls. 20-21; *Cartas, patentes alvarás*, 628, fls. 14, 17-18.
17. HAG : *PRA*, 8089, fls. 2-3v.
18. Teotonio R. de Souza, "Goa-Mahe Trade Links (Late 18th - Early 19th Centuries) : A New Source Material", *Studies in Maritime History*, (ed.) K. S. Mathew, Pondicherry, 1990, p. 168.
19. HAG : *MR*, 152A, fl. 134v.
20. Walter Rodney, *How Europe Under-developed Africa*, London/Tanzania, 1976.
21. HAG : *MR*, 152A, fls. 134v-135.
22. HAG : *MR*, 152A, fl. 135; 168D, fl. 1020; 178A, fl. 256v.
23. HAG : *Moçambique*, 1446, fl. 95; *MR*, 168D, fl. 1020v.
24. HAG : *MR*, 152A, fls. 135-135v.
25. HAG : *MR*, 158A, fl. 220; 168D, fls. 1020v-1021.
26. HAG : *Moçambique*, 1445, fls. 20-20v; *MR*, 152A, fls. 134v-136.
27. HAG : *MR*, 152A, fls. 136-136v.
28. HAG : *MR*, 152A, fl. 136v.
29. HAG : *MR*, 152A, fls. 136v-137.
30. HAG : *MR*, 168D, fl. 1022.
31. HAG : *MR*, 167A, fls. 146-146v.
32. HAG : *Moçambique*, 1445, fls. 17, 22v.
33. HAG : *MR*, 167A, fl. 149.
34. HAG : *PRA*, 8089, fl. 17v.
35. HAG : *PRA*, 8089, fls. 17v-18.
36. HAG : *PRA*, 8089, fls. 18-18v.
37. HAG : *PRA*, 8089, fls. 18v-19.
38. HAG : *PRA*, 8089, fl. 19v.
39. HAG : *PRA*, 8089, fl. 22; *Cartas, patentes, alvarás*, 628, fls. 196-204.
40. AHU : *Moçambique*, Caixa 65, doc. no. 25.
41. AHU : *Moçambique*, Caixa 54, doc. no. 5.
42. HAG : *MR*, 178A, fl. 250v.
43. HAG : *MR*, 178A, fls. 251-251v.
44. HAG : *MR*, 178A, fl. 251v.
45. HAG : *MR*, 178A, fl. 251v.
46. HAG : *MR*, 178A, fls. 252v-253.
47. HAG : *MR*, 178A, fl. 253.
48. HAG : *MR*, 178A, fls. 254v-255v.
49. HAG : *MR*, 178A, fl. 255v.
50. HAG : *MR*, 178A, fls. 253v-254v.
51. HAG : *CR*, 1638, doc. dated 14 March 1782; 1642, doc. dated 26 March 1790; 1643, doc. dated 11 March 1793; 1651, doc. dated 22 March 1806.
52. AHU : *MI, Maço* 138, no. 130, doc. dated 5 Nov. 1790.
53. AHU : *MI, Maço* 138, no. 130, doc. dated Sept. 1790.

54. ANTT : *Casa da India*, no. 741: *passim*
55. HAG : *MR*, 166, fl. 266.

The following is a list of Goan merchants and the amount of pepper and textiles despatched by them to Lisbon in 1809 :

Merchants	Textiles (in bales)	Pepper (in bales)
Venkatesha Naik Coraleiro	20	
Rama Kamat	8	10
Anta Parab Lawande	5	25
Vithoba Sinai Dhempe	4	
Narayan Naik	5	
Venku Sinai	2	
Narayan Parab Lawande	2	
Vasu Sinai Khazani	2	
Lakshman Pai	1	
Vaman Parab Sinari	10	25
Venku Chattim (Shet) Khalap	5	
Vithoba Sinai Shetye	1	
Molu Kamat	1	
Kushta Sinai Dhempe	1	
Venkatesha and Narayana Kamat	10	15

AHU : *MI*, Maço 186, no. 176, doc. dated 28 Sept. 1809.

56. BPA : *India*, 46-XIII-24, fls. 5-100 : *passim.*
57. HAG : *MR*, 125B, fl. 643v; 176A, fl. 249; Refer to Figure 7.
58. HAG : *MR*, 189, fl. 33.
59. XCHR : *MHP* (Portuguese), doc. dated 18 Oct. 1810.
60. Gervase Clarence-Smith, *The Third Portuguese Empire, 1825-1975, A Study in economic imperialism*, Manchester/Dovey, 1985, p.25.
61. HAG : *Correspondencia de Damão*, 1060, doc. dated 9 Jan. 1792; 1061, fls. 8-39; *MR*, 207B, doc. dated 17 Jan. 1827.
62. See Appendix 3.

5

BIG TRADE : HIGH ON OPIUM

Existing literature on Indo-Portuguese history reveals that no serious effort has been made to examine in depth the various phases of the Portuguese opium trade. Its rise and fall, how far it proved to be a windfall for the Indo-Portuguese merchants, the *Estado da India* and Portugal, the extent to which the British Opium Monopoly was threatened and the measures undertaken by the British authorities to contain its growth and development are precisely what this chapter is concerned with.

Prior to the classic periods of Greece and Rome, several species of *papaver somniferum* were found growing in plentiful in India. Even at such an early date the value of these plants as resources of oil or as medicine was not unknown. Poppy cultivation in India was at first confined to coastal regions for local consumption. It had not assumed any commercial importance. From Abul Fazl's *Ain-i-Akbari* we gain the impression that in the fifteenth century the key opium-producing regions of India were Fatehpur, Ghazipur and Allahabad. By the eighteenth century the opium-producing belt included the entire Himalyan range, Punjab, Malwa and other parts of Central India. Therefore there existed two major sources of supply: Bengal which produced the Patna and Banaras varieties and Central India, the Malwa variety.

Beginnings of the Portuguese Opium Interlude

The rise and development of the Portuguese opium commerce was closely linked with the opium policy of the English East India Company. It would therefore not be out of order to examine briefly the subtle role played by the Company in propelling it into prominence.

In the eighteenth century, the English East India Company conducted an extensive trade in Chinese silk, tea and porcelain. Unfortunately Chinese demand for British goods was negligible. At the end of the eighteenth century, the English East India Company bought an average of 4,000,000 silver taels of tea from China each year while the value of British products — woollen fabrics, metals and cotton — imported into China from 1781 to 1793, amounted to only one-sixth of the value of the teas China exported to Britain. So to get teas and silk, Britain had to pay large sums of silver. This continuous drain of treasure from England to China brought a perplexing problem to the forefront, that of tackling a one-sided trade.[1] However things soon turned for the better when with the acquisition of Diwani rights over Bengal, Bihar and Orissa in 1765, sizable opium-producing regions came within the Company's reach. In 1773 it established a monopoly over opium cultivation in India and by the closing decade of the century monopolised opium manufacture and sale. The Company came up with a novel scheme of getting rid of the Indo-Chinese trade imbalance. The willingness of the Chinese to accept raw cotton and opium, products of British India, was ascertained. The resultant complex trading network that emerged provided for the all-important tea investment.

While the Indian cotton trade with China did not gain much momentum, opium took firm roots. The official Canton trade in cotton staple soon came to be overshadowed by the rising traffic in opium. Before 1767 China's opium imports from India never exceeded 200 chests per year. The Chinese government permitted the import of opium to be used as a medical ingredient. But since the government of British India adopted the criminal policy of large scale opium exportation to China, by 1800 about 2000 opium chests reached the Chinese shores and this assumed mammoth proportions of more than 7500 chests in 1830.[2]

The British, however, did not participate in the distribution of the drug in China as opium was a contraband item in that country. Opium was not openly marketable due to the Chinese embargo. It was the avowed policy of the Company to confine itself to its production and distribution in India. Factories were erected at Calcutta to process opium mixtures that catered to the tastes of Chinese addicts. It managed the production so well that its trade-mark earned reputation and acclaim as a hall-mark of quality. It however encouraged the trade and allowed it to remain largely in the hands of private traders. The drug was bought at public auctions and then transported to China in country vessels. The traders would then deposit the proceeds from opium sales in China in the Company's Canton Treasury in exchange for bills of exchange on the

Board of Directors or the Bengal Government.[3]

Matters came to a head when in the early nineteenth century, the English East India Company began to restrict Bengal opium production with the primary objective of improving its quality. Under this self-imposed restriction the Company selected the most fertile land for poppy cultivation and improved the packing to make the Company's stamp on Bengal opium chests a symbol of quality. The Company had extracted a high price from every chest sold.[4] With eyes set on increasing revenues, what the British failed to foresee was that its policies would give rise to a large scale system of operation outside the orbit of Company control. It seemed evident that the opium traders would evade the payment of high prices for Company opium, for this would cause sharp inroads into their opium profits. They had to find ways and means to circumvent this obstacle. One alternative left to them was to switch from the high-priced, high quality Bengal opium to the inferior non-Company Malwa opium. What must have assisted them a great deal was the changing political scenario. With the suppression of the Marathas as a political force and with the elimination of the Pindaris, peace was restored and poppy cultivation in Central India became more popular with the peasants making a comfortable profit. Increased production led to the availability of cheap Malwa opium. Generally speaking, native traders would smuggle Malwa opium from Central India to the Portuguese ports that lay in its proximity — Daman, Diu and Goa — to the far-off, Portuguese Far Eastern settlement of Macao.

Nature and Network of the Trade

In Malwa, the cultivator paid annually to the government of Sindhia or of Holkar a sum of Rs. 15 for each *bigha* of land sown with poppy seed. This meant about Rs. 45 to 50 for each acre of land under cultivation. The production was said to yield much more monetarily, out of which the farmer defrayed the expenses of seed, implements and husbandry, labour and his own livelihood.

The cultivator himself was usually the manufacturer of Malwa opium. But it was often the saukars who would receive opium from the cultivators in a crude state.[5] The process of manufacturing involved the extraction of juice from the poppy, preserving it in vessels until it assumed a firmness in lesser and larger lumps, packing it either in earthern-ware or in baskets of bamboo work, oblong in shape of various sizes with slender stalks and leaves of plants, and covering the packaging with coarse cloth and later with strong leather (sheep skin). Good quality opium was moderately firm in texture, of a dark yellow colour, when held in the light, but nearly black in the mass and free of gritness. The value increased within a short time but ceased to do so with age.[6] A basket contained at times 5 *seers* and at other times 10 *seers* of opium, each *seer* costing Rs. 40. Therefore a basket of Malwa opium was worth between Rs. 200 to Rs. 400. The name of the maker was usually superscribed on the package. It was by means of some peculiarity in the stitching, that those who carried on the traffic could judge whether the material was adulterated or not. The mode of adulteration was by mixing flour with the fresh juice. In this state, Malwa opium was despatched to the markets and ports of Gujarat and Kathiawar.[7]

From a single document drawn from British records we get a picture of the chief Malwa opium marts in Central India of which Ujjain supplied the maximum in 1821, namely 250 out of 700 loads. This formed about 35.71 per cent of the total. Indore provided the minimum, 25 chests, that is about 3.57 per cent of the total. (See Table 5.1). The opium was transported in conveyances of all denominations. It was hidden in boxes apparently containing jingely oil, of which a small quantity appeared at the head. The oil did not harm the opium. At times the opium was concealed in loads of grain or dry grass, saw-dust or bales of cotton in bullock-carts or among ballast in coasting vessels. Frequently the opium was conveyed by horsemen who got it sewn to the folds of their saddles.[8] The natural concern of the opium dealers was to spare no efforts to escape official detection and the payment of vexatious duties. In 1803, tolls, duties and imposts amounted to Rs. 2.5 per *maund* at Dholkar, Rs. 4.2 per *maund* at Fatehpur, Rs. 1 per *maund* at Broach, 1 anna per *seer* at Baroda and 4.5 per cent duty at Dhollera.[9]

TABLE 5.1 : MARTS IN MALWA FROM WHENCE OPIUM WAS EXPORTED TO THE DECCAN AND GUJARAT, 1821

Marts	Total no. of loads in Malwa Opium	No. of loads exported to Deccan	No. of loads exported to Gujarat
Ujjain	250	100	150
Nolye	100	50	50
Rutlam	100	25	75
Kachrode	50	10	40
Mundisore	100	50	50
Kahjehanpur	75	50	25
Indore	25	25	
Total no. of loads	700	310	390

Source: BA : *RD*, 10/10, 1821, p. 101.

The trade was left almost to itself unchecked and secure in its transit to Broach, Jumbasoor, Daman, etc. on the west coast of India.[10] While the bulk proceeded to Macao and China via the Portuguese ports and Bombay, a great quantity was also exported to Haldywar for exportation to Arabia, Persia, Batavia, Penang, Sumatra, the islands of the Indonesian archipelago and Manila. The rest found its way to Bassein and the other ports of the Konkan from where it was dispersed into the interior of the peninsula.[11] The ports of Gujarat and those of Portuguese India and the country intervening between Malwa and them not being British, nor subject to British control, afforded every facility for the prosecution of a clandestine commerce.

Even when the restrictions appeared, such was the strong profit motive for smuggling that the opium dealers would discover other channels to escape them. A powerful combination was formed with native agency houses located at Bombay to clandestinely operate the Malwa trade in defiance of all vigilance that could be conducted.[12]

The Daman Connection

Of all the Portuguese enclaves on the west coast of India, Daman became the principal centre handling two-thirds of the opium exports in the 1820s. Malwa opium was conducted to Daman initially via Gujarat, Kathiawar and Kutch. Some arrived in smaller quantities via the Ghats, east of Daman.[13] To avoid the restrictions it was later conveyed from the places of growth to Pali, a province of Ajmer, governed by Raja Man Singh, independent of British domination, to Jaisalmer and then to Karachi in Sind. Coasting vessels displaying Portuguese flags would then transport opium from Karachi to Daman. It took about twenty days to reach Pali from whence it was transported by camels to Karachi, involving a period of two months, provided the party did not encounter British authorities on the way. A minimum of fifty camels were loaded with opium. One camel load of Malwa opium equalled 8 *pucca maunds* or 10 *kuccha maunds* or 15 Daman *maunds*. Therefore a minimum consignment of 50 camels involved 400 *pucca maunds* or 500 *kuccha maunds* or 750 Daman *maunds*. The rest were burdened with water and provisions so essential for the tedious journey across the desert of Sind upto Karachi. At Karachi coastal ships belonging to the Amirs were laden with the opium cargoes and within ten days would arrive at Daman where opium was deposited for re-exportation and onward carriage to China and Macao.[14] Normally it took about 90 to 100 days for one consignment of opium to reach Daman from the place of production.

Even though Diu was located nearer to Karachi than Daman, the sources reveal distinctly that the opium traders openly demonstrated their preference for the latter. The reasons for this are obvious. To the opium dealers, Daman provided excellent port facilities for importation, re-exportation and distribution. Its strategic location on the western sea-board made it a convenient port of transit where opium dealers could converge. Most of the merchants and capitalists involved in the opium traffic were settled at Bombay. From this port they could easily conduct their transactions and correspondence with Daman. Such was the profitable nature of the trade via Daman that it caused several opium merchants to flee from the British dominions in India and take sanctuary at that port.

Every effort was made by the Portuguese authorities to protect and stimulate the Daman Malwa opium trade. The Portuguese Viceroy Conde de Rio Pardo and the *Junta de Fazenda* in 1820 permitted the re-exportation of opium at Daman not only in Portuguese but in foreign vessels tco, to any area the owners desired to visit.[15] The duties imposed were set artificially low. Re-exportation duties charged at Daman were moderate, 4 per cent in the case of Portuguese vessels destined for Macao. But Portuguese and foreign vessels unwilling to ship their cargoes to Macao were required to pay 5 per cent re-exportation duty, besides emoluments (*lagimas*) and without the benefit of 15 per cent discount permitted at Daman.[16] For a long time the authorities had even toyed with the idea that it would be more profitable and appropriate if Portuguese ships sailing directly to Macao had to pay 3 per cent duty at Daman, while those proceeding elsewhere paid double and foreign vessels paid treble.[17] But this idea was immediately abandoned probably on the grounds that such a taxation scheme would serve as a deterrent to foreign vessels making a beeline for Daman. Later on due to pressure from the mercantile classes, the duties were lowered from 4 per cent to 2-1/2 per cent in the case of Portuguese vessels and from 5 per cent to 4 per cent in the case of foreign ones.[18] This encouraged the traders to don Portuguese colours. What probably prompted the authorities was the realisation that Malwa opium was not a product of Daman and that trade in this drug was mainly operated by the British subjects. The stringent regulations of the British government had made them shift their network of operations directed towards Karachi and the *Estado* ports, which in turn enriched the Portuguese Indian treasury. They began to feel that this lucrative commerce should be preserved at all costs and as long as possible with liberal concessions and port facilities. Daman was looked upon as the locus for immediate and future prosperity in the East. The Daman authorities were quick to realise that Macao's insistence that opium should be unloaded in Portuguese ships led to the decline of the commerce in opium at that port. Liberal concessions alone would serve to entice vessels to Daman.

Daman was a scene of bustling activity. Both Karachi and Daman were visited by French, Danish, American and even Arab ships. Usually vessels of 200 tonnage were engaged in the trade.[19] Among the foreign vessels touching the port of Daman, one finds references to an American ship *Alexander* which acquired 800 chests of opium and was permitted to move directly to Canton in 1818. In 1820 the Danish vessel Hooghli under the command of Captain Peter Johnson was denied such permission. Johnson was obstructed from departing with his consignment of 525 chests of opium for Canton.[20]

How much Malwa opium was exported to China via Daman? We have three sets of figures which could enable us to arrive at definite conclusions. Opium exports of Daman in 1820-21 was a low 678 chests (Table 5.2). This was presumably due to the sales at Bombay and the Mandarin campaign against opium importation in China. But the situation improved immediately. Opium exportation from Daman was more or less steady until 1826-27. Over the period 1821-27 it averaged 1,757-1/2 chests per annum according to British sources.

TABLE 5.2 : DAMAN OPIUM EXPORTS TO CHINA, 1820-29

Year	Number of Chests
1820-21	678
1821-22	2255
1822-23	1535
1823-24	2063
1824-25	1563
1825-26	1605
1826-27	1524
1827-28	3881
1828-29	3500

Source: BA : *RD*, 32/279, 1829, p. 420.

Almost the same trend can be observed in the customs records of Daman, that is, an average opium exportation of 1822 *picos,* 2 *arrobas*, 17 *arrateis* and 10 *onças* per year for the period 1824-27. (See Table 5.3).

Each chest contained about 1 *pico* and 6 or 7 *arrateis*. This works out to an average of 1,735 chests.

TABLE 5.3 : DAMAN MALWA OPIUM RE-EXPORTATION, 1824-28

Period	Quantity			
	picos	*arrobas*	*arrateis*	*onças*
Jan 1824- May 1824	2200	03	06	00
Aug 1824- May 1825	1670	01	29	12
Oct 1825- June1826	1719	00	26	03
Oct 1826- May 1827	1700	00	08	12
Oct 1827- May 1828	4131	02	17	03

Source: AHU : *MI*, Maço 95, no. 94, doc. dated 5 March 1829.

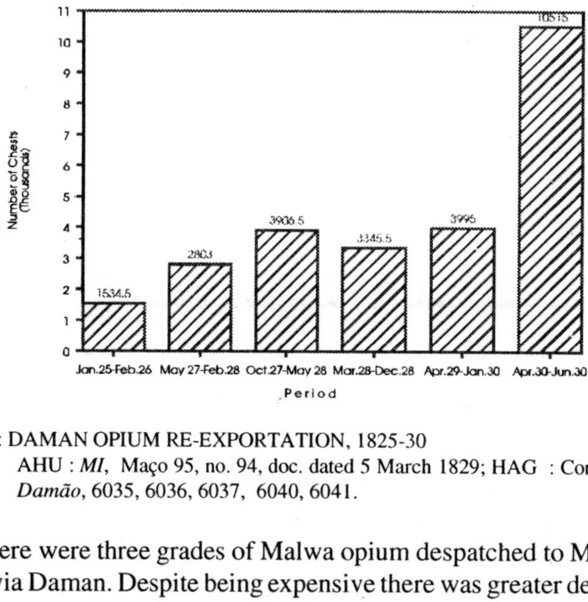

FIG. 5.1 : DAMAN OPIUM RE-EXPORTATION, 1825-30

Sources: AHU : *MI*, Maço 95, no. 94, doc. dated 5 March 1829; HAG : Compiled from *Damão*, 6035, 6036, 6037, 6040, 6041.

There were three grades of Malwa opium despatched to Macao and China via Daman. Despite being expensive there was greater demand for Malwa opium of the first grade. Tables 5.4, 5.5 and the Daman customs records testify to this. From Table 5.4 we gather that out of a total of 1,013 chests on board the *Castro* which departed from Daman for Macao on 29th April 1823, 847 chests (76.79 per cent) were of the first grade, 124 chests (11.24 per cent) were of the second sort and 132 chests (11.97 per cent) were of the third grade.

TABLE 5.4 : OPIUM DESPATCHED TO MACAO ON BOARD THE SHIP CASTRO, 29TH APRIL 1823

Merchants	Number of opium chests			Total value		
	First type	Second type	Third type	*xerafins*	*tangas*	*reis*
Rogerio de Faria	366	-	-	519720	0	00
Rogerio de Faria	-	39	-	42900	0	00
Rogerio de Faria	-	-	132	52800	0	00
Naurogi Rustamogi	-	9	-	9900	0	00
Daniel Mariano Rebeiro	25	-	-	35500	0	00
Racique Valobo	25	-	-	35500	0	00
Caugi Beramogi	-	1	-	1100	0	00
Beramogi Bicagi	101	-	-	143420	0	00
Beramogi Bicagi	-	43	-	47300	0	00
Dearamo Dulobo	25	-	-	35500	0	00
Caramochande Amarchande	15	-	-	2100	0	00
Amarchande Daramochande	54	-	-	76680	0	00
Amarchande Daramochande	-	1	-	1100	0	00
Mulchanda Ira'	3	-	-	4260	0	00
Manachande Areachande	54	-	-	76680	0	00
Mody Dorabaça Nacervangi	160	-	-	227200	0	00
Mody Dorabaça Nacervangi	-	31	-	34100	0	00
Caramochande Areachande	18	-	-	25560	0	00
Total	847	124	132	1391940	0	00

Source: Antonio Francisco Moniz Junior, *Noticias e Documentos para a Historia de Damão Antiga. Provincia do Norte*, vol. II, Bastora, 1900, p. 174.

The above-mentioned grades of Malwa were undoubtedly priced differently. From 1825 to 1829 the price of Malwa opium at Daman was on the rise (Table 5.5). This coincided with the increasing exports of Malwa opium via Daman. However rise in prices was sharper in April 1825-February 1828 compared to March 1828-January 1830. In the later period restrictions dictated the situation. Around mid-1830, a slide in prices was observed. This was in all probability due to the excessive supply and easy availability of Malwa opium.

The price of Malwa opium was generally lower than that of its Bengal counterpart irrespective of its grade.[21] This was on account of its superior quality. The only exception was with respect to the years 1827-30. This development might have been due to the delayed effects of the programme of increased production of Bengal opium introduced in the early 1820s.

TABLE 5.5 : PRICE OF VARIOUS GRADES OF MALWA OPIUM AT DAMAN, 1825-30

Period	First Grade (In *rupias*)	Second Grade (In *rupias*)	Third Grade (In *rupias*)
April 1825- Dec. 1825	800	637 1/2	257 1/2
Feb. 1826- Feb. 1828	1200	975	409
March 1828- Oct. 1828	1437 1/2	1125	462
April 1829- Jan. 1830	1475	1325	525
April 1830	837 1/2	587 1/2	287 1/2

Sources: HAG : Compiled from *Damão*, 6035, 6036, 6037, 6040, 6041.

In China the price of Daman Malwa opium rapidly declined from $660 in June 1830 to $560 per chest in June 1831. This development was the result of excessive supply of the said opium in Macao and the Chinese markets. According to the Jamsetjee Jejeebhoy papers, on 20th February 1835 the price stood at Rs. 1,141 to Rs. 1,150 per chest. This dropped to Rs. 1,100 on 18th April 1835 and Rs. 1,075 on 30th April 1835. Stagnation had probably set in the Far Eastern markets.[22]

According to Table 5.6 the bulk of opium cargoes from Daman were shipped to Macao and Lintin. The rest which was hardly of significance was despatched in coastal vessels to Alibagh and Bhavnagar. Occasionally in a single month between one to three consignments would move to Alibagh and Bhavnagar. This was negligible compared to the 119 and 244 consignments that left for Macao and Lintin in May 1828 and May 1829 respectively.

From the Daman customs records, we gather that *Cassador, Santo Antonio, Angelica, Dezempenho, D. Manoel de Portugal, Sebastião, Doirado, S. Francisco de Paulo, Esperança* and *Camoens* were ships that paid duties at the port of Daman during 1825-30 and transported opium either to Macao or Lintin. But the Macao customs records have a slightly different tale to tell. In addition to the above-mentioned ships, others like *Conde de Rio Pardo, Fenix, Leticia, Deligente* and *Eliza* had also brought opium from Daman to Macao during the said period.[23] One wonders if these ships escaped the notice of the Daman customs authorities and received opium clandestinely. This surely and certainly must have affected the opium revenues of Daman.

From the official Daman records one gathers that during 1825-30, 13 of those engaged in the Daman-based Malwa opium trade were Christians, either *Canarins, casados* or pure Portuguese, 11 were banias and 4 Parsees.[24] Other leading opium dealers at Daman according

to British sources were Kurumchand Hurukchand, Manikchand Kurumchand, Ratanchand Heerachand, Mulchand Heerachand and Haribhay Moorsha. They imported opium in coastal boats into Daman from Karachi, Kutch and other ports of Sind.[25] Mulchand Heerachand was the agent of Moteesa Banya, a great opium trader at Bombay.[26] Kurumchand Hurukchand was a correspondent of Mahomed Soostary also based at Bombay.[27]

TABLE 5.6 : SHIPMENTS OF MALWA OPIUM THAT LEFT DAMAN, 1825-30

Month/Year	Number of shipments destined to					Total
	Macao	Lintin	Number of Macao or	Alibagh	Bhavnagar	shipments
January 1825	-	-	-	2	-	2
April 1825	3	-	-	-	-	3
May 1825	68	-	-	3	2	73
October 1825	-	-	-	1	-	1
December 1825	-	-	-	1	-	1
February 1826	-	-	-	1	1	2
May 1827	48	-	-	2	-	50
December 1827	3	-	-	1	-	4
February 1828	-	-	-	1	-	1
March 1828	-	-	1	-	-	1
April 1828	23	-	26	-	-	49
May 1828	98	-	21	-	-	119
Oct.-Dec. 1828	-	-	-	2	-	2
April 1829	8	1	-	-	-	9
May 1829	206	38	-	3	-	247
June 1829	10	-	-	-	-	10
January 1830	-	-	-	3	-	3
Apr.-June 1830	14	47	-	2	-	63

Sources: HAG : Compiled from *Damão*, 6035, 6036, 6037, 6040, 6041.

On 29th April 1823 opium cargoes were despatched to Macao on board the vessel *Castro* by merchants at Daman (Table 5.4). We observe that of the 14 exporters of opium 8 were banias which formed 57.14 per cent, 4 were Parsees that is 28.57 per cent and 2 were Christians amounting to 14.29 per cent. Rogerio de Faria despatched 366 opium chests of the first grade, 39 of the second sort and 132 of the third grade. The chests were worth 615,420-0-00 *xerafins*, which formed 44.21 per cent of the value of the total cargoes aboard the *Castro*. This points to Rogerio de Faria as the principal exporter of opium to the Far East among the Portuguese subjects at Daman.

Antonio Pereira, Venkatesha and Narayana Kamat and Venku

Shet Khalap were amongst the Goa merchants involved in the flourishing Malwa opium commerce on the western coast of India.[28]

One must bear in mind that the Daman opium trade was primarily controlled by merchants at Bombay and that just one-fiftieth part of the Daman Malwa shipping was in the hands of Portuguese subjects.[29] Remington Crawford & Co., Adam Skinner & Co., Leckie & Co., Patrick Stewart & Co., Ritchie Zinlay & Co., Shotton & Co., Rogerio de Faria & Co., Motichund Amichund, Pestonjee Merjee, Jamsetjee Jejeebhoy, Hormusjee Dorabjee, Franjee Cowasjee, Bomanjee Hormusjee, Guilder & Co., and Beckwill & Co., were amongst the outstanding agency houses located at Bombay dealing in Malwa opium.[30]

It was not only merchants from the west coast of India that were involved in the Daman opium trade, but also those at Calcutta, Macao and China. For instance, in the early 1820s Magniac and Company based at Canton had no less than five ships transporting Daman opium consigned to them. Jardine Matheson, Samuel Rupell, John Richardson were among other Malwa opium importers at Canton.[31]

Table 5.7 provides us a picture of the area-wise extent of mercantile participation in the Daman opium commerce in the early 1820s. It reveals the predominant role played by the Bombay/*Estado* merchants.

TABLE 5.7 : AREA-WISE INVOLVEMENT OF THE MERCHANTS IN THE DAMAN OPIUM TRADE, 1821-23

Year	Areas		
	Bombay/*Estado* (per cent)	Calcutta (per cent)	Macao (per cent)
1821	66	34	
1822	86.71	8.86	4.43
1823	86.20	2.30	11.50

Source: BA : *RD*, 79/1823, pp. 466-467.

As regards the profits accrued by merchants, we could make an estimate for the year 1820-21. According to a British source the cost price of one chest of Malwa opium of four Surat *maunds* was Rs. 800 for the first grade, Rs. 700 for the second and Rs. 660 for the third. The expenses involved for road concealment and customs duties amounted to Rs. 632 per chest. The selling price in the case of each of the three grades of opium was Rs. 1,900, Rs. 1,800 and Rs. 1,760 respectively. The net profit per chest irrespective of its quality/grade was Rs. 468.[32] We have

considered earlier that during 1820-21 678 chests of Malwa opium were exported via Daman (Refer to Table 5.2). The net profit derived from the sale of these chests would amount to Rs. 317,304. When we compare this figure with the average gross profit (Rs. 1800 x 678 = Rs. 1,220,400) we discover that almost one-fourth of the capital involved in the Malwa opium trade went straight into the hands of the opium dealers, and that at a time when the Daman opium exports were poor. Though we have the selling price of opium for the subsequent years, we do not have any information relating to cost price, customs duties and other expenses which were bound to fluctuate and vary in the course of time. If we consider the net profits on Malwa opium for the years following 1821, assuming that the cost price, selling price, customs duties and other expenses were those maintained in 1820-21 we observe that in 1827-28, the net profit on 3,881 chests amounted to Rs. 1,816,308, in 1829-30 on 3,995 chests it amounted to Rs. 1,869,660 and in 1830 on 10,515 chests it amounted to Rs. 4,921,020. (Refer to Tables 5.2, 5.3 and Fig. 5.1). Thus Rs. 317,304 can be accepted as a lower net profit limit for the period 1820-30 and Rs. 4,921,020 the upper limit.

The Malwa opium trade of Daman did yield rich returns. According to Table 5.8 more than half of the annual revenues of Daman were derived from opium. It seems likely that the value of the annual importation and re-exportation of opium at Daman amounted to forty lakhs of rupees in 1823 and around one crore of rupees in 1830, and this despite the fact that the duties were artificially low.[33] It earned for the *Estado* average opium revenues to the tune of about two and half lakhs of *xerafins* annually.

TABLE 5.8 : CUSTOMS REVENUES OF DAMAN, 1823-30

Year	Opium Revenues (In rupees)	Total Revenues (In rupees)
1823	56210-2-62	91210-2-62
1824	65305	102305
1825	43185	83185
1826	87936-3-50	129936-3-50
1827	67905-3-37	113905-3-37
1828	190000	239500
1829	274000	325500
1830	375000	426500

Source: BA : *PD*, 20/404, 1830-31, doc. dated 2 May 1831.

Table 5.9 indicates that in 1824 the revenues derived from opium

commerce amounted to 146,936-1-22 *xerafins*, in 1825-26, 197,858-0-37 *xerafins* in 1827-28, 410,402-3-17 *xerafins* and in 1829, 616,868-0-18 *xerafins*. During 1825-29, on an average the opium trade yielded the Customs Department of Daman 344,479-1-45 *xerafins* per year. In 1828-29 Portuguese ships leaving Daman were issued licences to proceed to Macao or Lintin or other places of their choice in the Far East. The outcome of this move was that Daman opium revenues climbed up to 616,868-0-18 *xerafins*. The total income derived was remitted to Goa.

TABLE 5.9 : DAMAN OPIUM REVENUES, 1824-30

Year	(In *xerafins*)
January - May 1824	146936-1-22
August 1824 - May 1825	97167-2-28
October 1825 - June 1826	197858-0-37
October 1826 - May 1827	152788-3-03
October 1827 - May 1828	410402-3-17
22nd April - 3rd June 1829	616868-0-18
January - July 1830	579101-0-16

Source: AHU : *MI*, Maço 95, no. 94, docs. dated 5 March 1829, 7 July 1829.

In all probability revenue from Malwa was channelled into ostentatious display. Edifices erected in the new capital *Nova Goa* in the 1820s and 1830s, the network of bridges and roads, public buildings like the police station (*Quartel Militaria*) and the Customs House owe their origin to opium capital. Huge sums of money had also been expended to promote hygiene. For instance salt marshes and inundated rice fields were cleared.[34] Capital accumulation had led to architectural expression and a modicum of material prosperity.

The echoes of intermittent strife between the liberals and the conservatives in Portugal were heard loud and clear in Goa. The latter during the 1820s and 1830s underwent a phase of political turmoil and instability. One observed the seesawing of fortunes, at times in favour of the liberals and other times in favour of the conservatives. Apparently the liberal faction was funded by opium traders. As mentioned earlier the Bombay-based Rogerio de Faria employed opium capital in 1835 to raise a force against the Goa Government with the view to reinstating the deposed ex-Prefect Bernardo Peres da Silva.[35]

In the absence of evidence we are unable to determine whether Portugal profited from the lucrative Portuguese Malwa opium interlude. One wonders whether a portion of the Daman opium revenues was routed from Goa to Portugal. In the light of the fact that these revenues were so essential to prop up the *Estado*'s sagging economy, this seems unlikely. That the Indo-Portuguese opium traders made some contribution to the mother-country seems to be a remote possibility. According to Clarence-Smith a few rich Hindus might have acquired titles in return for payments of some kind.[36]

The Macao End

The Portuguese had also been active at the other end. A brisk trade in opium was plied at Macao. The Chinese authorities had banned the importation of opium at Canton, where the English East India Company conducted its licit trade. So the opium dealers peddled their wares at Macao where there was greater demand and which was accepted as a safer distribution centre compared to Whampoa. The Macao government welcomed the entry of opium, because around 1810 the finances of Macao were in dire straits, largely due to recently terminated wars with the Chinese pirates.[37] Since 1804 the Chinese waters had been infested with pirates, a source of critical times for the city of Macao and its commercial activity. This growing menace was efficiently dealt with after the Portuguese armed forces waged a fierce battle involving an expenditure of about 200,000 *patacas* of which 10,000 *patacas* was paid by the Imperial Chinese government in accordance with a convention signed by both parties.[38]

Why did the opium dealers turn to Macao for their smuggling activities? The Portuguese were advantageously placed in the opium trade in the Far East. Macao was considered to be the only port through which opium, whether Bengal or Malwa variety, could be safely smuggled by the Portuguese agency houses to China. It was accepted as a safer distribution centre than Whampoa. The Macao Portuguese were able to profit from their long-standing collaboration with the Chinese officials. They knew how to get things done, being well-acquainted with the Chinese habit of falling a prey to bribery and corruption. Other factors that probably provided Macao a favourable position in the Indo-Chinese opium trade, was the un-paralleled advantage of possessing a civilian station where members of the foreign trading communities, subject to stringent Chinese regulations, could retire from April to September. This was the time for establishing business ties and clinching business deals.

The opium commerce conducted at Macao was however subjected

to certain restrictions. The local authorities there refused to permit opium landings at the port except from Portuguese and Spanish ships. The opium traders were expected to display Portuguese colours and employ Portuguese agents in order to pursue the lucrative trade at Macao.

The opium trade of the early nineteenth century enabled Macao to reach fresh heights of prosperity. It enabled her to establish direct commercial contacts with the Portuguese enclaves in India — Goa, Daman and Diu. These settlements provided the Portuguese at Macao unthought of opportunities for engaging themselves in a flourishing trade with China. As the Portuguese were in possession of trading stations both in China and India, they could ship goods from India to China and vice versa, without hindrance. The Portuguese ships were the only carriers of Malwa opium after the English East India Company prohibited its loading on Bombay vessels in 1813.[39] Macao soon rose to the enviable position as the opium mart of China.

How much Malwa opium was imported into Macao? During 1797-1815 an annual average of just 17 chests of Malwa opium arrived at Macao from Portuguese India, especially Goa, probably for medicinal use.[40] The upper limit of import was 53 chests and the lower limit 3 chests. But we see a gradual increase in imports during 1817-35 from a minimum of 249 chests in 1817 to a maximum of 4,397.5 in 1835. The import figures for the period 1817-35 provide an average import of about 1,843 chests per year that is 108 times more than that of the earlier period 1797-1815.

During 1797-1817 just one ship carried opium to Macao from the *Estado da India* every year. Since 1818 a minimum of 1 ship and a maximum of 7 ships arrived at Macao laden with Malwa opium acquired at Daman, Goa and Bombay. The reasons for this shift are not far to see. Since 1818, after the termination of the Pindari War peace prevailed in Central India — a situation which favoured Malwa opium production. Moreover, since 1820 Malwa opium was becoming popular in China and this stepped up the demand for it.

From Table 5.10 we observe that during 1802-19 there was a steady inflow of Bengal opium into Macao, amounting to a total of 33,576.25 chests or an average of 1,975 chests per year. This compared favourably with a maximum of 260 Malwa opium chests entering Macao during the same period. But this picture changed dramatically over the years 1820-35. There was a sharp decline in Bengal opium imports. In 1831 a meagre 16 chests of Bengal opium entered Macao.

Among those deeply involved in the nineteenth century opium

commerce at Macao reference can be made to Albino G. de Araujo, Widow of Paiva & Sons. and Barão de S. Joze de Porto Allegre.[41] Their opium business network covered Bengal as well as the west coast of India. One of their chief suppliers of Malwa opium was the Bombay-based Rogerio de Faria.[42]

TABLE 5.10 : MACAO OPIUM IMPORTATION, 1802-35

Year	From West Coast of India (Number of Chests)	From Bengal (Number of Chests)
1802	10	2108
1803	14	1149 1/2
1804	-	811 3/4
1805	32 or 52	1660 (?)
1807	13 or 14	1770
1808	-	1572
1809	-	2813
1810	-	2559 (?)
1811	-	2987
1812	53	2562
1813	11	3441
1814	4	2888
1815	3	1883
1816	114 (?)	1080 (?)
1817	249	1549
1818	260	1638
1819	-	1105
1820	972	1386
1821	1224	1809
1822	2030	1090
1823	1208	1183
1824	420 1/2	1238 (?)
1825	2046 1/4	567
1826	1883 1/2	220
1827	1914	313
1828	4291 1/2	97
1829	3630 1/2 + 5 sacks	-
1831	2713	16
1832	3007 1/2	49
1833	1596	58 1/2
1834	2948 1/2	16
1835	4397 1/2	128 1/2

Sources: AHU : *Moçambique*, Caixa 34, 35, 37; HAG : *Macau*, 1298-1302, 1305-13, 1315-20, 1322-27, 1329-30, 1332, 1334, 1336, 1338, 1340-41.

Not only Portuguese vessels but also British, Spanish and American ships were engaged in the Macao opium commerce as Table 5.11 demonstrates. They were carriers of both Bengal and Malwa varieties of opium, as well as Turkey opium. In 1820 British ships brought 1,221 chests of Bengal opium and 1,222 chests of Malwa opium to Macao. Portuguese ships on the other hand shipped in 1,500 chests of Bengal opium and 1,609 chests of Malwa opium in the same year.[43] Macao thus earned considerable revenue by way of port charges and other fees and duties. Although we are unable to make an estimate of the income acquired by the Macao government from port duties and other fees due to lack of adequate data, we know that in 1823, a duty of 16 *taeis* per *pico* was charged at the port of Macao.[44] From Table 5.10 we observe that 1,208 Malwa opium chests and 1,183 of the Bengal variety entered the port in 1823 (2,391 chests in all). Each chest contained 1 *pico* and about 6 to 7 *arrateis*. This meant that the 2,391 chests equalled either 2,503 or 2,522 *picos*. The duty charged was therefore either 40,048 or 40,352 *taeis*.

TABLE 5.11 : OPIUM SHIPMENTS TO MACAO, 1821

Nationality of Ships	Nature of Opium Bengal (no. of chests)	Malwa (no. of chests)	Turkey (no. of chests)
British	115	-	-
Portuguese	1700	1149	60
Spanish	150	-	-

Source: Hosea Ballou, Morse, *The Chronicles of the East India Company Trading to China*, 1635-1834, vol. IV, Cambridge, 1926, p. 21.

British Controls : Efforts at Containment

Since the beginning of the nineteenth century, the English East India Company felt threatened by the sudden rise and development of the Malwa trade. As its opium monopoly was being endangered, it began to make determined efforts to arrest its further growth and to bring about its eventual elimination.

When in 1803 the British authorities first learnt of the slow but steady flow of Malwa opium into Bombay from Surat and the northern ports of Gujarat, it instituted a thorough enquiry into the matter.[45] Elaborate reports on the nature of the Malwa trade operating on the west coast of India especially at Bombay, Surat, Dhollera, Fatehpur,

Dholkar, Cambay and Kathiawar convinced them of the need to take immediate steps to nip the problem in the bud.[46] Accordingly towards the end of 1803 circulars were issued not only in English but also in vernacular languages, prohibiting the cultivation of poppy in Company territories.[47] The Customs Masters at Bombay and Surat were directed not to permit the import and export of opium except what was purchased at Company sales in Bengal. The owners of the vessels navigating under the British flag were warned against receiving Malwa opium on board under pain of forfeiture and additional penalties.[48] From the records we gather the impression that there was opposition to the prohibition in Gujarat as opium had been produced on a limited scale for internal consumption since ancient times.[49]

It was in 1804 that the advent of Malwa opium in the Chinese market drew for the first time the serious attention of the supercargoes at Canton. In that year they learnt that 100 piculs of Malwa opium had been shipped to Whampoa from Goa, by a Parsee merchant.[50] In 1805 the supercargoes informed the Government of the arrival of 100 chests of Malwa at Macao from Goa. Their letter contained an element of alarm and called for timely action.[51] Though the trade in opium did not appear to have been carried on to any great extent yet it was felt that its continuance would affect significantly the revenue derived from the Bengal opium monopoly. Representations were therefore made to the Viceroy of Goa who solemnly agreed to prohibit the shipments of opium from Goa and issued instructions to his subordinates at Daman and Diu to take similar action. It was most likely that these steps would fail to produce the desired results, because smuggling opportunities were too valuable to be sacrificed and the Portuguese government was not expected to rigorously enforce regulations against a system from which it derived no small benefit. To keep the Portuguese in check, the English adopted a devious method of imposing a heavy tax on Portuguese ships arriving at Calcutta to which however the former responded by compelling the opium dealers to don Portuguese colours in order to unload their cargoes at Macao. Indeed this rivalry assumed a formidable intensity in the ensuing decades.[52]

During 1805-10 a lull in the Malwa trade was observed. This was probably due to the unsettled state of the Malwa territories disturbed by Pindaris, culminating in the Pindari War.[53] British occupation of Goa, Daman and Diu during 1799-1815 might have also served to clamp down on the trade operating on the west coast. What probably affected the Malwa opium trade was the ban on exportation of Malwa opium via Bombay in 1813. At Macao too the trade was suspended owing to Chinese piracy as Table 5.10 seems to suggest. Therefore until 1815 the trade in Malwa opium held no real threat to the Bengal monopoly.

Prior to 1818, the English East India Company was rather disadvatageously placed with respect to Malwa opium since the entire Malwa opium producing belt was in the hands of the native rulers, beyond the reach of the British political control, though the Second Anglo-Maratha War had no doubt relatively improved this position. Therefore, all that the Company could do was to prohibit British subjects from participating in the trade and prohibit its loading on Bombay vessels. It could persuade at times the native chiefs to cooperate with the British Government in preventing the passage of opium through their lands. Attempts were made to restrict poppy cultivation in their areas through agreements with some of the chiefs, including the Gaikwad. But these policies could not be pursued for long in the face of stiff opposition raised by the Court of Directors.[54]

This situation altered dramatically and drastically with the collapse of the Mughal authority, when the English East India Company emerged as the paramount power in India. It was obvious that with the Treaty of Mandasaur (1818) the *de facto* sovereignty of the Malwa region passed into the hands of the Company's government. The acquisition of Bassein, and all the territory surrounding the Portuguese settlement of Daman, together with the establishment of supremacy over Kathiawar, Gujarat and Myhee Kaunta, placed in British hands the chains of control over the Malwa trading network. It was expected to give the British the necessary fire-power to contain and eventually extinguish the Malwa trade. This was not to be. The restoration of peace and security in Central India after the termination of the Pindari War accelerated poppy production and opium commercial activity via the west coast of India.

Despite British presence in the *Estado* ports, opium arrived at Goa from Daman and later proceeded to Macao. The British envoy C. S. Schyler stationed at Goa informed the Bengal government in April 1816 about the departure of the vessel *Angelica* with 106 chests of opium for Macao.[55] The Macao government provided the Malwa opium commerce its official sanction and recognition in view of the benefits that the State stood to gain from its existence.[56]

During 1815-20 the British authorities in India adopted further measures designed to meet the threat posed by Malwa to Company interests.

While it was the avowed policy of the British Government to

prohibit the production of Malwa opium in Company territories, it began to formulate plans to step up the rate of production of Bengal opium. The cultivation of poppy was resumed in areas where it was earlier halted. Collectors of revenue were appointed as deputies to the opium agents. In order that they should develop real interest in the production of the item, they were allowed a commission on any increase that would occur in production in their districts. This expansion of poppy cultivation in Bengal resulted in the availability of cheap Company opium. But this experiment did not produce the desired results.[57]

In a bid to meet the challenge of Malwa the Company made attempts to coerce independent rulers in the Malwa region into cooperating with the British. In 1816 an agreement was signed with Holkar, according to which, cultivation of opium in his lands was not to exceed 5,000 *maunds*. Of these, 1,000 *maunds* were to be utilised for internal consumption and the rest was to be handed over to the Company at the rate of 30 Farrukhabadi Kaldur of Rs. 120,000. Furthermore, the British at the end of each season would pay to the State a commission of Rs. 100,000 in Ujjain or Indore currency. The British also agreed to pay a sum equivalent to the net profit derived from the sale of 200 chests of opium each containing 14 *punseries*. Similar type of agreements came to be applied to other native states in the course of time.[58]

Regulation I of 1818 introduced a set of restrictions also aimed at encompassing the Central Indian rulers. The closure of the port of Jumbasoor to the exportation of opium was an important step directed towards closing an outlet of Malwa opium to Daman.[59] The Regulation called upon the native rulers to discourage the entry and departure of Malwa opium in their territories. They were required to enforce the payment of a duty of Rs. 12 per *seer* on opium entering their lands. At first Gaikwad's government manifested an aversion for the restrictions but later expressed desire to give effect to the Regulation I of 1818.[60] In April 1819 Gujarat was exempted from the operations of the said Regulation. The free entry of opium for internal consumption was permitted.

In 1820 the British government passed the Regulation II of 1820. Accordingly letters were addressed to the Rajahs of Dhurrumpor and Paint calling upon them to prohibit the transit of opium through their territories to the sea coast to Daman. Similarly the native agents at Goga and Dhollera received instructions to use every means in their power to detect any opium which could be brought or taken away from the ports under their jurisdiction.[61] Efforts were made to prevail upon the chieftains of Myhee Kaunta to give effect to the Regulation I of 1818 and

Regulation II of 1820 within their respective principalities.[62] Captain Pottinger of Sind was instructed to exercise utmost vigilance over the opium trade through Khandesh leading to Daman.[63] The Rana of Porbhandar in January 1822 readily agreed to use his exertions to meet the wishes of the British government with respect to the illicit traffic in opium.[64]

But soon, based on the letters and reports submitted by the Resident of Baroda, Collector of Northern Konkan, Customs Master of Bombay, the Agent of Porbhandar and Nawab of Cambay, it was evident that despite the best efforts of the British to curtail the passage of Malwa opium to Daman, and from thence to Bombay and Alibagh and finally to China, the trade persisted and thrived. The streams, creeks and inlets on the west coast provided ample oportunities for the secret rendezvous of opium smugglers.[65]

It seems evident that the restrictions imposed by the British government till 1820 in fact stimulated the clandestinely operated commerce and led to the stupendous increase in Malwa opium consumption in China. The energetic restrictive measures meant to control the Malwa opium trade, not only through British territories, but also through those of the allies and vassals of the British government, proved counter-productive. In fact, they stimulated the ingenuity and adventuresome spirit of the speculators to devise plans to counteract them by seeking a circuitous route for the transit of the trade. Opium found its way to Karachi and thence to the ports of Daman and Goa, the localities which afforded every facility as emporia for the opium trade on the western side of the Indian peninsula, and was later consigned to eastern markets in ships belonging to the Portuguese and other foreigners. The tranquil state of Malwa after the Pindari war leading to an increased cultivation of poppy, was favourable to the success of a plan which gave vent to so valuable a product.

There were various schemes adopted by the speculators and dealers to evade and escape the British dragnet. The boats sailing along the west coast laden with opium had the habit of flying their colours according to their convenience. When they approached a foreign port, they did not always hoist the English flag, but one resembling that of the vessels of the port they touched.[66] The fishing dinghys of Karachi, for example, were disguised so as to have every appearance of being engaged in that operation and thus safely conveyed opium to Daman.[67]

The Bombay government tried hard but failed to penetrate the production centres and internal markets feeding Daman, Bombay and other ports on the west coast of India. This demonstrated the widespread pervasiveness and strength of the Malwa opium network which was definitely a force to reckon with.

Meanwhile, Malwa consumption was on the rise. Its quality, though inferior to Bengal opium, was improving. Besides it yielded a greater proportion of smokeable extract than the Bengal drug. According to some experiments conducted in 1821 for the purpose of ascertaining the comparative purity and value of the two varieties of opium and detecting the nature and extent of foreign ingredients contained in them, Patna 53 1/2 yielded 27 1/2 or 51 per cent pure extract while Malwa 53 1/2 yielded 41 1/2 or 77 per cent pure extract.[68]

Malwa opium became the favourite of the great masses of China with the exception of the wealthy and it was cheap and certainly safe to speculate in. It fetched much more profits than its Bengal counterpart.[69] Malwa opium was made up of small cakes which were infinitely better adapted to facilitate its transit packed in picul boxes which were more convenient, being a smaller sort than the British one.[70] Since the 1820s the Malwa opium exports to China surpassed those of Bengal opium.[71] There was much demand for Malwa and this goes to prove the growing popularity for the drug among the Chinese masses. During 1800-19 the average shipment of Bengal opium to China amounted to 2,793 chests while those of Malwa averaged 1,318, that is, less than 50 per cent of the Bengal variety. But over the years 1819-39 the average export of Bengal opium chests equalled 7,644 chests while Malwa opium exports amounted to an average of 9,393 chests, more than seven times than that shipped during 1800-19.

Likewise figures on the consumption of Malwa opium at China reveal that during 1822-28 there was a minimum consumption of 4,000 chests and a maximum consumption of 6,308 chests per annum.[72] Thus an average of 5,170 chests of Malwa opium having a value of Rs. 4,863,138 were consumed per year during 1822-28. During the same period an annual average of 3,267 chests of Bengal opium worth Rs. 3,753,325 was consumed. The general demand for Malwa opium continued unabated.[73]

In 1820 the Bengal government consulted the Bombay authorities on the practicality of establishing an opium monopoly at Bombay. Malwa opium could be brought for sale to Bombay. What probably prompted the authorities was the fact that from Bengal opium sales the government derived a revenue of about 70 lakhs of rupees annually, but from Malwa nothing. What was irritating was that the trade in Malwa had been fostered and increased by the enterprise of British merchants and carried on with the help of British capital in promotion of Portuguese interests. It was hoped that the establishment of the monopoly would be found equally advantageous to the Company and the dealers of Malwa by giving them the opportunity of selling without risk and at a fair and reasonable profit.[74] Deliberations on the matter led to certain definite conclusions. It was felt that the sale of 4,000 chests of Malwa opium of 2 factory *maunds* should be conducted at Bombay on the lines of the public sales conducted at Calcutta.[75]

The first Bombay sale of 1,500 Malwa opium chests was conducted in the first week of April 1821. It netted in a profit of Rs. 928,000, while the 1822 and 1823 Malwa sales brought in Rs. 720,000 and Rs. 496,000 respectively.[76] Although an average annual profit of seven lakhs of rupees had been realised from the 1821-23 Malwa opium sales at Bombay, the high prices paid namely Rs. 2,024, Rs. 2,007 and Rs. 1,764 for the 1821, 1822 and 1823 sales respectively by the Bombay government and the limited quantity allowed to be brought to the sales, an average of about 1,500 chests, had produced effects contrary to those desired by the authorities. The clandestine trade was still successfully prosecuted via the circuitous route to Karachi to supply the full demand in Bombay and the west coast, which equalled 4,000 chests at least.[77]

Malwa opium sales continued to be held at Bombay until 1828, leaving a precarious margin between cost and sale prices.[78]

In a fresh bid to meet the challenge posed by the clandestine Malwa opium commerce, the British government tried to apply diplomatic pressure on the Lisbon government to prohibit the exportation of Malwa opium through the Portuguese ports in India but this did not produce the required effect. At one time in the early 1820s, the British government even toyed with the idea of exchanging some of its possessions for Portuguese India. It was probably felt that to counteract the illicit trade via the Portuguese settlements in the vicinity of the Bombay Presidency, the occupation of Daman and Diu would help. Though Goa would be open to the prosecution of the opium trade, it would be by no means convenient, and it would be definitely difficult for the opium dealers to use Goa as the base of operations instead of Daman and Diu. Their expenses would be enhanced. The matter of ceding any of the British colonies in the West Indies or other part of the world, or entering into negotiations with the Portuguese to suppress the trade on condition of receiving from the British government annually the value of the concessions was also taken up for consideration.[79]

An inquiry was instituted to derive information on the public resources of Daman and Diu. The inquiry was conducted in secrecy so as not to cause alarm.[80] In the absence of documents one is not able to know the outcome of the inquiry, whether the British did take up the matter for negotiations with the Portuguese authorities and whether their proposals were turned down or whether the matter was temporarily abandoned.

The British authorities launched a fresh attack on the baneful Malwa trade. In a far-reaching move, they concluded restrictive treaties during 1825-27 with the petty rulers of central and western India. It was discovered that opium was still being conveyed from Malwa to Pali, to Jaisalmer and thence to Karachi and from Sind it was shipped to Daman. The need to prevail upon the Raja of Jaisalmer to restrict the traffic through his territories was brought to the attention of the government. Consequently, a letter was despatched to the agent in Rajputana, calling upon him to use his best endeavours and ploys to bring about this coup.[81] Other attempts were made to coerce the other native rulers to restrict the production and transit of Malwa opium through lands under their jurisdiction. The Resident of Hyderabad was instructed to start similar negotiations with the Nizam.[82] In 1824, Captain Cobbe successfully concluded a treaty with the Maharaja of Udaipur. The said Maharaja, in lieu of a handsome compensation of 40,000 Sonat rupees, conceded to prevent the sale and transit of opium through his domains. Highly gratified by the success of Cobbe, the Resident of Indore was particularly instructed to be active in arriving at similar treaties with native chiefs under his authority. Caufield, the Agent at Kotah, entered into an agreement with the State of Kotah in August 1825 for a period of six months. The British authorities, however, wanted a more permanent arrangement and expressed their preparedness to pay one lakh of rupees as compensation to the ruler to prevent the exportation of opium to coastal areas. Captain Alves entered into an agreement with the authorities of Ajmer in September 1826. They agreed to cooperate with the restrictive policy of the government. Similar agreements were reached with the rulers of Bundi, Dhar and Dewas who agreed to curtail cultivation as well as to prevent the passage of opium through their dominions.[83] The government seemed determined to see that no Malwa opium would seep its way into Portuguese territories.

The restrictive measures of the Company came under severe pressure. The first to raise the banner of revolt and to openly oppose the system, was the State of Kotah. The Raja of Kotah had been hostile to a policy which only served to cramp the internal commerce and economy of his State. Much opposition to the policies also came from British circles.[84] The measures had been oppressive to the people and unpalatable and offensive to their rulers. The revenues of the Raos of Kutch were diminished to the tune of at least 50,000 crores per annum, and most of the tributary and feudatory chiefs suffered in the same way.[85] This demonstrated that the treaties had been ruinous to the internal commerce of Malwa and Rajputana and made sharp inroads into the independence and sovereignty of the native States. Smuggling activities continued to be rampant. They were too profitable to be abandoned by the dealers and speculators in Malwa opium. In spite of the restrictive measures they were carried on uninterruptedly. This was obvious from the opium exports via Daman as indicated in Table 5.2. In fact during 1827-29 a sharp rise in exportation was observed. In 1827-28 3,881 chests, in 1828-29 3,500 chests and in 1829-30 7,500 chests were exported from Daman.[86] Some of the native States like Jaipur, Kishengargh and Gwalior had conveniently avoided coming within the purview of the restrictive policies. This provided the outlets for the Malwa drug to be transported to Portuguese ports. The opium dealers successfully thwarted the plans of the British authorities by channelling their cargoes through routes beyond the orbit of the British restrictive system. Furthermore, the public sentiments had been so hostile to the restrictions that even though the native rulers were well disposed towards fulfilling their engagements, they found it difficult to put the system into complete effect. The interference of the British local agents too, was an irritant.

In 1829 the Bengal authorities passed a resolution stating their decision to abstain from any direct interference in the growth and transit of opium throughout Central India, confining the restrictions to British territories.[87] Thus the oppressive restrictive system encompassing the independent native states of Central India came to a welcome end.

Once again the British government cast its covetous eyes on Portuguese India. On 26th May 1830 William Astelle, Robert Campbell and George Smith, signatories to a confidential letter from the East India House, London, addressed to the Governor General of British India, sought information on the possibilities of purchasing the Portuguese territories in India. Information was demanded on the annual receipts of the Portuguese customs revenues during the previous 8 years at each port, the amount of trade carried on at each of the Portuguese ports in terms of tonnage, nature of the imports and exports, value and the like, the expenditure of the Portuguese government in India and the manner in which the surplus revenue if any was transmitted to Portugal.[88] Accordingly detailed reports were submitted on both Daman and Diu. A report on Diu revealed that its revenue amounted to 90,000 *xerafins* annually.[89]

As regards Daman it was reported in 1831 that the annual receipts of the Portuguese government from Daman amounted to Rs. 460,137-2-0. It was derived from the snuff farm, gambling houses, salt pans, etc. The annual expenditure was estimated at Rs. 75,000, covering expenses on government officials, secretaries and servants, the judicial department, the customs house establishment, the treasury and military establishments, repairs to public buildings, etc.[90] We have no information of the outcome of these inquiries.

Contraction, Stagnation and Decline

Realising that there was no way in which it could contain the Malwa trade the British authorities had to give up their dog-in-the-manger attitude and change tactics. They hit upon a novel plan aimed at dealing with the Malwa problem and turning it into an asset. It was estimated that more than one crore of rupees was invested in this trade chiefly by the merchants of Bombay from which the Government derived no revenue. In the year 1829-30 7,500 chests were exported by Daman and the exports were expected to touch 9,000 in 1830-31. The need was felt to convert this clandestine trade via Daman into a legitimate trade via Bombay.[91] A proclamation was issued on the 23rd November 1829 permitting the export of Malwa directly to Bombay on the payment of a fee for passes at the rate of Rs. 250 per chest of 140 lbs. weight.[92]

This duty was however found to be too steep by the opium merchants. This was probably why it was decided to set aside the matter for some time and accordingly no passes were issued.[93]

On 12th September, 1831 the Bombay government issued a fresh proclamation permitting the free transit of Malwa opium via Bombay on the payment of a duty of Rs. 175 per chest of 140 lbs. weight.[94] This step taken by the British authorities was definitely popular, not only because the route from Malwa to the sea via Bombay was direct involving less expense and wastage of time and energy than by the circuitous route via Daman, but also because shipment at Daman was also a little expensive, a sum of Rs. 45 being charged by the Portuguese merely for the cover of their flag.[95] The transit pass system must have been welcomed for other reasons: The extensive trade in Malwa through Daman owed its existence to the prohibition imposed on the transit of the drug via Company territories. The capital employed in it was principally that of Bombay merchants, who could not find employment for their capital at Bombay and therefore resorted to Daman where they incurred considerable risk as to the quality of the purchase as well as shipping them on foreign bottoms. They definitely preferred an arrangement closer at home.

The new system showed encouraging results from the very start. The duties collected on the transit of Malwa opium went on increasing year by year and proved to be a valuable source of Company revenue as represented by Table 5.12.

TABLE 5.12 : REVENUES DERIVED BY THE BRITISH FROM THE TRANSIT PASS SYSTEM, 1830-35

Years	Chests	Revenues (In rupees)
1830-31	4621	808675
1831-32	10630	1860250
1832-33	7998	1399650
1833-34	10860	1900500
1834-35	6966	1219020

Source: IOL : *RLB*, L/E/3/349, p. 144.

However, in 1834-35, passes supplied for 6,966 chests brought in a revenue of Rs. 1,219,020 much less than those of the previous three years and Rs. 681,480 less than that of 1833-34 (Table 5.12). This can most definitely be attributed to smuggling. Incidentally, since the inception of the pass system Malwa opium continued to reach Daman, much to the exasperation of the British authorities. Though 8,000 chests went by the direct route to Bombay, about 3,000 were transported by the circuitous route to Daman. In 1831, 4,628-1/2 Malwa opium chests were exported from Daman.[96] During 1834-35 5,600 chests left Daman for China.[97] It was therefore in the hope of diverting the trade from Daman that the price of the passes was dropped from Rs. 175 to Rs. 125 in 1825.[98].

The trade via Karachi still persisted as Table 5.13 seeems to suggest. The fee of Rs. 125 per pass continued to exist till 1843. It was then raised to Rs. 200 once the Portuguese connection was no more effective.[99]

Undoubtedly the *Estado da India* was badly hit by the pass system. With the introduction of the transit pass system in 1831 opium revenues of Daman dropped sharply (Table 5.14). In 1832 they dropped to 123,157-2-32 1/2 *xerafins*. During 1838-40 the average annual revenues from opium fell sharply to 37,865-4-38 *xerafins*. The export of Malwa opium to China via Daman fell to 2,700 chests in 1834.[100] The Portuguese reacted by lowering the tariffs at Daman to lure back some of the traffic in the mid-1830s. The tariff war between Daman and Bombay became so bitter that the British actually blockaded the Portuguese port for a while in 1838. By 1840, nine-tenths of the Malwa opium was being exported through Bombay and one-tenth via Daman, while earlier two-thirds passed through Daman and one-third through Bombay.[101]

TABLE 5.13 : ARRIVAL OF OPIUM CONSIGNMENTS AT DAMAN FROM KARACHI, 1837

Date	Quantity
9th March	64 bales, 5 chests, 2 sacks
13th April	84 bales, 2 sacks
27th April	96 bales, 72 chests
29th April	28 bales, 78 chests
14th May	61 bales, 44 chests
18th May	142 bales, some chests (?)
23rd May	132 bales
23rd May	136 chests, 84 bales

Source: *Damão*, 6055, fls. 1-470 : *passim.*

TABLE 5.14 : DAMAN OPIUM REVENUES, 1832-40

Year	Revenues (In *xerafins*)
1832	123157-2-32 1/2
1838	64501-1-15
1839	22469-3-25 3/4
1840	26626-4-14 1/4

Sources: HAG : *Correspondencia de Damão*, 1081, 20 June 1832; Carlos Xavier "Daman Port and Shipyards (1800-1875)" *Purabhilekh-Puratatva*, vol. III, no. 1, Jan.-June 1985, p. 10.

Even in the early 1840s the British were disturbed with the Malwa problem. Several options were explored as to how best to secure control over Karachi, the only remaining outlet of the Portuguese Malwa opium trade. It still caused harm to the opium monopoly. It was felt that it would be possible to tempt the Amirs of Sind with a liberal offer, to farm the sea customs revenues for a limited term, that even for a short period, in case the Amirs objected to renewal of the farm, the Malwa opium commerce would come under British control and surveillance. All efforts could then be made to stamp out the trade through every outlet of the River Indus, and things could be placed on a sound footing. Another option considered was the imposition of high customs duties in Sind to discourage and stifle the trade. It was felt that the Amirs would have no objection to imposing higher duties on opium entering and passing through their dominions. They would have to be handsomely compensated for losses. The export duty levied on the drug at the rate of Rs.5-1/2 per 8 *pucca maunds* brought in over 1 lakh of rupees, besides tolls levied on the frontiers near Rajputana.[102] In 1843 the British put an end to all speculations by occupying Sind. The Malwa route via Karachi to Daman was thus cut off.[103]

At the Far Eastern end several events caused the opium commerce to take a turn for the worse, destroying the credibility of Macao as a hub of the thriving opium commerce. The trickle of opium flow into Macao turned into a flood, making it increasingly unsafe. All of a sudden the Chinese government woke up to the dangers of opium addiction and began to take a firm line to stem the flood of opium into China. In the wake of a systematic campaign launched by the mandarins against opium smugglers in 1820-22, the drug trade at the Macao port came to a stand still. Furthermore, the Chinese authorities began to increase their interference in the Portuguese settlement, which strictly speaking was not a colony but was leased to Portugal. In 1800 a mandarin was stationed in the city of Macao. This unsettled state of affairs coupled with the insistence on the part of the Macao government to seek Portuguese colours and to operate through Portuguese agents were a source of discouragement to the opium dealers and drove them from Macao at first to Whampoa, and later to Lintin (Table 5.15). When the question arose of finding a safe and permanent depôt for opium storage and distribution the Macao government staked its claim, but the opium traders demonstrated their preference for Lintin located at the mouth of the Pearl River.[104]

Alarmed at this move to undermine and undercut the Macao-based opium commerce, the Macao government formulated plans for equalizing the duties charged on British and Portuguese shipping, if the English East India Company would agree to hold Malwa sales at Bombay. But nothing emerged from these proposals.[105] Even a domestic popular upsurge directed against the foreigners involved in the trade ended in a fiasco and could not save Macao from economic ruin.[106] In a bid to lure back some of the opium commerce to its port, the Macao authorities announced belatedly in 1823 a reduction in the customs duties to be paid by foreigners and nationals bringing their cargoes in Portuguese ships. Henceforth they would have to pay 16 *taeis* per *pico*. The duty was further dropped to 7 *taeis* and 2 *mazes* per *pico*.[107] By 1828 the opium traders and brokers had practically abandoned Macao. Lintin henceforth began to play a key role in the opium commerce. Lintin was a regular place of rendezvous for shipping, particularly during the winter months when the open anchorage gave shelter from the prevailing north-east monsoon. Instead of 8 receiving ships there were over 20 and the number of opium chests grew from a few thousands to about 30,000. It was here that unbridled smuggling prevailed on an ever increasing scale. A smuggling network based at Lintin encompassed China's coastal provinces and hinterland providing outlets for the opium traffic to practically all the towns of China.[108] From Table 5.10 one gathers that the entry of Bengal opium chests into Macao fell rapidly from 1825 onwards. Over the years 1825-35 a total of just 1,465 chests were imported into Macao, that is an average of 163 chests per annum.

TABLE 5.15 : OPIUM SHIPMENTS TO WHAMPOA, 1821

Nationality of Ships	Nature of Opium		
	Bengal (no. of chests)	Malwa (no. of chests)	Turkey (no. of chests)
British	1245	1369	15
Portuguese	-	-	-
Spanish	-	-	-
American	-	-	437

Source: Morse, vol. IV, p. 21.

The smuggled Malwa opium which came via Daman was Macao's last hope. In this case too the opium dealers opted for Lintin since 1828.[109] They were able to launch a successful attack against this remnant of the Macao privilege, by driving a wedge between the Portuguese authorities in India and the government of Macao. At the intercession of Rogerio de Faria, the Portuguese authorities permitted the opium merchants to bypass the claims of Macao and to ship their cargoes to Lintin. They were able to secure at a price, licenses from the Goa or Daman authorities to conduct their business operations at Lintin, instead of Macao. For instance, Rogerio de Faria was issued one such passport in 1828 permitting his ship *D. Manoel de Portugal* to be loaded with opium for Lintin.[110] A hue and cry was raised by the Macao government over such passports as they were detrimental to its interests. It would deprive the *Alfandega de Macao* of duties, freight charges and commissions. It was observed that the duties derived from Malwa opium arriving from the west coast of India formed the only remaining means of preserving the city from utter destruction and ruin. The Malwa trade served as the only source of subsistence for its inhabitants.[111]

It was obvious that Rogerio de Faria wielded much power with the Portuguese authorities at Goa and Daman. It was also obvious that it was a question of Daman versus Macao. It was necessary to keep the Daman end going for the survival of the *Estado* was at stake.

The authorities at Goa issued a *Portaria* on 31st March, 1828 introducing the passport system which upheld that the opium merchants and dealers could ship their cargoes from Daman to wherever it was found convenient to them. In this matter they received the backing and support of the Lisbon authorities.[112] But the Daman government was not blind to the predicament of Macao. To discourage opium transportation to Lintin, it fixed different rates of customs duty on opium moving to Lintin and Macao.[113] It was public knowledge that merchants of Macao would load thousands of opium chests at Calcutta and Bombay annually in British ships and direct them to Lintin and other parts of China without paying the customary 22 *patacas* per chest at Macao if opium was transported in Portuguese ships. In 1829 almost 400$000 *patacas* were sent to Bombay for opium to be transported in British ships to Lintin thus depriving the *alfandegas* of Macao and Daman duties on them.[114] This contributed to the mounting debt of Macao. If the merchants of Macao themselves displayed such a lack of patriotism for their settlement, where their agency houses, families and fortunes were located, no better behaviour and attitude could be expected of Indian merchants like Rogerio de Faria, the British traders and brokers, or from the Goa and Daman authorities.[115]

For a time Macao openly defied its Goa overlord. We have the instance of the seizure of the vessel *D. Manoel de Portugal*, which carried a passport issued by the Government of Daman and a copy of the *Portaria* of 31st March 1828 exempting it from calling at Macao and paying customs duties. It could export Malwa opium wherever it was found convenient, and could even proceed directly to Lintin. On reaching the islands of China on 8th July 1828, it was intercepted and detained by the Macao authorities. Customs payments were demanded. At first the Captain of the ship refused to make the payment but later kept a security amount and obtained the release of the ship.[116] Rogerio de Faria, the proprietor of the vessel brought the happenings at Macao and the resultant loss incurred to the attention of the Goa authorities. Thereupon, the Macao authorities were ordered to return to Rogerio de Faria and his legitimate trustees the duties that had been charged on the cargo of the ship.[117]

William Jardine, Samuel Rupell and John Richardson, the agents of Rogerio de Faria in China also reacted sharply to the unjust and violent seizure of *D. Manoel de Portugal* and to the forcible extraction of duties on the grounds that the ship had not entered the sphere of control of Macao. The Macao government justified its behaviour stating that ships bearing Portuguese flags could not bypass Macao after entering Chinese waters. They had to call at Macao and pay port duties.[118]

One can review the Daman-Macao opium connection with the help of Table 5.6. Until 1827 the bulk of the opium cargoes from Daman, that is, about 89.71 per cent were shipped to Macao and the rest was carried in coastal vessels to Alibagh and Bhavnagar. Matters underwent a radical change in 1828 with the introduction of the passport system. Shippers were permitted to transport opium cargoes to any area of their choice in the Far East. Thus began the movement of opium cargoes to Lintin. While in 1828, 121 shipments proceeded to Macao, 48 were permitted to move either to Macao or Lintin and 3 to Alibagh. In 1829, 224 shipments moved to Macao, 39 directly to Lintin and 3 to Alibagh. In 1830 only 14 ships moved to Macao, 47 to Lintin and 5 to Alibagh. Thus in 1828 from 89.71 per cent, the shipments to Macao dropped to 70.35 per cent. About twenty-eight per cent of the shipping was directed to either Macao or Lintin and 1.74 per cent to Alibagh. In 1829 shipments that moved directly to Macao amounted to 84.21 per cent, those directly to Lintin 14.66 per cent and those proceeding to Alibagh about 1 per cent. In 1830, 71.21 per cent of the shipments proceeded directly to Lintin, 21.21 per cent to Macao and 7.58 per cent to Alibagh. The final nail in the coffin of the Malwa opium commerce was driven by the lethal transit pass system initiated by the English East India Company in 1831. The traffic in opium at Macao came to be suspended and its economic fabric was gravely undermined.

In sheer desperation, the Macao government retaliated by prohibiting the residence of all foreign merchants including the British, at their settlements. The Select Committee in China reported to the British authorities in India that it was formally intimated by the government of Macao of the orders received from Portugal banning the residence of foreign merchants, including the English unless they brought licences from Lisbon.[119]

Governor General Bentinck addressed a strong protest to the Governor General of Portuguese Asia. He reminded the Portuguese authorities that Macao was the spot set apart by the Imperial Government of China for the residence of foreigners resorting to China for trade. The harsh communication from Bentinck was an indication of the extent to which the British had moved to challenge the very presence of the Portuguese at Macao. Under such pressure Portugal had to rescind its stand and issued instructions permitting residence to all foreigners without exception at Macao.[120]

The opium trade at Macao which formerly brought much wealth and glory to that port had dwindled by 1830 to a trickle.[121]

Macao was totally dislodged from the Chinese opium network and entered the final throes of decay. It was eventually overshadowed by the development of Hong Kong in its vicinity.[122]

Although the Portuguese Malwa opium on the west coast of India enjoyed a brief flowering, the connection was not entirely destroyed because earlier the Turkish variety had been a minor component of the Portuguese trade. In 1859 the Portuguese authorities authorised the revival of re-exportation of Turkish opium from their ports. In the 1870s ambitious plans were underway to cultivate opium on a large scale in Moçambique.[123]

Probably the British sought to ensure the ultimate end of the Portuguese opium trade through the Anglo-Portuguese Treaty of 1878, which contained a stipulation prohibiting the cultivation, manufacture and export of opium in Portuguese India.[124]

REFERENCES AND NOTES

1. The Compilation Group, *The Opium War*, History of Modern China Series, Peking, 1976, pp. 8-9.
2. *Ibid.*, p. 5.
3. *Historical Statistical Monographs of Commercial Crops of India, Poppy (Opium)*, Gokhale Institute of Economics and Politics, Pune, 1981, pp. 11-12; Michael Greenberg, *British Trade and the Opening of China, 1800-1842*, New York/London, p. 12.
4. Tan Chung, "The Britain-China-India Trade Triangle, 1771-1840", *Essays in Modern Indian Economic History*, (ed.) Subyasachi Bhattacharya, Delhi, 1987, pp. 119-120.
5. BA : *RD*, 7/1821, p. 668.
6. Andrèw Ljungstedt, *An Historical Sketch of the Portuguese Settlements in China*, Boston, 1836, p. 316.
7. BA : *RD*, 7/1821, pp. 34-41.
8. BA : *RD*, 7/1821, p. 670; 13/13, 1821, p. 197.
9. BA : *RD*, 7/1821, pp. 38, 49-52.
10. BA : *RD*, 7/1821, pp. 34-41.

11. BA : *RD*, 7/1821, pp. 34-41; HAG : *Correspondencia de Damão*, 1072, fl. 136v.
12. BA : *RD*, 79/1823, p. 302.
13. BA : *RD*, 13/13, 1821, p. 197.
14. HAG : *MR*, 205A, fl. 41v.
15. HAG : *MR*, 205A, fls. 43-43v.
16. HAG : *Provisões*, 1591, fl. 177.
17. HAG : *MR*, 205A, fl. 48.
18. Gervase Clarence-Smith, *The Third Portuguese Empire, 1825-1975 A study in economic imperialism*, Manchester/Dovey, *1985*, pp. 26,28.
19. HAG : *MR*, 205A, fl. 42v.
20. HAG : *MR*, 198B, fls. 487v-490v.
21. See Appendix 7.
22. BUL : *J.J. Papers*, no. 351, pp. 122, 129, 133.
23. See Appendix 8.
24. Mulchand Ira, Joze Simão dos Remedios, Inacio Bauptista Gomes, Felis (?) Hilario de Azavedo, Racique Vallobo, Caugi Beramogi, Rogerio de Faria, Naurogi Rustamogi, Daniel Mariano Ribeiro, Beramogi Bicagi, Dearamo Dulobo, Caramochande Amarchande, Mody Dorabossa Nassarvanji, Caramochande Areachande, Lalu Valobo (?), João de Noronha, Antonio Fernandes da Silva, João Thomas de Aquino, Gopala Lalu, Anacleto Francisco Thome de Souza ....P.(?), Joze Francisco de Oliveira, Maylal Narana, Joze Maria Siqueira, Anv China, Francisco Xavier, Francisco Pedro de Lemos, Quecobad Dorabossa, Naranabay Dearamo and Dearamo Pan Vallobo are names that figure in the customs records of Daman as opium dealers during 1825-29.
25. BA : *RD*, 28/80, 1823, p. 110.
26. BA : *RD*, 13/13, 1821, pp. 253-254.
27. BA : *RD*, 18/42, 1822, p. 350.28. HAG : *AG*, 6826, fls. 119, 129, 137, 144.
29. Clarence-Smith, *op. cit.*, p. 26.
30. BA : *RD*, 7/335, 1831, fl. 59.
31. Greenberg, *op. cit.*, p. 127.
32. BA : *RD*, 13/13, 1821, pp. 197-198.
33. BA : *PD*, 20/204, doc. dated 8 May 1823; 89/1190, 1840, p. 275.
34. M. J. Gabriel Saldanha, *Historia de Goa (Politica e Arquelogica)*, vol. I, Bastora, 1898, pp. 250-251.
35. BA : *GD*, 20/23, 1821-23, doc. dated 16 Sept. 1821; 12/344, 1836, pp. 99, 107, 153, 165-166, 171-172, 174, 177; 13/345, 1836, pp. 38-39; 14/346, 1836, pp. 11, 25, 36, 52, 94, 207, doc. dated 30 June 1835; Teotonio R. de Souza, "Capital Input in Goa's Freedom Struggle : The Bombay Connection", *Indo-Portuguese History, Old Issues, New Questions*, (ed.) Teotonio R. de Souza, New Delhi, 1984, pp. 103-107, 111.
36. Clarence-Smith, *op. cit.*, p. 26.
37. HAG : *Provisões*, 1587, fl. 148.
38. HAG : *Macau*, 1303, fls. 31, 70; *MR*, 185, fl. 58.
39. Clarence-Smith, *op. cit.*, p. 25.
40. See Appendix 8.
41. Other Macao-based merchants engaged in the opium trade were Antonio Pereira, Joaquim Joze Ferreira Viega (?), Antonio G. de Silveira, D. L. Calvo & Co., Joaquim Joze dos Santos, M. Francisco Marques, João de Noronha, Antonio Fernandes de Silva, Joze Joaquim Barros, Nicolao Tolentino da Costa, Francisco Xavier Lança, Joaquim de Souza, Antonio Joze Gonsalves Pereira, China Alam, Angelo Antonio da Silva,

João de Deos de Castro, Caetano Vicente Joze de Silva, Felis Vicente da Rocha, Justimano Viera Ribeiro, Constantino Joze Lopes, Boaz Joaquim Botelho, Francisco dos Remedios and Emedio do Rozario. HAG : *Macau*, 1320, fls. 424-426.

42. HAG : *MR*, 205B, doc. dated 6 Dec. 1828.
43. Hosea Ballou Morse, *The Chronicles of the East India Company Trading to India*, 1635-1834, vol. III, Cambridge, 1926, p. 383.
44. HAG : *Macau*, 1327, fls. 424-426.
45. BA : *RD*, 79/1823, p. 303.
46. BA : *RD*, 7/1821, pp. 29-32, 49-52.
47. BA : *RD*, 7/1821, p. 17.
48. BA : *RD*, 7/1821, pp. 7-9.
49. IOL : *ARLB*, L/E/3/11, doc. dated 11 Dec. 1816.
50. J. Kumar, *Indo-Chinese Trade, 1793-1833*, New Delhi, 1974, p. 49.
51. BA : *RD*, 79/1823, p. 305; IOL : *BD*, E/4/1022, pp. 190-192.
52. Kumar, *op. cit.*, p. 50.
53. See Appendix 8.
54. Kumar, *op. cit.*, p. 49.
55. BA : *RD*, 7/1821, pp. 89-90.
56. HAG : *Macau*, 1312, fls. 518-518v.
57. Kumar, *op. cit.*, p. 135.
58. Kalpana Sharma, "Opium Trade in the Holkar State, 1816-1856", *Proccedings of the Fourth All India Maratha History Seminar*, (ed.) S. K. Bhatt, May 1979, p. 116.
59. BA : *RD*, 7/1821, p. 341.
60. BA : *RD*, 7/1821, pp. 407-409, 415, 420.
61. BA : *RD*, 13/13, 1821, fls. 217, 221, 225, 273-274.
62. BA : *RD*, 13/13, 1821, p. 5.
63. BA : *RD*, 13/13, 1821, p. 243.
64. BA : *RD*, 18/42, 1822, pp. 12-13.
65. BA : *RD*, 7/1821, pp. 91-92, 407-635 : *passim*; 13/13, 1823, pp. 149-150, 155, 157.
66. BA : *RD*, 18/42, 1822, p. 4.
67. BA : *RD*, 13/13, 1821, p. 282.
68. BA : *RD*, 16/40, 1822, pp. 9, 11, 23-24.
69. Celsa Pinto, "Goa-based Overseas and Coastal Trade (18th-19th Centuries)" *Goa Through the Ages*, vol.II, (ed.) Teotonio R. de Souza, New Delhi, 1989, p. 202.
70. BA : *RD*, 10/10, 1821, pp. 475-476.
71. See Appendix 5.
72. See Appendix 6.
73. See Appendix 6.
74. IOL : *ARLB*, L/E/3/11, p. 98.
75. BA : *RD*, 79/1823, pp. 315-316, 318.
76. BA : *RD*, 79/1823, pp. 323-324, 326-327.
77. BA : *RD*, 79/1823, pp. 327, 331; 32/279, 1828, p. 416.
78. BA : *RD*, 32/279, 1828, p. 446.
79. BA : *PD*, 20/404, 1830-31, doc. dated 18 Feb. 1823.
80. BA : *PD*, 20/404, 1830-31, docs. dated 8 May 1823, 8 Sept. 1823.
81. Kumar, *op. cit.*, p. 138.
82. *Ibid.*, p. 140.
83. *Ibid.*, pp. 141-142.
84. *loc. cit.*
85. BA : *RD*, 32/279, 1828, pp. 432-433, 454-455, 457, 459.

86. IOL : *RLB*, L/E/3/346, p. 333.
87. BA : *RD*, 32/279, 1828, p. 460.
88. BA : *PD*, 20/404, 1830-31, doc. dated 26 May 1830.
89. BA : *PD*, 20/404, 1830-31, doc. dated 10 Jan. 1831.
90. BA : *PD*, 20/404, 1830-31, doc. dated 9 April 1831.
91. IOL : *RLB*, L/E/3/346, p. 333.
92. IOL : *RLB*, L/E/3/346, p. 334; *ARLB*. L/E/3/11, p.137.
93. BA : *RD*, 32/279, 1829 p. 661; HAG : *MR*, 206A, fl. 108.
94. BA : *RD*, 7/335, 1831, doc. dated 12 Sept. 1831.
95. Kumar, *op. cit.*, p. 147.
96. BA : *RD*, 40/507, 1833, p. 229, 239.
97. IOL : *RLB*, L/E/3/349, pp. 259-260.
98. IOL : *ARLB*, L/E/3/11, p. 178.
99. BA : *RD*, 40/507, 1833, p. 229; Historical Statistical Monographs, *op. cit.*, p. 112.
100. BUL : *J. J. Papers*, vol. 358, p. 140.
101. Clarence-Smith, *op. cit.*, p. 26.
102. BA : *PD*, 89/1190, 1840, pp. 275-277v; *SRBG*, no. XVII, Bombay 1855, p. 218.
103. Clarence-Smith, *op. cit.*, p. 26.
104. *Ibid.*, p. 28; Greenberg, *op. cit.*, pp. 132-133.
105. Greenberg, *op. cit.*, p. 133.
106. *Ibid.*, pp. 132-133.
107. HAG : *Macau*, 1327, fls. 354-354v; 1334, fl. 210.
108. The Compilation Group, *op. cit.*, pp. 12-13.
109. HAG : *Damão*, 6036, fls. 1-36 : *passim*; 6037, fls. 1-39 : *passim*.
110. HAG : *Macau*, 1327, fls. 324-339, 340; *MR*, 205A, fl. 44.
111. HAG : *Macau*, 1327, fls. 348-348v.112. HAG : *MR*, 205B, doc. dated 14 Feb. 1829.
113. In 1829 and 1830 the duty per chest at Daman if the vessel would move to Lintin was Rs. 88 and Rs. 50 respectively but if the vessel was bound for Macao the duty per chest was fixed at the rate of Rs. 58 and Rs. 30 respectively. In 1831 the duty on 140 lbs. of opium at Daman destined for Lintin was charged at the rate of Rs. 36-0-70 for the first sort, Rs. 26-1-40 for the second sort and Rs. 11-2-60 for the third sort. In the case of opium available at Daman to be shipped to Macao, the customs duties charged on 140 lbs. of opium of the first, second and third sort were Rs. 19-6-60, Rs. 14-2-04, and Rs. 6-1-60 respectively. BA : *RD*, 11/292, 1830, p. 143; 7/335, 1831, pp. 173-175.
114. HAG : *MR*, 205B, doc. dated 14 Feb. 1829.
115. HAG : *MR*, 205B, doc. dated 31 Jan. 1829.
116. HAG : *MR*, 205B, doc. dated 31 Jan. 1829.
117. HAG : *MR*, 205B, doc. dated 31 Jan. 1829.
118. HAG : *MR*, 205B, doc. dated 22 July 1828.
119. HAG : *Macau*, 1334, fl. 100, *Canton Register*, no. 4, vol. 4, 19 Feb. 1831.
120. HAG : *Macau*, 1334, fl. 77v, *Canton Register* no. 20, vol. 4, 15 Oct. 1831; *MR*, 200A, fls. 298-298v.
121. BA : *RD*, 8/336, 1831, doc. dated 12 Jan. 1831.
122. Greenberg, *op. cit.*, p. 49.
123. Pinto, *op. cit.*, p. 185.
124. We have evidence that opium was being produced earlier in Moçambique. In February 1812, 48 arrateis of opium were imported into Goa from Moçambique. *loc. cit.*

6

BIG TRADE : DRAINING AFRICA OF PEOPLE, IVORY AND GOLD

Arab writers like Alberuni, Idrisi and Ibn-ul-Wardi have testified to the age-long, well-organised mutually advantageous exchange network between the East African littoral and India even before the European presence in the Indian Ocean.[1] While gold was the primary product furnished by Moçambique and Sofala to India, ebony wood, ivory and slaves too were bartered for victuals, textiles, glass beads and the like. The celebrated explorer of the Dark Continent, David Livingstone hinted at the existence of similar commercial links between East Africa and India with the coming of the Portuguese.[2]

Trade in Human Cargoes

Even in the period under review the western sector of the Indian Ocean was a scene of brisk and bustling activity. Ships were seen transporting black slaves procured from Sena and other districts up to Quelimane, Tete, Zumbo, Moçambique, islands of Querimbo, Sofala, Inhambane and other areas along the east coast of Africa.[3] The Portuguese Indian traders figured prominently and were well-entrenched in the traditional slave-trading nexus linking the west coast of India and East Africa. They served as agents and middlemen and were particularly active in nothern Moçambique, Cape Delgado, Sofala, Zambezi and Quelimane. Some of them conducted business on behalf of merchants domiciled in Brazil and Portugal, but how much they shipped on their own account remains obscure.

Lisbon merchants with Asian connections, such as Jose Nunes de Silveira, Vicente Tomas dos Santos and Tomas Marie Bessone, were also active in the nineteenth century Moçambique slave trade.[4] Whether they had links with the Goa-Moçambique slave trade network needs further study.

The figures for slave exports in and around the Indian Ocean are difficult to determine, though Benchley's wild guess has placed the figure as high as 200,000 annually.[5] Those pertaining to Goa in the early nineteenth century were considerably minuscular in number.[6] More substantial slave cargoes proceeded to Daman and Diu.[7] Eleven slaves in 1804-05, 90 in 1817-18 and 243 in 1824-29 came from Moçambique to Diu. We see that the shipping of human cargoes was comparatively low during 1804-05, probably due to the insecurity on the high seas caused by the French. But it picked up momentum from 1809 onwards. In the case of Daman, 115 slaves were shipped from Moçambique to Daman in 1827-29 forming a yearly average shipping of 38 slaves. In 1831-32, 43 slaves while in 1833 78 slaves were transported to Daman. Thus the increase over the years was marginal.

It must be borne in mind that slave figures have been drawn from official records and would not be of help to ascertain the clandestine shipping of human cargoes across the Indian Ocean. However the available evidence demonstrates conclusively that the traditional slaving commerce between East Africa and Portuguese India existed, though at a very low level.

On comparing Daman's annual slave imports with those of Diu, during the years 1828-32 one observes that Diu seemed to have a slight edge over Daman in the slave trade. However if one compared Daman's average annual slave imports of the period 1804-33 with those of Diu the picture appears to be different (Refer to Fig. 6.1)

There was a spurt in the trade as a new slave trading channel in the western Indian Ocean was opened during 1770-1830. It hinged around the French islands in the region. Abandoned by the Dutch in 1710, claimed by the French in 1715 and later re-named Isle de France, Mauritius emerged into a strategic centre of French power. In the 1740s, La Bourdonnais built it up as a base of operations against the English in India. By the mid- eighteenth century, Isle de France and her satellites Bourbon (Reunion), Rodrigues and Mascarenhas began to experience an upswing in plantation economy — coffee and sugar production. This led to the development of plantation slavery.[8] Initially the French bought slaves in the established markets of Madagascar and the Comoros, but these markets failed to satisfy French needs.[9] In the later part of the eighteenth century slaves were procured from Moçambique and other parts of East Africa directly, or through agents located in the *Estado da India*.

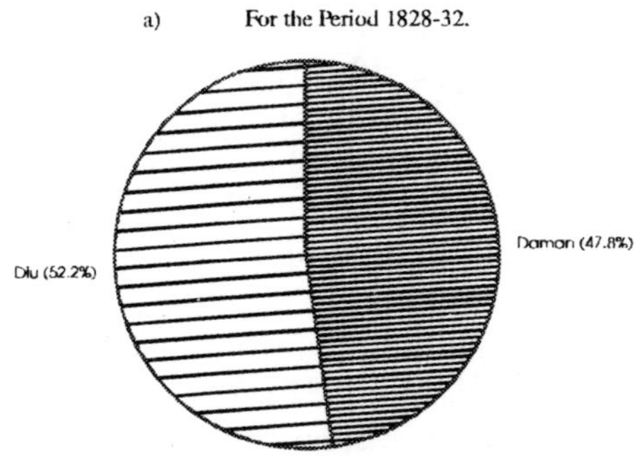

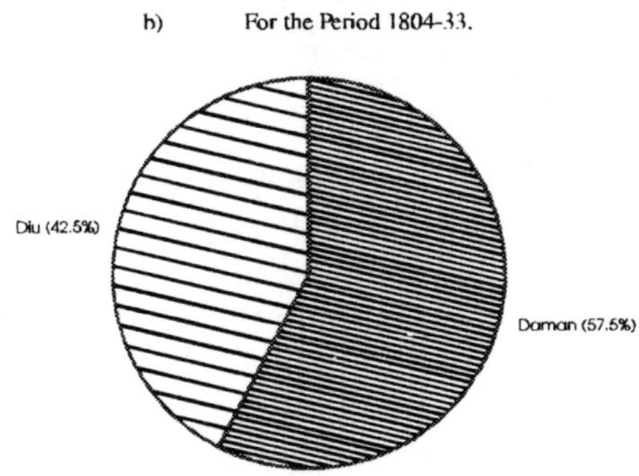

FIG. 6.1 : EXTENT OF SLAVE MOVEMENT FROM MOÇAMBIQUE TO DAMAN AND DIU

Sources: HAG : Compiled from *Dio*, 4952, 4953, 4956, 4959, 4960, 4963, 4965, 4967, 4969; Compiled from *Damão*, 4839, 4841, 4842, 4846, 4848.

Although slaves of African origin were shipped to Asia since times immemorial, no highly organised slave trading network comparable to that in the Atlantic developed in the Indian Ocean until the mid-eighteenth century. The French, drawing on their Caribbean experience, built up a *traite de noirs* that revolved round their insular possessions in the East.[10]

Moçambique needed grain and other victuals as well as arms and ammunition. It expressed its willingness to exchange slaves for such essential items. Besides slaves, the French also brought back cargoes of ivory, gold, and dog-whelk. Apart from Moçambique, the French conducted their trade at Kilwa and enabled it to reach pre-eminence on the East coast of Africa as a slave-trading mart. French slave imports reached their peak during the 1780s when nearly 10,000 slaves were being transported annually from East Africa.[11]

The decree of 1811 reiterated the Portuguese open door policy to ships arriving from Brazil and the French islands in the Indian Ocean in search of slaves to be employed on sugar plantations. This further stimulated the slave traffic.[12]

The Mhamais were involved in the Goa-Moçambique-Mauritius slaving nexus. They supplied slaves from Moçambique to Frenchmen like Coronat and Warnet at Poona, to Boyer, De Court, Canaple, Chalamont based at Mahe, to Michel at Pondicherry and to Berbier and the Monnerons at Mauritius. We find repeated requests made to the Mhamais in the Mhamai House Papers for the despatch of slaves.[13] For instance, in April 1788, Canaple requested the Mhamais to arrange for a young kaffir, 18 to 20 years of age, for which he was prepared to pay Rs. 190. He indicated his expectations: the kaffir had to be intelligent, trust-worthy and capable of conversing in Portuguese, he had to be clean and free of odour and one who could be employed in the kitchen.[14] In March 1796, Monneron at Mahe requested the Mhamais to assist his friend, Ian Murbeck, to purchase slaves at Goa at a reasonable rate.[15]

The customs records too provide evidence on the involvement of the Mhamais and other Goan merchants in the Mauritius-oriented slave commerce. In December 1775, Jose Xavier despatched to Mauritius 70 adult and big-built kaffirs priced 100 *xerafins* each, 12 medium-sized kaffirs for 70 *xerafins* each, 10 small-sized kaffirs for 50 *xerafins* each, 24 negresses for 100 *xerafins* each, and 60 small-sized negresses for 50 *xerafins* each.[16] On 16th and 21st October, 1789, Venkatesha Kamat despatched from Goa to Mauritius, 50 slaves worth 725 *xerafins* and 6 slaves valued at 860 *xerafins* respectively.[17] Similarly, in February 1790 Venkatesha Kamat shipped for the French based at Mauritius, a cargo of 4 big-built kaffirs priced 180 *xerafins* each, 3 *mulatos* for 125 *xerafins* each, 2 small-sized negresses and 3 small-sized kaffirs for 100 *xerafins* each.[18]

In the early 1790s the boom period came to a sad end as the slave market entered a period of slump. The writing was on the wall for the French - Mhamai slave connection. Europe was embroiled then in a series of wars, the echo of which was heard loud and clear in the Indian Ocean region. The Revolutionary period also, created local problems in the French possessions in the East, chiefly because of their stubborn refusal to adopt anti-slavery legislation initiated by the Revolutionary Government.[19]

Though Mauritius continued for some time to be an active slave-trading base, its capture by the British in 1810 and the presence of the British troops in Goa in 1799 until the end of the Napoleonic era, checked the free flow of slave cargoes and effectively clamped down on the slave trading circuit linking Moçambique, the French islands and Portuguese Goa.[20]

Besides direct trade with Moçambique, negro slaves would reach Goa via Surat, Daman, Diu and even Bombay.[21] For instance, in November 1817, one kaffir and one slave arrived at Goa from Bombay. Again, in the same year, one kaffir was transported to Goa from Surat by Henriques to be delivered to Domingos Barboza.[22]

Many African slaves transported to Goa reached other destinations in the Indian Ocean region. The customs records demonstrate quite obviously that slaves were despatched to Macao from Goa.[23] Those engaged in the trade were mainly Christians. Out of the 28 merchants engaged in the Goa-Macao slave trade during 1796-1829, only one was a Hindu namely Kushta Sinai Dhempe and the others were all Christians (96.55 per cent).[24] At the request of their Bombay-based business associate, Rogerio de Faria, the Mhamais dispatched slaves to Macao.[25] In 1804, slaves were sent to Colombo from Goa on the account of the Government of Ceylon.[26] In 1813, once again on the recommendation of Faria, the Mhamais rendered assistance to Charles, of Bruce Fawcett & Co. of Bombay, to purchase slaves at Goa for the Government of Ceylon.[27]

The available documentation demonstrates the steady rise in the prices of slaves over the years during the period under review. During 1771-75, the price of slaves was comparatively low, 100 *xerafins* for an adult, 70 *xerafins* for a medium-sized, and 50 *xerafins* for a young kaffir. An adult negress was priced at 100 *xerafins* and a young one at 50 *xerafins* each. But in 1783, the price rose to 150 *xerafins*, 120 *xerafins* and 85 *xerafins* for a big-built, a medium-sized and a small-sized kaffir respectively. During 1789-1800, the price rose further up to 180, 125 and 100 *xerafins* for a large, a medium and a small kaffir respectively and to 150 and 100 *xerafins* in the case of a large and a medium female slave respectively. The revolutionary wars and the Napoleonic era disturbed the peace of the Indian Ocean and made slave shipping unsafe, which in turn made slave supplies scarce and highly priced. In the 1820s the price of slaves was further hiked to 200, 180 and 120 *xerafins* for a large, a medium and small-sized kaffir respectively. A negress fetched 160 *xerafins* and a young one between 120 to 140 *xerafins*.[28] This upswing may have been due to anti-slavery measures adopted by the British authorities to restrict the flow of slaves across the Indian Ocean.

The slave trading between Moçambique and the *Estado da India* was dominated by Christian merchants. This especially pertained to Goa and Daman.[29] Slaves were brought into Goa to cater to the needs of convents, churches and the Christian population. There was little or no demand for slaves amongst the Hindus and Muslims in Goa.[30]

From available customs records we find that during 1804-33 the *Estado da India* drew a revenue amounting to 5303-3-14 *xerafins* from the Moçambique-Daman-Diu slave trade (Table 6.1). During 1827-33 the Daman *alfandega* contributed 2129-2-16 *xerafins* while during 1804-32 that of Diu contributed 3174-0-58 *xerafins*.

TABLE 6.1 : REVENUES DERIVED BY DAMAN AND DIU FROM THE SLAVE TRADE WITH MOÇAMBIQUE, 1804-33

Year	Diu (In *xerafins*)	Daman (In *xerafins*)
1804	43-3-18	
1805	25-1-45	
1809	169-0-07	
1817	545-3-05	
1818	185-4-30	
1824	110-0-48 (?)	
1825	325-2-56	
1826	241-2-31	
1827	118-1-30	
1828	789-3-32	627-1-45
1829	631-0-24	328-0-47
1830	27-3-37	367-0-20
1831-32	78-4-25	
1833	688-2-54	

Sources: HAG : Compiled from *Dio*, 4952, 4953, 4956, 4959, 4960, 4963, 4965, 4967, 4969; Compiled from *Damão*, 4839, 4841, 4842, 4844, 4846, 4848.

If we are to consider the earnings of the *Estado da India* from the Diu-Moçambique slave commerce in the context of the total revenues accrued from the Diu-Moçambique trade, we observe that the annual average slave revenues obtained during 1804-32 amounted to 264-2-36 *xerafins* while that derived from the Diu-Moçambique trade in its entirety during 1804-32 averaged 20,551-4-02 *xerafins*. (See Tables 6.1 and 6.2). In brief the revenue collection from the Diu-Moçambique slave trade formed just 1.29 percent of the total revenue collection involved in the Diu-Moçambique commerce. Similarly when we compare the revenues accrued by Daman from the slave commerce with Moçambique during 1827-33 with the total revenue benefits it derived from the Moçambique commerce during 1827-40 that is an annual average revenue of 425-4-27 *xerafins* and 14,829-2-56 *xerafins* respectively, we observe that the Daman-Moçambique run yielded revenues to the tune of 2.87 percent of those derived from the total trade of Daman with Moçambique. This indicates that the place of the slave commerce in the overall Daman-Moçambique trade was more significant than its place in the Diu-Moçambique trading nexus.

TABLE 6.2 : TOTAL REVENUES DERIVED BY DAMAN AND DIU FROM THE MOÇAMBIQUE TRADE, 1804-40

Year	Daman (In *xerafins*)	Diu (In *xerafins*)
1804	19278-0-40	
1805	28761-4-51 3/4	
1806	25941-0-51	
1807	12237-2-44 1/2	
1808	12067-1-50 3/4	
1809	16461-0-40 3/4	
1817	15432-0-57 1/2	
1818	27459-4-24 1/2	
1819	11536-2-11 1/2	
1824	17551-1-53	
1825	22823-1-06	
1826	33356-2-41 1/2	
1827	25647-0-45	
1828	22259-0-14 1/2	35438-4-30 1/2
1829	21680-0-53	30247-1-40
1830	23367-1-55	
1831	16858-2-14	15007-3-47 1/2
1832	5147-3-53	2412-1-53 1/2
1839	6355-4-41	
1840	5858-2-51 3/4	

Sources: HAG : Compiled from *Damão*, 4839, 4841, 4842, 4848, 4849, 4851; Compiled from *Dio*, 4952, 4953, 4956, 4960, 4963, 4965, 4967, 4969.

A world-wide resentment against the odious slave trafficking was spearheaded by England in the early nineteenth century. Initially it did not press for the suppression of the Portuguese slave commerce. Although Britain banned trading in slaves by its subjects in 1807, its real concern with Portugal was not the outlawing of slave trading but rather the obtaining of commercial concessions in Brazil which had been closed to British commerce by high customs barriers. In the face of Portuguese reluctance to ban the slave trade, Britain yielded on this subject to the Anglo-Portuguese Treaty of friendship and alliance of 1810, and formally recognised the rights of the Portuguese nation to trade in slaves but insisted on the restriction of the movement of slaves to Portuguese dominions.[31] In fact in England itself prohibition was not taken seriously until the parliamentary reform in 1833. The decrees of the Congress of Vienna of 1815 had made it possible for England to take steps to suppress the foreign slave trade and at the same time to carry out a bouyant smuggling business. From 1807 to 1847, 5,000,000 human beings were carried from Africa to the English colonial territories with the actual suffrance of the government.[32]

Since the signing of the Treaty of 22nd January, 1815 at Vienna, followed by the additional convention of 28th July, 1817, England spared no efforts to solicit Portuguese collaboration and to pressurise Portugal to suppress the slave commerce. A royal decree was issued by the Portuguese government in 1818, at the behest of England, prohibiting the traffic in slaves in Portuguese possessions north of the Equator. Transgression involved stiff penalties: forfeiture of ship and cargoes; the immediate liberation of slaves; ship officials would be heavily fined, dishonoured and exiled to Moçambique for a period of five years; insurance of the ship would be nullified and those guilty of insuring such a ship would suffer the payment of a fine, equivalent to thrice the value of the premium.[33]

As the slave trade persisted despite heavy British patrolling on the high seas, the Portuguese authorities issued another decree on the 10th December 1836 calling for the total abolition of the slave trade in all the Portuguese dominions. This measure was however not rigidly enforced. Three years later an act passed by the British Parliament empowered British cruisers to intercept and detain Portuguese slavers and slave traffickers and to haul them before the British Admirality Court instead of the Mixed Commissions, known for their leniency. This act was repeated in 1842 when Portugal solemnly undertook to suppress the inhuman trade with a heavy hand.[34] In 1849, Gil Joze Conceição a Portuguese official was instructed to keep a vigilant eye over the coast of Goa in keeping with the Portuguese policies and moves directed against slave trafficking.[35]

Although British measures to suppress the slave commerce did affect the overall volume of slaves being sent across the Indian Ocean or the Atlantic, it helped to accelerate the illicit movement of slaves to the remote creeks and inlets, especially river systems with multiple mouths into the sea and then across the Atlantic Ocean to America and the Indian Ocean to western India especially in the 1840s.

Moreover, in their efforts to rigidly enforce anti-slavery regulations, the British authorities were at times faced with peculiar situations. For instance in September 1853, the British apprehended the ship *Quatro de Abril*, on its way from Moçambique to Daman suspected of transporting five African slaves. It was the commander's contention that the five African boys had been brought as servants as permitted by Article V of the Anglo-Portuguese Treaty of 1842 and were not intended for slavery. The matter was taken up before the Supreme Criminal Court.[36]

Despite restrictions the slave trade persisted in Portuguese India. However the official import figures for Goa and Daman during 1837-39 did not exceed 20 slaves.[37] On 7th November, 1847 the sale of a slave named João aged 30, transported from Moçambique was conducted at Goa.[38] In 1855 there were only 134 slaves in Goa and Daman and none in Diu.[39]

Surprisingly, in 1859 the Goa government requested Moçambique to despatch 200 blacks to serve in the army which had been drastically reduced due to a high mortality rate. It was felt that as the blacks were accustomed to the climate they would serve well.[40] Undoubtedly it was only by the last quarter of the nineteenth century around 1878, that most, if not all traces of black slaving disappeared in the *Estado*.

Ivory Trade

Since their appearance in the Indian Ocean waters in the sixteenth century, the Portuguese took charge of the ivory trade of East Africa. Under Portuguese supervision, a steady supply of ivory reached the shores of Portuguese India throughout the sixteenth and the seventeenth centuries. In conformity with an agreement concluded in 1686 with the Mahajans of Diu (*Mazanes de Dio*), the merchants of the *Estado* were permitted to despatch ships laden with Indian merchandise including rice for Moçambique. Their return cargoes included the prized ivory.

The East African trade with the *Estado* in ivory continued to persist in the period under study. Regular shipments of ivory made their appearance at each of the ports of Goa, Daman and Diu.[41] For instance Francisco Soares, scribe at the Customs House at Diu, certified the entry of 370 *candis*, 5 *maons* and 3 *ceiras* of ivory in the year 1767, which produced revenues amounting to 55,538-0-13 *xerafins* at the rate of 150 *xerafins* per *candil*.[42] In 1805 the Goa-based João Baptista Goethals freighted his ship *Nossa Senhora dos Milagres* to Moçambique and returned with ivory cargoes to be delivered to certain merchants of Daman.[43] In the year 1822, a large consignment of ivory came from Portuguese East Africa to Daman on board the vessel *Anna Feliz*, paying 2573 *xerafins* as customs duties.[44]

The Zambezi valley in the eighteenth century emerged as the principal artery through which ivory flowed from the interior to eastern coastal Africa. The *prazos* lining the banks of the river Zambezi became the base of operations for the *mussambazes*, the professional traders who penetrated the interior in search of ivory supplies.[45] In the extreme south, the Indo-Portuguese traders traded in ivory with Inhambane and Cape Delgado. The latter in fact was one of the keys to the ivory trade. The Portuguese had dealings with three major chieftancies that controlled the region. Inevitably the trade suffered from the constant friction between the chiefs, and this in turn affected the volume of ivory exports, which although fairly regular, remained low.[46] Ivory could be bought here at the rate of half a rupee per pound which brought the trader a profit of 400 per cent to 800 per cent.[47] One also witnessed the rise of Zanzibar as a centre of the East African trade in the early nineteenth century. The Zanzibar trade in ivory was financed by banias. Half of their imports at Zanzibar in 1811 consisted of cloth from Kutch and Surat. Each year they wintered in East Africa until September to dispose off their merchandise and to lay their hands on ivory.[48]

At this stage it is significant to note that existing documentation underlines the fact that the Portuguese East African ivory in the period under study was in a state of decline. Liberalisation policies adopted by the Portuguese authorities in keeping with the free trade doctrines of the times and with the view to placating Britain caused a serious dent in the commerce. It had to face the challenges posed by British, Dutch and French competition in East Africa. Despite the reduced state of the trade, capital was accumulated and fortunes were made by Indo-Portuguese merchants.

The total value of the Moçambique-Daman ivory trade for the period 1827-33 stood at 289,742-01-15 *xerafins* that is an annual average value of 57,948-2-03 *xerafins*. In 1840 the value of the aforesaid trade fell dramatically to 5,858-2-51 3/4 *xerafins*, because by this time ivory resources were getting exhausted in East Africa and the trade was reduced to a trickle. In the case of the Moçambique-Diu ivory commerce, its value during 1804-09 amounted to 861,546-1-46 1/4 *xerafins* or an average of 172,309-1-21 per year. However over the years 1824-32 the total value was reduced marginally to 708,517-0-41 1/2 *xerafins* or an annual average value of 118,086-0-57 *xerafins.*[49]

Figure 6.2 helps us to conclude that the ivory trade was more extensively conducted at Diu than at Daman and that the former drew greater material benefits from the ivory import trade.

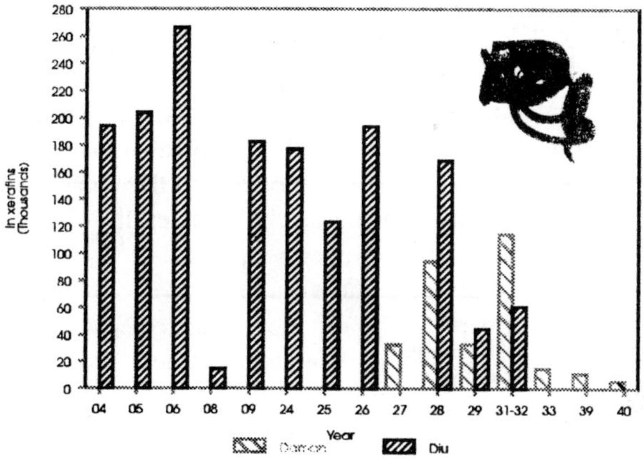

FIG. 6.2: TOTAL VALUE OF IVORY CARGOES SHIPPED TO DAMAN AND DIU FROM MOÇAMBIQUE, 1804-40

Sources: HAG : Compiled from *Damão*, 4839, 4841, 4842, 4846, 4848, 4849; Compiled from *Dio*, 4952, 4953, 4956, 4959, 4960, 4963, 4965, 4969.

Ivory transported from East Africa to Portuguese India would proceed to Lisbon, Macao and elsewhere.[50] According to the Macao customs records, during 1796-1802, on an average about 71.6 tusks of ivory were re-exported by Goa and Daman to Macao. During 1811-17 about 24 *quintais* of ivory arrived at Macao (Table 6.3). Ivory consignments were re-exported to Bombay, Surat and other ports to the north. Thus in April 1813, Caramochande Areachande of Daman informed the Mhamai brothers Venkatesha and Narayana of the despatch of ivory to Surat in accordance with their instructions.[51]

From Table 6.4 we observe that the *Estado da India* despatched tusks to Bombay, Jumbasoor, Bhavnagar and Dhollera in the Bombay Presidency. As regards Bombay during 1819-26 the upper limit of ivory exports touched 60,700 tusks in 1824-25 and the lower limit 4,632 in 1820-21. On an average Portuguese India exported 22,084.57 tusks annually to Bombay during the said period. In the case of Jumbasoor and Amode, Daman and Diu conducted a flourishing trade in ivory with them. Over the period 1818-26 Daman exported an annual average of 78,425.29 tusks to

Jumbasoor and Amode while Diu despatched 53,634.14 tusks. Hence it is clear that Daman's trade with Jumbasoor and Amode was more extensive than that of Diu. Both Daman and Diu exported ivory tusks to Bhavnagar and Dhollera though this trade was sporadic. I have come across just one reference to ivory being shipped to Bhavnagar from Goa. Ivory cargoes occasionally proceeded to Goga. In 1816-17 Diu exported 2,250 tusks to both Bhavnagar and Goga.

TABLE 6.3 : IVORY CONSIGNMENTS FROM GOA AND DAMAN TO MACAO, 1796-1817

Year	Ship	*quintais*	(Quantity) tusks	sacks
1796	Santo Antonio		74	
1797	Luis e Almas Santos		219	
1798	Nossa Senhora da Luz		4	
1800			30	
1802	Esperança		31	
1803				4
1811	Conde de Sarzedas	3		
1812	Angelica		14	
1813	Angelica	25		
1814	Angelica		15	
1815	Angelica	61		
1816	Angelica	5 (?)		
1817	Rainha dos Anjos	2		
	Angelica	24		

Sources: HAG : Compiled from *Macau*, 1295-98, 1305, 1307-11.

Who were the participants in the Moçambique ivory trade? During 1775-1824 the Christian merchants seemed to have established their predominance in the Goa-Moçambique ivory commerce.[52] In the case of the Diu-Moçambique run all 13 merchants involved in 1783 were banias.[53] The merchants who participated in the Daman-Moçambique ivory trade during 1823-40 were a mixed lot.[54] Six of them were banias, four Christians and the rest Muslims.

Ivory tusks brought from Moçambique to Goa were utilized to produce figurines. In 1807 Dineur commissioned the Mhamai brothers to procure two dozen ivory figurines representing couples of different castes of India with their respective names engraved in Portuguese. In case the Goan craftsmen were able to produce figures in different Indian dresses, the brothers were requested to execute the order for four dozen ivory figurines.[55] Ivory statues were also in demand to adorn churches and other centres of religion.[56]

TABLE 6.4 : IVORY RE-EXPORTATION OF THE *ESTADO* TO BOMBAY PRESIDENCY, 1816-26

Year	Bombay (No. of Tusks)	Jumbasoor & (No. of Tusks)		Amode (No. of Tusks)		Bhavnagar (No. of Tusks)		Dhollera (No. of Tusks)
		Daman	Diu	Goa	Daman	Diu	Daman	Diu
1816-17						2250*		
1818-19		185600	39150		14090	10485		
1819-20	13147	117708	58780		494	5286		
1820-21	4632	34640	79008				127	
1821-22	11810	81647	78665	4219		5025		
1822-23	6116	74432	24420		1612	2000		
1823-24	30396							
1824-25	60700	47690	55010					15600
1825-26	27791	7260	40406				41200	

Sources: BA : *MRIEC*, vol. 16/17, 30 April 1817; vol. 18, Part II, 8 Oct. 1819; vol. 19, 30 April 1820; vol. 20, 30 April 1821, 31 Oct. 1821; vol. 21, 30 April 1821, 31 Oct. 1822; vol. 22, 30 April 1823, 31 Oct. 1823; vol. 23, 31 Oct. 1824; vol. 24, 30 April 1825, 31 Oct. 1825; vol. 25, 30 April 1826, 31 Oct 1826.

Note: * Figure in common with Goga.

During 1804-39 the *Estado* derived revenues totalling 178,141-3-42 *xerafins* from the Moçambique-Daman-Diu ivory commerce. Diu supplied 126,317-3-42 3/4 *xerafins* during 1804-32 and Daman provided 51,823-0-00 *xerafins* during 1818-1839 (Table 6.5). If we compare the ivory revenue figures of Daman with its total revenue collection for the period 1827-39, we observe that they amounted to 24,308-3-24 *xerafins* and 103,807-0-32 1/4 *xerafins* respectively (Tables 6.2 and 6.5). In brief the ivory revenue collection amounted to 23.42 per cent of the total revenue of Daman. On the otherhand if we analyse the ivory revenue figures of Diu and compare them with the total revenue collection for the years 1804-32, we observe that they amounted to 126,317-3-42 3/4 *xerafins* and 349,380-3-39 1/4 *xerafins* respectively. Thus the Diu-based ivory trade amounted to 36.15 per cent of the total revenue yield. The place of the ivory commerce in the Moçambique-Daman-Diu trade was much more significant compared to that of the slave trade.

By the 1830s ivory around the ports of northern Moçambique was growing scarce, and though ivory supplies could be acquired from the interior of Africa they moved to Zanzibar where the Omani Arabs imposed less onerous duties than the Portuguese. Ivory exports from southern Moçambique were expanding, yet the trend discernible was the diversion of these supplies to western markets. Furthermore, the *prazos* were in a state of flux owing to the abolition of feudal tenure by Portugal in the 1830s and the Nguni menace.[57] In spite of such a state of affairs, ivory cargoes continued to be shipped to the *Estado* even in the 1840s.

TABLE 6.5: REVENUES DERIVED BY DAMAN AND DIU FROM THE MOÇAMBIQUE IVORY TRADE, 1804-39

Year	Daman (In *xerafins*)	Diu (In *xerafins*)
1804	10933-4-27	
1805	12687-1-50 1/4	
1806	15010-0-20 3/4	
1808	818-0-36	
1809	10288-4-16 3/4	
1817	9451-3-59	
1818	16816-2-19	9781-2-23
1819	10697-4-17	7617-2-37 1/2
1824	6593-3-19	
1825	7562-3-28	
1826	11375-4-34 1/2	
1827	2228-3-56	
1828	7792-3-46	9519-0-20 1/2
1829	2664-2-13	2867-3-17
1830	5582-1-58	
1831-32	9443-3-41	6227-1-15 1/2
1833	1246-3-01	
1839	932-1-47	

Sources: HAG : Compiled from *Dio*, 4952, 4953, 4956, 4959, 4960, 4963, 4965, 4969; Compiled from *Damão*, 4839, 4841, 4842, 4846, 4848, 4849.

Trade in Precious Metals and Bullion

The liberalisation of trade in 1769 brought about dramatic structural changes in the economic system of East Africa. The Luso-Atlantic slave trade caused a spectacular increase in the circulation of gold and silver coins in Moçambique. This situation drew hordes of banias from the *Estado da India* to East Africa causing the massive outflow of precious metals and bullion to western coastal India throughout the eighteenth century. The banias continued to exert a firm hold over the Moçambican economy, extracting as much profit as they could from the helpless East African natives and remitting their vast accumulated fortunes back home to India.[58]

We have plenty of evidence of the arrival of gold, silver and bullion in Portuguese India. On 1st November 1785, Mochande Premogy, Vady Gichande and Morargy Amaidas brought from Moçambique to Diu 160, 24-1/2 and 49 *patacas* respectively. Morargy Amaidas and Migogy Canacondas brought 10 and 35-1/2 *maticaes* of gold dust, respectively.[59] Similarly, in the same year 3,112 1/2 *patacas* and 1,510 *maticaes*, 1 *quarto* and 6 *graons* of gold arrived at Diu from Moçambique in a vessel belonging to Mulgi Raghunath.[60] In October 1793, 1 *marco*, 3 *onças* and 4 *oitavas* of gold were shipped into Goa by Venkatesha Kamat.[61] On 27th October 1795, gold consignments of 4 *onças* and 2 *oitavas*, 7 *onças* and 2 *oitavas*, and 9 *marcos* and 6 *onças* were brought on board the vessel *S. Anna* into Goa by Vithoba Kamat Mhamai, Rama Naik and Venkatesha Kamat respectively.[62]

The lively trade between the *Estado* and East Africa in gold was fed by Sofala, Sena and other districts upto Quelimane, Tete, Zumbo and Manice identified as key centres of gold supply.[63] Linschoten wrote in 1506, that gold came to India primarily from the lands of Monomatopa and Sofala. He refers to Monomatopa as a mine of gold that *Portingales* called *Botonga* and *ouro em po*.[64] To Tavernier, the purest and finest gold was derived from the lands of Monomatopa and was extracted without great difficulty by excavating the ground only to a depth of two to three feet. At times and at certain places in the region, gold was found on the surface of the ground in nuggets in all kinds of shapes and weights. He also mentions the availability of an inferior kind of gold dust at Mouran in several rivers which joined the Sena.[65]

From Fig. 6.3 we observe that the value of the Diu-based trade in precious metals and bullion was more than that of Daman and Goa. The average value of the *Estado's* bullion trade with Moçambique during 1804-39 amounted to 297,408-4-48 *xerafins*, that of Goa totalling 22,949-1-51 *xerafins*, of Daman 88,363-2-15 *xerafins* and of Diu 186,096-0-42 *xerafins*.[66] Therefore we can conclude that the bullion flow into Diu was more extensive than that into the other two Portuguese enclaves.

Apart from Moçambique, bullion would also arrive at Goa from Lisbon, Macao and Brazil.[67] On 13th November, 1792, 147 *meyas doblas* and 3,288 *reis* arrived from Lisbon.[68] On the following day, 71 *meyas doblas* and 275 *reis* together with 721 *patacas* and 542 *reis* were brought to Goa from Lisbon. Bullion brought from the metropolis was gainfully employed in procuring Indian textiles, spices, saltpetre and other Asian products, much sought after in Portugal.

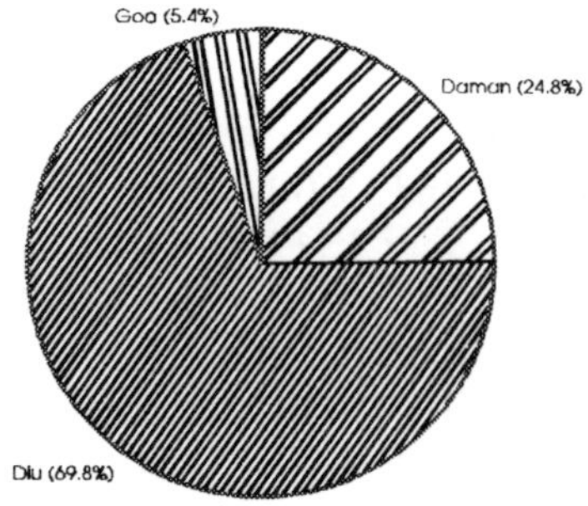

FIG. 6.3 : TOTAL VALUE OF THE *ESTADO*-MOÇAMBIQUE BULLION TRADE, 1804-39.

Sources: HAG : Compiled from *Dio*, 4952, 4953, 4956, 4959, 4960, 4963, 4967, 4969; Compiled from *Damão*, 4839, 4841, 4842, 4846, 4848, 4849; AG, 2668, fl. 2; 11318, fls. 2-12; 9869, fls. 1v-2.

The official records indicate that the prices of gold, silver and bullion arriving from Moçambique remained more or less stable during the period under study. The price of gold, gold-dust and gold articles in 1791 was 450 *xerafins* per *marco* and remained so at least till 1826. The cost of silver was 40 *xerafins* in 1816 and was the same in 1826. *Patacas* and *meyas doblas* were valued at 4-4-00 *xerafins* and 36 *xerafins* respectively in 1816 and possessed the same value in 1826.[69]

There was definitely lucre in the gold and bullion trade for the *Estado*. It added substantially to the State coffers in terms of customs duties levied. This is indicated by Table 6.6.

The revenues derived by the *Estado* during 1827-39 from the Daman-based bullion trade amounted to 8,824-4-49 *xerafins* that is only 8.50 per cent of the total revenues of Daman drawn from its trade with Moçambique during the same period (Tables 6.2 and 6.6). Diu on the otherhand obtained during 1804-32 revenues to the tune of 64,721-1-22 1/4 *xerafins* from its bullion import trade with Moçambique. This formed 18.52 percent of the total customs revenues collected at Diu for the said period. As regards the bullion revenues collected at Goa, Table 6.6 demonstrates that during 1824-38, duties imposed on bullion arriving from Moçambique amounted to just 590-2-51 *xerafins* that is an average of about 147-3-12 *xerafins* per annum. From the above analysis we thus conclude that Diu profited the most from the bullion trade with Moçambique.

The trade also stimulated currency and coinage in the State. It appears that bullion and precious metals arriving from Moçambique made its way to the Goa Mint (*Casa da Moeda*) as raw material for the production of Portuguese coins.[70] However, the greatest beneficiaries were the merchants engaged in the contraband trade in gold. Despite stringent regulations demanding the registration of gold at the *Casa da Moeda* within eight days of its arrival at the port of Goa, much of the gold was probably, illegally transported to the mainland mint at Ponda.[71] Gold would also flow out of the Portuguese dominions for the purchase of tobacco and pepper in Kanara.[72] Gujaratis and cloth merchants would exchange their wares at Goa for gold. Precious metals were hoarded by the natives of Goa in their natural form or as ornaments at home or on the mainland to enhance and enrich family fortunes.

TABLE 6.6 : REVENUES DERIVED BY THE *ESTADO* FROM THE BULLION TRADE WITH MOÇAMBIQUE, 1804-39

Year	Goa (In *xerafins*)	Daman (In *xerafins*)	Diu (In *xerafins*)
1804			1840-2-29 1/2
1805			3286-2-58 3/4
1806			3167-1-30
1807			485-0-16 1/2
1808			1217-2-24 1/2
1809			5255-0-49
1816			
1817			5348-1-46
1818			4614-3-39 1/2
1824	372-2-45		2201-3-54
1825			4927-2-06
1826			14854-1-00
1827		3177-4-09	
1828		2987-1-14 1/2	9587-3-52 1/2
1829		2248-1-18	5253-0-15
1830			2539-2-51
1831-32		386-2-12	142-1-30
1833	201-2-36	24-4-00	
1834	6-4-30		
1838	9-3-00		
1839		0-1-55 1/2	

Sources: HAG : Compiled from *Damão*, 4839, 4841,4842, 4846, 4848, 4849; Compiled from *Dio*, 4952, 4953, 4956, 4959, 4960, 4963, 4967, 4969; AG, 8125, fls. 3-34 : *passim*; 9869, fls 1-5v; 11318, fls. 2, 5, 8, 12.

As regards the merchants engaged in the Goa-Moçambique bullion trade, in 1824-38 all of them were Christians.[73] But in Daman the involvement in the bullion commerce with Moçambique in 1800-27 was an all bania affair.[74] Occasionally we come across the participation of Christians. João Manoel Luis and Fr. Lourenço dos Milagres participated in the said trade in 1826. The same can be said with reference to Diu. According to the official records, nearly all the participants in the trade in 1804 were banias. A few Muslims and Parsees figured in it.[75]

The State entered into gold contracts to dispose off the gold brought from Moçambique so as to be employed and invested in saltpetre and other items of Asia to be shipped to Lisbon. During 1767-69 the contracts were exclusively with Hindu businessmen.[76] Once again we have evidence of the predominance of the Hindus in the Goan economy. We also observe that the quantity of gold assigned to a contractor in the said period was never more than 6 *marcos*, 5 *onças* and 7 *oitavas*. On an average about 4 *marcos* were assigned to a contractor. The price of gold under the contracts ranged between 401 *xerafins* and 450 1/2 *xerafins* per *marco*. Moreover the contract had a maximum value of 2,814-4-50 *xerafins* and never fell below 444-0-07 *xerafins* during the said period.

By the 1830s gold production in the Zimbabwean plateau revealed a marked decline for technical reasons as the miners were in no position to pump out water when they reached the water-table. Moreover, gold reserves in this region were rapidly getting exhausted.[77] Accordingly, the gold flow to the west coast of India was gradually reduced to a trickle.

REFERENCES AND NOTES

1. Teotonio R. de Souza, "The Afro-Asian Church in the Portuguese Estado da India", *African Church Historiography : An Ecumenical Council Perspective*, (ed.) Ogbu U. Kale, Nairobi, 1986, p. 57.
2. William Francis Rea, *The Economics of the Zambezi Missions 1580-1759*, Roma, 1976, pp. 117, 120.
3. HAG : *MR*, 152A, fls. 134-134v; AHU : *Moçambique*, Caixa 38, doc. no. 27, doc. dated 5 March 1782.
4. Gervase Clarence-Smith, *The Third Portuguese Empire, 1825-1975, A study in Economic Imperialism*, Manchester/Dovey, 1985, pp. 35-36.
5. Celsa Pinto, "Goa-based Overseas and Coastal Trade (18th - 19th Centuries)", *Goa Through the Ages*, vol. II, (ed.) Teotonio R. de Souza, New Delhi, 1989, p. 188.
6. *Ibid.*, p. 206; HAG : *AG*, 2668, fl. 2; 6809, fls. 282, 403; 9256, fl. 46; 6810, fls. 474-508 : *passim*; 6814, fls. 26, 55, 117, 729; 9258, fls. 39, 342-343; 9260, fls. 3-5; 9261, fls. 2-5, 233-239, 278; 9254, fls. 1, 192, 216, 335, 763-771 : The chief participants in the Moçambique-Goa channel in 1796, were Antonio Lourenço, Domingos João Manoel de Macedo, Joze Manoel de Conceição, Tome de Miranda, João Antonio Alvarez, Manoel Antonio Fernandes, Jeremias Luis Roiz, Matheus Fernandes, Antonio Joaquim de Matheus, Antonio de Noronha; *AG*, 9246, fls. 201-213 : In 1811-1813, those actively involved were Inacio Xavier Unhão, Vicente de Rocha, Diogo Francisco

Menezes, João Rozario and others. Slaves were despatched to Joaquim Floriano de Rocha, Florenço de Remedios and Inacio da Silva in Goa.

7. See Appendix 9.
8. Pinto, *op. cit.*, p. 190; Holden Furber, *Rival Empires of Trade in the Orient, 1600-1800*, Minnesota/Oxford, 1976, pp. 14, 275.
9. M. D. D. Newitt, "East Africa and Indian Ocean Trade Network 1500-1800", *India and the Indian Ocean, 1500-1800,* (eds.) Ashin Das Gupta and M. N. Pearson, Calcutta, 1987, p. 218.
10. Furber, *op. cit.*, p. 318.
11. Pinto, *op. cit.*, p. 190; Newitt, *op. cit.*, pp. 218-219.
12. A. Rita-Ferreira, "Moçambique e Os Naturais de India Portuguesa", *II Seminário Internacional de Historia Indo-Portuguesa*, Lisboa, 1985, p. 622.
13. Teotonio R. de Souza, "French Slave Trading in Portuguese Goa", *Essays in Goan History*, New Delhi, 1989, pp. 120-128; XCHR : *MHP* : passim.
14. XCHR : *MHP* (French), vol. 3, fl. 99; Teotonio R. de Souza, "Goa-Mahe Trade Links (Late Eighteenth-Early Nineteenth Centuries) : A New Source Material", *Studies in Maritime History,* (ed.) K. S. Mathew, Pondicherry, 1990, p. 170.
15. XCHR : *MHP* (Portuguese), doc. dated 11 March 1796.
16. HAG : *AG*, 8114, fl. 106.
17. HAG : *AG*, 6807, fls. 307, 317, 735.
18. HAG : *AG.*, 6327, fl. 163.
19. Pinto, *op. cit.*, pp. 190-191.
20. Souza, "French Slave Trading in Portuguese Goa", pp. 128-129; Pinto, *op. cit.*, p. 191.
21. HAG : *AG*, 6334, fl. 629; 9261, fls. 11, 13, 23, 30; Pinto, *op. cit.*, p. 207.
22. HAG : *AG*, 6826, fl. 37.
23. Refer to Appendix 10.
24. *Ibid.*
25. Pinto, *op. cit.*, p. 191.
26. P. P. Shirodkar, "Slavery in Coastal India", *Purabhilekh-Puratatva*, vol. III, no. 1, Jan.-June 1985, p. 36.
    This is indicated in the letter dated 31st December, 1804, of Sir William Clarke, in charge of the British occupation forces of Goa, to the Government of Bombay.
27. Souza, *op. cit.*, p. 129.
28. The *Alfandega de Goa* records provide details on slave pricing.
29. HAG : *AG*, 6809, fls. 228, 282, 403; 6810, fls. 474-508 :*passim*; 6814, fls. 26, 55, 117, 729.
30. HAG : *AG*, 6317, fls. 30-32.
31. Clarence-Smith, *op. cit.*, p. 30.
32. Max Weber, *General Economic History*, (transl.) Franck H. Knight, New York, 1961, p. 224.
33. HAG : *MR*, 196A, fls. 175, 194-195.
34. Clarence-Smith, *op. cit.*, p. 30; BNL : *Regulação para a Navegação de Passageiros com Escravos*", doc. dated 5 Oct. 1846.
35. HAG : *Moçambique*, 1449, fl. 42.
36. HAG : *MR*, 227, doc. dated 26 Nov. 1853.
37. Jeanette Pinto, "Slavery in Portuguese Goa, 1510-1842", Unpublished Thesis, University of Bombay, 1985, p. 45.
38. HAG : *MR*, 222, fl. 428.
39. HAG : *Escravos*, 2976, fl. 2v; 2977, fls. 1-4; 2978, fls. 2-2v; 2979, fls. 2v-4; 2980, fl. 3; 2981, fls. 2-2v; 3016, fls. 2v-3; 3017, fls. 2-2v; 3018, fls. 2v-5; There were 41

slaves in Ilhas, 9 in Salcette, 49 in Bardez, 1 in New Conquest areas, 34 in Daman and none in Diu.

40. HAG : *Moçambique*, 1449, fls. 81v-82.
41. HAG : *Damão*, 4846, fls. 13-13v; 4847, fl. 247; 4848, fls. 26, 56, 95; 4849, fls. 14-16; 4850, fl. 14; *Dio*, 5665, fls. 166-173; *AG*, 6323, fls. 142-181 : *passim*; 6331, fls. 492, 616, 655; 6802, fls. 428, 491; 6807, fls. 332-630 : *passim*; 6814, fl.55; 8114, fls. 1, 154; 8115, fls. 68-92v, 8117, fls. 31, 116; 8119, fls. 242-243.
42. HAG : *PDCF*, 1156, fl. 144.
43. HAG : *RGF*, 2153, fl. 73.
44. A. F. Moniz, A visit to Daman, *The Examiner*, 8 March, 1913, p. 13.
45. Newitt, *op. cit.*, p. 214.
    Basically the *prazo* was an agricultureal enterprise. Concessions were granted initially by African chiefs and later by the Portuguese Crown which ensured tenure over the land. The tenant or *prazeiro* enjoyed the privilege of exercising jurisdiction over the free Africans in his area, accepted tributes from them and counted on their assistance in times of war. His slaves would cultivate for him whatever land he needed within his jurisdiction.
46. *Ibid.*, p. 215.
47. HAG : *MR*, 161E, fls. 1034-1034v.
48. Asiya Siddiqi, "Some Aspects of Indian Business under the East India Company", *State and Business in India : A Historical Perspective*, (ed.) Dwijendra Tripathi, New Delhi, 1986, pp. 6-7.
49. See Appendix 11.
50. HAG : *AG*, 9270, fls. 1v-2, 11v-12.
51. XCHR : *MHP* (Portuguese), doc. dated 17 April 1813.
52. HAG : *AG*, 6323, fls. 142-181 : *passim*; 6331, fls. 492, 616, 655; 6802, fls. 428, 491; 6807, fls. 332-630 : *passim*; 6814, fl. 55; 8114, fls. 1, 154; 8115, fls. 68-92v; 8117, fls. 31, 116; 8119, fls. 242-243.
53. HAG : *Dio*, 5665, fls. 166-173.
54. HAG : *Damão*, 4846, fls. 13-13v; 4847, fl. 247; 4848, fls. 26, 56, 95; 4849, fls. 14-16; 4850, fl. 14.
55. XCHR : *MHP* (French), vol. 6, fl. 39.
56. Fundação Calouste Gulbenkian, *A Expansão Portuguesa e a Arte do Marfim*, Lisboa, 1991, pp. 39, 43-44, 58-60, 63, 68-69, 76-78, 91, 139, 156, 161, 166, 171, 174, 178, 186-188; Bernardo Ferrão de Tavares e Tavora, *Imaginária Luso-Oriental*, Lisboa, 1983, pp. 49, 52, 183.
57. Pinto, *op. cit.*, p. 187; Clarence-Smith, *op. cit.*, p. 34.
58. Rita-Ferreira, *op. cit.*, pp. 622-624.
59. HAG : *Provisões*, 7926, fls. 38-39.
60. HAG : *Provisões*, 7926, fls. 37-38.
61. XCHR : *MHP* (Portuguese), doc. dated 29 Oct. 1793.
62. XCHR : *MHP*, doc. dated 27 Oct. 1793.
63. HAG : *MR*, 152A, fls. 134-134v.
64. Arthur Coke Burnell, (ed.) *The Voyage of John Huyghen Van Linschoten to the Indies*, vol. I, New Delhi/Madras, 1988, p. 31.
65. Jean-Baptiste Tavernier, *Travels in India*, vol. II, London, 1925, pp. 125, 127.
66. Refer to Appendix 12.
67. HAG : *AG*, 9869, fls. 1v-2; 11318, fls. 2-12; *MR*, 203A, fls. 294v-250; Celsa Pinto, "At the Dusk of the Second Empire : Goa-Brazil Commercial Relations 1770-1825", *Purabilekh-Puratatva*, vol. VIII, no. 1, Jan.-June 1990, pp. 53, 67-69.
68. XCHR : *MHP* (Portuguese), docs. dated 13 Nov. 1792, 14 Nov. 1792.

69. HAG : *AG*, 8125, fls. 11-30; 11318, fls. 2-12.
70. HAG : *PDCF*, 2754, doc. dated 13 Jan. 1813.
71. Teotonio R. de Souza, "A Study on Indo-Portuguese Coinage and the Working of the Goa Mint", pp. 9-10.
72. Pinto, *op. cit.*, p. 44.
73. HAG : *AG*, 9869, fls. 1-4v, 25; 11318, fls. 2-12.
74. HAG : *Damão*, 1061, fl. 124, 136, 194, 321, 419, 420; 1063, doc. dated 9 Nov. 1815; 1070, doc. dated 8 Oct. 1822; 1071, doc. dated 22 Oct. 1824; 1073, doc. dated 3 June 1827.
75. HAG : *Dio*, 4952, fls. 24v-29.
76. Refer to Appendix 13.
77. Pinto, *Goa-based Overseas and Coastal Trade*, p. 187; Clarence-Smith, *op. cit.*, p. 34.

7

SMALL TRADE : ESSENTIAL INGREDIENTS, TEXTILES, TOBACCO AND TIMBER

Although trading in luxury and high-value commodities occupied the centre-stage of the Portuguese Indian Ocean commercial system even in the late eighteenth-early nineteenth centuries bulk, low-value goods and essentials like coarse textiles, tobacco, timber and the like had figured significantly in the commercial world of the *Estado da India*. Each of them had their respective roles to play. Coarse textiles by and large, formed the largest component of the bulk cargoes leaving the ports of Portuguese India. Tobacco imports, while serving to cater to the needs of the tobacco-addicted folk of the Estado were a source of considerable revenue for the Portuguese treasury. Timber was essential for ship-building.

Textiles

From the sixteenth to the eighteenth centuries, particularly in the decades prior to 1770, fine Indian textiles, from Madras, Bengal, Surat, Diu, Daman and other parts of India were being forwarded to Portugal, Brazil and West Africa. That this trade in textiles was a source of rich returns, was demonstrated by the fact that the Lisbon vessels brought to India bullion belonging to Lisbon-based merchants or their crew especially for the purpose of procuring Indian fabrics for sale at Lisbon, Bahia and elsewhere.[1] Moreover, privately operated shipping conveyed cargoes of Indian cotton fabrics to South-East Asia, China, Japan and East Africa.

Since the 1780s trade in finished cotton goods underwent major structural changes. The picture that emerges from the official records is one of infinite variety, colour and movement. The trickle of the mid-eighteenth century developed into a flood.

The quality and texture of the fabrics that figured in the said trade were very diverse as reflected in the customs house records, in the invoices for export in private business papers, and in the price and tariff lists of the late eighteenth-early nineteenth centuries. There were calicoes of very coarse quality for daily use by the poor and muslins and silks of delicate softness for the elite. There were piece-goods, household articles, such as table cloths, serviettes, curtains and bed linen and those of apparel, such as skirts, kimonos, scarves, *lungis, dupattas, ornis, dhotis* and *pudvins*.[2]

From the available price lists it appears that tafetas, raw silk (*seda crua*), *molmols, panos sadins, morins,* and velvet (*veluda*) could be categorised as the more expensive textiles. The moderately-priced textiles included *cutinias, cadeas, coromandeis, chellas, chitas, zuartes, savaigagins, marchas, beatilhas, canequins, anagoas, sanas, durgogins, tofulis, tiadas, naguinas* and *biloras*. The cheaper category of textiles included *tucorins, bartingis, botians, carlaganis, panos de cafre,* and *palangapuço*.[3] From shipping lists it is evident that the moderately-priced and cheaper varieties of textiles figured more prominently in the export trade of Portuguese India in the late eighteenth-early nineteenth centuries.

The textile trade of Portuguese India appears to have operated in two distinct ways. There was firstly a bi-lateral trade between the *Estado* ports and the other ports of India and Asia. Locally produced goods were marketed in exchange for other goods. Daman, for instance, exported varieties of home-produced textiles namely, *tiadas, canequins, chitas, anagoas, beatilhas, zuartes, bartingis, cutinias, savaigagins, cadeas, tufolis*, and household products such as table cloths, serviettes, pillows, cushions and bed-linen.[4] Diu on the other, manufactured and exported *panos de joris, panos de begagis, panos de durgogins, panos picotilhos, chellas, anagoas, bartingis, chondrins, cutinias, chitas, marchas, naguinas, savaigagins*, besides bed-linen, handkerchiefs, thread, pillows, skirts and the like.[5]

The *Estado*-based bilateral trade assumed another dimension — the import of textiles from certain parts of Asia for home consumption. Varieties of Chinese textiles such as damasks, *retroz, tabias*, velvet, satin designated as *setim preta, setim mandarin, setim de cantão, setim de cores, setim laurado* and other silks were shipped to Portuguese India to cater to the tastes of the elite.[6] From Persia, the *Estado* imported a variety of piece-goods and fabrics, such as *girabolos* of gold, silver and silk, *dorains*, self-coloured and printed velvets, *alcatigas, cambolins, tirmoens* and carpets.[7]

The other trading pattern was in the nature of a transit trade via Goa.

Indian textile products drawn from various supply centres of coastal India were brought to Goa. After paying a re-exportation fee they would be shipped across the Indian Ocean to East Africa and beyond the Cape of Good Hope to Lisbon, Angola and Brazil. The massive outflow of textiles as reflected in the customs house records indicates the demand for such goods in the overseas markets.

A reversal in Portuguese trading policies provided the stimulus for the massive scale trans-shipment of Indian textiles via the *Estado da India*. Prior to 1783, exhorbitant duties levied at Goa, severely restricted Goa's overseas trade. Just one or two ships docked at the port of Goa. The *Alvará Regio* of 8th January, 1783 marked a departure from the earlier stance adopted by the Portuguese authorities. Several import/export duties were abolished. All merchandise re-exported from this port was taxed a low 4 per cent trans-shipment fee.[8]

The 1790s spurt in the outflow of cotton products owed its origin to Portugal's neutrality during the European wars and the fact that it was at peace with France. Portuguese merchants especially those of the *Estado da India*, could easily ship their textile cargoes into the European continent while other traders were hampered by the British blockade.[9]

The outflow of textiles from Daman and Diu to Moçambique was substantial. This is demonstrated by Fig. 7.1.

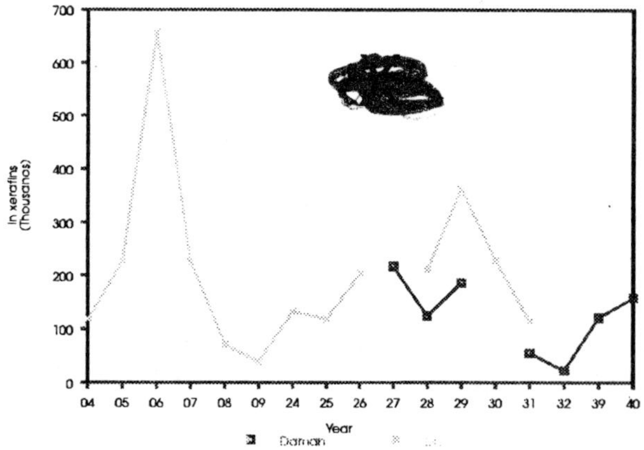

FIG 7.1: TOTAL VALUE OF THE TEXTILE TRADE OF DAMAN AND DIU WITH MOÇAMBIQUE, 1804-40

Sources: HAG : Compiled from *Damão*, 4839, 4841, 4842, 4846, 4848, 4849, 4851; Compiled from *Dio*, 4952, 4953, 4956, 4959, 4960, 4963, 4965, 4969.

The export trade of both Daman and Diu in textiles brought substantial gains for the *Estado da India* as indicated in Table 7.1. As regards Daman, in 1827, out of the total revenues amounting to 25,647-0-45 *xerafins* derived by it from its trade with Moçambique the textile revenues totalled 19,980-0-40 *xerafins*, that is, about 77.90 per cent of the total revenues. In 1831, the textile revenues amounted to 6,580-1-40 xerafins. This formed about 39.03 per cent of the total revenue of 16,858-2-14 *xerafins*. In 1832, the revenues drawn from the textile exports amounted to 2,591-2-50 *xerafins*. This amounted to about 50.34 per cent of the total revenues that is 5,147-3-53 *xerafins*. It seems that the textile revenues acquired by Daman ranged between 40 and 80 per cent of the total revenues drawn from the Daman-Moçambique trade (Tables 6.2 and 7.1).

TABLE 7.1: REVENUES OBTAINED BY DAMAN AND DIU FROM ITS TEXTILE TRADE WITH MOÇAMBIQUE, 1818-40

Year	Diu (In *xerafins*)	Daman (In *xerafins*)
1818	14865-0-54 1/2	
1819	11536-2-11 1/2	
1824	8209-2-37	
1825	9123-1-06	
1826	12990-3-20 1/2	
1827		19980-0-40
1829	26597-3-20 1/2	16054-1-41
1830	15613-1-08 1/2	
1831	6487-3-08	6580-1-40
1832		2591-2-50
1839		4416-2-08
1840		5858-2-51 3/4

Sources: HAG : Compiled from *Damão*, 4839, 4841, 4842, 4846, 4848, 4849, 4851; Compiled from *Dio*, 4956, 4959, 4960, 4963, 4965, 4969.

Almost the same trend was observed in the case of Diu. In 1818 the textile revenues of Diu amounting to 14,865-0-54 1/2 *xerafins* formed about 54.13 per cent of the total revenues from its trade with Moçambique totalling 27,459-4-24 1/2 *xerafins*. (See Tables 6.2 and 7.1). In 1825 the revenues from the textile trade amounted to 9,123-1-06 *xerafins* that is about 39.97 per cent of the total revenues, 22,823-1-06 *xerafins* acquired from the Moçambique trade. In 1829 the textile revenues of Diu from its Moçambique trade amounted to 26,597-3-20 1/2 *xerafins* that is about 87.93 per cent of the total revenues 30,247-1-40 *xerafins*.

The export of textiles from Goa to Moçambique was also considerable as indicated in the records.[10] These fabrics were usually drawn from Daman, Diu and Gujarat. In 1791 for instance, a cargo of textiles was despatched to Moçambique on board the ship *Ferdinand.*[11] In 1835, 12 shirts of long cloth material were shipped by *Maria* to Moçambique from Goa.[12] On board the same vessel, Victor Mariano Araujo exported *carlaganis.*[13]

There was a steady flow of Indian fabrics to Lisbon since the 1790s up to the 1820s.[14] Table 7.2 shows us that in 1790-92 two ships arrived at Lisbon laden with cotton products from Goa and the Malabar coast. They were meant for the *Sociedade de Rebeiro, Hubens e Companhia.*

TABLE 7.2: ARRIVAL OF TEXTILES AT LISBON, 1790-92

Date	Ship	Nature and Quantity	
Sept. 1790	Rainha	240	*fardos* of Surat textiles
	dos	265	*fardos* of Balaghat textiles
	Anjos	1	*fardo* of Daman textiles
July 1791	Princeza	429	*fardos* of Surat textiles
	de	16	*fardos* of Balaghat textiles
	Portugal	2	*fardos* of Diu textiles
Sept. 1792	Rainha	680	*fardos* of Surat textiles
	dos	290	*fardos* of Balaghat textiles
	Anjos	9	*fardos* of Diu textiles
		1	*fardo* of Daman textiles

Source: AHU : *MI*, Maço 47, no. 310, doc. dated Sept. 1790.

In March 1793, 1159 *fardos* and 131 *trouxas* of Indian textiles worth 41,862-0-33 41/82 *xerafins* were transported to Lisbon from India on board the vessel *Nossa Senhora de Bellem* captained by Joze Francisco de Perne. The expenses incurred at Goa and in the northern enclaves were 1,166-1-21 1/2 (?) and 2,198--3-27 *xerafins* respectively. The commission charged was 4 per cent.[15]

Besides textiles from Surat, Balaghat, Daman and Diu available on the west coast of India, Lisbon merchants had a fascination for textiles available at Bengal and Madras. Private Lisbon shipping would in fact proceed directly to the east coast to scour the ports for textiles and commodities in demand in Europe without touching the west coast of India.[16] All that the Lisbon merchants were concerned with was promoting their business interests and piling up fortunes. They experienced no twinge of conscience when they moved directly to the Coromandel coast without docking at the *Estado* ports. The Lisbon government seemed indifferent to this at least till 1799, even though it affected the interests of the *Carreira da India.*

Textiles imported into Portugal from India were later exported to England, France, Russia, Italy, Holland and the United States.[17]

The Mhamai brothers were agents for Lisbon-based traders. Francisco Antonio de Moraes made a request to the Mhamais for *zuartes, coromandeis, chitas, cadeas*, and *panos de cafre,* in May 1800.[18] In December 1805, Balaghat textiles were exported from Goa to Lisbon on board the ship, *Rainha dos Anjos*, captained by Antonio Garcia Alves, on behalf and on the account of the Mhamais.[19] There were other *Estado* merchants engaged in the textile trade to Portugal. In 1787, textile goods were transported to Lisbon on board the ship *Triumfo* by Anta Sinai and Co., Babaji Sinai Cabadi and Co., João Rodrigues Velho, Ari Sinai and Co., Govinda Sinai and Co., Jacinto Domingos and Co., Jose Gomes Matias, Antonio de Fonseca, Joaquim Estanislaus de Souza, Ignacio Alberto de Oliveira, Jose Custodio de Silva, Anta Naik and Co., Alexandre Jose Monteiro, Anta Bhandari, Francisco de Silva Pomar, Panduranga Naik Sardessai, Roghunath Naik, Vithoji Naik and others.[20]

On the Goa-Brazil route Simão de Rocha Loureiro, Domingos Alvares Loureiro, João Gomes Duarte, Thomas Loureiro, Venkatesha and Narayana Kamat, Venku Shet Khalap, Anta Parab Lawande, João Baptista Goethals, Narayan Parab Lawande, Narayan Bulla Naik and Co., Joze Joaquim de Fonseca, Thomas Pedro Moller, Joaquim Mourão Garcez Palha, Antonio Joze Viegas, João Manoel Correa, and Narayan Naik were active as textile traders.[21] In 1815 Gervazio Peres Ferreira, owner of the ship *Espado de Ferro* revealed his desire to dispatch 500 *fardos* of textiles involving 54,000 pieces worth 353,100 *xerafins* to Brazil.[22]

Expansion of the Indian textile commerce in the late eighteenth and early nineteenth centuries did stimulate textile production which in turn provided labour opportunities. It must be noted, however, that manufacturing techniques and processes underwent no structural changes.

Daman and Diu were important centres of textile production supplying fabrics that formed a portion of textile cargoes shipped to Portugal, Brazil, Angola, Moçambique, South East Asia and Macao. From Table 7.3 we observe that the centres of textile production at Diu were the city of Diu (*Praça*), Brancavara, Monxivara, Passo do Covo and Podame. Chief amongst them was the main city and the market place (*Praça*). All the painters resided here during 1810-14. The highest concentration of weavers was found at the market-place and the rest at Brancavara, Moxivara, Paso do Covo and Podame. In a given year during 1810-14 there were about 323 weavers as against the 53 painters. The weaver population outnumbered the painters in Diu by more than six times. As regards the social composition of those involved in textile production at Diu, out of the 232 weavers found in Diu in 1816, 162 of them were Hindus and 36 were Parsees (the rest were Dores (?) and Colles(?)).[23] Thus 69.83 per cent of the weaver population consisted of Hindus and 15.52 per cent Parsees.

In Daman the centres of weaving were located at Upper Daman (Damão de Sima), Doler, Ambavary, Chão de Jamporis, Damão Pequeno, Fora de Jampa, Carivary and Varacunda.[24] During 1810-12, most of the weavers were found at Damão Pequeno. Out of about 667 weavers, 201 were located here. This formed 30.13 per cent of the weaver population of Daman. In the subsequent years from 1814 onwards till 1828 Carivary, Jampa Fora and Varacunda began to grow more in industrial importance compared to Damão Pequeno. Out of an average number of 340.5 houses of weaving 12.11 per cent were found at Damão Pequeno, 20.26 per cent at Fora de Jampa, 24.08 per cent at Carivary and 26.87 per cent at Varacunda. The latter was therefore the principal centre of weaving during 1814-28.

The weavers of Daman belonged to either the Hindu or the Muslim community. During 1810-12, the Muslim weavers were in the majority.[25] They formed 82.01 per cent of the average number of 667 weavers. The Muslim weavers continued to dominate the scene in the subsequent period. In fact during 1824-28 they grew in strength and importance. The average number of Muslim houses of weaving formed 86.53 per cent of the average total of 340.5 weaving houses located at Daman.

During 1814-28 an average of 479.75 looms were available at Daman for 340.5 weaving houses that is 1.41 per house.[26]

As for the dyers of Daman, all of them belonged to the Hindu community. During 1814-28 there were on an average 30 of them functioning at Ambavary, Chão de Jamporis, Damão Pequeno and Jampa Fora districts of Daman. But as regards printers during the same period their houses were mainly concentrated at Chão de Jamporis, Damão Pequeno and Jampa Fora, 59.24 per cent at Cháo de Jamporis, 36.63 per cent at Damão Pequeno and the rest at Jampa Fora. Almost all the printers were Hindus. During 1823-28 there existed on an average only one Muslim house of textile printing.

Thus we can conclude that in Daman weaving was mainly handled by the Muslims and printing and dyeing by the Hindus.

Textile manufacture was also conducted at Goa on a limited scale.

TABLE 7.3:WEAVERS, DYERS AND OTHER ENGAGED IN TEXTILE PRODUCTION AT DIU, 1810-16

Districts	1810		1811		1812		1814		1816	
	Weavers	Painters	Weavers	Painters	Weavers	Painters	Weavers	Painters	Weavers	Dyers
Market Area (Praça)	261	57	258	56	241	53	238	47		
Brancavara	66	64	59	53						
Monxivara	2	2	2	1						
Paso do Covo	6	6	6	4						
Podame	8	7	5	4						
Total	343	57	337	56	313	53	300	47	232	81

Sources: HAG : *MR*, 191D, fl. 1187; 192B, fl. 566; AHU : *MI*, Maço 188, no. 173, doc. dated 17 Nov. 1810; Maço 192, no. 206, doc. dated 6 Dec. 1811; Maço 193, no. 201, doc. dated 11 Dec. 1812; Maço 198, no. 196, doc. dated 10 April 1814; Maço 201, no. 193, doc. dated 4 Jan. 1817.

The Royal Factory of Cumbarjua (*Fábrica Real de Cumbarjua*) was probably set up in 1783 to produce cotton textiles to meet the local need for clothing and to stimulate trade.[27] It produced cotton textiles such as *beatilhas, zuzuartes, ardians, tucorins, botians, panos de cafre, chitas, cadeas,* and *coromandeis,* in imitation of textiles produced at Surat.[28] These manufactures were shipped to Portugal, Moçambique and other distant countries.[29]

In December 1787 the *Fábrica de Cumbarjua* produced 25,880 pieces worth 12,487-3-14 *xerafins*. The expenditure involved was 8,934-3-9 1/4 *xerafins*. Therefore the net profit amounted to 3,553-0-4 3/4 *xerafins*.[30] But in 1792-94 it ran at a loss. Its income that year was 10,766-3-44 *xerafins* while its expenditure amounted to 32,201-4-32 1/4 *xerafins*. Therefore the loss involved amounted to 21,435-0-48 1/4 *xerafins*.[31] It was probably to overcome such losses that the *Fábrica de Cumbarjua* came to be managed by an Administrator (*Administrador*). In 1798 it was administered by and on the account of Luis Joze de Souza Machado de Morais Sacramento.[32] On his death the *Fábrica de Cumbarjua* came to be administered by a well-known Goan merchant Antonio Pereira.[33] Goods produced by the Royal Factory of Cumbarjua were exempt from the payment of customs duties.[34] This implied that the State was keen to foster textile production.

Textile factories were also located at Betim, Taleigão, Mandur, Divar, Talaulim and Mapuça.[35] But some of them had to be closed down at least for a short while. Probably shortage of raw material could have been behind such closures. In the early 1790s efforts were being made to accelerate textile production. It was suggested that the cultivation of *linho canhamo* and cotton should be promoted. This would be essential for *lonas*.[36]

Silk-producing factories were established at Betim, Chimbel and Porpangim.[37]

During the period under study, Goa had to import items essential for weaving and dyeing. In 1841-45 it imported sizable quantities of indigo, glue, *gulgul*, indigo water, *azeite de gergelim*, white thread, combs for weaving and dyeing, dyes and the like.[38]

Circumstances were soon to change. With the political and economic winds of change blowing over India in the late eighteenth - early nineteenth centuries, the trade in Indian fabrics was badly affected. It had to face unrelenting competition from manufactured cloth produced in Europe. The consolidation of British colonialism in India coupled with the rise of free trade doctrines permitted the British machine-made fabrics to enter India unhindered. The opening of the Portuguese ports in 1808, led to the glutting of East African and Brazilian markets with cheap Manchester textiles which struck a devastating blow to the *Estado's* thriving trade in textiles. During the peak year 1816, this trade accounted for 10 per cent of Portugal's trade with Asia. By 1828, this was drastically reduced to 1.4 per cent and thereafter it was virtually non-existent.[39]

Tobacco

It was originally introduced into India from South America by the Portuguese in the beginning of the seventeenth century. Tobacco was grown in the open field, the plant consisting of green leaves almost one foot in length and 6 to 8 inches in breadth. These were plucked, dried and later exported. In Portuguese India tobacco was consumed extensively for smoking, sniffing and chewing. Few people could be persuaded to give up the habit once acquired however highly tobacco was taxed and however inferior the grade, quality and state of the product. In Ponda, Canacona, Pernem and Bicholim, for instance they had such a passion for smoking, that they even went to the extent of mixing tobacco with betel leaf probably in times of tobacco scarcities.[40]

Tobacco addiction in Goan society demanded regular supplies from Portugal. Tobacco available in the home-market was Bahian or Virginian, furnished by Britain or even that grown and prepared illegally in Portugal. Table 7.4 demonstrates that during 1824-28 the annual average shipment of tobacco and snuff from Portugal was worth 24,904$140 *reis*. Prior to 1770 the average supply of snuff from Portugal touched about 40,945 *arrateis* per annum but between 1770-1824 the annual average supply shot up to about 83,203 *arrateis* that is more than double of that shipped to the *Estado da India* prior to 1770.[41] With the money acquired from the sale of tobacco, Portugal expected to obtain Indian cotton textiles. Thus in February 1775, Indian cotton products from Surat, Porto Novo, Patavar and Diu valued at 33,800-3-30 *xerafins* were acquired out of funds raised from tobacco sales.[42]

The *naos* leaving Lisbon for India would also collect tobacco rolls at Moçambique for onward delivery at the port of Goa. Thus in 1827, Goa received 20 barrels of tobacco weighing 757 arrobas and 10 *arrateis* from the *Companhia de Moçambique*.[43] From Goa tobacco would later move to Daman and Diu.[44]

Tobacco supplies would arrive from the south. Thomas Dineur at Mahe would consign tobacco cargoes to the Mhamais for sale in the

Portuguese dominions. In fact there was a contract in existence with the Mhamais for looking after tobacco sales.[45] In January 1809, Thomas Dineur despatched on board the *pattamar Bhowany*, 77 bales of tobacco weighing 10 *candis*, 14 *maons* and 30 *arrateis*.[46] Dineur commissioned the Mhamais to dispose off this consignment as profitably as possible. When the Mhamais informed Dineur of their inability to dispose off the consignment, Dineur expressed surprise, as he failed to understand why the brothers could not sell a small quantity of tobacco at a time when Portuguese government had awarded them the Tobacco Contract *(Renda)* and when there were possibilities of their retaining the contract for a second term as the Brazilian ships had not arrived.[47] Dineur later received communication that his tobacco had been rejected by the State authorities. He instructed the brothers not to send the tobacco back since its entry into Malabar would not be permitted, but to store it in their warehouse for some prospective buyer from the north.[48] In October 1810, in reply to a query posed by the Mhamais, Dineur informed them that 100 bales of tobacco were available at Thomas Warden's place that the payment was to be made either by bill of exchange or in the form of salt to be delivered at Mahe or Canary.(?)[49]

Table 7.4: TOBACCO IMPORTS FROM PORTUGAL ON THE ACCOUNT OF THE *FAZENDA REAL*, 1824-28

Year	Quantity		Value (In *reis*)
1824	32000	*arrateis* of snuff	9600$000
	32000	*arrateis* of snuff	9600$000
1825	5703	*arrobas* and 8 *arrateis* of Brazilian tobacco	13687$000
	32000	*arrateis* of snuff	9600$000
1826	656	*arrobas* of Brazilian tobacco	1574$000
	5503	*arrobas* and 16 *arrateis* of Virginian Tobacco	19812$000
	32000	*arrateis* of snuff	9600$000
1827	5528	*arrobas* and 8 *arrateis* of Virginian Tobacco	19901$700
	32000	*arrateis* of snuff	9600$000
1828	5985	*arrobas* of Virginian Tobacco	21546$000

Source: HAG : *MR*, 206B, fls. 376, 377.

Tobacco from Ponani and Bengal also made their appearance at Goa.[50] In 1816, a cargo of 570 *arrobas* and 4 *arrateis* of tobacco came from

Ponani.[51] Tobacco was also bought at Mangalore where it was brought by tobacco cultivators/middlemen from remote regions.[52]

Tobacco was especially brought to the New Conquest areas by the traders of the *Carreira de Balagate* in bullock carts and sold at the rate of 5 to 6 *xerafins* per *maon* of 25 *arrateis* and the local traders and contractors sold it to the people for 11 to 12 *xerafins* per *maon*.[53]

Daman and Diu, besides receiving regular tobacco supplies from Lisbon, Moçambique and the south, received tobacco cargoes from Cambay and Jumbasoor. On 7th February, 1824, 6 *fardos* of tobacco valued at 492 *xerafins* were brought to Daman by Amaidas Tricamo.[54]

The price of tobacco available in the south went on fluctuating in the early nineteenth century. In 1800 it was available at the rate of 215 *xerafins* per candil. In 1808 critical times caused by French privateers was responsible for the price shooting up to 300 *xerafins*. In 1809 and 1811 it dropped to 216 *xerafins* and 230 *xerafins* respectively.[55]

Since its establishment in 1675, the *Administração de Estanco Real* would enter into monopoly contracts.[56] The procurement and distribution of tobacco and the farming of revenue were handled entirely by contractors almost all of whom were Hindus. This task was assigned usually for a term of three years. In fact auctions were held in each area and the contract was awarded to the highest bidder. The system saved the limited Portuguese administrative manpower to take care of the more important task of defence and supervision. It provided the Government ready cash which the contractors paid in advance.

The system certainly had its drawbacks. The contractors in their bid to make profits over and above the figures determined in their contracts, would resort to the severest means to extract tobacco revenues. The latter resorted to blatant forms of coercion and extortion. In fact such vexations led to the loss of Pernem taluka in 1759.[57] The rentiers would also indulge in contraband activities. Contraband tobacco was often housed in the homes of the innocent who were later subjected to searches by the soldiers.[58] Such was the state of affairs prior to 1775 that caused the State authorities to take remedial steps.

The *Estado* was seized with another problem of alarming proportions in the early 1770s. Tobacco revenues collected by the local monopoly (*Estanco Real*) through a system of farming formed one of the principal sources of income of the *Estado*. In 1745 the tobacco revenues amounted to 210,000 *xerafins*. In the years immediately preceding and following 1750 the revenues never fell below 200,000 *xerafins*.[59]

Since then a pronounced constant decline was observed as follows:[60]

1764	175,900 *xerafins*
1767	160,000 *xerafins*
1770	135,000 *xerafins*
1773	119,000 *xerafins*

Thus we observe that when compared to the revenues collected in 1745, those of 1773 registered a shortfall of 91,000 *xerafins* or 43.33 per cent.

The steady erosion of tobacco revenues cannot be ascribed to a fall in the population of Goa or to pressures of wars, invasions or other calamities likely to influence the consumption of tobacco and other such substances. The justification offered by the tobacco contractors especially by Vithogi Sinai Nerlikar, was that the downward slide was due to the occupation of the southern ports by Hyder Ali Khan, which in their opinion had triggered off a sharp rise in the cost of tobacco and utter confusion in the trading system in the south.[61]

Apart from dwindling revenues, the financial situation in Portuguese India was further aggravated by the bullion drain. Gold and silver coinage was being syphoned off to the ports of Kanara and other neighbouring areas. Payments made by the tobacco revenue farmers to Hyder Ali Khan were in gold and silver while those made by them to the *Fazenda Real*, were in *bazarucos* and other such coins of little value.[62]

The responsibility for such disconcerting circumstances could be laid at the door of the tobacco contractors.

In the later part of the eighteenth century, tobacco revenue farming was a monopoly enjoyed by a few Hindu business houses. They were free to transact in gold and silver outside the confines of Goa. In their quest to maximize profits they would scour the Malabar for cheap and consequently inferior tobacco. The same was transported to Goa in country craft and deposited in their warehouses to be later directed to areas marked out for tobacco sale. Before the disposal of inferior tobacco especially that found useless for consumption, it was soaked in a concoction of pepper water. Tobacco subjected to such treatment came to be artificially strengthened and later disposed off in the province of Salcette. These and other excesses were the order of the day in Portuguese Goa under the *Estanco Real*. It was evident that the prime concern of the contractors was personal enrichment. Their appetite for wealth never seemed to ebb even at the cost of irreparable damage done to public health. Tobacco was sold in the environs of Ilhas and Bardez at the rate of 2 *xerafins* per *arratel*, while that supplied to the military officials, soldiers and the white population was available at the rate of 6 -1/2 *tangas* an *arratel*.[63] This unfair price discrepancy for the same item in the same State was a source of much resentment and complaint.

The tobacco contractors also deliberately falsified figures and demonstrated low consumption. They claimed that the annual consumption of tobacco in Goa amounted to 223 *candis* or 3572 *arrobas*.[64] In the light of the fact that the statistical records reveal that the population of Goa, Bardez and Salcette totalled 233,712 it implied that every individual consumed not more than half an *arratel* annually. This was far from plausible. In reality the contractors would purchase the bulk of their tobacco supplies at the ports of Calicut, Tellicherry and Ponani and this did not fall below 400 *candis* or 7,200 *arrobas*.[65] It therefore becomes evident that the domestic consumption was double the quantity cited by the contractors.

Not unexpectedly the situation caused unremitting concern to the Portuguese Government. It had to wrestle with a thorny problem afflicting the *Estado*. Therefore to enhance and streamline tobacco revenues of the State, it conceived policies designed to break the *modus operandi* of the contractors and to curtail their illegal activities that syphoned income away from the financially pressed treasury. In 1773 the ideal solution envisioned was the admission of Brazilian tobacco into Portuguese Asia on a very large scale with a view to eventually establishing a tobacco trading network in India on the lines of the Virginian tobacco trading system in existence in British India. In fact one can comment that it had been sheer negligence on the part of the Portuguese authorities not to have given considerable thought to this matter earlier even though Brazilian tobacco was acknowledged to be far superior to its Virginian counterpart. The British as usual had manifested a great deal of shrewdness and sound business acumen. Their tobacco trading nexus in India ironically encompassed Diu.[66]

The first consignment of Bahian tobacco made its appearance at Goa in 1776. Since then one witnessed the periodic remission of tobacco cargoes from Brazil despite turmoil and turbulence in the first quarter of the nineteenth century, brought on by the Napoleonic Wars followed by the shifting of the Portuguese Court to Rio de Janeiro in 1808, finally culminating in Brazil's break-away from Portugal.[67] This ostensibly marked a major change in the tobacco policies of the Portuguese authorities. It signalled an important departure from traditional approaches.

With the introduction of Brazilian tobacco in Goa the administration of the *Estanco Real* underwent drastic alterations. To eliminate the abuses earlier practised by the contractors, the tobacco monopoly came under the direct control and jurisdiction of the *Fazenda Real* which began to exercise a tighter rein over the system. Contracts for the sale of tobacco, initially granted for a period of one year were later substituted by triennial contracts. Under no circumstances were the contractors permitted to procure tobacco from any part of India for sale in Goa. A decree was issued on 12th April, 1776 prohibiting the entry of tobacco from the ports controlled by Hyder Ali Khan. Such restrictions were imperative to safeguard the local monopoly from eventual extinction.[68] As soon as the vessels laden with Bahian tobacco touched the shores of Goa the tobacco bales and rolls were unloaded and deposited in the godowns of the *Estanco Real*. To counter the practice of *botoens* and other vexations, they were rigorously inspected by the *Junta* before distribution and sale. The *Junta* was empowered to burn stocks of poor quality tobacco and adulterated mixtures shipped from Brazil.[69] The policy of burning bad Brazilian tobacco one observes sharply contrasted with the earlier system when the contractors supplied Malabar tobacco to the people of Goa irrespective of quality. Under no circumstances was such tobacco consigned to flames.

The contractors initially bought Brazilian tobacco at the government warehouses at the rate of 2 *tangas* and 9 - 1/2 *reis* per arratel. This was later disposed off in the Old Conquest areas at the rate of 8 *tangas* per *arratel* and the New Conquest regions at diverse rates varying from province to province.[70] These differences in prices probably arose due to the fact that these areas were predominantly occupied by Hindus who were not accustomed to smoking tobacco acquired from the West and were traditionally dependent on Balaghat for cheap tobacco supplies.

The new tobacco system in operation in Goa since 1776 was later introduced in Daman and Diu. Orders were issued to introduce the use of Brazilian tobacco in these areas and to impede the entry of tobacco from the *Canaes*.[71] In 1779 the amount of tobacco required was 240 candis for Goa, 40 *candis* for Diu and 138 *candis* for Daman.[72]

For sometime the system functioned well.[73] All the contracts during 1775-1825 were assigned to Saraswat brahmins. The price of a contract during the said period ranged from 322,089-0-00 xerafins (1786-88) to 575,851-2-30 *xerafins* (1820-22). On an average the contracts were priced at 467,613-3-15 *xerafins*. The first triennial contract assigned to Govind Sinai Malia from 1777 to December 1779, yielded 127,500 *xerafins* per year which we see was an improvement upon the yield of 1770-73 contract to the extent of 8,500 *xerafins* per year.[74] But soon difficulties were encountered in meeting local demands. In January 1780 it was observed that merchant ships that came to Asia from Lisbon would touch Portuguese America and buy tobacco snuff there at the rate of 300 *reis* or less an *arratel*. This snuff was later transported to Goa in barrels, tins and bottles and sold to convents, the military and in various parts of Goa for two *pardaus* an *arratel* or even less. This contraband in snuff severely affected the revenues of the State. The tobacco contractors were expected to pay the State five *pardaus* per *arratel* and were expected to sell at the rate of 5-1/2 *pardaus* per *arratel*. They were unable to sell tobacco at this rate. A request was made to the Lisbon government to enforce strict measures to prevent the sale of snuff at Brazil to private ships proceeding to Asia.[75]

Moreover, Bahian tobacco was often in short supply.[76] Such scarcities could be ascribed to repeated delays in the arrival of Bahian tobacco shipments at Goa. Shortages also occurred due to the practice of burning Brazilian tobacco that was useless for consumption. The arrival of such tobacco could in all probability be ascribed to administrative lapses and laxity in enforcement of regulations. Thereupon it was found expedient to turn to supplies from Ponani and the southern ports on the Malabar coast. At times tobacco was also shipped from Bengal, Surat, Corda, Balaghat and Jumbasoor.[77] During 1775-1825 an annual average of about 16,428 *arrobas* of Bahian tobacco were shipped to Goa but proved insufficient to satisfy the needs of the *Estado da India*[78]. In fact since 1780 the State was compelled to acquire tobacco from other parts of India to make up for the shortage of Bahian supplies. On an average during 1780-1825 about 224 *candis* of tobacco were purchased in other parts of India for an average annual amount of 74,569-1-17 *xerafins*. The situation was critical during 1795-97 when just 4,109 *arrobas* and 24 *arrateis* of tobacco arrived from Bahia. This led to the purchase of a sizable quantity of tobacco in other parts of India, 544 *candis*, 2 *quintais*, 2 *arrobas* and 14 *arrateis* for a sum of 55,145-1-34 *xerafins* to overcome this deficit. This undoubtedly proved detrimental to the financial interests of *Estado da India*. It led to exhorbitant tobacco pricing, causing undue hardships to the tobacco-addicted Goan population.[79]

To offset the problems arising out of frequent scarcities of Bahian tobacco, the *Fazenda Real* found it justifiable to abstain from burning stocks of inferior Bahian tobacco and to supply it to the people via the contractors. A spate of proposals were made to tide over the crisis. It was decided to furnish the contractors with special licences enabling them to purchase tobacco in India. It was stipulated that the said tobacco was to be stored in government godowns and was to be subjected to similar scrutiny as in the case of Brazilian tobacco before distribution and sale.

Stiff penalties would be imposed on those found guilty of flouting the regulations.[80]

Notwithstanding these measures adopted by authorities, the furtive clandestine operations of the contractors continued unabated. On 29th January, 1819 during the rule of Governor Conde de Rio Pardo an edict was promulgated compelling the smoking of tobacco supplied only by the *Estanco Real.* It also stated that the contrabandists ran the risk of exile to Moçambique for a period of five years and the confiscation of personal property.[81]

To curb the nefarious activities of the tobacco contractors as well as to protect their privileges since there were often loud protests and complaints about infringements into their respective jurisdictions, the government prescribed certain rules and regulations applicable in New Conquest areas.[82] Wholesale and retail sale of tobacco including cigars and cheeroots by contractors, their administrators and agents demanded the holding of a license. The contractor was expected to sell good quality tobacco, fit for consumption in public places in the district under his jurisdiction and not beyond. He was not to distinguish between persons when conducting tobacco sales nor to sell at rates higher than those prescribed in the contract. In the province of Zambaulim the retail price of tobacco was not to exceed 4 tangas per *arratel* and the wholesale price 3-1/2 *tangas* per *arratel.* Every six months the weights and measures used were to be inspected.

Contraband tobacco would be seized and publicly burnt in such a manner that none could use it. A *fidalgo* found guilty of dealing with contraband tobacco would suffer the loss of property and would be exiled to Africa for a period of six years. Introduction of tobacco from any foreign land would involve him an additional penalty of ten years of exile to Diu. Confiscation of property, five years exile to Moçambique and on introducing tobacco from foreign lands an additional punishment of ten years of exile to Angola were what one had to face if one was a noble. The penalties were more stringent in the case of commonfolk. If caught indulging in clandestine activities they would have to face loss of property, whipping and five years of forced labour probably on the galleys. Introduction of tobacco from foreign lands for commercial purposes meant additional whipping and forced labour for ten years. Soldiers found guilty of selling tobacco even in limited quantities would lose their service and would be exiled to Angola for a term of five years. All military officers were required to imprison soldiers discovered to be indulging in illegal tobacco sale and intimate their seniors about the matter. Failure to do so would cost them their posts. They would even be stripped off their ranks.[83]

In the first decade of the nineteenth century a need was felt to abolish the *Renda do Tabaco da Folha*. Its functioning was found to be highly vexatious and aggressive. But it was still found to be a lucrative source of revenue to the State. In 1809 it yielded revenues amounting to 167,000 *xerafins*, 180,700 *xerafins* in 1813, 178,500 *xerafins* in 1816, 188,300 *xerafins* in 1819 and about 190,000 *xerafins* by 1820.[84] Thus on an average the tobacco revenues during 1809-20 amounted to 180,900 *xerafins*.

In 1840 Governor General Barão do Candal gave the matter of abolition considerable thought. He issued a circular on 7th March, 1840 to different corporations and competent authorities, eliciting their opinions on the retention or extinction of the said *Renda*. Almost everyone voted in favour of extinction. Joze Joaquim Lopes, the successor of Barão do Candal did not hesitate to give official sanction to this near unanimous verdict. By the *Portaria* of 27th October 1840, the *Estanco Real* was abolished and with it the notorious *Renda do Tobaco da Folha*. Thereafter customs duties were levied on imported tobacco.[85]

Timber

Blessed by nature with rich luxuriant forest growth, Daman featured prominently in the thriving coastal trade in timber. The district of Nagar Haveli, was particularly rich in varieties of wood such as teak (*teca*), *sisso, kher, hedú, sadrá, assane, calicanty, palasse, sivaņe, apteira, tenasse, timbri, jambol, babul* and *biá*.[86]

Besides the aforesaid varieties of wood, Daman exported *patingas*, bamboos, *quita, rajalu, curee, wajal, nulderwa* to Bombay, Surat, Amode, Jumbasoor, Dhollera, Goga, Bhavnagar and Broach in the Bombay Presidency, Muscat, Diu and even Goa.[87] Table 7.5 suggests that the total value of Daman's timber export trade with Bombay during 1802-26 amounted to Rs. 502,920 or an annual average of Rs. 26,469.47.

Daman's said trade with Amode, Jumbasoor, Broach, Dhollera, Bhavnagar, and Goga during 1818-26 had a total value of Rs. 149,064. (Table 7.6)

If we consider the annual average value of the timber trade that Daman conducted during 1818-26 with each of the areas of the Bombay Presidency we come up with figures like Rs. 5,183.67 for Bombay, Rs. 5,972.57 for Amode and Jumbasoor, Rs. 618.2 for Broach, Rs. 12,799.5 for Dhollera, Rs. 4,312.33 for Bhavnagar and Rs. 747 for Goga. (Table 7.6) Thus Daman's timber export trade was mainly carried on with

Dhollera in the early nineteenth century. The total value of Daman's timber exports to the Bombay Presidency during 1818-26 thus amounted to Rs. 29,633.27 per annum. Industrial expansion put pressure on Bombay to import wood in bulk from Daman.

TABLE 7.5: VALUE OF THE TIMBER AND WOOD EXPORTS OF PORTUGUESE INDIA TO BOMBAY, 1802-26

Year	Value (In rupees)
1802-03	79483
1803-04	66673
1804-05	3389
1806-07	10036
1807-08	73014
1808-09	125386
1809-10	17455
1810-11	2933
1811-12	19838
1812-13	17569
1813-14	13718
1815-16	31812
1816-17	10512
1818-19	3321
1820-21	1483
1822-23	5103
1823-24	8897
1824-25	9843
1825-26	2455

Source: Compiled from *MREIC*, vols. 1-3, 5/6, 8-15, 16/17, 20-25.

TABLE 7.6: VALUE OF TIMBER EXPORTS OF DAMAN TO AREAS IN THE BOMBAY PRESIDENCY OTHER THAN BOMBAY, 1816-26

Year	Amode and Jumbasoor (In rupees)	Broach (In rupees)	Dhollera (In rupees)	Bhavnagar (In rupees)	Goga (In rupees)
1816-17			6084	3253*	
1818-19	8077	1473	31415	3291	
1819-20	12463		6810	4066	
1820-21	5424	700		9000	
1821-22	9303	121	9219	3017	
1822-23	1255	654	11076		790
1824-25	2736	143	2215	5500	
1825-26	2550		16062	1000	704

Sources: BA : Compiled from *MREIC*, vols. 16/17, 18, Parts I and II, 19-25.

Note: * This is in common with Goga.

Daman was Goa's chief supplier of ships and country vessels used in the country trade. It provided teak, *patingas* and furniture. From Daman, wood was despatched to Portugal too.[88] Daman in turn imported *pao preto* from Moçambique.[89]

Daman earned the Portuguese world acclaim as a ship-building centre. Brazilian ships and slave galleys and even ships of private traders engaged in the Indo-Chinese trade were constructed at Daman. The following ships for instance were built at Daman.[90]

Ship	Ton	Owner
Elizabeth	255 1/2	Nursidas Pussotoma
Gloriozo	490	Rogerio de Faria
Kurovie	324	Mohamed Takey
Sulamaney	329	Framjee Cowasjee
Anna Felix	324	Premchand Curimchand

Among the Portuguese ships constructed at Daman mention can be made of the frigate *Francisco Xavier* built in 1770 at the cost of 111,970-2-34 1/2 *xerafins.*[91] Other ships built at Daman were frigates *Santa Anna e S. Joaquim,* in 1761, *Real Fedelissima* in 1777, *Temivel Portuguesa* in 1778 and *chalupas S. Pedro de Alcantra* in 1771 and *N. Senhora das Necessidades e S. Joze* in 1772.[92] The above-mentioned vessels were built at the orders placed by Lisbon. Macao and Moçambique too placed orders for the construction of ships at Daman. In 1816 funds were despatched by Macao through *Tenente Coronel* Vogal for the construction of two frigates.[93] Five thousand *cruzados* were despatched in 1819 from Moçambique to Daman for the construction of two ships. In August 1819 Moçambique found itself in the critical situation of being attacked by enemies on all sides. Ships were required to guard its coastline.[94] A ship was built for the *Capitania de Moçambique* in 1825.[95]

Bamboos formed a significant part of Goa's export cargoes.[96] The customs records indicate that Goa exported 36,750 bamboos in 1844 and 28,100 in 1849.[97] Goa shipped to Muscat timber in the form of bamboos, *cana-fistula*, beams and *patingas.*[98] In 1835-36 Lada Shet, Ramu Shet and Acabagi Shet despatched bamboos from Goa to Macao.[99] Timber was also exported from Goa to Moçambique.[100] In February 1843 the ship *Quatro de Abril* captained by Mussagy Velgy, anchored at Goa, but destined for Moçambique, was carrying a consignment of wood belonging to Iria Kamat Mhamai.[101] According to an official price list the price of bamboos at Goa ranged between 20 and 50 *xerafins*.[102]

To cater to the needs of the Goa Shipyard and the *Arsenal de Goa* much teak wood was imported from the south. *Canoas* and *tonas* too would arrive from this region.[103] In May, October and December 1774, 2 medium-sized *tonas* and 1 large *tona* were imported from southern ports.[104] Likewise in December 1835, 1 *canoa* was brought to Goa by Babi Naik from the south.[105] Since timber production was low in Goa, efforts were stepped up to promote the growth of timber trees. In 1778 there were 19,848 such trees found in Ilhas, 15,459 in Bardez and 38,323 in Salcette.[106]

As in the case of tobacco and liquors timber revenue-farming was practised in Goa during the period under review.[107] Timber contracts were triennial in character.[108] Table 7.7 provides us details of the timber contractors during 1761-81.

TABLE 7.7: GOA TIMBER REVENUE CONTRACTORS, 1761-81

Revenue Contractor	Contract Assigned In	Value of the Contract per year (In *xerafins*)
Roullu Sinai	1761	260-0-00
Lakshman Sinai	1765	270-0-00
Lakshman Sinai	1769	200-0-00
Lakshman Sinai	1773	150-0-00
Govinda Sinai	1775	225-0-00
Ramage Naik	1781	151-0-00

Source: HAG : *Rendas*, 7849, fls. 51, 76, 108v, 135, 149v, 249v.

REFERENCES AND NOTES

1. HAG : *PDCF*, 1156, fl. 130v.
2. See Appendix 14.
3. HAG : *AG*, 6375, fls. 4-201 : *passim; MR*, 148, fls. 728-811v.
4. HAG : *MR*, 148B, fls. 744v-745v; *RGF*, 2273, fls. 40-41; XCHR : *MHP* (Portuguese), doc. no. 11826.
5. HAG : *MR*, 148B, fls. 748-750; *Dio*, 8042, fl. 94; *AG*, 6375, fls. 107-117; *RGF*, 2273, fls. 40-41.
6. HAG : *AG*,6375, .fl. 8. From the Mhamai House Papers we gather that Carlos Joze Pereira from Macao sent aboard the ship *Thereza*, on the account of the Mhamais a silken bordered bed-cover along with other goods. Its price was fixed at 110-00 *patacas*. XCHR : *MHP* (Portuguese), doc. dated 27 Dec. 1807.
7. HAG : *MR*, 148B, fl. 751.
8. XCHR : *MHP* (Portuguese), doc. dated 11 Feb. 1789.

9. Pamela Nightingale, *Trade and Empire in Western India, 1784-1806*, Cambridge, 1970, p. 161.
10. HAG : *CR*, 1642, doc. dated 16 March 1790; 1643, doc. dated 11 March 1806; ANTT: *Casa da India*, 1501, doc. dated 2 March 1790.
11. ANTT : *Casa da India*, 1500, fls. 12-14, 40.
12. AHU : *MI*, Maço 190, no. 204, docs. dated 16 Feb. 1816, 24 March 1816, 10 May 1816.
13. BPA : *India*, 46-XIII-24, fls. 5, 30, 40, 48, 51, 54, 59, 82, 100, 107.
14. XCHR : *MHP* (Portuguese), doc. dated 20 May 1800.
15. XCHR : *MHP* (Portuguese), doc. dated 31 Dec. 1805.
16. HAG : *MR*, 166, fls. 266-271v.
17. HAG : *AG*, 6347, fls. 134-233, 342-343; 6350, fls. 5-27, 647-653; 6355, fls. 18-238, 593-634 : *passim*.
18. HAG : *MR*, 195C, fl. 304.
19. XCHR : *MHP* (Portuguese), doc. dated 7 Jan. 1808; *MR*, 178A, fl. 267; *Moçambique*, 1445, fl. 29v; 1446, fl. 182; *AG*, 2247, fls. 2-3, 272; 2668, fls. 30-30v; 6318, fls. 1-302 : *passim;* 6325, fls. 79-95; 6327, fls. 549, 749; 6810, fls. 720-773 : *passim*; 8117, fls. 324, 335-360 : *passim;* 9258, fls. 122-334 : *passim.*
20. HAG : *MR*, 161E, fl. 1019v.
21. HAG : *AG*, 8128, fl. 3v.
22. HAG : *AG*, 8128, fl. 3v.
23. AHU : *MI*, Maço 201, no. 193, doc. dated 14 Jan. 1817.
24. See Appendix 15.
25. See Appendix 15.
26. See Appendix 15.
27. HAG : *MR*, 164F, fl. 1609; *Cumbarjua*, 1962, fls. 4-5.
28. HAG : *MR*, 179A, doc. dated 23 April 1800, fl. 325; *Cumbarjua*, 1962, fl. 34; *AHU: MI*, Maço 119, no. 117, doc. dated 14 Jan. 1793. In 1787 the price of *beatilhas* produced at the *Fábrica de Cumbarjua* was as follows :

Textiles	Factory Rate (In *xerafins*)	Rate at Royal Arsenal (In *xerafins*)
Beatilha branca	3-0-00	4-2-36
Beatilha verde	3-1-15	3-2-30
Beatilha encardenado	4-3-00	4-2-30
Beatilha azul	3-2-30	3-1-15
Beatilha amarelho	3-2-03	3-3-45

29. AHU : *MI*, Maço 119, no. 117, doc. dated 11 Jan. 1793.
30. HAG : *MR*, 169B, fl. 687.
31. HAG : *MR*, 176A, fl. 275.
32. HAG : *MR*, 179A, fl. 325.
33. HAG : *MR*, 183B, fl. 398.
34. HAG : *MR*, 183B, fl. 401.
35. HAG : *MR*, 164F, fl. 1611; 179A, fl. 325; AHU : *MI*, Maço 92, no. 101, doc. dated 1 March 1792.
36. HAG : *MR*, 183B, fl. 400; AHU : *MI*, Maço 92, no. 101, doc. dated 1 March 1792.
37. AHU : *MI*, Maço 99, no. 86.
38. HAG : *MR*, 220B, doc. dated 23 Dec. 1846.

39. Gervase Clarence-Smith, *The Third Portuguese Empire, 1825-1875: A study in Economic Imperialism*, Manchester/Dovey, 1985, pp. 24-25.
40. HAG : *MR*, 161D, fl. 2044.
41. See Appendix 17.
42. AHU : *MI*, Maço 122, no. 114, doc. dated 1775.
43. Celsa Pinto, "Goa-based Overseas and Coastal Trade (18th-19th Centuries)", *Goa Through the Ages*, vol. II, (ed.) Teotonio R. de Souza, New Delhi, 1989, p. 180.
44. HAG : *Provisões*, 1586, fls. 56, 180, 465, 758-759.
45. XCHR : *MHP* (French), vol. 6, fl. 174.
46. XCHR : *MHP* (Portuguese), doc. dated 29 Jan. 1809.
47. XCHR : *MHP* (French), vol. 6, fls. 178-178v.
48. XCHR : *MHP* (French), vol. 6, fls. 180-180v.
49. XCHR : *MHP* (French), vol. 6, fls. 188-188v.
50. HAG : *RGF*, 2216, fl. 207.
51. HAG : *RGF*, 2287, fl. 343.
52. ANTT : *Ministerio do Reino*, 1000, undated doc.
53. HAG : *MR*, 164G, fl. 1735; RGF, 2274, fl. 27.
54. HAG : *Provisões*, 1584, fls. 111, 178, 179, 195, 270; 1585, fls. 159, 162v, 241, 244; 1587, fl. 182, 195; 7922, fls. 48, 66v, 80v; 7924, fl. 63; 7926, fls. 18v-19, 73, 87v; 7927, fls. 8-8v, 34, 37-37v; 7932, fls. 9, 31, 73v, 113; 7933, fls. 95v, 191.
55. HAG : *MR*, 195E, fls. 953, 955; RGF, 2287, fl. 342.
56. HAG : *MR*, 202D, fl. 385v; See Appendix 17.
57. HAG : *MR*, 161D, fls. 2045-2045v.
58. HAG : *MR*, 161D, fl. 2045.
59. Celsa Pinto, "At the Dusk of the Second Empire : Goa-Brazil Commercial Links, 1770-1825", *Purabhilekh-Puratatva*, vol. VIII, no. 1, Jan.-June 1990, p. 44.
60. *loc. cit.*; HAG : *MR*, 164G, fls. 1711-1711v.
61. HAG : *MR*, 159C, fls. 684v-685.
62. HAG : *MR*, 159C, fls. 682, 686.
63. HAG : *MR*, 164G, fls. 1710-1711.
64. HAG : *MR*, 159C, fls. 691-691v.
65. HAG : *MR*, 159C, fl. 692.
66. HAG : *MR*, 159C, fls. 692v-693.
67. HAG : *MR*, 164G, fls. 1722-1723v; 171B, fl. 566; 172B, fl. 833; 178B, fl. 789; 181B, fl. 574; 187B, fl. 552; 189, fls. 372, 376.
68. HAG : *MR*, 159C, fls. 687v-688, 690v.
69. HAG : *MR*, 164G, fl. 1713.
70. J. M. Carmo Nazareth, "Monopolio do Tabaco na India, *O Oriente Português*", vol. III 1906, p. 95.
71. HAG : *MR*, 159C, fl. 707; 161D, fl. 2008; 168D, fl. 1085.
72. HAG : *CR*, 1637, doc. dated 29 Dec. 1779.
73. See Appendix 16.
74. HAG : *MR*, 159C, fl. 682; DUP, vol. V, *Centro de Estudos Historicos Ultramarinos*, Lisboa, 1967, p. 167.
75. AHU : *MI*, Maço 132, no. 140, doc. dated 2 Jan. 1780.
76. Carmo Nazareth, op. cit., p. 95.
77. HAG : *MR*, 199B, fl. 432; 202D, fl. 384v.
78. See Appendix 16.
79. HAG : *MR*, 164G, fl. 1713v.
80. HAG : *MR*, 164G, fl. 1720.

81. Miguel Vicente de Abreu, *O Governo do Vice-Rei Conde de Rio Pardo*, Nova Goa, 1869, p. 119.
82. HAG : *Feitorias*, 9701, doc. dated 14 July 1709; 9702, fl. 112.
83. Felippe Nery Xavier, *Bandos*, vol. I, Pangim, 1840, pp. 136-143.
84. Carmo Nazareth, *op. cit.*, pp. 97-98.
85. *Ibid.*, pp. 98-99.
86. See Appendix 18.
87. BA : *MREIC*, vol. 16/17, doc. dated 30 April 1817; vol. 18, Part I, docs. dated 30 April 1819, 8 Oct. 1819; vol. 18, Part II, docs. dated 30 April 1819, 8 Oct. 1819; vol. 18, Part II, docs. dated 30 April 1819, 1 March 1819; vol. 19, doc. dated 30 April 1820; vol. 20, doc. dated 30 April 1821; vol. 21, doc. dated 30 April 1822; vol. 22 doc. dated 30 April 1823; vol. 24, doc. dated 30 April 1825; vol. 25, doc. dated 30 April 1826.
88. HAG : *AG*, 2247, fl. 145.
89. HAG : *Damão*, 4848, fl. 10.
90. BA : *CD*, 23/1824, p. 27.
91. AHU : *MI*, Maço 121, no. 111, doc. dated 26 Feb. 1772; BPA : *India*, 51-XIII-25, fl. 100v.
92. AHU : *MI*, Maço 129, no. 143, doc. dated 14 May 1779.
93. AHU : *MI*, Maço 205, no. 190, doc. dated 11 Dec. 1816.
94. HAG : *Estrangeiros*, 1226, fls. 2-3.
95. AHU : *MI*, Maço 223, no. 208, 16 Dec. 1825.
96. BA : *MREIC*, vol. 1, doc. dated 1 Sept. 1803; vol. 2, doc. dated 1 Sept. 1804; vol. 3, doc. dated 1 Sept. 1805; vol. 5/6, doc. dated 31 Oct. 1807; vol. 8, doc. dated 31 Oct. 1808; vol. 9, doc. dated 31 Oct. 1809; vol. 10, doc. dated 31 Oct. 1810; vol. 11, doc. dated 31 Oct. 1811; vol. 12, doc. dated 31 Oct. 1812; vol. 13, doc. dated 31 Oct. 1813; vol. 14, doc. dated 31 Oct. 1814; vol. 15, doc. dated 31 Oct. 1815; vol. 16/17, doc. dated 31 Oct. 1817; vol. 20, doc. dated 31 Oct. 1821; vol. 21, doc. dated 31 Oct. 1822; vol. 22, doc. dated 31 Oct. 1823; vol. 23, doc. dated 31 Oct. 1824; vol. 24, doc. dated 31 Oct. 1825; vol. 25, doc. dated 31 Oct. 1826.
97. HAG : *MR*, 218B, fl. 776; *AG*, 9265, fls. 43v-44.
98. HAG : *AG*, 6337, fl. 2; 6342, fls. 3-6.
99. HAG : *AG*, 8126, fls. 14v, 16-16v.
100. HAG : *MR*, 218B, fl. 776.
101. XCHR : *MHP* (Portuguese) doc. dated 9 Feb. 1843.
102. HAG : *AG*, 9267, fl. 11.
103. XCHR : *MHP* (Portuguese), doc. dated 13 Nov. 1793; HAG : *AG*, 6811, fls. 40-346: *passim*; *Provisões*, 1587, fl. 189; 7932, fl. 192.
104. HAG : *AG*, 6319, fls. 96-143 : *passim*.
105. HAG : *AG*, 8126, fl. 15.
106. AHU : *MI*, Maço 126, no. 142, doc. dated 1 March 1778.
107. HAG : *AG*, 6337, fls. 2-77: *passim*.
108. HAG : *Rendas*, 7849, fls. 51, 76, 108v, 135, 149v, 249v.

8

SMALL TRADE : NETWORKING THE 'TRIFLING': VICTUALS AND SPICES

The available evidence points to the existence of a lively coastal trade in victuals such as rice, wheat, coconuts, salt and other essentials. Country vessels at intervals would sail up and down the western littoral of India well-laden with such provisions required to meet the daily consumption needs of the people. Spices, one time luxuries, shipped round the Cape of Good Hope to cater to the tastes of Europeans, were now reduced to the status of essentials and figured significantly in the coastal trade of western India.

Victuals

Coconuts

Coconut cultivation was undertaken on a large scale in Portuguese India in all areas that were not hilly or serviceable for the cultivation of rice and along the coast. Coconut trees such as *madd, birla-madd* and *sasur-madd* were produced in abundance in Goa. Daman however, concentrated on the production of *cajuri*.[1] It was therefore, logical that coconuts would form the bulk of consumer goods exported from Portuguese India. *Pattamars* from Goa, piled with coconuts and coconut products would proceed northwards to Bombay, Gujarat, Daman and elsewhere along the west coast of India. The Customs records are full of entries on the despatch of coconut cargoes from Nova Goa, Salcette and Bardez. In 1789 Venkatesha Kamat despatched 10,000 coconuts to the north.[2] In 1826 448,885 coconuts and 34 *candis* and one *maon* of copra were exported from Goa to Bombay and 186,100 coconuts and 25 *candis* and 12 *maons* of coir to Daman.[3] Coconuts were also shipped to Moçambique as a part of the provision cargoes. In 1808, 1000 coconuts and 11 *maons* and 4 *canadas* of coconut oil left the *Estado* on board the *Pedro de Alcantara* for Moçambique.[4] In November 1800, 2000 coconuts were despatched to Muscat from Goa.[5]

Despite the availability of coconuts in abundance in Goa, it imported 2,263,000 coconuts in 1759, 2,258,500 in 1760, 2,257,050 in 1763 and 119,700 in 1770.[6]

Coconut cargoes would arrive from Calicut, Mahe and other southern ports.[7] The Mhamai records provide evidence of the entry of coconuts from the south. In November 1804 Brown and Dineur had dispatched to Goa a cargo of 27,200 coconuts priced at Rs. 22 3/4.[8] On the same day the said company shipped 58,400 coconuts from Tanur.[9]

Coconuts were often consigned for sale in Goa. By a letter dated 25th September 1804, Brown and Dineur instructed the Mhamais to dispose off 60,500 coconuts that had been sent aboard the coastal vessel *Lacmy*. The proceeds were to be converted into *Sultani* or *Bahaduri pagodas* or *meyas doblas* and a part of the proceeds was to be used to purchase salt.[10]

Table 8.1 indicates that during 1765-78, 49,012,786 coconuts arrived at Goa from the southern ports. This formed an average yearly cargo of 3,500,913.2 coconuts. During the said period, 7671 *candis* and 10.25 *maons* of copra too were shipped to Goa from the south. This means that on an average 547 *candis* and 19 *maons* of copra were imported into Goa from the south every year. As against this 9,722,728 coconuts were exported by Goa or an annual average of 6,94,480.57 coconuts. As regards copra a total amount of 14,160 *candis* and one *maon* were exported during 1765-78. This meant a yearly average of 1011 *candis* and 9 *maons.*

In 1804-05 coconuts had become scarce in the south because of a bad harvest of rice and the subsequent dependence on coconuts for food.[11] Therefore, in September 1804, coconuts were very expensive and were being sold at the rate of Rs. 20 to 25 per thousand at Tellicherry and could fetch a price of Rs. 80 to 90 at Bombay.[12] In August 1805 Brown and Dineur informed the Mhamai brothers that tender coconuts were available at the rate of Rs. 25 per thousand and mature ones at Rs. 28. But by December 1805, the price had dropped to Rs. 15 in the case of tender coconuts and Rs. 25 in the case of mature ones. Coir too was in short supply and it was being sold at Rs. 35 to 40 per *candil* in 1805.[13] By 1812, the situation had improved the price of coir then being Rs. 26 to 27 per *candil.*[14]

TABLE 8.1 · GOA'S IMPORTS AND EXPORTS OF COCONUTS AND COPRA FROM AND TO THE SOUTH, 1765-78

Year	Coconuts		Copra			
	Importation	Exportation	Importation		Exportation	
			Candis	*Maons*	*Candis*	*Maons*
1765	3784550	594090	375	15 1/2	81	02
1766	1903600	703170	327	15	650	18 1/2
1767	1582350	456520	414	11	478	07
1768	1946500	496600	350	09 1/2	392	10 1/2
1769	1543500	373050	265	03	203	14
1770	1176200	193350	279	16	66	10
1771	3627500	225220	454	17	354	11 1/2
1772	7569206	1128805	710	19	888	15 1/4
1773	7635690	2002094	330	00	1626	04 1/4
1774	1093015	625833	507	17 1/2	981	07 1/4
1775	3772495	1164465	1095	12	2316	15 1/2
1776	4292983	191073	270	15 3/4	1781	05 1/4
1777	2793395	708738	865	02	1885	10
1778	6291802	859720	1422	17	2452	10

Source: HAG : *MR*, 169B, fls. 457-458.

In the early 1780s the issue that gripped the attention of the State authorities was whether to permit the importation of coconuts and coconut products from the south despite the fact that the *Estado* was rich in the commodity.[15]

The influx of coconuts from the south had adversely affected the market value of coconuts available in Goa. Earlier priced at 80 to 100 *xerafins* per thousand, the price since the late 1770s dropped appreciably.[16] In 1779 the price was never higher than 35 *xerafins* per thousand and in 1780 it fell to 25 *xerafins*.[17] This in turn had a profound impact on the *Fazendeiros* who no longer felt motivated to promote coconut cultivation and in fact totally neglected it.[18] Moreover, local coir manufacture particularly in the province of Bardez faced the prospect of extinction.[19]

After weighing the matter carefully, the authorities issued an order banning the entry of coconuts from the south and stating quite definitely that transgression would invite severe punishment.[20] But in March 1781 it reversed its decision on being convinced by certain vested interests that the economy of the *Estado* was at stake. A new order provided a *carta blanche* to the merchants to import coconuts from the south.[21] This was evidently a step taken to please the merchants.

The issue of banning the imports of coconuts from the south surfaced once again for discussion and debate. A representation made by traders highlighted the need to continue to permit the importation of coconuts from the south.[22] They argued that this branch of commerce served as a feeder for the Balaghat trade. The merchants of Balaghat would arrive at Goa with provisions like wheat, paddy, rice, spices, *nachenim, urid,* gram and textiles and would depart with mercandise consisting of copra and salt. A ban on the entry of coconuts from the south would cause a shortfall in the supply of coconuts in Goa.[23] Not finding enough copra to meet their needs, for locally produced coconuts would not be enough for provisioning even one-third of their annual needs, the *Balagateiros*, they argued, would in all probability resort to acquiring copra forcibly or clandestinely, inducing a sharp climb in prices.[24] There was every possibility that the *Balagateiros* would turn to Vengurla, Rarim and other areas to conduct their trade. If the Goa-Balaghat trade was stopped, the State treasury (*Fazenda Real*) which derived an annual income of about 20,000 *xerafins* in the form of customs duties would suffer a severe loss. The local people too would be subjected to undue hardships due to scarcity of provisions.[25] Moreover the merchants of Goa conducted their trade on certain lines. The trade in coconuts procured from the south provided opportunities for financing the rice trade. Capital raised on the commerce in coconuts during the months of October to December could be employed to purchase rice from the south in the month of January.[26]

João Ozorio, in charge of collecting *lagimas* at the Panjim check-post and involved in the importation and exportation of coconuts brought from the south, had different views to express.[27] He presented a case distinctly in favour of prohibition. To him, free entry of coconuts from the southern ports spelt the doom of local coconut production and sale. It posed a threat to the livelihood of the *Fazendeiros* who no longer found it profitable to undertake coconut cultivation.[28] Even the *Fazenda Real* suffered a serious economic setback. He argued that it was in possession of palm-groves confiscated from the Jesuits, at Ilhas, Bardez and Salcette from which it used to derive an annual produce of ten lakhs of coconuts. The sale of these coconuts when the price was high, that is, between 50 and 90 *xerafins* was a substantial source of revenue.[29] Futhermore, it incurred a loss of *foros* imposed on coconut plantations and *dizimos* collected from coconut tree rentiers.[30] The loss and agony caused to the people was much more. He emphasized that the State should adopt a policy of protecting home production as practised in other civilised countries of Europe and Asia.[31] He probably referred to Portugal's prohibiting the entry of liquors to protect its wine industry. Great Britain too not only prohibited the entry of wheat but favoured its exportation.[32]

João Ozorio also argued that although a ban on the entry of coconuts from the south would disrupt the Balaghat trade, and cause the *Balagateiros* to turn to Rajapur, Vengurla and Rarim for coconut supplies, locally produced coconuts and coconut products could be marketed elsewhere. For instance, earlier shipments of 50 lakhs of coconuts and copra would move to the northern ports.[33] He rejected the viewpoint that people would face food shortages due to a halt in provisions descending from the Ghat areas. He observed that areas that produced wheat, paddy, cereals and condiments in the Ghats were Mangaum, Padgaum, Azarem, Gavansem, Chanaguinnem, Zambarim, Shapur, Belgaum (?), Khanapur, Kittur, Dharwar, Hubli, Callaganj and Alxy which did not consume nor import copra and salt from Goa. Textiles, he noted manufactured at Patavar, Conchi, Narrana, Penta, Sagara, Maetal, Bagalkot (?), Talikota, Corgiguy, Callagaty, and Forgolla would be brought to Goa in exchange, not for coconuts and copra but for bullion. The markets to which copra proceeded were Chikodi, Kolhapur, Mirgaum, Vodgaum, Sangli (?), Casagaum, and Oiragar from where neither victuals nor textiles arrived.[34]

The Government decided to resolve the issue once and for all. As a step in this direction it decided to make further investigations relating to the manufacture of coir in the provinces of Bardez and Salcette, which catered significantly to the needs of the State Shipyard (*Arsenal Real*). The latter had an excellent workshop for providing cord for ship-rigging and caulking.[35] Accordingly, viceregal orders were issued binding the Inspectors (*juizes*) of the *Communidades* of Ilhas, Bardez and Salcette to supply information as to which villages in their respective jurisdictions produced coir, approximately how much was produced annually, how many men and women were engaged in its manufacture, their conditions and privileges of employment and the quality of coir demanded. Furthermore, suggestions were invited as to who should be entrusted with the task of manufacturing this item and the conditions necessary for the protection of this industry.[36] It was found out that in Salcette coir manufacture was conducted at Mormugão, Vaddem, Chicalim, Sancoale, Cortalim, Quelossim, Utorda, Betalbatim, Cavelossim and Sernabattim. These centres produced 60 *candis* of coir annually and 29 men and 132 women were gainfully employed in its manufacture.[37] In Bardez, coir was produced at Siolim, Oxel, Anjuna, Arpora, Calangute, Nerul and Candolim. It was of two varieties, namely fresh water coir produced in summer and salty water coir produced in the months of October and November. The latter kind was sold at the rate of 24 *xerafins* per *candil* and the former at the rate of 20 *xerafins*. Salt water coir depended upon fresh coconut husks.[38]

The matter of importation of coconuts from southern ports was put to vote. Of the merchants of Goa (Ilhas) engaged in the coconut trade, 25 of them voted against prohibition. So too did the Customs Superintendent, who supplied two charts on the volume of coconuts and copra which entered and left Goa together with duties collected during 1776-78 and 1779-81 respectively, indicating that a fall in revenues to the tune of 52,207-3-28 *xerafins*, had occurred during 1779-81, the period when prohibition was enforced.[39] The thirteen merchants of Bardez engaged in the commerce in coconuts unanimously voted in favour of the entry of coconuts from the south, while the lone merchant of Salcette João Ozorio staunchly stood against such imports.[40] The Municipalities of Ilhas and Salcette voted in favour of prohibition and demanded the suspension of the existing orders permitting entry.[41] But the Municipality of Bardez which had earlier favoured prohibition later changed its stand.[42] As regards the *Fazendeiros* of Goa, 34 favoured banning while 147 expressed their preference for the entry of Malabar coconuts. In the province of Bardez 64 *Fazendeiros* stood for prohibition while 2,634 voted against it. In Salcette 2,955 *Fazendeiros* voted for a ban on the admission of coconuts from the south.[43] Most if not all the merchants of Bardez and Ilhas engaged in the coconut trade favoured the free entry of coconuts from the south. Likewise 81.22% of the *Fazendeiros* of Goa and 97.63% of those of Bardez opposed prohibition. This indicates that merchants and *Fazendeiros* of Bardez and Goa (Ilhas) drew considerable benefits from the Goa-Balaghat commerce and were keen to protect it at all costs. The *Estado* authorities observed after examining the pros and cons of the controversial issue that prohibition of the entry of coconuts from the south would have damaging consequences for the State economy. But also stressed that coconut cultivation in Goa should not be neglected since its people used coconuts extensively as a food item especially in the form of coconut oil. The coir, jaggery and liquor production too needed State protection. Therefore they arrived at a decision that while the entry of coconuts from the south was not to be banned, the importation of coconut husks and oil were to be prohibited.[44] From the complaints and representations made by the people of Salcette in 1830, it seems that coconut products continued to enter Goa.[45]

The State stand on the importation of coconuts from the southern ports is an indication that it was more interested in appeasing the merchants and protecting their interests than in protecting its agricultural system and the Goan economy. However, the State had also to think in terms of customs revenues that it derived from the importation of coconuts from the south. As indicated earlier during the period of the prohibition, (1779-81) there was a drop in revenues to the tune of 52,207-3-28 *xerafins* as compared to the earlier period (1776-78).

Figure 8.1 demonstrates the effects of the State policy of free entry of coconuts from the south implemented in 1785. We see that the income of State was more from imports of coconuts and copra than from exports.

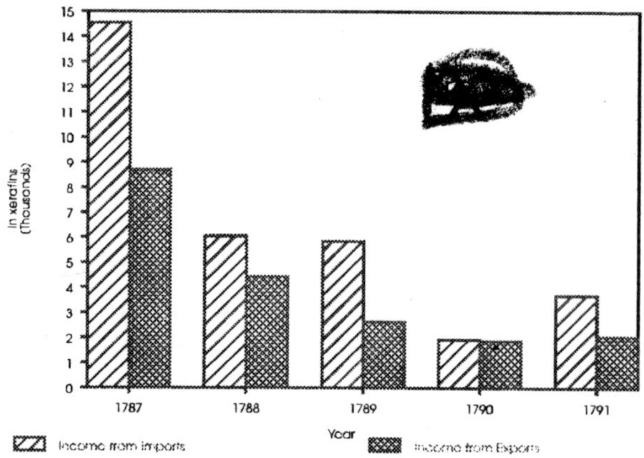

FIG. 8.1: INCOME DERIVED FROM COCONUTS AND COPRA AT GOA, 1787-91
Source: HAG *: MR*, 173, fl. 284.

Coming to the volume of Goa's coconut imports during 1787-91 when the free entry of coconuts from the south was permitted, Table 8.2 reveals that a total number of 5,428,892 coconuts were imported averaging 1,085,778 coconuts per year. About 7,204 *candis* and 4 *maons* of copra or an average annual amount of 1,440 *candis* and 17 *maons* of copra were imported during the aforesaid period. If we compare these import figures with those of 1765-78, the period prior to free entry of coconuts from southern ports, a drop in coconut importation was observed during 1787-91 to the extent of 2,415,135 coconuts while the increase in copra imports amounted to 892 *candis* and 18 *maons* (Tables 8.1 and 8.2).

As regards the exports trade during 1787-91 a total of 4,773,660 coconuts or an annual average of 954,732 coconuts were exported, while copra exports amounted to a total of 4,651 *candis* and 6 *maons* or an average per year of 930 *candis* and five *maons* (Table 8.3). When we compare these export figures with those for the years 1765-78 we observe an increase in the quantity of coconuts exported during 1787-91 to the tune of 2,60,252 coconuts and a decrease in copra exports in the same period to the extent of 81 *candis* and 4 *maons* (Tables 8.1 and 8.3). The increase in Goa's coconut exports must have served to stimulate and boost coconut production in the area.

Table 8.2: VOLUME OF THE GOA-BASED IMPORT TRADE IN COCONUT AND COPRA, 1787-91

Year	Number of Coconuts	Copra (in *candis*)
1787	3125326	2800-00
1788	721099	1568-12
1789	526800	1638-18
1790	447253	350-14
1791	608414	846-00
Total	5428892	7204-04

Source: HAG : *MR*, 173, fl. 284.

TABLE 8.3: QUANTITY OF COCONUTS AND COPRA EXPORTED BY GOA, 1787-91

Year	Number of Coconuts	Copra (in *candis*)
1787	2181520	2034-07
1788	1008800	1112-01
1789	685690	590-04
1790	456500	418-04
1791	441150	496-06
Total	4773660	4651-02

Source: HAG : *MR*, 173, fl. 284.

In 1844, 11,769,152 coconuts, 2,101 *candis* and 13 1/2 *maons* of copra together with coconut oil, were exported by Goa.[46] In 1849, 15,292,349 coconuts and 1,839 *candis* of copra were a part of the export cargoes of Goa.[47]

In 1831-32 an official price list demonstrates the value of coir imported into Goa. The price of coir from Maldives ranged between 17 1/2 to 22 1/2 *xerafins* per quintal that from Cochin between 14 and 20 *xerafins* a quintal and that from Calicut between 12 and 17 1/2 *xerafins* a quintal. Distance, resulting in higher transportation charges, was at the root of this price differentiation. In 1831-32 locally produced coconuts fetched a price of 20 *xerafins* per thousand while that imported from the south cost 25 *xerafins* per thousand. Copra on the other hand cost 10 *xerafins* per quintal whether locally produced or imported from the south.[48]

Coming to the value of Goa's trade in coconuts we have considered that in 1778 the price of coconuts ranged between 80 and 100 *xerafins* per thousand. From Table 8.1 we gather that 6,291,802 coconuts were imported in that year. Therefore Goa's import trade in coconuts in 1778 was valued between 503,344-0-08 and 629,180-0-01 *xerafins*. In 1780 the price of coconuts stood at 35 *xerafins* per thousand and in 1804-05 at 25 *xerafins*. Let us assume that the price of coconuts ranged between 25 and 35 *xerafins* during 1787-91. During the said period Goa's coconut imports on an average amounted to 1,085,778 and therefore it valued between 27,144-2-15 and 38,002-1-09 *xerafins*. During 1787-91 the average coconut exports per year totalled 954,732. Therefore Goa's export trade in coconuts during the said period had a value that ranged between 23,868-1-30 and 33,415-3-06 *xerafins*.

Rice

Rice was another commodity featuring significantly in the Estado-based coastal trade. Rice cultivation was conducted extensively in Goa. Any available land favourable for rice production was put to use. It was in lands called *addis, batlem* or *moroddes, quero, dulpi, molay*, and *bawal, khari* or *gally* where rice was cultivated. Among the varieties of rice produced, mention can be made of *asgó*, produced in Ilhas, *xittó*, *patni* and *quendal* produced in Salcette, *domagó* and *khonchori* in Bardez and *sall, pacharil, domagó,* and *xittó* in New Conquest areas.[49] *Coxerim* and *derabo* were the two main varieties of paddy. During 1777-80 *coxerim* fetched a price of 6 *xerafins* per *candil* while *derabo* cost 3-1-45 *xerafins* per *candil*.[50]

However the annual rice production of Goa was much less than the need. It was probably enough for just six months. According to Manoel Joze Loureiro the *Estado* consumption of rice was 1 million *fardos* per annum.[51] Therefore rice supplies in bulk would move from areas of surplus production to Goa. Goa's rice imports stood at 162,145 bales in 1757. This fell to 146,246 and 138,036 bales in 1779 and 1780 respectively. Pombaline efforts to boost agricultural production during the 1770s was probably responsible for this. In 1824 Goa imported 24,327 bales of rice and this figure climbed up to 47,197 in 1846.[52]

Throughout the sixteenth and seventeenth centuries Goa demonstrated how heavily dependent it was on Kanara for rice. About 3 to 4 convoys would leave Kanara for Goa every year in the sixteenth century.[53] In the 1630s the value of the rice trade from Kanara alone stood at Rs. 450,000.[54] Basrur in Kanara was a major source of rice supply to Goa. It exported an annual average of 1,975,000 kg of rice during 1611-16, 1,530,000 kg in 1623 and an average of 27,500,000 kg per annum during September 1625-March 1628.[55] Mangalore, Honavar, Kalianpur and Ponani were other sources of rice supply in Kanara.[56] Supplies would also come from the north, Malabar and overland from the Ghat region. People in Goa did not apply themselves sufficiently to the cultivation of the lands they possessed, except in relation to their own wants and personal subsistence, and definitely with no view to commerce. Therefore many of the lands remained uncultivated and even the rice fields which might have produced two crops in a year produced only one crop.

Vitalji Kamat, Keshav Parab Cawandy, Vithoji Sinai Dhempe and the Mhamai brothers were involved in the flourishing trade in rice along the west coast of India. Brown and Dineur would often consign rice cargoes from Mangalore and Ponani to the Mhamais for sale in Goa. In August 1805 there was a shortage of Mangalore rice as gathered from the Mhamai records. However, Brown and Dineur informed the brothers that the export of Ponani rice would be resumed as there had been a good harvest.[57] In September 1791 the Bombay-based Herjee Jevanjee consigned 120 sacks of rice to the Mhamais for disposal at Goa.[58]

Daman, however had enough rice for its needs. This may be inferred from the regular rice supplies that proceeded to Goa and across the Indian Ocean to Moçambique from Daman. In 1794 Arcachande Ira of Daman despatched 46 *candis* of rice to Moçambique on board the vessel *Azia Feliz*.[59] Likewise in the same year Javer Cuxal sent on board the ship *Nossa Senhora das Augustias e Porto Seguro* 343 sacks of fine rice.[60] In February 1802 *Anna Joaquina* transported 20 sacks of fine rice and 32 sacks of thick rice to Moçambique from Daman.[61] In January 1808, 18 *candis* of rice were shipped on board *Pedro de Alcantara* to Moçambique.[62]

The price of rice in 1831-32 ranged between 6 and 8 *xerafins* per sack of 5 *arrobas*.[63]

Usually the rice merchants got their supplies from the peasants through their agents. Sometimes the cultivators themselves brought their rice cargoes to the merchants and sold them at the acceptable prices. It is difficult to ascertain just how profitable this business was for the cultivators. Usually the merchant class and their agents would fleece the cultivators because of their weak financial position. But it appears certain that with the increasing demand for rice by the Portuguese and the dependence of the merchants on the peasants, their position did improve. They could bargain extensively for favourable rates especially when rice was in short supply.

Wheat

Wheat was cultivated in Portuguese India, on a limited scale at Nagar-Haveli in Daman. Excessive rain was a handicap. To meet the wheat requirements of the people of Goa, regular wheat supplies came to Goa from Daman, Diu, Bombay and the Ghat areas.[64] In 1826 Goa imported 5 *candis* of wheat from Daman at the rate of 34 *xerafins* per *candil* and an equal amount from the south at the rate of 35 *xerafins* a *candil*.[65] In 1849 Goa's wheat imports amounted to 3989 *candis*.[66] In fact traders along western coastal India found a favourable market situation at Goa for the sale of wheat and would constantly call upon the Goa merchants to sell off their wheat cargoes. In 1791 Herjee Jeevanjee consigned 201 sacks of wheat to the Mhamais for disposal at Goa.[67]

In 1831-32 the price of wheat at Goa was 10 *xerafins* for a *candil* of *ancia* variety, 7 *xerafins* per *candil* of *calea* variety and 6 *xerafins* per *candil* of *polê* variety.[68]

Arecanuts

The arecanut or the betelnut tree is a thin graceful palm 50 to 60 feet high widely cultivated at Goa where water for irrigation purposes was available throughout the year. The arecanut formed one of the main ingredients of the mixture known as *pan supari* which was used for chewing. This mixture was said to aid digestion and to protect teeth from decay.

Arecanuts produced in Goa were of two varieties, red and white. The former was a superior sort. Locally produced arecanuts were exported in bulk to Bombay and other places in the north. About fifty ships laden with arecanuts, coconuts, coir and other goods proceeded annually to the north from Goa.[69] In 1826 Goa exported to Bombay 1080 *candis* and 14 *maons* of red arecanuts and 1,015 *candis* and 8 *maons* of white arecanuts priced at 60 and 40 *xerafins* per *candil* respectively.[70] In 1826 Goa also exported 19 *candis* and 2 *maons* of red arecanuts to Daman.[71]

Arecanuts were also exported to Macao, Muscat and Moçambique. In 1800 white arecanuts priced at 40 *xerafins* per *candil* were despatched to Muscat.[72] Table 8.4 reveals the increasing demand for arecanuts from Goa in Macao in the early nineteenth century. In 1844 Goa's arecanut exports were worth 260,170-3-7 *xerafins.*[73] In 1849 Goa exported 6,350 *candis* of arecanuts.[74]

TABLE 8.4: ARECANUT CONSIGNMENTS TO MACAO FROM GOA AND DAMAN, 1796-1832

Year	Ships	Quantity				
		picos	*gunes*	*pessas*	*sacos*	*quintais*
1796	Galeria	347				
1797	Luis e Almas Santas		461			
1798	Nossa Senhora da Luz		250			
1800		275818				
1802	Esperança			10		
1805	Bella Julia				5	
1811	Conde de Sarzedas					163
1813	Angelica					472
1816	Angelica					187
1817	Angelica					30
1823	Angelica					1900
	Santo Antonio					1700
1825	Dezempenho					2583
1826	Angelica					20(?)
1828	Eliza					535
1829	Angelica					1000
1832	Eliza	9257				

Sources: HAG : Compiled from *Macqu*, 1295-99, 1305, 1308, 1310-11, 1322, 1324-25, 1329, 1332, 1336.

Arecanuts were also imported from the Malabar which produced them in abundance.[75] Malabar arecanuts were however boiled and dried before use.

Salt

Salt was one of the chief items of export of the *Estado da India*. Daman salt was transported to the Malabar coast and Calcutta. Salt extracted from the salt-works at Nerul in Goa was despatched by local merchants to

Bombay and the south.[76] In February 1808 Thomas Dineur requested the Mhamais to help Vithoba of the coastal vessel *Laxmy* to buy Nerul salt.[77] In June 1811 Dineur inquired whether the Mhamais were willing to enter into a contract to supply 400 *cumbos* of Nerul salt at the rate of Rs. 12 per *cumbo* before the year terminated and that the penalty for every *maon* short supplied would involve a deduction of Rs. 5. The payment would be made in three instalments, the first at the time of signing the contract, the second when half the delivery was made, and the last one when the entire order was executed.[78] In February 1822 Suba Kamat dispatched 376-1/2 *cunbos* of salt to Alleppey (Table 8.5). In 1844 Goa's salt exports totalled 59,579 *candis* and 6 *maons* while in 1849 they amounted to 74,284 *candis*.[79]

TABLE 8.5: SALT SHIPMENTS MADE BY SUBA KAMAT FROM GOA TO ALLEPPEY, 1822

Ship	Tindal	Quantity(In *Cumbos*)
Revulnath Persand	Sucundnaik	17
Maha Laxmi	Shaikh Abdullah	34
Salamity	Shaikh Ebrahim	26
Esvonty	Shaikh Mohamed	13
Salamity	Shaikh Huson	14
Durga Dowlat	Tucker	80
Sanjao	Senivar	40
Salamity	Abdul Coader	16
Palky Salamity	Mookoond	25 1/2
Sacry Salamity	João	35

Sources: XCHR : *MHP*, doc. nos. 1360, 11623, 9270, 5136, 5137, 11551, 16739, 19486, 5982, 5207, 5387, 5290, 11620, 11621, 20998.

According to local statistics there were 658 salt extractors at Goa, 84 at Daman and 24 in Diu in 1850.[80]

Locally produced salt was extensively employed in the fishing industry. On days when the catch was abundant, the fishermen found it impossible to dispose off all the fish. As the climatic conditions in India did not permit fish to remain for more than five hours, the surplus fish was salted and dried. A substantial quantity of salt was required to increase the fertility of fields and palm groves. In Portuguese India the cooking of rice and fish demanded the use of much salt. The actual average annual need of a person was a minimum of 32 lb.

Fruits

In the Mhamai documentation we observe the regular despatch of mangoes to the south and Bombay. Mango exports by sea were almost exclusively operated by means of country crafts. Fifteen baskets of mangoes were sent to Brown and Dineur at Mahe in 1793.[81] Similarly, 475 mangoes loaded on the *pattamar* of Rama Tandel, were received by Joakin Lewis at Bombay in 1794.[82] In May 1809 Joakin Lewis of Bombay requested the Mhamais to dispatch 200 to 300 mangoes comprising of some afonso mangoes and others of good quality.[83]

There were no regular and continuous tracts used exclusively for the cultivation of mango except in extremely rare cases and that too in an area not exceeding one square mile. Mango production was nevertheless much higher in Ilhas than elsewhere in Goa, its soil being favourable for mango cultivation and growth. There were many varieties of grafted trees, but the most popular was afonso. Ungrafted trees were of numerous varieties but their fruits were not much appreciated except for pickles and chutneys. Such preserves were exported to Moçambique and neighbouring ports. In January 1808, 43,100 mangoes for pickle were exported from the *Estado* to Moçambique on board the vessel *Pedro de Alcantara*.[84] Eleven *maons* and 12 *barris* of salted mangoes were sent from Goa to Bombay in 1826.[85] Each *barril* was worth 10 *xerafins*. In 1849, 100 *almudes* of mango preserves (*conservas de mangas*) were exported from Goa.[86]

Sugarcane, pineapple and cashew fruits were other local fruits shipped to Bombay[87] (Table 8.6) A massive programme was launched to promote cashew-fruit growing. In 1778 there were 4,515 cashew trees in Bardez and 10,648 trees in Salcette.[88]

TABLE 8.6: FRUIT AND VEGETABLE EXPORTS OF GOA, 1844

Type	Quantity (In *xerafins*)	Total Value (In *xerafins*)	Duties Collected
Figs	3787400	1362-1-00	3787-0-00
Mangoes	1152200	9217-3-00	5761-0-00
Pineapple	43732	874-3-12	437-0-00
Sugarcane	8800	44-4-00	15-0-00
Potatoes	442	3536-0-00	110-0-00

Source: HAG : *MR*, 219B, fl. 867.

Fish

A sizable part of the population was exclusively employed in the fishing industry all along the sea-coast of Goa and other enclaves of Portuguese India. In 1850 there were 3,306 fishermen in Goa, 1393 in Daman and 403 in Diu.[89] The fish caught was so abundant at times that it became extremely difficult to dispose it off at a nominal rate. Such fish was dried and salted. But the major part of such hauls was sold for manuring purposes in either its fresh or dried form.

The bulk of the fish produced was consumed locally and the remainder made its way to British India. Goa would transport salted fish to Bombay and other nearby ports.[90] Daman exported not only salted fish but also fish maws and shark fins (*azas de tubarão*). Deep sea fishing was conducted by Daman fishermen between Diu and Jaffrabad. A large quantity of salted fish proceeded directly from this region to several Konkan ports, principally Bhiwandy in Tanna collectorate, which was noted as a market for fish and fish products from whence traders would convey their goods to distant areas beyond the Ghats. The fish cargoes brought to Daman proceeded to Dhurrampor and Bansda(?) where they were bartered for grain. Fish maws and fins were despatched to Macao and China via Bombay. The Khojas residing at Daman were actively involved in this trade.[91] Shark fins and fish maws were also directly exported from Goa to Macao. One *pico* of shark fins worth 48 *xerafins* was exported in 1800 by João de Noronha.[92] In the same year the well-known Goan merchant Ignacio Xavier Unhão despatched two *picos* of shark fins to Macao.[93] Shark fin cargoes would also move to Bombay from the port of Goa. In 1826, 5 *candis*, and 2-3/4 *maons* of shark fins were exported to Bombay.[94]

Salted and pickled fish (*peixe tamarinho*) too formed a part of the export cargoes of Goa moving to Bombay, Moçambique and other areas. In 1826, 386 *barris* of pickled fish were despatched from Goa to Bombay.[95] In 1844, 69 small *barris* of pickled and salted fish worth 15,797 *xerafins* were a part of Goa's total exports.[96]

Domesticated Birds

The exports of Goa included domesticated birds, such as ducks, geese, fowls, chickens and turkeys. Such items would move to Bombay, Daman, the southern ports as well as to Moçambique. Canaple made repeated requests from Mahe to the Mhamais for such birds. The requests were born out of the need to meet the scarcity of food supplies caused by Tipu Sultan's embargo and wars.[97] Boyer, also based at Mahe, would request for provisions to tide over difficulties caused by Tipu Sultan's embargo. Thus on 26th November 1789 he requested the Mhamais to despatch 100 ducks, 100 turkeys and 400 chickens for breeding.[98] He repeated the request in February 1790 and even later.[99] In a letter dated 25th November 1789, to the Mhamais, we gain the impression that Brown and Dineur had earlier ordered for birds but had not yet received them. It mentions that a sepoy named Domingos would be sent to acquire 10 pairs of turkeys, 6 pairs of ducks and some chickens.[100]

In 1826, 127 pairs of chickens at the rate of 5 xerafins each and 366 pairs of turkeys at the rate of 4 *xerafins* per pair were exported by Goa to Bombay.[101] Daman in the same year received 6 pairs of turkeys.[102] In January 1808 on board the ship *Pedro de Alcantara* 50 chickens were despàtched to Moçambique.[103]

It is also interesting to note that the expenditure records of various convents and hospitals of Goa indicate that the latter were major consumers of chicken and other food items like eggs, coconut oil, rice, wheat, butter, vegetables, fish, beef, pork, vinegar, sugar and milk.[104]

Sugar

Indigenously produced sugar called jaggery was of two kinds, that derived from toddy and sugarcane respectively. Jaggery production undoubtedly occupied a prominent place in the Goan economy. Sweets which formed a major part of the diet of the people demanded not only the manufacture of jaggery but also the import of sizable quantities of sugar from Macao and China.[105]

Sugar also arrived at Goa from Bombay, Bengal, Siam, Batavia, Manila, Mauritius, and even Brazil.[106] Such sugar was either granulated, powdered, or candied. In 1826 Goa obtained granular and fine sugar worth 30,601-1-52 1/2 *xerafins* from Bombay. This consignment included sugar from Bengal.[107] Sugar from Macao was furnished to the Royal Hospital (*Hospital Real*), the Military Hospital (*Hospital Militar*) and the Royal Arsenal of Goa.[108] For instance in 1838, 60 *arrobas* of fine sugar and 4 *arrobas* of the granular kind were supplied to the pharmacy of *Hospital Militar.*[109] Though much of the sugar imported was locally consumed, some this sugar would proceed to Moçambique.[110] In 1794, the ship *Azia Feliz* carried one *candil* of powdered sugar from Daman to Moçambique.[111] In 1802, 28 *balças* of granular sugar and 32 sacks of fine sugar were despatched to Moçambique from Daman.[112] (See Table 8.7)

TABLE 8.7: VICTUAL EXPORTS FROM DAMAN TO MOÇAMBIQUE, 1840

Date	Ship	Merchant	Goods
30th Jan 1840	Domingi	Francisco Sebastião de Souza	6 *fardos* of wheat
31st Jan 1840		Gulamo Amogy	1 *candil* of fine rice
31st Jan 1840		Gulamo Amogy	30 sacks of fine rice
31st Jan 1840		Salmogi Vallogi	13 sacks of fine rice
1st Feb 1840	Estrelade Damão	Cassam Obai	5 sacks of rice
1st Feb 1840	Estrelade Damão	C.M. Montes	37 bottles of castor oil
1st Feb 1840	Estrelade Damão	Avivalobe Bogoane	4 *balças* of granulated sugar
1st Feb 1840		Cassabai Abdul Caremo	6 *tureens* of rice
1st Feb 1840	Fate Islamo	Mamod Faquir	2 *candis* of rice
1st Feb 1840	Estrelade Damão	Ismalgi Vassangi	1 sack of wheat
1st Feb 1840	Estrelade Damão	Ismalgi Vassangi	1 sack of white arecanuts
4th Feb 1840	Estrelade Damão	Musagi Vallagy	5 sacks of powdered sugar 2 *baleas* of granulated sugar, 5 tins of butter

Sources: HAG : *Damão*, 4851, fls. 2v-7v; 4853, fls. 1-14v.

In 1831-32, the price of powdered sugar from China ranged between 5 and 10 *xerafins* per *arroba*, that of Bengal between 4 and 10 *xerafins*, that of Batavia between 5 and 6 *xerafins*, that of Manila between 6 and 8 *xerafins*, that of Brazil between 3 and 8 *xerafins* while fine sugar from Mauritius cost 3-1/2 *xerafins* an *arroba*.[113] One can infer from this that Brazilian sugar was of an inferior kind.

Cashewnuts

Cashewnuts with or without a coating of sugar were often shipped to Bombay, Mahe and other ports on the western littoral of India during the period under study.[114] In February 1789, Canaple instructed the Mhamais to send two or three *maons* of cashewnuts.[115] In September 1804, Brown and Dineur expressed a desire for cashewnuts.[116] In 1789 cashewnuts were exported to the north.[117] In 1826 37 *quintais*, 3 *arrobas* and 3 *arrateis* of cashewnuts were exported from Goa to Bombay.[118] In 1844, 8,725 *arrobas* and 28 *arrateis* of cashewnuts worth 36,273-0-00 *xerafins* were exported from the port of Goa.[119]

Local Liquors

In Goa country liquors were manufactured chiefly from coconut toddy and the juice of the cashew fruit. In Daman and Diu liquor was produced from *cajuri toddy*. Two varieties of liquor, *feni* and arrack, were manufactured at distilleries from both coconut extract and coconut toddy. *Feni* was of a superior kind, its alcohol percentage being higher. To produce *feni*, double the quantity of toddy or cashew juice and double the time of distillation were required. *Feni* was said to be an effective cure for rheumatism, asthma and other maladies. In 1850 there were 3,764 toddy tappers in Goa, 1,192 in Daman and 58 in Diu. Besides there were 2,843 distillers of liquor in Goa and 202 in Daman.[120] Of the three Portuguese enclaves Goa specialised in liquor production.

Goan liquors would arrive at Bombay, Daman, Diu and the south. In 1789, *feni* was despatched to both the north as well as the south.[121] In 1826, 2 *candis* and 3 *maons* of coconut *feni* and 10 *maons* of cashew liquor arrived at Bombay from Goa. Coconut *feni* was priced at 100 *xerafins* per *candil* and cashew liquor at 2 *xerafins* per *maon*.[122] In the same year, 1 *candil* and 6 *maons* of *feni* and 19-1/2 *candis* of cashew liquor were transported to Daman from Goa.[123] Arrack was quite a favourite item of import at Moçambique.[124] The official records provide ample evidence to indicate the regular flow of Goan liquors to East Africa. In December 1795, Vicente Joze Lopes de Laura dispatched 9 *maons* of cashew liquor to Moçambique.[125] In 1828 Estevão Pinto despatched feni and cashew liquors to Moçambique.[126]

As in the case of tobacco, local liquor revenues were also farmed in the *Estado da India*.[127] In 1766, we have the case of Merlu, a Parsee residing in Daman who held a triennial contract worth 4,220-1/2 *xerafins* per annum.[128] In Goa, Dulba Sinai of Panelim was assigned the contract for the triennial 1770-73 at 11,290 *xerafins* per year. Likewise the arrack contract for Bardez was assigned to Lakshman Sinai for the same period at the rate of 17,500 *xerafins* per year.[129]

One of the principal sources of income of the State was in the form of duties imposed on imported and exported liquors. From an undated document we are able to gather an idea of the revenues of the State from arrack in a single year. Probably in the year 1771, Ilhas yielded 11,059-0-28 *xerafins*, Salcette 27,421-0-28 *xerafins* and Bardez 18,230-2-28 *xerafins*.[130] Table 8.8 also provides a glimpse of the income that the State obtained from customs duties on liquor.

Table 8.8: LIQUOR CUSTOMS REVENUES OF THE *ESTADO DA INDIA*, 1776-77

(In *xerafins*)

Year	Ilhas	Salcette	Bardez	Daman	Diu
1776	4458-0-36 1/4	6454-2-30	5000-0-00	1216-1-22	205-0-00
1777	4473-0-02 1/2	2151-2-30	5000-0-00		

Source: HAG : *CR*, 1634, doc. dated 1 April 1777.

Tea

Tea would come to Portuguese India from Macao, China and Bombay. By the ship *Santa Clara* tea was brought to Goa from Macao in May 1800 by Roque de Rego.[131] Two *quintais*, 3 *arrobas* and 46 *arrateis* of tea arrived at Goa from Bombay in 1826.[132] This tea was of various brands and types designated *chá haisson, chá perola, chá preto, chá verde* and *chá bay*.[133] In 1831-32, tea was priced in Goa as follows : *chá bay* at 50 to 60 *xerafins* per chest of half *pico, chá perola* between 125 and 150 *xerafins* and *chá preto*, three *xerafins* an *arratel*.[134]

Tea despatched to Goa was usually for local use although some of it reached Moçambique.[135] Eduardo Popham informed the Mhamais that he was sending 5 cases of tea to be sold at the best possible price, preferably 1-1/4 rupees per pound. His instructions to the Mhamais were to sell the tea profitably and find out the prospects of selling tea at Goa, Tellicherry or Cochin.[136]

Spices

Another major segment of *Estado* imports were pepper and spices which formed an essential ingredient in cooking for the wealthier classes as well for the commonfolk. They also had medicinal use.

Pepper, an item of international significance in the sixteenth century, was in the period under review of importance in the western coastal trade. It was produced in abundance in the entire stretch of territory from Cape Comorin to Kanara, an area disturbed by the political designs and intrigues of Tipu Sultan and the rivalry between the French and the British. Malabar, Cannanore, Calicut, Cochin and Quilon were the chief sources of pepper supply. While the quality of Cannanore pepper was reportedly the best in the region, Portuguese India received bulk supplies from Calicut. Cochin pepper was relatively cheaper and of an inferior variety. Quilon was of lesser importance than Cochin in the pepper trade though the pepper available there was of the same grade as that procured from Cochin. Mahe too was another centre of pepper supply. Merchants dealing with pepper produced in Malabar were mostly Indianized descendants of Arab migrants called Moplahs or Mappilas. In Kanara, the leading pepper growers were at Honavar, Basrur and Mangalore. The price of Kanara pepper was higher than that supplied by Malabar. Kanara pepper was obviously far superior.[137]

Pepper was also produced in Goa though on a small scale. In 1778 we observe that there were 21,020 pepper trees in Ilhas, 40,508 in Bardez and 74,408 in Salcette.[138]

Spices such as nutmeg, cloves, mace, cardamom and cinnamon were far more limited in their consumption as seen from the low volumes that were imported. Cardamom was produced in the region between Cannanore and Chale near Calicut,but was imported from the ports of Cochin and Calicut.[139] Cloves were obtained from South East Asia especially Moluccas. Usually clove cargoes of this region were transported to the port of Malacca and then shipped to the *Estado*.[140] Mauritius and other French islands in the Indian Ocean too supplied cloves to Goa.[141] Ginger, a food item, believed to have medicinal value was derived from the south. Beladi ginger was produced in the vicinity of Calicut and in the interior while Dely ginger was produced in the area between Mount Dely and Cannanore. The former was also grown in Bengal. Mace and nutmeg, products of Banda came to Goa via Malacca. Tamarind was collected from the regions of Malabar and Gujarat.[142] Cinnamon came from Ceylon while a coarser variety came from Cochin, Calicut and Basrur.[143]

Cinnamon cargoes also arrived at Goa from Solor. They were said to be superior to that obtainable on the Malabar coast. In the post-1765 period cinnamon from Solor was sold at the rate of 360 *xerafins* per *candil* while that of the Malabar coast was available at the rate of 80 *xerafins*.[144]

From Mhamai documentation we gather that the Indo-Portuguese merchants were extensively involved in the *Estado*-based spice trade along the west coast of India. Brown and Dineur would despatch spices to Goa and other areas to the north at regular intervals. 1789 was however a critical year. In October 1789 Brown and Dineur informed the Mhamais that there was little chance of procuring any pepper. The Mappilas had either fled or were refusing to conduct business fearing that Tipu Sultan would pass through Mahe. They were unwilling to enter into contracts even for exorbitant rates.[145] By 1805 the crisis sparked off by Tipu Sultan had apparently blown over. In December 1805 Brown and Dineur informed the Mhamais that since the English East India Company had not bought pepper that particular season, there was an abundance of that spice. Brown and Dineur offered to buy 300 to 400 *candis* of pepper on Mhamai's account at the rate of Rs. 138 per *candil* of 640 pounds.[146] In July 1806 Brown and Dineur informed the Mhamais that the price of pepper had dropped to Rs. 100 per *candil* and had been exempted from customs duties up to 31st December 1806.[147]

In 1814 Thomas Dineur informed the Mhamais that there was little old pepper left in the region and that it was selling at the rate ranging between Rs. 130 and Rs. 135. There were indications that the new pepper would be expensive and should the Bombay Presidency decide to send banias to procure it as in the preceding year the price was expected to shoot up to Rs. 180 to Rs. 200.[148] It was obvious that the Mhamais faced stiff competition from the banias of the Bombay Presidency with respect to the spice trade.

Some of the spices acquired from the south were sent to Lisbon in the period under review, though not on the scale at which they were shipped in the sixteenth century. In 1800 a cargo of textiles, pepper and cinnamon was despatched from Daman on board the ship *Rainha dos Anjos*. The ship touched Goa before its onward voyage to Lisbon.[149] The Mhamais too would despatch regular supplies of spices to Portugal and other parts of Europe on demand and on their own account. In March 1799 the Mhamais were required to send a chest of cinnamon procured from Ceylon to Lisbon.[150]

As in the case of Indian textiles, Lisbon merchant ships would pay a visit to the ports on the Coromandel coast for pepper and cinnamon without touching the ports of the *Estado da India*. In July 1814, 4139 sacks of pepper obtained at Madras formed a part of the cargo of the ship *Nossa Senhora da Paz Rozalia* on its homeward-bound journey.[151] In 1815 three ships acquired cargoes of spices at Bengal.[152]

Pepper was acquired from middlemen. The latter bought pepper from the cultivators. They would then transport it by cart, oxen or river boat to the markets inland or along the coast, and sell there to exporters and distributors. Most middlemen were independent operators who acted as agents for wealthy coastal merchants. It is quite difficult to ascertain the profits accrued by the middlemen. Although sale prices are known in certain instances there appears to be no corresponding information about rates at which the middlemen paid the growers. The pepper cultivators had frequently to pledge their pepper in advance to middlemen. The latter would at most times acquire the next season's crop for a cash advance.

Pepper was apparently bought on contract.[153] Usually the Indo-

Portuguese merchant acquired pepper from the exporters and distributors or even the middlemen on the payment of an advance of half of the total amount. The remaining amount was paid on delivery or receipt of the goods. Payments were normally made in cash or in the form of bills of exchange. The significance of the Estado-based trade in spices lies in the fact that although the turnover was not large, the margin of profit was great.

REFERENCES AND NOTES

1. A. B. de Bragança Pereira, *Etnografia da India Portugueza*, vol. II, Nova Goa, 1923, p. 401.
2. HAG : *AG*, 6807, fl. 467.
3. HAG : *AG*, 2668, fls. 33, 34v-35v.
4. HAG : *Provisões*, 1586, fl. 933.
5. HAG : *AG*, 6810, fl. 62.
6. Felippe Nery Xavier, *O Gabinete Litterario das Fontainhas*, vol. II, Nova Goa, 1847, p. 162.
7. XCHR : *MHP* (French), vol. 6, fls. 72-72v, 228-228v.
8. XCHR : *MHP* (French), vol. 6, fl. 63.
9. XCHR : *MHP* (French), vol. 6, fl. 65.
10. XCHR : *MHP* (French), vol. 6, fl. 52.
11. XCHR : *MHP* (French), vol. 6, fl. 35v.
12. XCHR : *MHP* (French), vol. 6, fl. 37.
13. XCHR : *MHP* (French), vol. 6, fls. 84-85, 78-78v.
14. XCHR : *MHP* (French), vol. 6, fl. 216v.
15. HAG : *MR*, 161F, fl. 1015.
16. HAG : *MR*, 161F, fl. 1525.
17. HAG : *MR*, 161F, fls. 1015, 1017.
18. HAG : *MR*, 161F, fl. 1017.
19. HAG : *MR*, 161F, fls. 1492-1518.
20. HAG : *MR*, 161F, fl. 1492.
21. HAG : *MR*, 161F, fl. 1505.
22. HAG : *MR* 161F, fl. 1528v. Daquea Kamat, Keshav Kamat, Venkat Kamat, Mukund Sinai, Venku Pai, Rama Sinai, Vassu Parab, Phondu Parab, Vithogi Sinai, Venkatesh Kamat, Venkat Naik, Bhikya Kamat, Rogu Kamat Mhamai, Malu Parab, Venku Kamat, Polpotea Naik, Rama Kushta Sinai, Vithoba Sinay and Keshav Parab were the traders who signed the memorandum.
23. HAG : *MR*, 161F, fl. 1526v-1527.
24. HAG : *MR*, 161F, fl. 1526v-1527.
25. HAG : *MR*, 161F, fls. 1527-1527v.
26. HAG : *MR*, 161F, fls. 1527v-1528.
27. HAG : *MR*, 161F, fls. 1540-1540v.
28. HAG : *MR*, 161F, fl. 1541v.
29. HAG : *MR*, 161F, fls. 1541v-1542.
30. HAG : *MR*, 161F, fl. 1542.
31. HAG : *MR*, 161F, fl. 1543.

32. HAG : *CR*, 1638, undated doc.
33. HAG : *MR*, 161F, fl. 1544.
34. HAG : *MR*, 161F, fl. 1544v.
35. HAG : *MR*, 161F, fl. 1493.
36. AHU : *MR*, Maço 140, no. 132, doc. dated 15 March 1782.
37. HAG : *MR*, 161F, fls. 1500-1500v.
38. HAG : *MR*, 161F, fls. 1503-1503v.
39. HAG : *MR*, 161F, fl. 1508.
40. HAG : *MR*, 161F, fl. 1508.
41. HAG : *MR*, 161F, fl. 1508.
42. HAG : *MR*, 161F, fls. 1507v-1508.
43. HAG : *MR*, 161F, fl. 1509; AHU : *MI*, Maço 141, no. 131, doc. dated 8 Feb. 1782.
44. HAG : *MR*, 161F, fls. 1510-1510v.
45. AHU : *MI*, Maço 232, no. 233, doc. dated 12 March 1830.
46. HAG : *MR*, 218B, fl. 776.
47. HAG : *AG*, 9265, fls. 43v-44.
48. HAG : *AG*, 9267, fl. 36v.
49. Bragança Pereira, op. cit., pp. 397, 399; *Administração das Communidades das Ilhas de Goa, O Arroz Cultura, Producção e Consumo em Goa*, Nova Goa, 1909, p. 4.
50. AHU : *MI*, Maço 135, no. 133, doc. dated 5 April 1781.
51. BNL : *Collecção Pombalina*, Cod. 666, fl. 1v.
52. Felippe Nery Xavier, *O Gabinete Lilterario das Fontainhas*, vol. II, Nova Goa, 1847, p. 161.
53. Pearson, *Merchants and Rulers of Gujarat, The Response to the Portuguese in the Sixteenth Century*, Berkeley/New Delhi, 1976, pp. 46-47.
54. *loc. cit.*
55. Sanjay Subrahmanyam, "The Portuguese, the port of Basrur and the rice trace", *Merchants, Markets and the State in Early Modern India*, (ed.) Sanjay Subrahmanyam, Delhi, 1990, p. 35.
56. XCHR : *MHP* (Portuguese), doc. dated 8 Feb. 1809; HAG : *RGF*, 7709, fl. 373.
57. XCHR : *MHP* (French), vol. 6, fls. 79-80.
58. XCHR : *MHP* (Portuguese), doc. dated 6 Sept. 1791.
59. AHU : *Moçambique*, Caixa 69, doc. no. 95.
60. AHU : *Moçambique*, Caixa 69, doc. no. 95.
61. AHU : *Moçambique*, Caixa 92, doc. no. 53.
62. HAG : *Provisões*, 1586, fl. 933.
63. HAG : *AG*, 9267, fl. 6.
64. AHU : *MI*, Maço 95, no. 94.
65. HAG : *AG*, 2668, fls. 8v, 20v.
66. HAG : *AG*, 9265, fl. 45v.
67. XCHR : *MHP* (Portuguese), doc. dated 22 Aug. 1791.
68. HAG : *AG*, 9267, fl. 94.
69. AHU : *MI*, Maço 81, no. 104.
70. HAG : *AG*, 2668, fl. 33.
71. HAG : *AG*, 2668, fl. 35.
72. HAG : *AG*, 6810, fls. 694, 702-703, 766.
73. HAG : *MR*, 218B, fl. 776.
74. HAG : *AG*, 9265, fl. 43v.
75. XCHR : *MHP* (Portuguese), doc. dated 17 Oct. 1779.

76. XCHR : *J. N. Fonseca Papers. An Account of Daman for Bombay Presidency Gazetteer*, doc. dated 7 July 1875, p. 37; *MHP* (French), vol. 6, fl. 25v, 257-258; *MHP* (English), docs. dated 20 Jan. 1822, 21 Jan. 1822, doc. nos. 10871, 10877, 10883, 13812, 13827, 13884.
77. XCHR : *MHP* (French), vol. 6, fl. 153v.
78. XCHR : *MHP* (French), vol. 6, fl. 204.
79. HAG : *MR*, 218B, fl. 776; *AG*, 9265, fls. 43v-44.
80. BNL : *Mapa Geral, Estatistica e Historica da India Portuguesa*, 1850.
81. XCHR : *MHP* (Portuguese), doc. dated 15 April 1793.
82. XCHR : *MHP* (English), doc. dated 31 July 1794.
83. XCHR : *MHP* (English), doc. dated 5 May 1809.
84. HAG : *Provisões*, 1586, fls. 933-934.
85. HAG : *AG*, 2668, fl. 34v.
86. HAG : *AG*, 9265, fls. 43v-44.
87. HAG : *MR*, 219B, fls. 867-868.
88. AHU : *MI*, Maço 136, no. 142, doc. dated 1 March 1778.
89. BNL :*Mapa Geral, op. cit.*
90. HAG : *MR*, 224, doc. dated 30 Nov. 1850.
91. XCHR : *J. N. Fonseca Papers, An Account of Daman for the Bombay Presidency Gazetteer*, pp. 27-28.
92. HAG : *AG*, 6810, fl. 309.
93. HAG : *AG*, 6810, fl. 315.
94. HAG : *AG*, 2668, fl. 33.
95. HAG : *AG*, 2668, fl. 34v.
96. HAG : *MR*, 218B, fl. 776.
97. XCHR : *MHP* (French), vol. 4, fls. 5, 7, 22, 65, 67-67v, 78, 118.
98. XCHR : *MHP* (Portuguese), doc. dated 26 Nov. 1789.
99. XCHR : *MHP* (Portuguese), docs. dated 10 Feb. 1790, 20 Aug. 1792.
100. XCHR : *MHP* (Portuguese), doc. dated 25 Nov. 1789.
101. HAG : *AG*, 2668, fl. 34v.
102. HAG : *AG*, 2668, fl. 35v.
103. HAG : *Provisões*, 1586, fls. 933-934.
104. HAG : *Conventos*, 7500, fls. 1-243v : *passim*; 7502, fls. 40, 42, 88, 97; 7503, fls. 1-180 : *passim*; 7886, fls. 1-39, 46-63v : *passim*; 7887, fls. 1-173v : *passim*; 9458, fls. 1-234v : *passim*; 9459, fls. 1-20, 23-35v : *passim*; 9471, fls. 2-142 : *passim*.
105. BNL : *Fundo Geral*, Cod. 466, fls. 3v-100v : *passim*.
106. XCHR : *MHP* (Portuguese), docs. dated 30 Nov. 1788, 12 Dec. 1812, 24 Nov. 1813; *MHP* (English), docs. dated 11 Feb. 1812, 19 Feb. 1812, 17 April 1812, doc. nos. 47, 2761, 2762, 3312; *AG* 9267, fls. 7-7v.
107. HAG : *AG*, 2668, fl. 10v.
108. HAG : *Macau*, 1294, fls. 105-106; 1317, fls. 229-230; 1324, fls. 253-254; 1325, fl. 26.
109. HAG : *Macau*, 1343, doc. dated 3 May 1838.
110. XCHR : *MHP* (Portuguese), doc. dated 8 April 1799; *AG* 6325, fl. 31; 6810, fls. 765, 766, 767; 8117, fl. 360.
111. AHU : *Moçambique*, Caixa 69, doc. no. 95.
112. AHU : *Moçambique*, Caixa 92, doc. no. 53.
113. HAG : *AG*, 9267, fls. 7-7v.
114. HAG : *AG*, 6319, fls. 31-312 : *passim*; XCHR : *MHP* (Portuguese), doc. dated 1789; *MHP* (French) vol. 4, doc. dated 29 Dec. 1781.

115. HAG : *MHP* (French), vol. 4, fl. 16.
116. HAG : *MHP* (French), vol. 6, fls. 45-45v.
117. HAG : *AG*, 6807, fl. 289.
118. HAG : *AG*, 2668, fl. 12v.
119. HAG : *MR*, 218B, fl. 776.
120. BNL : *Mapa* Geral, op. cit., 1850.
121. HAG : *AG*, 6802, fl. 499; 6807, fls. 560, 572.
122. HAG : *AG*, 2668, fl. 34.
123. HAG : *AG*, 2668, fl. 35.
124. HAG : *AG*, 6325, fls. 23-72 : *passim*; 6810, fl. 753; 8117, fl. 357; 8128, fl. 16; *Moçambique*, 1445, fl. 28v.
125. HAG : *AG*, 8114, fl. 219.
126. HAG : *AG*, 6816, fl. 590.
127. Bragança Pereira, *op. cit.*, pp. 182-183.
128. HAG : *PDCF*, 1156, fls. 104-105.
129. HAG : *Rendas*, 2599, fls. 10, 16.
130. AHU : *MI*, Maço 22, no. 9, undated doc.
131. HAG : *AG*, 6810, fl. 174.
132. HAG : *AG*, 2668, fl. 12v.
133. HAG : *AG*, 9267, fls. 31v-32
134. HAG : *AG*, 9267, fls. 31v-32.
135. HAG : *AG*, 2247, fl. 12; *MR*, 217A, docs. dated 7 Jan. 1843, 16 Jan. 1843; *AG*, 6318, fls. 160v, 220; 6816, fl. 613; 8128, fl. 173.
136. XCHR : *MHP* (French), vol. 5, fls. 115-116v.
137. Afzal Ahmed, "Portuguese Trade on the Western Coast of India in the Seventeenth Century (1600-1663)", Unpublished Thesis, University of Baroda, 1984, pp. 74-75.
138. AHU : *MI,* Maço 126, no. 142, doc. dated 1 March 1778.
139. Ahmed, *op. cit.,* pp. 142-143.
140. The Mhamai ships would touch Batavia for cloves. In a letter received by the Mhamais in August 1791 from Joaquim Xavier Moraes S., we learn that the ship Salvamento belonging to the Mhamais was impounded at Batavia along with cargo consisting of 200 *cates* of cloves on board. XCHR : *MHP* (Portuguese), doc. dated 17 Aug. 1791.
141. HAG : *AG*, 9267, fl. 40v.
142. Ahmed, *op. cit.,* pp. 145-150.
143. HAG : *AG*, 9267, fls. 1-98v.
144. AHU : *Timor*, Caixa 3, doc. 1.
145. XCHR : *MHP* (French), vol. 4, fls. 69-70.
146. XCHR : *MHP* (French), vol. 6, fl. 92.
147. XCHR : *MHP* (French), vol. 6, fl. 96.
148. XCHR : *MHP* (French), vol. 6, fls. 247-247v.
149. XCHR : *MHP* (Portuguese), doc. nos. 12980, 12981.
150. XCHR : *MHP* (Portuguese), doc. dated 15 March 1789.
151. AHU : *MI*, Maço 47, no. 310, doc. dated 13 July 1814.
152. AHU : *MI*, Maço 190, no. 204, docs. dated 24 March 1816, 10 May 1816.

Ship	Cargoes
Gram cateta	100 boxes of pepper
65 boxes of cinnamon	
Principe do Brazil	620 sacks of pepper
Triumfo	63 boxes of cinnamon
1000 sacks of pepper	

153. XCHR : *MHP : passim*; Ahmed, *op. cit.*, pp. 90-92.

9

SOME CONCLUSIONS

This study of the *Estado da India* has been an attempt to explain the nature and extent of Portuguese participation in the intra-Asiatic commercial system at a time when the world was moving from the age of mercantilism to that of free trade. This was also a period when Anglo-French struggle for supremacy in Europe, America and even on the Indian sub-continent and the Indian Ocean occupied the centre-stage, disrupted world peace and eventually gave way to England's ascendancy and pre-eminence as the nerve-centre of the capitalist world system.

Existing literature on the maritime history of Portuguese India tends to dismiss the eighteenth and nineteenth centuries as periods of no importance to the *Estado* and Portugal. Most Indo-Portuguese historians are too often obsessed with the commerce of Portuguese India in the sixteenth century and fail to appreciate the remarkable growth of trade in the subsequent centuries. To deny the existence of a thriving trade in the said centuries is to fly in the face of facts. The sources point to the existence of a lively trade in luxuries and essentials emanating from the *Estado da India* in the late eighteenth-early nineteenth centuries with a precise peak reached in the 1780s-1790s and a slide observed in the 1820s-1830s. Such trends of expansion and contraction were discernible in the case of trade in opium, slaves, gold, ivory, textiles and tobacco. Commerce in timber, spices, and victuals however, continued to thrive even beyond the mid-nineteenth century.

The Portuguese country trade of the late eighteenth-early nineteenth centuries was privately operated by Portuguese settlers and officials in their entrepreneurial capacities, and by ethnic Indians, chiefly by Saraswat brahmins and the banias. Much of the trade was clandestinely operated enabling them to pile up fortunes with little proceeding into the State treasury.

This unofficial commercial participation had its deep-seated roots in the nature of Portuguese colonialism and the prevailing situation in Portugal.

Since the sixteenth century, one of the methods adopted by the home country was to promote settlement with the view to building up a pliant and submissive population in far-off Asia, paving the way for political domination and economic exploitation. This policy however, boomeranged. The poor salaries provided to the Portuguese settlers by the authorities had to be supplemented by other sources of income. Spurred on by the growing indifference displayed by the Lisbon authorities to their woes, they turned with a vengeance towards the profitable interport trade of Asia. With miles and miles of ocean waters separating Portugal and its eastern imperial possessions, with not more than 10,000 able-bodied European and Eurasian soldiers in all in Asia and 100 warships in Indian Ocean waters, and with an administrative system in the East beset with ills, it was almost impossible for Portugal to effectively curb the illicit private trading in Portuguese Asia.

The Pombaline dictatorship made concerted efforts to foster the development of the commercial class. Pombal had seen capitalism at work in England and desired that metropolitan Portugal and her colonies should attain a similar prosperity. Thanks to his policies, the growing entrepreneurship and indigenous capitalism in the *Estado* received a boost and this further stimulated participation in the thriving interport trade of Asia.

Since the Napoleonic invasion of Portugal in 1807, the home-country was plunged into decades of political chaos and anarchy together with a deepening economic crisis which left its authorities exercising a tenuous hold over the far-flung eastern empire. It was no wonder that contraband, basic to Portuguese colonialism, assumed fresh heights in Portuguese India leading to accumulation of wealth.

Events in the *Estado da India* also provided the merchants opportunities to conduct their commercial activities with a minimum of State interference. The *Estado*, constantly plagued by fiscal difficulties and troubled with constant revolts and factional strife, was in no position to dictate terms to the merchants. All that it was concerned about was survival. Ironically, it was the un-official commercial involvement of the Portuguese in India that explains the survival of the *Estado.* Prior to 1770 the *Fazenda Real* was running into deficit as indicated by Fig. 9.1. Matters improved with State attempts at customs reorganisation and especially with the passing of the Alvará of 1783.

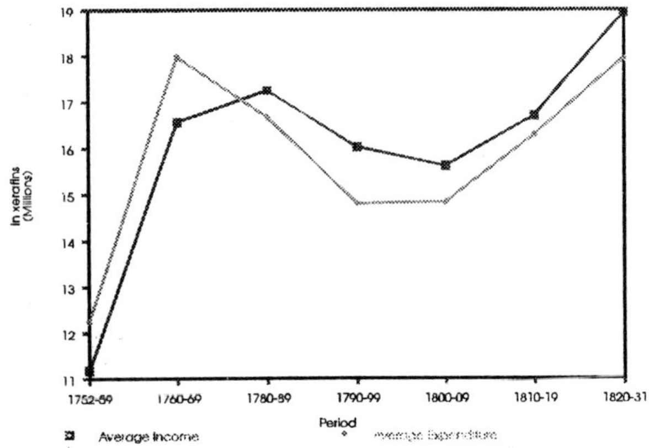

FIG. 9.1: INCOME AND EXPENDITURE OF THE STATE TREASURY, 1752-1831

Sources HAG : Compiled from *CR*, 1632, 1638, 1640, 1642-43, 1645-1652, 1654-1655, 1664, 1666,2409-2414, 2417, 2419, 2421-2423, 2567; *MR*, 125B, fl. 643v; 126A, fl. 57; 127B, fl. 388; 129B, fl. 572; 130B, fl. 476v; 131B, fl. 416; 132B, fl. 677v; 133B, fl. 472v; 135B, fl. 495v; 137A, fls. 125v, 205; 138D, fls. 1052, 1165; 140B, fl. 619; 142C, fl. 900; 145B, fl. 445; 171A, fl. 347; 176A, fls. 63, 249; 178B, fls. 531v-532; AHU : *MI*, Maço no. 279, doc. dated 20 Jan. 1761.

Incoming and outgoing commercial goods brought in revenues which kept the *Estado* going. Figure 9.2 demonstrates this.

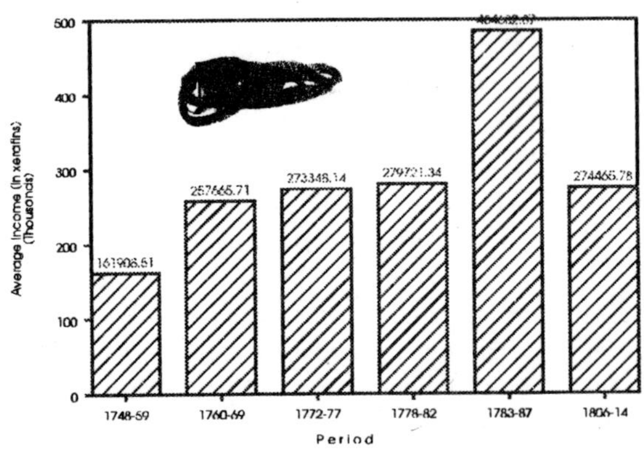

FIG. 9.2: INCOME OF THE GOA, SALCETTE AND BARDEZ CUSTOMS, 1748-1814

Sources: Claudio Lagrange Monteiro de Barbuda, *IDJ*, Nova Goa, 1841, p. 25; HAG : *MR*, 121B, fls. 626-626v; 122B, fls. 421-422; 123B, fls. 614-615; 125B, fls. 632-633v; 126A, fls. 49-50v; 127B, fls. 391-392; 129B, fls. 562-563; 130B, fls. 467-468; 131B, fls. 407-410; 132B, fls. 669-670; 133B, fls. 463-464; 135B, fls. 486-487v; 137A, fls. 82v-205; 138D, fls. 996v-1043v; 140B, 569v-609v; 145B, fls. 387v-438v; 161B, fls. 606, 610; 171B, fl. 493; 176A, fls. 166-168; 178B, fls. 457-480; 191B, fls. 1299v-1300; *CR*, 2408, fls. 92v-94.

The general pattern from the mid-eighteenth century onwards, is one of Indo-Portuguese merchants transacting with both European and Asian counterparts in the Indian Ocean region who conducted a trade in goods, both the splendid and the trifling, and who associated themselves with the trade in victuals, essential for general well-being or in slaves, opium, tobacco and liquors that did incalculable harm. The motivation that governed such behaviour was none other than the craving for substantial profits. The viceroys and even the clergy were not free of this greed. They felt no qualms of conscience when they received human cargoes from Moçambique and later dispatched some of them to Macao and other parts in the Indian Ocean region. The merchants had, however, to work within the framework of the British monopoly. This did not deter them. They would seek gaps in the control system, much to the chagrin and dismay of the British authorities.

In the absence of relevant documentation one is unable to quantify the profits derived by the merchants from the intra-Asiatic trade and to indicate the extent of the fortunes made. However, with the assistance of piecemeal and circumstantial evidence, we are able to conjure a picture of business prosperity.

For a brief spell of time, the Crown in the late eighteenth century, focussed its attention on the *Estado*-based Asiatic trade. Motivated by dreams of restoring in Portuguese India its former glory, it enacted commercial legislation aimed at liberalising Portuguese Asian commerce. This was in sharp contrast with the promotional efforts of the *Estado* authorities whose sole concern was to shield high-powered officials involved in the Asiatic trade and ascertain the *Estado's* chances of survival. The *Estado* depended heavily on the trade for customs revenues to boost its economy. There was no thought of promoting prosperity, merely of survival. The Crown efforts at promoting prosperity in the East, did yield fruit until Britain decided that under no circumstances should Portuguese India prosper even marginally, at the cost of British India.

A review of the late eighteenth-early nineteenth centuries trading system of Portuguese India reveals that its destinies were intimately bound with and subordinated to British interests in India and the rest of the world and was therefore linked with the European-based capitalist economy, having England as its epicentre.

That the *Estado* had to succumb to British pressures becomes evidently clear on many an occasion. For instance, the flourishing illegitimate Portuguese Malwa opium trade was thrown out of gear by the British transit system introduced in 1831 aimed at providing protection to the English East India Company's opium monopoly.

The same attitude and trend are discernible from the British policies towards the traffic in human beings. With the emergence of a capitalist system, slavery was envisaged as a social anachronism and the slave trade as unprofitable, hindering social and material progress. It was these considerations which drove England to launch an offensive on a massive scale against the inhuman practice of slaving. At every stage since the Congress of Vienna, the British sought to apply pressures on Portugal to end its eighteenth century legitimate trade in slaves which was the mainstay of the Luso-Atlantic economy. The second Portuguese empire founded on slaves, sugar and gold was brought to a disastrous end by none other than England, Portugal's so-called traditional ally. Similar was the case of the Portuguese slave commerce across the Indian Ocean. In 1847, England went to the extent of subjecting ports, bays, creeks and rivers in the Portuguese dominions where illicit slave trafficking was common, to severe surveillance.

Paradoxically, while England sought to project the image of serving the cause of humanity by outlawing slavery and slave-trading, it was guilty of practising slavery with another label "indentured labour" in its indigo and other plantations in India and elsewhere till the twentieth century with no other purpose in mind but to prop up its export-oriented cash-cropping system. Then again, it did not hesitate to encourage opium-trafficking in China, realising fully well that opium-smoking enfeebled the faculties of mind and body.

Indian textiles from times immemorial formed the principal item of export in the Indian Ocean region, yielding rich profits and thereby reinforcing the image of a self-sufficient India. The trade in these commodities reached fresh peaks in the period under study only to be seriously menaced by the glutting of European, Brazilian and Indian markets with cheap British-made goods. Portuguese India was badly hit by this development. The re-export trade in Indian textiles met with a sad end to satisfy the whims and fancies of England.

Even the coastal trade came to be subordinated to British control. This trade was mainly restricted to Bombay and a glimpse of the balance sheets demonstrate that the value of Goa's imports from Bombay far exceeded that of its exports. In fact, Goa-based traders and businessmen conducted their business operations mainly with the assistance of their counterparts domiciled at Bombay. The Mhamai correspondence makes references to John Hester Cherry, David Scott and Co., Forbes Smith and Co., Joakin Lewis, Charles Russell and Co., and Alexander Adamson of Bombay. The Goa merchant predominant in the medieval and pre-modern Asian trade, had now to play a passive role, to accept British protection and to work within the framework of their control in the emerging world economy.

The climax was yet to come. The imperial dream of promoting prosperity in Goa and restoring it to its former glory by constructing a railway line linking Goa and the British Indian railway network, led to the signing of the Anglo-Portuguese Treaty of 1878. But this dream was rudely shattered. The British salt monopoly and the *Abkari* system under the Treaty left the economy of the *Estado* in shambles. The economic independence and dignity of the *Estado* was bartered away for a few concessions. While the Portuguese colonialism on the west coast of India was badly eroded, the Treaty underlined the preponderance of Britain. The latter went all out to enhance its position of pre-eminence in India and its status as the nerve centre of the capitalist world economy.

Despite the fact that the commercial system of the *Estado da India* was the target of many a British official policy and which in the course of time came to be drastically reduced, it was this private commercial network which kept the *Estado* going and averted the otherwise inevitable doom of Portuguese India. It was the linchpin that held together the last relics of the Portuguese eastern empire which ultimately enabled the Portuguese in Asia to outlast their competitors, for their *Estado da India* lingered on till 1961.

This present study certainly leaves much to be desired. Its purpose will however be served if it proves that not only the sixteenth century but also the eighteenth and nineteenth centuries were commercially significant to the *Estado da India*. Secondly, I hope it will stimulate further studies on the commercial system of Portuguese India in the eighteenth and nineteenth centuries. Fresh research could be undertaken to examine the nature of the Portuguese country trade in the second half of the nineteenth century and subsequently in the twentieth century up to 1961. Till the mid-nineteenth century, the emphasis was still on luxury goods. But by the end of the nineteenth century, when the trade dwarfed in volume and value, it was restricted to essentials. Goa, the once-glorious entrepôt of the commerce between the East and the West, dwindled into insignificance. It lost all its commercial attractions for ships dispatched from Europe, East Africa and Brazil. Its export trade was limited to Bombay, the bulk of its cargo being coconuts, salt, arecanuts, poultry and fruits. It would be a worthwhile and scholarly contribution to Indo-Portuguese historiography to examine the commercial system of Portuguese India even in this state of decline. A true historian should not merely be embroiled in glories. Shades and shadows also have their stories to tell.

BIBLIOGRAPHICAL ESSAY

A. ARCHIVAL SOURCES

1. State Papers from the Historical Archives of Goa

Monções do Reino is one of the largest and most important series of records in the Goa Archives. It deals with instructions, letters and reports received at Goa every year from Portugal in the monsoon season, that is, during June-September, with enclosures containing copies of replies despatched from Goa during the period, December to March. Thus the correspondence in this series was closely associated with the monsoons.

I have consulted volumes 125A to 230 of this collection covering the period 1750 to 1850. Most of them are in good condition. Some of the volumes contain documents that are moth-eaten or illegible. They throw light on the political and economic happenings in the *Estado da India*. Valuable information on the commercial system of Portuguese India can be obtained from MSS 146, 148A, 148B, 154, 158A, 159C, 161A, 161B, 161D, 161F, 163B, 164F, 164G, 167A, 167B, 167C, 167D, 168C, 169B, 170C, 171B, 173, 174B, 176A, 176B, 177A, 178A, 179A, 179B, 180A, 181B, 183B, 184B, 187A, 192B, 193A, 195C, 195E, 196A, 198B, 202D, 205A, 205B, 206C, 207B, 217A, 217B, 218B, 219B, 220B, 221, 224 and 228. Details on regulations and conditions at the *alfandegas* are found in MSS 148B, 192B and 193A. MS 179A contains an interesting document on the plan for the establishment of a private trading company in 1799. One finds information on the tobacco monopoly in Goa and the import of Brazilian tobacco in MSS 154, 159C, 161D, 164G, 167C, 170C, 176A, 202D, 206B and 207B. MS 161A contains a rare document on the establishment of an agency house in Portuguese India. Details on the Daman opium trade are available in MSS 205A and 205B. MS 206A contains information on the attempts made to establish the *Feitoria de Siam*. Valuable information on the coconut trade of Goa and the conflict between the *Fazendeiros* and coconut merchants over the entry of coconuts into Goa from the southern ports can be derived from MSS 161F; 167D, 169B, 173 and 176B.

The *Monções do Reino* series contains documents that shed light on the nature of the textile industry in Portuguese India. Details on textile production in Daman and Diu can be found in MSS 169C, 193A, 195B, 195C, 198B, 198D, 200B, 202C and 204B. The working of the *Fábrica de Cumbarjua* is examined in MSS 164F, 169B, 174B, 175, 176A, 179A, 191B and 202D. Information on agricultural production in Goa is available in MSS 157B, 158A, 161D, 163B, 164F, 168D, 170C, 171B, 174A, 177B, 178A, 179A, 180B, 181A, 182, 183A, 185, 186, 187B, 188, 190A, 191D, 192A, 193A, 195B, 198E, 200A, 202C, 204A, 206A, 209, 210A and 211. The demography of the *Estado da India* can be drawn from MSS 162B, 163A, 163B, 164E, 167A, 168D, 169C, 170B, 176B, 179A, 180B, 181A, 182, 183A, 184A, 185, 186, 187B, 188, 190C, 191D, 192B, 193A, 195D, 197B, 198D, 200A, 200B, 202B, 202C, 204A, 207B, 209, 210A, 211, 216B and 218B. Statements of income and expenditure of the *Fazenda Real* in the period under study can be drawn from MSS 125B, 126A, 127B, 129B, 130B, 131B, 132B, 133B, 135B, 137A, 137B, 138B, 138D, 140B, 142C, 145B, 171A, 171B, 176A, 178B, 190C, 191B, 197B and 198B.

The Goa Archives is also the repository of a large collection of Customs Records (*Alfandegas*) rich in information on the maritime trade of Portuguese India. The records are in a fairly good condition. They contain entries on the arrival and departure of ships, the nature and value of imports and exports, the merchants involved, the levies imposed and the revenues collected. Commercial legislation, correspondence, tariff charts, registers and receipts also figure in these records.

Of significance are the customs records dealing with income derived from imports and exports (*receitas*). Those on Bardez and Salcette demonstrate that trade via the *alfandegas* of Bardez and Salcette was mainly restricted to neighbouring ports and those along western coastal India. The Goa Customs records, on the other hand, reveal a more broad-based trade through the port of Goa. We observe the arrival and departure of goods to and from Lisbon, Macao, Moçambique, Brazil, Muscat and other distant lands. The customs records on Daman and Diu shed light on the trade in Indian textiles, slaves, ivory and bullion. MSS 4952-53, 4956, 4959-60, 4963, 4965 and 4969 refer to ships arriving at Diu from Moçambique, while MSS 4839, 4841-42, 4844, 4846, 4848-49, 4851 are records on ships arriving at Daman from Moçambique. MSS 6035-37, 6040-42, 6055, 6057, 6061 and 6070 contain valuable information precisely on the Daman opium trade. MS 6132 and 6374 refer to opium-shipping with reference to Diu and Goa respectively. The *Estado*-based timber trade is examined in MSS 5917, 6082-83, 6319-20, 6329, 6335, 6337, 6343 and 6362.

Information on brokerage, freighting, warehousing, trans-shipment and re-exportation at the port of Goa can be drawn from MSS 6622, 6804, 6827, 8127 and 9869 respectively. MS 2668 is a rare document running into 40 folios. It provides details on the quantity, quality and value of goods imported into and exported by Goa in 1826. At the end of this document one finds a list of ships that arrived and left the port of Goa in that year. MSS 8125, 9869 and 11318 are records that indicate the entry of bullion and precious metals into Goa in the years 1816-17, 1824, 1833 and 1838. Of significance too, is the price list (*Pauta*) of 1831-32 found in MS 9267. This document runs into 98 folios. A document on the prices of textiles from Surat and Balaghat despatched to East Africa and Rio de Janeiro in 1826 is found in MS 2247. MS 6813 is significant for commercial legislation passed by the State and the Crown.

Correspondecia para o Reino (Correspondence with Portugal) includes correspondence directed to Portugal on matters of administration and commerce prevailing in the *Estado da India*. Information on the income and expenditure of Portuguese India can be found in MSS 1632, 1638, 1640-43, 1645-52, 1654-55, 1657-64, 1666, 2409-14, 2417, 2419-23, 2567. Causes of the decay and commercial decline of the *Estado* in the late eighteenth century can be examined in MS 2408. MS 1654 contains details on the income derived in 1809 by the *Alfandegas* of Goa, Salcette and Bardez and the *Estanco Real de Tobaco*. The textile trade with Lisbon is considered in MSS 1638, 1642-43 and 1651. Details on saltpetre despatches to Lisbon are found in MSS 1633 and 1637. MS 1638 makes a reference to the prohibition of coconuts from the south. MS 1634 contains a document that throws light on the income derived by Goa in 1776-77 on liquors and meats.

Registos Gerais de Fazenda (The Miscellaneous Revenue Records) are full of details on the internal and coastal trade of the *Estado*, its merchants and other miscellaneous information on economic matters. MSS 2275-76 and 2281 contain information on the import of rice. MS 2276 in particular provides a list of merchants of Goa and the capital invested by them in the import of rice from Sind. Details on timber are available in MS 2275, on arrack and meats in MSS 2271 and 2278 and on tobacco in MSS 2271, 2275-76 and 2278. The latter contains a document in which we find that Christian and Hindu merchants made a representation to be exempted from the importation of American tobacco as it was bad for health. They were accustomed to tobacco from the

Canaes. MS 2155 contains a rare document on the manner in which goods were officially despatched from the *Estado* to Moçambique. We find that by an order issued on 7th November 1823 it was announced that the Goa Government would despatch a ship to the port of Moçambique and that merchants should within six days make a declaration stating the quantity and nature of the goods they were desirous of despatching to the said port. In case the total cargo fell short of the requirement for shipping the said vessel, the merchants could transport their cargoes to Moçambique on a ship belonging to Natu Saugi of Diu. After paying the necessary freight charges, the merchants could despatch their goods to Diu. They were required to appoint agents and attorneys to handle their transactions at Diu.

A list of Hindu and Muslim merchants in the provinces of Ilhas, Bardez and Salcette in 1800 is found in MS 2279. Similarly MS 2277 contains a list of merchants of Goa involved in the trade in silk and piece-goods. The Sivapoy Tarrif is available in MS 2280. MS 2287 indicates the State debts of the Mhamais in 1815-16. MS 7954 compares the prices of goods at Goa and Diu in the 1820s. A chart on weights and measures (1803-05) is found in MS 2281. Income of various *alfandegas* during the period under study can be gathered from documents found in MSS 2154, 2287, 2297-98, and 2635. Details on the *Fábrica de Cumbarjua* are available in MSS 2158, 2277 and 2278.

The Historical Archives of Goa also houses twenty-six volumes relating to correspondence from Moçambique (*Correspondencia de Moçambique*). They are in a fairly good condition. They throw light on the *Estado*-Moçambique relations prior to the termination of the Union and after. I have consulted MSS 1443-48, that is, the volumes relating to the period of my study. MSS 1445-46 contain valuable information on the attempts made to activate the commerce of Moçambique with Portuguese India in the 1780s.

The *Correspondencia de Macao* (Macau Correspondence) at the Goa Archives is equally significant. Most of the volumes are in a bad state and falling apart. MSS 1295-1302, 1305-13, 1315-20, 1322-27, 1329-30, 1332, 1334-36, 1338-42, 1345 and 1356 include charts on the imports of Macao. I have consulted these charts for the import of opium, ivory, bullion, textiles, fish maws, shark fins, birds and spices from Portuguese India. The same volumes supply details on items imported from Macao into Goa for the Royal Hospital (*Hospital Real*), Military Hospital (*Hospital Militar*) and the Royal Warehouses (*Armazens Reaes*)

Other details on the Daman-Macao opium trade can be found in MS

1311 where a suggestion was made in 1817 to conduct auctions for the sale of Malwa opium at Daman. MS 1312 provides a statement of comparative profits and losses in the case of Bengal and Malwa opium trade during 1816-19. MS 1320 provides information on the arrival of five ships at Macao in 1822 loaded with Daman Malwa opium. MS 1327 contains correspondence on the detention of *D. Manoel de Portugal* by Macao authorities in 1828. MSS 1334 and 1342 contain details on the stagnation of the opium market in Macao in the 1830s.

The *Provisões da Fazenda* (Supplies) too contain valuable information relating to the late eighteenth-early nineteenth centuries. For instance, MS 1586 contains details of provisions exported and despatched to Goa for furnishing the Military Hospital, Royal Arsenal and the Royal Warehouses. MS 1587 contains a document indicating a list of items, their quantity and value despatched to Moçambique in 1808 on board the vessel *Pedro de Alcantara*. This volume also contains a reference to the financial straits of Macao due to Chinese piracy in the first decade of the nineteenth century.

Petições Despachadas no Conselho da Fazenda (Despatched Petitions) too are in a fairly good condition. I have examined just three volumes MSS 1156-58 on the period under review. MS 1156 refers to complaints made by Goa merchants on the banning of Lisbon ships touching the ports of Brazil in 1767. MS 1158 has information on the presence of Armenians in Goa.

The Processos Judiciaes (Records on Judicial Suits) contain documents on suits filed by and against merchants. Details on the commerce of Portuguese India in the late eighteenth-early nineteenth centuries can be obtained from these volumes. MS 2491 has information on the business matters of Narayan Kamat. Details on a suit filed against Dulba Sinai, a revenue farmer for wood and arrack in 1766, is provided in MS 2546. We have valuable information on the tobacco monopoly and trade in MSS 2654 and 2664. MS 2654 also contains valuable documents on rice acquired by Goa from Mangalore, Kalianpur and Basrur in 1759 being later diverted to Anjediva. MS 2757 deals with a suit involving the Goa merchants, Ganaba Sinai Nerlikar and the Mhamais.

Estrangeiros (Records on Foreigners) form a valuable source of information on the Portuguese Indian trade. MS 1225 contains information that Bombay merchants, namely, Motichund Amichund, Merwanjee Dossabhai, Jamsetjee Jejeebhoy, Jehangir Cowasjee, Mohammed Syed, Shapurchund Harichund and Mancherjee Fordunjee had contacted Rogerio de Faria in 1819 requesting the intervention of his agent at Goa with the

Viceroy to take action against the Commander Archibald Cameroon of the brig, *Alliance*, whose ship was loaded with goods at Malacca and Penang and was consigned to the above-mentioned merchants at Bombay. However the said commander had touched Goa and was disposing off the cargo on his own account. MS 1226 too contains an important document stating that foreign ships laden with merchandise from Bhavnagar and Surat had proceeded directly to the port of Moçambique without touching Daman and Diu. This was damaging to the *Fazenda Real*. The volume also contains a document referring to Kushta Sinai Dhempe as the constituent of Virchande Givane of Diu. MS 1661 has information on Rogerio de Faria purchasing a printing press worth 7310-2-47 *xerafins* for the Goa government in 1825. MS 1227 and 1230 indicate that João de Faria was the Portuguese agent at Bombay till 1843.

Fianças (Sureties) series MSS 1850-51 provide valuable information on shipping arrivals at Goa in 1841-42.

Arrematação das Rendas (Records of Revenue Farming) contain information on triennial contracts which permitted the contractors to collect revenues from the import of tobacco, foodstuffs and several other minor items. MSS 1940, 4470, 7849-51 and 7853 relating to the period under review are full of such details. The *Escravos* (Records on Slaves) series especially MSS 2976-81 are registers of slaves found in the Tiswadi, Bardez, Salcette, Daman, Diu and the New Conquest areas.

The *Portarias do Governo* are volumes on government grants and orders. They shed light on the Portuguese administrative system. Many of them reorganised the customs administration. MS 1410 in particular is significant for the tax-structure introduced in 1840.

Cartas, Patentes, Alvarás (Letters, Patents and Royal Orders) provide information on the commerce of Portuguese India. MS 628, for instance, is rich in commercial legislation with documents relating to opinions elicited from merchants on the *Regimento* of 1774, the plan of 1786 to promote commerce between the *Estado* and Moçambique. duties on the import of liquors, toddy and jaggery, the entry of coconuts from the southern ports and the like.

Ordens Régias or Royal Orders is another important series of documentation which enables us to get a better picture of the administrative system of colonial Portuguese India.

Regimentos e Instrucções consist of bye-laws and instructions received from kings and viceroys with reference to any matter of administration. The *Regimento de Alfandega de Goa* of 1774 is found in MS 1418.

The *Cumbarjua* series contain documents on the *Fábrica de*

Cumbarjua. MSS 2052-67 are mainly concerned with the accounts of thi: royal factory. MS 1962 contains information on the price of textiles produced at the factory and later sold to the Royal Arsenal in the year 1787.

The *Conventos* (Convents) series include books on the annual income and expenditure of the Convents of *Santo Augustinho, S. João de Deus, Santa Barbara, Convento de Cabo* etc. The volumes indicate that one of the main items of expenditure of the convents were provisions like, fowls, eggs, butter, oil, vinegar, sugar, vegetables, meats, rice, fish and the like.

2. State Papers from the Bombay Archives

The *Revenue Department* volumes of the period 1821-45 are significant for the study of the Malwa opium trade via Portuguese territories. I have examined 80 volumes of this series in which it is obvious that the Portuguese Malwa opium commerce was a threat to the Bengal Opium Monopoly. It was a source of apprehension to the British authorities and concerted efforts were made to annihilate it. The steps taken by the British upto 1830 can be studied in MSS 7, 9/9, 10/10, 13/13, 16/40, 18/42, 25/49, 79, 28/80, 29/81, 19/103, 20/104, 9/119, 5/137, 6/138, 31/184, 22/213, 38/234, 29/235, 32/279 and 11/292. Information on the introduction of the transit pass system and the revenues collected by the British under this system is available in MSS 5/333, 6/334, 7/335, 8/336, 13/428, 12/429 and 44/588.

Political Department volumes in the Bombay Archives like the Revenue Department volumes are in excellent condition. MS 20/404 provides information on how the British authorities were contemplating on gaining control over Daman and Diu in 1830. An enquiry was made into the sources of revenue of both these areas. MS 89/1190 is another volume containing interesting and useful information on the plans and strategies of the British to gain control over Sind and thus terminate the Portuguese Malwa trade. It may be recalled that despite the pass system, Malwa trade continued to reach Daman via Sind. MSS 92/1088, 89/1190, 90/1191, 91/1192, 74/1289, 75/1290, 69/1396, 103/1525, 104/1526, 105/1527, 84/1617, 85/1618, 86/1619, 87/1620, 98/1982, 99/1983 and 100/1984 contain information on the efforts by the British government in India to suppress the Malwa trade via Sind.

Due to lack of time at my disposal I was able to scrutinise just 17 diaries of the *Commercial Department* series. MS 23 (1824) contains useful information on the ships built by Bombay merchants at Daman in the early 1820s.

I consulted 5 volumes of the *General Department* series. Volumes 12/344, 13/345 and 14/346 contain interesting details on the deposition of Bernardo Peres da Silva Prefect of the *Estado da India* in 1835 and the efforts made by Rogerio de Faria at Bombay to restore him to power.

The *Miscellaneous Records : External and Internal Commerce* series presents a wide picture of the commercial system of the Bombay Presidency. MSS 1-25 relating to the period 1802-26 provide information on the trade that existed between the Bombay Presidency and the *Estado da India*.

3. State Papers at Lisbon

The Overseas Historical Archives (*Arquivo Histórico Ultramarino*) of Lisbon is rich in documentation for the seventeenth century and thereafter. This archives houses correspondence pertaining to the Overseas Council (*Conselho Ultramarino*) which played a pivotal role in the administration of Portugal's overseas dominions. The Overseas Council was set up in 1643 following the restoration of the independence of the Portuguese Crown in 1640. This council was a ressurected form of an earlier India Council (*Conselho da India*) created by Philip II of Spain in 1604 for supervising the administration of the Portuguese dominions in India. The India Council was suppressed in 1614 owing to clashes it had with the Crown Board of Justice (*Desembargo do Paço*) and the Public Revenue Council (*Conselho da Fazenda*) both of which had a say in the administration of the overseas dominions. With the creation of the Overseas Council, all such powers regarding the administration of the overseas possessions were passed on to it.

Over 200 bundles (*maços*) of loose documents on India (*Papeis Avulsos da India*) and 68 bundles of classified documents (*Documentos Organizados*) have added to my information on Portuguese India.

On the nature of commerce of Portuguese India in the late eighteenth-early nineteenth centuries, *Maços* 81, 86, 140 and 141 shed light on the coconut trade of Goa, especially the conflict between the merchants and the *Fazendeiros* over the entry of coconuts from the southern ports into Goa. *Maços* 126 and 140 provide details on tobacco brought from Brazil while *Maços* 108, 111 and 122 refer to the importation of tobacco from Portugal. Details on Moçambique and the nature of the trade between the *Estado da India* and East Africa can be deduced from *Maços* 94, 108, 111, 142, 194 and 214.

Efforts made by the State and the Crown to promote commerce in the

East is evident in *Maço* 81 which contains the plan of 23 January 1786 for promoting commerce between Portuguese India and East Africa. *Maço* 173 contains a document that states that by the *Alvarás* of 1783, 1789, 1795 and November 1800, Portugal sought to favour textile manufacture at Goa, Daman and Diu and to stimulate the commerce of Goa. The textile products of Goa and the Malabar were to be exported to Brazil, Africa, Azores and other islands.

Very useful information on the Lisbon Trade is contained in *Maços* 81, 86, 95, 97, 109, 112, 113, 125-26, 129, 135-36, 138-39, 148, 180, 185-86, 190 and 211. These documents contain details on shipping and the arrival of Asian products such as textiles, pepper, saltpetre, cinnamon and coffee from Goa and other ports of Asia at Lisbon.

The business relationship between the merchants of the *Estado da India* and their counterparts elsewhere in Asia as well as the State-merchant relationship can be drawn from *Maços* 87, 95, 121 and 138.

Details on the textile industry in the *Estado* are found in *Maços* 92, 95, 99, 102, 173, 188, 192-93, 197-98, 201, 204, 221 and 231. *Maço* 64 informs us that the *Fábrica de Cumbarjua* was not faring too well, that it was facing difficulties due to lack of raw material. Therefore the need was acutely felt for textiles from neighbouring areas like Balaghat. As regards the factories at Daman, the government made efforts to promote its development but did not interfere in its general functioning.

Rare information on the income of the *Alfandegas* of Goa, Bardez and Salcette can be obtained in *Maços* 142, 208, 224, 231, 233, 242 and 251. Population statistics figure in *Maços* 127, 150, 173, 189 and 246. Ship-building at Daman is revealed in *Maços* 121, 125-26, 129, 205, 223 and 231. A rare undated document in *Maços de India* provides information on weights and measures prevalent in western coastal India. Glimpses of agricultural production and development in Portuguese India can be obtained from *Maços* 110, 135, 139 and 142.

The *Caixas de Moçambique* housed in the *Arquivo Histórico Ultramarino* relating to the late eighteenth-early nineteenth centuries generally focus on political, administrative and commercial matters. These documents are catalogued and organised in files each bearing a date. A *caixa* contains at least five files.

There is much information on the commerce of Moçambique with Mauritius in the above-mentioned *caixas*. *Caixas* 33 and 34 for instance provide information on the outflow of slaves to Mauritius and other islands in the Indian Ocean. Very few of the documents in the *Caixas de Moçambique* that I examined make a reference to India. The value of ivory and other exports from Moçambique to India is determined in documents available in *Caixas* 90 and 92. *Caixa* 62 contains a document indicating the income derived by Moçambique from the import of textiles from Goa and the export of ivory and gold to India. In *Caixa* 54 we find a statement of the income derived by Moçambique from its trade with the *Estado.* *Caixa* 135 includes a document that sheds light on the duties imposed at Moçambique on goods arriving from the *Estado* and on slaves, gold and ivory leaving the port. A description of the textiles manufactured at Goa, Daman and other places in India is provided in a document found in *Caixa* 47.

I could consult only fifteen *Caixas de Macau* dated 1810-20. Those of the later period were not made available to me as the processing and cataloguing work was not over. *Caixas* 30 and 31 provide details on piracy in the South China seas which did much harm to Macao's commerce in the first decade of the nineteenth century. In *Caixas* 33 and 34 we find useful information on Macao's opium trade. Precise information on the Malwa opium trade is available in *Caixas* 38-40 and 43. Details on tariffs are found in documentation in *Caixa* 35.

The inventory on Timor at the *Arquivo Histórico Ultramarino* indicated that *Caxias de Timor* 3, 4, and 5 would be of significance to me. I could, however, scrutinize the documents included in only two *caixas* numbered 3 and 4. They are bundles of loose papers still to be catalogued. *Caixa* 5 was not made available to me as the work of processing its documents was not completed. *Caixa* 3, document no. 1 running into twenty-four folios contains valuable information on the general economic situation in Timor. It makes a reference to cinnamon being transported from Solor to Goa in the eighteenth century. This cinnamon was said to be superior in quality to that available in the Malabar.

The National Archives of Lisbon (*Arquivo Nacional de Torre do Tombo*), has manuscripts of *Casa da India* relating to the late eighteenth-early nineteenth centuries. They are in good condition and fairly well-preserved. MSS 741, 787, 884-885, 889-90, 917, 919-20, 928, 1202, 1210 and 1213 contain details on the arrival of Asian textiles at Lisbon. MSS 1500 and 1501 refer to the cargo of textiles, pepper and other commodities despatched from Goa to Lisbon on board the vessels *Nossa Senhora de Bellem* and *Nossa Senhora de Conceição e Santo Antonio* in the early 1790s. Information on the income and debts of the *Fazenda Real* of Goa (1773-88) is found in MSS 1489-90, 1513 and 1514. Details on ivory imports received by the *Casa da India* are recorded in MSS 1541-52. As regards the series *Ministerio de Reino*, I was able to consult *Maços* 999 and 1000. *Maço* 999 contains an interesting document that throws light on the merchant-state relationship in the *Estado*. We find details on efforts made to curb smuggling activities in *Maço* 1000. It also contains information on tobacco purchases made at Mangalore. Documents of the *Conselho da Fazenda* and *Junta Real Fazenda do Estado da India* series are in bad condition and are therefore not available for consultation.

The Ajuda Library (*Biblioteca do Palácio de Ajuda*) contains valuable documents on the sixteenth and seventeenth centuries. It however houses very few documents relating to the eighteenth and nineteenth centuries. Nevertheless, certain documents on India and Moçambique contained a mine of information. MSS 51-XI-19 and 54-XIII-22 throw light on the income and expenditure of the *Estado*. Details on shipbuilding at Daman are available in MS 51-XIII-25. One finds a description of Moçambique and its commercial system in MS 54-V-12. The gold mines of Monomotapa are described in MS 51-VII-34.

The National Library of Lisbon (*Biblioteca Nacional de Lisboa*) houses the *Collecção Pombalina* which contains a few valuable documents that throw light on the commerce of the Estado in the late eighteenth-early nineteenth centuries. MS 666 contains a letter dated 24 February 1808 written by Manoel Joze Loureiro, known to be deeply involved in the interport trade of Asia and the trade with Lisbon and Brazil. He states that the *Estado* consumed a million bales of rice annually and subsisted mainly on fish. Relating to commerce, he mentions that Goa being midway on the Malabar coast, had opportunities to conduct trade with the Coromandel and by land with the interior of India including the Ghat region. Although European merchants felt that in Goa there was no capital with which to load their ships, the writer feels that Portugal could still benefit from Goa, as it did in the past. Ships from Portugal obtained permission to visit British ports alleging that there was no market in Goa. They would participate in the coastal trade (*cabotagem*) for Bengal and Coromandel textiles. They therefore paid duties at foreign ports and avoided payment of duties at Portuguese ones. The writer was of the opinion that there were merchants in Goa who could obtain 1000 bales of merchandise to load a ship. The writer stresses that this was his personal experience. This document reveals that even in the early nineteenth century, Goa had the potential for commercial greatness that it enjoyed in the earlier centuries. The *Regimento de Alfandega de Goa* of 1774 is found in MS 460. MS 633 contains a letter dated 25 April 1808 refering to the flight of the royal family of Portugal to Brazil escorted by a squadron of the British navy. Proposals to bring Goa and other Portuguese possessions in India under British protection to counteract the designs of the French are also found in this codex. The latter also contains the convention arrived at between Conde de Sarzedas, Viceroy of Portuguese India and Captain Courtland Schuyler in 1808.

Documents on Portuguese India in the eighteenth and nineteenth centuries in the *Fundo Geral* series of the *Biblioteca Nacional de Lisboa* are mainly in the form of microfilms. Codex 466 is a rare codex running into a hundred folios. It contains details on revenue contracts (*Arrematação das Rendas*) of the period 1746-51. Names like Venku Naik, Rama Sinai, Pandu Kamat, Dulba Sinai, Massena Sinai, Vithoji Sinai Dhume, Vithoji Sinai Nerlikar, Rama Kamat, Vassu Kamat and Deuba Prabhu figure in the codex as revenue farmers for liquors, gold, tobacco, copra, rice, textiles and spices. Codex 10758 reveals the value of duties collected by the *Alfandega de Goa* in 1784. Codex 10801 reveals the causes for the decline of the *Estado da India* in 1802.

The *Biblioteca Nacional de Lisboa* is also the repository of the *Mapa Geral Estatistica e Historica da India Portugueza* (1850). Besides providing demographic information, it provides details on *dizimos* collected on rice, coconut and salt at the various *alfandegas* of the *Estado*. The total number of coastal and fishing vessels employed in the *Estado* and a statement of income and expenditure of the *Estado* figure in this chart.

4. Records from the India Office Library, London

The India Office Library houses records entitled *Abstracts of Revenue Letters* from Bengal, Madras and Bombay. MS L/E/3/11 has references to the need to establish an opium monopoly at Bombay in 1820 with the view to protect the Bengal Monopoly. It also contains information on the revenue arising out of the sale of opium transit passes during 1831-34.

The *Revenue Letters from Bombay* (Board's Copies) and the *Revenue Despatches to Bombay* (Board's Copies) are also significant in throwing light on the Malwa opium trade prior to 1837. MSS L/E/3/40-42, L/E/3/45-48 make pointed references to the trade and the efforts made by the British to contain the Daman Malwa Trade. MS L/E/3/340 contains an interesting proposal made by Mr. Warden that the Bengal Government should consign annually to Bombay a quantity of opium for consumption in western India. MS L/E/3/346 contains a document which provides a bird's eye-view of the nature of the Malwa opium trade since 1817. Details on transportation charges, sea customs, insurance and the like are found in this document. MS L/E/3/346 also contains proposals for introducing the pass system. MS L/E/3/347 has valuable information on the amount of revenue realised by way of passes during 1830-35.

The *Bombay Despatches* is another significant source of information on the Malwa opium trade. MSS E/4/1022, E/4/1034, E/4/1038, E/4/1041, E/4/1044, E/4/1046-49, E/4/1057, E/4/1059, E/4/1065, E/4/1068-69 indicate this. A document in MS E/4/1022 refers to the commencement of the Portuguese Malwa Trade in the year 1804. MS E/4/1044 has information on revenues derived from the Bombay opium sales. MS E/4/1061, on the other hand, has references to revenues accrued from the sale of passes.

Information on the Portuguese slave trade at Daman and Diu are available in MSS E/4/1065 and E/4/1067.

The *Bombay Proceedings* particularly MSS P/419/56-58 and the *Finance : Bombay Letters and Closures Received* series especially MSS L/F/3/598 and L/F/3/600 contain details on the Malwa opium commerce. The same can be said of the *Home Miscellaneous Series*. MS Home/Misc/762 contains details on the net profit derived by the British authorities from opium sales conducted at Bombay during 1820-23.

The series *Political and Secret Proceedings* in the India Office Library contains a sub-series called *Minutes of the Secret Committee*. MS L/PS/1/10, in this set of records, contains a document dated 22 December 1807 that states "the Royal Family of Portugal have (sic) quitted that country and transferred the royal residence to the Brazils" (sic). The letter also revoked the earlier order passed for taking possession of the Portuguese settlements in India and cautioned the Bengal Government against any attempt of the French to obtain possession of them. MS L/PS/5/323 in the *Bombay Secret Letters* sub-series refers to Miguel de Lima e Souza asking permission to use the badges of knighthood conferred on him (Portuguese Order of Christ).

There are Portuguese records in the India Office Library. Translations of the *Conselho Ultramarino* series MS I/3/151-54 compiled by F. C. Danvers throw light on the state of agriculture and the general economy of Portuguese India in the 1770s. MS I/3/151, in particular, goes into details on the neglect of agriculture in Goa and the need to promote pepper, cotton, coffee and cinnamon cultivation.

Another useful series is *Noticias da India*. MS I/3/113 describes the port of Daman while MS I/3/119 provides a description of Goa.

5. Private Papers in Goa

The Mhamai House Papers are available in the Xavier Centre of Historical Research (Goa). Three-fourths of the papers are written in the old Kannada script and rare are the scholars that can handle them. A sizable number of papers are in Modi script and many others are in Gujarati and Sanskrit. There are only two papers in Persian. They are deeds of obligation to repay cash borrowed by Sayed Zainul Abedin Khan from the Mhamais in 1781 during his visit to Goa on his way to Mauritius to secure French military assistance against the English.

I had the good fortune to scrutinize the Mhamai papers in European languages. They form about a third of the total collection and these have been classified into four categories namely: (1) Incoming Correspondence in Portuguese, French and English. (2) *Borradores* (Draft Books) of Outgoing Correspondence in Portuguese and French. (3) Books of Accounts of commercial transactions on farmed revenues in Portuguese, French and English. (4) Copies of Judicial Porceedings in Portuguese. The documents are generally loose but are in fairly good condition.

The personal papers of the nineteenth century Goan historian J. N. Fonseca are also housed in the Xavier Centre of Historical Research. Of significance is the report on Daman prepared by J. N. Fonseca for the Bombay Presidency Gazetteer in 1875. It throws light on the topography, society and economy of Daman in the nineteenth century.

6. Private Papers in Bombay

The Jamsetjee Jejeebhoy Papers are housed in the Bombay University Library. They throw considerable light on the involvement of the Bombay merchants in the Daman Malwa Trade. MSS 351, 355, 358 and 375 contain information on the despatch of Daman Malwa opium consignments to the Far East and the price of such opium. MSS 349 and 358 contain invoices on the shipping of opium from Bombay to China in the 1830s. They were usually consigned to Jardine Matheson & Co. MS 351 contains a letter of Jamsetji Jejeebhoy to Rogerio de Faria. Faria had earlier raised loans to meet the expense of raising a force to recapture Goa and to re-install the deposed and exiled Bernardo Peres da Silva. The venture ended in a fiasco and Bernardo da Silva failed to keep his promises to pay off the loans. The above-mentioned letter held out the threat of business relations being broken with Faria if the loans were not paid off immediately.

B. PUBLISHED PRIMARY SOURCES

Selections from the Records of the Bombay Government vols. X and XVII are useful for information on Portuguese India. Vol. X contains a statistical report on the Portuguese settlements in India particularly the Census of 1848 prepared by Captain Kol. Treaties and agreements arrived at between Great Britian and Portugal during the period 1661 to 1850 especially relating to the suppression of the Portuguese slave trade (1815, 1842, 1847) are incorporated in this volume. Vol. no. XVII contains interesting details on the Malwa opium trade via Karachi.

Noticias e Documentos para a História de Damão Antiga Provincia do Norte by Antonio Francisco Moniz, vols. 2 and 4 (Bastora, 1917), contain useful documents on the Daman Malwa opium trade particularly during the Governorhip of Bernardo Peres da Silva. One is able to get acquainted with the political, social and economic history of Daman through these works.

Documentação Ultramarina Portuguesa, 5 vols. (Lisbon 1960-7), contain valuable documents on the Portuguese administrative system in the East. Details on the tobacco trade are available in vol. 5.

Documentation relating to public revenue and other aspects of administration are also found in the journal *O Oriente Português*. Volumes II, III, IV, XII and XIII are significant in this respect.

Instrucções Com que El Rei D. Joze I Mandou Passar Ao Estado da India No Anno de 1774, (ed.) Claude Lagrange Monteiro de Barbuda contains the Carta Regia of 10th February 1774 providing instructions to the Governor and the Archbishop of Goa. The third part of the book contains notes compiled by the editor on Jesuits, customs houses, the Ranes, the *gauncars*, the Marathas and the Bhonsles, the caste system in Goa, the *Relação de Goa*, the *Marinha de Goa* and the Royal Shipyards of Goa, Daman and Diu.

Miguel Vicente de Abreu's *O Governo do Vice Rei Conde do Rio Pardo*, (Nova Goa, 1869) while providing a picture of the rule of Conde de Rio Pardo, contains documents on the establishment of the *Feitoria de Siam* and the all-round commercial prosperity of the *Estado*.

Collecção de Bandos e Outras Differentes Providencias Que Servem de Leis, Regulamentos Para o Governo Económico e Judicial Das Provincias Denominadas das Novas Conquistas by Felippe Nery Xavier, 2 vols., (Panjim, 1840-50) include proclamations, decrees, royal orders and the like relating to the New Conquest areas. They throw considerable light on the trade in tobacco and victuals with the hinterland.

Felippe Nery Xavier's *O Gabinete Litterario das Fontainhas*, vols. II and III (Nova Goa, 1847) provide information on various religious orders, especially on the suppression of the Jesuits. A description of the villages, their agricultural production and even details on the importation of rice figure in these volumes.

C. SECONDARY SOURCES

Owing to the growing interest in maritime history in general and in Indian Ocean commerce in particular, several significant studies have made their appearance in the last two decades or so. Consultation of this secondary literature of a high order provides insights into the different branches of the Asian trade network and in the Portuguese country trade in particular.

Readers approaching the study of intra-Asian trade must first familiarize themselves with the global situation in which the Asian context can be examined. In this connection, Immanuel Wallerstein's, *The Modern World System*, 2 vols. (New York, 1974/1980) is significant. The first volume examines the decline and fall of the Spanish empire and the gradual emergence of the north-western states as leaders of a commercial capitalism. The second volume demonstrates how the period from 1600 to 1750 was dominated by the efforts of England and France (core areas), first to destroy Dutch hegemony and then to succeed to the top position. The two volumes are notable for their theoretical reflections and demonstrate a new trend in the historiography of the early modern period. G. V. Scammell, in *The World Encompassed* (Metheun/London, 1981) traces European expansion between 800 A.D. and 1650 A.D. The rise and fall of some empires, European exploitation and indigenous societies and the impact of Christianity on colonial territories are some of the themes examined. Another recent book by Philip D. Curtin, *Cross-Cultural Trade in World History* (Cambridge, 1984) focuses on 'trading diasporas'.

Indian Ocean Studies

There are studies which attempt with varying success a synthesized treatment of the trade flowing through the entire stretch of the Indian Ocean. C.G.F. Simkin's *The Traditional Trade of Asia* (London, 1968) is disappointing so far as the seventeenth century. The reader would, however, do well to consult K.N. Chaudhuri's *Trade and Civilization in the Indian Ocean. An Economic History from the Rise of Islam to 1750* (New Delhi, 1985) for a scholarly analysis and interpretation of the oceanic trade which stretched from the South China Sea to the eastern Mediterranean in the pre-modern era. Ashin Das Gupta and M.N. Pearson's (eds.), *India and the Indian Ocean 1500-1800*, Calcutta, 1987 and Satish Chandra's (ed.) *The Indian Ocean Explorations in History. Commerce and Politics* (New Delhi, 1987) seek to present a composite picture of maritime India and the history of the Indian Ocean. Giorgio Borsa's (ed.) *Trade and Politics in the Indian Ocean. Historical and Contemporary Perspectives* (New Delhi, 1990) is a very recent contribution to Indian Ocean studies. The book is divided into two parts: One dealing with the Indian Ocean as a system of trade in the sixteenth to the eighteenth centuries, the European penetration into it and the interaction between the European and the Indian merchants; the other examines the current strategic problems arising in the Indian Ocean zone from the superpower rivalries and the impact they made on the littoral society and policy.

European expansion and penetration in the context of the interport trade of Asia has been best studied in Holden Fuber's *Rival Empires of Trade in the Orient, 1500-1800* (Minnesota/Oxford, 1976). The book consists of two parts. The first part is the story of European commercial activity in the East. The second analyses the organisation and structure of the East India Companies, the commodities of the East India trade, growth and development of the country trade and the relations between the Europeans and the Asians. Rothermund Dietmar's *Asian Trade and European Expansion in the Age of Mercantilism* (New Delhi, 1981) is a useful addition to studies on Asian trade.

Some recent critical studies on the lines meant to strike a balance between Eurocentricism and Indocentricism produced by Immanuel Wallerstein and Niels Steensgaard have provoked keen academic interest in studies focussed on the Indian Ocean region. In his *The Modern World System*, vol. 2 (New York, 1980) Wallerstein has argued persuasively that Asia continued to exist as a part of the external arena of the emerging world economy at least until the mid-eighteenth century. This viewpoint has been further highlighted by Steensgaard in his essay "Asian Trade and the World Economy from the 15th to 18th centuries", *Indo-Portuguese History : Old Issues, New Questions*, (ed). Teotonio R. de Souza (New Delhi, 1984). He holds that though the Europeans were unable to establish effective control over the Indian Ocean, they were definitely very often in a position to interfere in its mechanisms. Both Wallerstein and Steensgaard are in agreement that the world witnessed a phenomenal development since 1750: the gradual incorporation of the Indian subcontinent and other

Indian Ocean littoral states including China, into the Europe-based capitalist world system having England as its epicentre. Wallerstein examines this notion in his "Incorporation of Indian Subcontinent into the Capitalist World Economy" *The Indian Ocean. Explorations in History. Commerce and Politics*, (ed.) Satish Chandra (New Delhi, 1987).

There are a number of regional studies. As far as possible, I shall refrain from citing the works based on Portuguese sources and those which examine Portuguese presence and activities in the Indian Ocean region, as the next section concentrates solely on studies on Indo-Portuguese history.

Surat, as the dominant trading emporium of the Indian Ocean has naturally been the subject of much study. M.N. Pearson's *Merchants and Rulers in Gujarat* (Berkeley, 1976) and Ashin Das Gupta's *Indian Merchants and the Decline of Surat C. 1700-1750* are a must for anyone wanting to understand the commercial importance of this great port in the sixteenth and eighteenth centuries respectively. The role of merchants at Surat is also well-examined in Michelguglielmo Torri's essay "In the Deep Blue Sea. Surat and its Merchant Class during the Dyarchic Era, 1759-1800" *IESHR*, 19, 3-4, July-December, 1982. In his essay "Trapped Inside the Colonial Order : The Hindu Bankers of Surat and the Business World during the Second Half of the Eighteenth Century", *Trade and Politics in the Indian Ocean. Historical and Contemporary Perspectives* (ed.) Giorgio Borsa (New Delhi, 1990), he has attempted to challenge the concept of the Anglo-Bania order advanced by Laksmi Subramaniam. O.P. Singh's *Surat and its Trade in the Second Half of the 17th Century* (Delhi, 1976) and B.G. Gokhale's *Surat in the Seventeenth Century* (London, 1979) are other contributions to studies on Surat. For Malabar, Ashin Das Gupta's *Malabar in Asian Trade*, 1740-1800 (Cambridge, 1967) is another fine work which focusses on Malabar's position in the Asian trade in the late eighteenth century. It epitomises the struggle of the local merchants in the face of repeated challenges posed by Tipu Sultan.

Holden Furber was the first to demonstrate the importance of private trade in his monumental work *John Company at Work* (Havard, 1948). *His Bombay Presidency in the Mid-Eighteenth Century* (Bombay, 1963) is on the same lines. To the European traders, Bombay Presidency might have lacked the attractions of Madras and Bengal, but by the mid-eighteenth century, the scenario began to change owing to a series of events. The volume examines how British power steadily grew in the Bombay Presidency through participation in the country trade and the cooperation of the economically powerful native communities, notably the Parsis and the Muslim maritime traders. Furber's influence on Pamela Nightingale is obvious. Her *Trade and Empire in Western India, 1784-1806* (Cambridge, 1970) examines the influence of commercial interests on the expansion of the British empire in Western India in the late eighteenth-early nineteenth centuries. She has clearly shown that in western India it was the private interest of country-traders that chiefly determined the course of the East India Company's annexations of territory both in Gujarat and Malabar. Asiya Siddiqi's paper "The Business World of Jamsetjee Jejeebhoy" *IESHR*, 19, 3-4, July-Decemeber 1982 and Lakshmi Subramaniam's "Bombay and the West Coast in the 1740s" *IESHR*, 18, 2, April-June 1981 are welcome contributions to the studies on the Bombay Presidency.

Bengal has been the subject of numerous studies. Based on Dutch sources we have the recent well-documented *The Dutch East India Company and the Economy of Bengal, 1630-1720* (Delhi, 1988) by Om Prakash. Equally significant are other works on Bengal and the East India Company. Holden Furber had made a profound impact on Amales Tripathi who begins his story where Furber leaves it. The general theme of his work *Trade and Finance in the Bengal Presidency, 1793-1833* (Calcutta, 1979) is the transition of the East India Company to a purely administrative body. The struggle between the private traders and the Company culminating in the termination of the Company's historic career as a joint stock trading corporation and the beginning of a millennium of the free traders in 1813, is well-analysed in this book, rich in statistical information. P.J. Marshall's *East India Fortunes : The British in Bengal in the Eighteenth Century* (Oxford, 1976) and Susil Chaudhuri's *Trade and Commercial Organisation in Bengal 1650-1720* (Calcutta, 1975) are other useful attempts to shed light on Bengal's place in the Asian trade. Turning to the Coromandel coast, we are fortunate to have the work *Merchants, Companies and Commerce on the Coromandel Coast 1650-1740* (Delhi, 1986) produced by Sinnappah Arasaratnam. It is the first detailed account of the commercial system along the Coromandel coast. It analyses the ebb and flow of the Coromandel trade, the crucial role played by the merchants and their dealings with the European companies and the political authority. His work however gives little or no importance to the Portuguese presence in the Coromandel region examined by Sanjay Subrahmanyam in his *Improvising Empire : Trade and Settlement in the Bay of Bengal, 1500-1700* (Delhi, 1990).

We are also indebted to the following valuable studies on the Indian Ocean : K.N. Chaudhuri's *Trading World of Asia and the English East*

India Company 1660-1760 (Cambridge, 1978) which offers a comprehensive history of the English East India Company from mid-seventeenth to mid-eighteenth centuries. The concepts of function and analysis have been applied to the analysis of the East India Company's structure and activities at home and abroad; the relevant essays in *The Cambridge Economic History of India*, 2 vols. (New Delhi, 1982/1984) especially Ashin Das Gupta's contribution entitled "Indian Merchants and the Trade in the Indian Ocean" vol. 1, (eds.) Tapan Raychaudhuri and Irfan Habib; M.N. Pearson's "Brokers in western Indian port cities: their role in servicing foreign merchants" *Modern Asian Studies*, 22, 3 (Cambridge, 1988); *Essays in Medieval Indian Economic History* (ed.) Satish Chandra, (New Delhi, 1987) particularly Irfan Habib's essay "The System of Bills of Exchange (Hundis) in the Mughal Empire"; (ed.) Sanjay Subrahmanyam's fine collection of essays in *Merchants, Markets and State in the Early Modern India* (Delhi, 1990); Dwijendra Tripathi's *State and Business in India. A Historical Perspective* (New Delhi, 1986) and finally *Studies in Maritime History* (ed.) K.S. Mathew (Pondicherry, 1990).

Indo-Portuguese Studies

All readers approaching the study of Indo-Portuguese history must rely on certain basic introductory works. The best introduction to Portuguese colonial history is C.R. Boxer's *The Portuguese Seaborne Empire, 1415-1825* (London, 1969). The book has a topical approach and does not seek to provide a chronological account of the developments. Another work by C.R. Boxer *From Lisbon to Goa, 1500-1750 : Studies in Portuguese Maritime Enterprise* (London, 1984) surveys the role played by the *Carreira da India* over three centuries. Good surveys of the Portuguese empire in the east are provided by George D. Winus and Bailey W. Diffie in their *Foundations of the Portuguese Empire, 1415-1580* (Minneapolis, 1977) which is based on an exhaustive study of the Portuguese literature and has a fine bibliography; M.N. Pearson's "The Portuguese in India". *The New Cambridge History of India*, vol. 1 (Cambridge, 1987) which examines themes such as early colonialism, pre-modern society, religious conversions and race relations; and Donald S. Lach's *Asia in the Making of Europe* (Chicago, 1965-) which is particularly useful for details on what the Portuguese writers in the sixteenth century saw and wrote in India. Of some importance is R.S. Whiteway's *Rise of the Portuguese Power in India* (London, 1899 and 1967) and of little or no importance is F.C.

Danvers, *The Portuguese in India* (London, 1894 and 1966) as general and introductory works. Without doubt, the best available works on the history of Portugal are A.H. de Oliveira Marques' *História de Portugal*, (Lisbon, 1980) and H.V. Livermore's *A New History of Portugal* (London, 1967)

The Portuguese and the Indian Ocean Trade

Voyagers and travellers have left accounts that throw light on the extent and nature of the Portuguese trade in the East in the sixteenth and seventeenth centuries. We find glimpses of the sixteenth century trade in *The Voyage of John Huyghen Van Linschoten to the East Indies*, 2 vols. (London, 1885); *The Book of Duarte Barboza* (ed.) Longworth Dames, 2 vols. (London, 1918-21) and *The Suma Oriental of Tomé Pires* (ed.) A. Cortisão, 2 vols. (Reprint, New Delhi, 1990). Jean-Baptiste Tavernier's *Travels in India*, (transl.) V. Ball, 2 vols. (London, 1925) and Nicolao Mannuci's *Storia do Mogor*, (transl.) William Irvine, 4 vols. (Calcutta Reprint, 1966) examine the seventeenth century Portuguese trading system. They write of a flourishing Portuguese trade in Bengal long after the fall of Hooghly in 1632.

One gains a total picture of the Portuguese activities in western India and the *cartaz* system from M.N. Pearson's *Merchants and Rulers in Gujarat. The Response to the Portuguese in the Sixteenth Century* (Berkeley, 1976). In this work Pearson's main concern is to explain why the Gujarati merchants and rulers behaved in the way they did in the face of the Portuguese challenge. Seventeenth century Portuguese country trade is best examined in C.R. Boxer's *Portuguese India in the Mid-Seventeenth Century* (Delhi, 1980). The book reviews three aspects of Portuguese rule in India during the mid-seventeenth century — conquest, navigation and commerce. A.R. Disney's *Twilight of the Pepper Empire. Portuguese Trade in South-West India in the Early Seventeenth Century* (Cambridge, 1978) and Niels Steensgaard's *The Asian Trade Revolution of the Seventeenth Century. The East India Companies and the Decline of the Caravan Trade* (Copenhagen, 1975) examine the decline of the Portuguese commercial system in the seventeenth century.

Coming to area-wise studies on the Portuguese presence and activity in the Indian Ocean region, for Gujarat we have M.N. Pearson's *Merchants and Rulers of Gujarat* (Berkeley, 1976), Ashin Das Gupta's fine monograph *Indian Merchants and the decline of Surat c. 1700-1750* (Wiesbaden, 1979) and K. S. Mathew's *Portuguese and the Sultanate of*

Gujarat. Portuguese activities in Malabar have been examined in K.M. Pannikar's *Malabar and the Portuguese* (Bombay, 1929). K.S. Mathew's *Portuguese Trade with India in the Sixteenth Century* (New Delhi, 1981), O.K. Nambiar's *The Kunjalis: Admirals of Calicut* (London, 1963) and Genevieve Bouchon's *Regent of the Sea. Connanore's Response to Portuguese Expansion 1507-1528* (Delhi, 1988) are valuable contributions to studies on Portuguese commerce in Malabar. For Kanara, B.S. Shastry's *Studies in Indo-Portuguese History* (Bangalore, 1981) is informative, as is Sanjay Subrahmanyam's fine essay, "The Portuguese, the port of Basrur and the rice trade, 1600-50" in *Merchants, Markets and State in the Early Modern India* (ed.) Sanjay Subrahmanyam (Delhi, 1990). Portuguese activities in the Bay of Bengal have yet to be researched adequately. J.J. Campos' *History of the Portuguese in Bengal* (Calcutta, 1919) contains some information of value but a better treatment of the Portuguese private trade in Bengal is provided by "The 'Shadow-empire' of Goa in the Bay of Bengal" produced by G.D. Winius, *Itinerario*, VII, No. 2, (1983). The first substantial study of the Portuguese presence and activity in the Bay of Bengal was produced by Sanjay Subrahmanyam. *Improvising Empire: Portuguese Trade and Settlement in the Bay of Bengal 1500-1700* has broken fresh ground in an otherwise neglected area of research.

Other regional studies of seminal importance are: M.A.P. Meilink-Roelofsz's *Asian Trade and European Influence in the Indonesian Archipelago Between 1500 and 1630* (The Hague, 1962) and G. D. Winuis' *The Fatal History of Portuguese Ceylon. Transition to Dutch Rule* (Cambridge, 1971). The former is an attempt to supplement and criticize the socio-economic studies of Schrieke and J.C. Van Leur. The book falls into two parts: An accurate and comprehensive account of the trade in the Malay Indonesian region before the arrival of the Europeans is produced. The rise of the commercial port of Malacca and the Asian trading community at a time when the Indonesian archipelago had been hardly affected by European penetration are themes examined in the first part of the book. In its second part the stress shifts to the European element.

Estado da India and the Country Trade

On Portuguese India one can consult certain introductory works. The travelogues: F. Pyrard de Laval's, *Voyage de Fran'ois Pyrard de Laval, contenant sa navigation aux Indes Orientales aux Moluques et ou Brésil*, 2 vols. (Paris, 1619), S. N. Sen's *Indian Travels of Thevenot and Carreri*

(New Delhi, 1949), Manoel Godinho's *Relação do Novo Caminho da India para Portugal* (Lisboa, 1974), *The Travels of Abbé Carré In India and the Near East*, (transl.) Lady Fawcett, (ed.) Sir Francis Fawcett, vol. 1, (New Delhi Reprint, 1990) and *The Travels of Pietro Della Valle In India*, No. LXXXIV, vol. 1 (London) are rich in descriptions on the port cities of Goa, Daman and Diu in the sixteenth and seventeenth centuries, the customs and traditions of the people, their political, social and economic life. Useful general information on the *Estado da India* can also be found in Jose' Nicolau da Fonseca's *An Historical and Archaelogical Sketch of the City of Goa* (New Delhi Reprint, 1986), Maria Francisco Bordalo's *Ensaio sobre a Estatistica do Estado da India* (Lisbon, 1862), A. B. Bragança Pereira's *Etnografia da India Portuguesa*, 2 vols. (Nova Goa, 1923) and A. Lopes Mendes, *A India Portuguesa*, 2 vols. (New Delhi Reprint, 1989). For more details on the history of Goa one can consult M.J. Gabriel Saldanha's *História de Goa*, 2 vols. (New Delhi Reprint, 1990).

The economic set-up of Portuguese India in the nineteenth century is well-examined in J.B. Amancio Gracias's, *Subsidios para a história económico-financeira da India Portuguesa* (Nova Goa, 1909). Antonio Anastasio Bruto da Costa's *As Communidades Agricolas de Goa. O Que foram, O Que são na actualidade* (Margão, 1879) sheds light on nineteenth century agrarian Goa. The above-mentioned works on the economic situation in Portuguese India are generally-speaking contemporary works. A very recent contribution Teotonio R. de Souza's (ed.) *Goa Through the Ages. An Economic History*, vol. II (New Delhi, 1989) is a detailed work on the economic scene in Goa from the pre-Portuguese times till 1961. Overseas and coastal trade, rural economy and society, the agrarian set-up, transport and communication are amongst the themes examined in this book. Teotonio R. de Souza's *Medieval Goa* (New Delhi, 1979) is another valuable contribution to studies on the economics of Portuguese Goa.

Coming to the Goa-based trade, of seminal importance are: M.N. Pearson's "The Port City of Goa : Policy and Practice in the Sixteenth Century", *Coastal Western India. Studies from the Portuguese Records* (New Delhi, 1981) for the sixteenth century; Teotonio R. de Souza's "Goa-based Seaborne Trade in the Early Seventeenth Century" *IESHR*, XII, (1975) Anthony Disney's "Goa in the Seventeenth Century", *The First Portuguese Colonial Empire* (ed.) Malyn Newitt, II (Exeter, 1986) and George Winius "Jewel Trading in the XVI and XVII Centuries", *Indica*, vol. 25, No. 1 for the seventeenth century; Teotonio R. de Souza's "French Slave-Trading in Portuguese Goa (1773-1791)", *Essays in Goan History*

(New Delhi, 1989) and "Goa Mahe Trade Links (Late 18th-Early 19th Centuries) : A New Source Material", *Studies in Maritime History*, (ed.) K.S. Mathew (Pondicherry, 1990) for the late eighteenth-early nineteenth centuries. The last two works are based on the private papers of the Mhamais, housed at the Xavier Centre of Historical Research, Goa. My survey of the Goa-based trade in "Goa-based Overseas and Coastal Trade (18th and 19th Centuries)", *Goa Through the Ages. An Economic History*, vol. II (ed.) Teotonio R. de Souza (New Delhi, 1989) is a preview to this thesis. I have also examined the economic relations between Goa and Brazil in "At the Dusk of the Second Empire : Goa-Brazil Commercial Links 1770-1825", *Purabhilekh-Puratatva*, VII, 1, Jan.-June 1990 and "The Goa-Brazil Trading Nexus as reflected in the Mhamai House Records", a paper presented at the Second Seminar on Latin-Amercian Studies, 25-26 Feb. 1991, Centre of Latin American Studies, Goa University.

For the Estado trade with Moçambique and the rest of East Africa in slaves, ivory, bullion and textiles one can consult M.D.D. Newitt's "East Africa and the Indian Ocean Network. 1500-1800", *India and the Indian Ocean 1500-1800*, (eds.) Ashin Das Gupta and M.N. Pearson (Calcutta, 1978) and S. Sadiq Ali's "India and Moçambique : Past and Present", *Purabhilekh-Puratatva*, VI, 1, Jan.-June 1988. A. Rita-Ferreira's "A Moçambique e Os Naturais da India Portugueza", II Seminário Internacional de História Indo-Portuguesa : ACTAS, (eds.) Luis de Alburquerque and Inácio Guerreiro (Lisbon, 1985) analyses the shylockian grip of the merchants of Portuguese India particularly the banias of Daman and Diu over the Moçambican economy. I.S. Gorerazvo Mudenge's "Goans in the Zambezi Valley", *Purabhikekh-Puratatva*, 11, 2, July-Dec. 1984 and H. Ellert's "Indo-Portuguese Imports and Trade Goods in Zimbabwe (1570-1900)", *Purabhilekh-Puratatva*, July-Dec. 1985 are other additions to Indo-Portuguese studies.

Useful details on the *Estado*-based slave trade can be obtained in P. P. Shirodkar's "Slavery in Coastal India", *Purabhilekh-Puratatva*, III, 1, Jan.-June 1985.

A bird's-eye-view of the nineteenth century Portuguese opium commerce can be obtained from the following: Michael Greenberg's *British Trade and the Opening of China 1800-1842* (New York/London first published in 1951), Gervase Clarence-Smith's *The Third Portuguese Empire 1825-1975. A study in Economic Imperialism* (Manchester/Dovey, 1985), and J. Kumar's *Indo-Chinese Trade 1793-1833* (New Delhi, 1974). The last two works throw light on various attempts made by the British authorities to contain the Malwa menace. A.F. Moniz's "Commercio do opio em Damão no governo do Perfeito Bernardo Peres da Silva", *O Oriente Portugues*, XI contains documentation on the Daman opium commerce.

The *Estado*-based tobacco trade is examined in J.M. Carmo Nazareth's "Monopolio do Tabaco na India", *O Oriente Portugues*, III, 1906. My earlier-mentioned effort "At the Dusk of the Second Empire : Goa-Brazil Commercial Links, 1770-1825", *Purabhilekh-Puratatva*, VII, 1, Jan.-June 1990 has references to the tobacco trade.

Studies on mercantile communities are also significant. The place of predominance occupied by the Hindus in the Portuguese Indian economy is examined in thoroughly researched papers by M.N. Pearson in "Indigenous Dominance in a Colonial Economy: The Goa Rendas 1600-1670", *Mare Luso-Indicum*, II, Geneve, 1973 and "Banyas and Brahmins: Their role in the Portuguese Indian Economy", *Coastal Western India* (New Delhi, 1981). T. R. de Souza's "Glimpses of Hindu Dominance of Goan Economy in the Seventeenth Century", *Indica*, XII, (1975) and G.V. Scammell's "Indigenous Assistance in the Establishment of Portuguese Power in the Indian Ocean", *Indo-Portuguese History: Sources and Problems*, (ed.) John Correa Afonso (Bombay, 1981) run on similar lines and stress that the Portuguese presence in the East depended on indigenous assistance.

Besides the aforesaid studies, T.R. de Souza's "Xendi Tax: A Phase in the History of Luso-Hindu Relations in Goa (1704-1841)", *Studies in Foreign Relations of India*, (ed.) P.M. Joshi (Hyderabad, 1975) and "Mhamai House Records : Indigenous source for Indo-Portuguese historigraphy", ISIPH-II : ACTAS Investigação Cientifica Tropical (Lisbon, 1985), Lakshmi Subramaniam's "Banias and the British : Role of Indigenous Credit in the process of Imperial Expansion in Western India in the Second Half of the Eighteenth Century", a paper presented to the Seminar on State and Business: A Historical Perspective (Ahmedabad, 1984) and M.N. Pearson's "Brokers in Western Indian port cities : their role in servicing foreign merchants", *Modern Asian Studies*, 22, 3, (1988) help to build a picture of the socio-economic world of the Hindu merchants on the west coast of India. One is introduced to the Christian Indo-Portuguese trader Rogerio de Faria in Teotonio R. de Souza's "Capital Input in Goa's Freedom Struggle : The Bombay Connection", *Indo-Portuguese History. Old Issues, New Questions* (ed.) Teotonio R. de Souza (New Delhi, 1984). The socio-economic organisation of the Parsis in western India can be drawn from Dosabhai Framji Karaka's *History of the Parsees*, 2 vols. (London, 1884), David L. White's "Parsis in the Commercial World of Western India 1700-1750", *IESHR*, XXIV, 2, April-June 1987 and Asiya Siddiqi's "The Business World of Jamsetjee Jejeebhoy" *IESHR*, XIX, 3 and 4, July-Dec. 1982. The role of Jewish merchants in Portuguese India is best examined in Walter J. Fischel's "Leading Jews in the Service of Portuguese India", Reprint from the *Jewish Quarterly Review*, XLVII, (July 1956) and A.F. Moniz's "Um Judeu Director de Feitoria Portugueza de Surrate", *O Oriente Portugues*, II, (1905).

There are other specialised studies relating to the commercial system of Portuguese India. Notable among them is Francisco Xavier Ernesto Fernandes' *Memória Histórico-Económica das Alfandegas do Estado da India Portuguesa* (Lisbon, 1899) which examines the customs administration of the *Estado da India* since its genesis until mid-nineteenth century. *His Regimen do Sal, Abkary e Alfandegas da India*, (Lisbon, 1905), J.A. Ismael Gracias' *O Imposto e O Regimen Tributario da India Portugueza*, (Nova Goa, 1898), J.M. do Carmo Nazareth's "Alfandegas Portuguezas no Oriente" *O Oriente Portugues*, VI, (1909) and A.F. Moniz's "A Alfandega de Damão", *O Oriente Portugues*, XI, (1914) are other useful contributions that add to our knowledge of the customs mechanisms and tarriff system in Portugese India.

As regards shipping, Casmiro de Siqueira Nazareth's "Barcos nativos da India", *O Oriente Portugues*, IX provides useful information. Coinage in Portuguese India is best described in A.C. Texeira de Aragão's *Descrição geral e histórica das moedas cunhadas em nome dos reis, regentes e governadores de Portugal*, III, (Porto, 1964). It contains a number of documents of the sixteenth to the eighteenth centuries. Those on the nineteenth century are few but significant. Teotonio R. de Souza's "A Study on the Indo-Portuguese Coinage and The Working of the Goa Mint", *Indian Numismatic Chronicle*, (1975) is a thoroughly researched paper deserving scholarly attention. A.F. Moniz's "As moedas dabu e sivrai em Damão" *O Oriente Portugues*, XI also contain useful data.

APPENDIX 1

GOA-BASED HINDU MERCHANTS, 1800

Merchants	Place of Residence
Widow of Gopal Kamat	Cumbarjua
Narayan, Suba and Ramchandra Sinai	Cumbarjua
Kusha Lakshman Custom, Laximana and Anta Pai	Cumbarjua
Shaba, Santu and Nararey Sinai Shirodkar	Malar
Gopal, Ramchandra and Narayan Naik	Cumbarjua
Venku and Narayan Sinai	Cumbarjua
Vasu and Suba Sinai Khazan	Cumbarjua
Narayan Naik Sinquerkar	Cumbarjua
Narayan Pai Kalapurkar	Cumbarjua
Shabi Kamat	Panelim
Vasu Sinai	Cumbarjua
Rama Pai	Cumbarjua
Govinda Sinai	Cumbarjua
Venkatesha Bhandari	Cumbarjua
Narayan Parab Lawande	Cumbarjua
Anta Naik	Cumbarjua
Narayan Kamat	Cumbarjua
Shaba Naik Karande	Cumbarjua
Govinda and Mukund Sinai Malia	Cumbarjua
Giridhar Kamat	Cumbarjua
Madavji Naik Dessai	Racaim
Vithoba Kamat	Cumbarjua
Gopal Naik	Cumbarjua
Naba Keni(?)	Cumbarjua
Anta Keni(?)	Cumbarjua
Anta Naik Serraf	Cumbarjua
Vitogy Naik Karande	Cumbarjua
Govinda Sinai Navelkar	Cumbarjua
Mollu Kamat	Cumbarjua
Vasu Sinai Balculy	Panelim
Gopal Kamat	Panelim
Keshav Parab Lawande	Panjim
Vaman Parab Sinari	Ribandar
Bomby & Shabi Parab Lawande	Ribandar
Raghunath Parab Lawande	Ribandar

Merchants	Place of Residence
Venkatesha Kamat	Panjim
Kushta Sinai Dhempe	Panjim
Raghunath and Sansgiri(?) Sinai Dhempe	Panjim
Santa Sinai Dhempe	Panjim
Balu Kushta Kamat	Panjim
Narayan and Rama Naik	Cumbarjua
Shiva(?) and Laxman Kamat	Panjim
Anta Kamat	Panjim
Venkat Parab	Panjim
Manogogy Sinai	Cumbarjua
Laxman Sinai Bicho	Panjim
Pandu Sinai	Panjim
Pandu Kamat	Panjim
Sadashiva and Venkatesha Shet Khalap	Mapuça
Pandurang and Vassudev Sinai Cabadi	Betim
Raghunath Naik	Verem
Raghunath Kamat	Verem
Keshav Naik	Verem
Keshav Pai	Verem
Vithoba Seguina and Damu Sinai Dondo	Verem
Gopala Kamat	Verem
Seguna, Kushta, Ganaba and Vissuanata Sinai Nerlikar	Verem
Ganesh and Vaman Sinai Zangal	Verem
Balu Kushta Naik	Verem
Rama Kamat Mhamai	Verem
Roulu and Nagogy Naik	Verem
Mall Parab Lawande	Pomburpa
Bara Shet	Panjim

Source: HAG : *RGF*, 2279, fls. 673 - 675.

APPENDIX 2

RETURNS FROM THE CUSTOMS HOUSES OF SALCETTE AND BARDEZ, 1772-97

Year	Bardez (In *xerafins*)	Salcette(In *xerafins)*
1772	24099-4-31	28489-1-15 1/2
1773	23391-2-04 3/4	35864-0-42 1/4
1774	21453-1-27 1/4	19338-0-14 2/3
1775	21740-1-23 1/2	20803-2-30 1/2
1776	22532-4-34	24840-2-39
1777	19666-0-21 1/2	21884-0-56 1/2
1778	18029-1-05	19251-3-03 1/2
1779	18160-2-38	23458-2-43 5/12
1780	18624-0-04	29423-2-49
1781	18201-1-45	21190-4-44
1782	18742-1-15 1/4	29757-1-45 1/2
1783	18555-1-42 1/4	25457-1-24 1/2
1784	22364-2-36 1/2	27357-1-38 1/2
1785	20039-3-01	23489-3-37 1/2
1786	18161-4-01 3/4	13439-3-12 3/4
1787	19694-0-59 3/4	14528-3-50
1788	20164-1-33 1/2	18024-1-56 1/4
1789	19986-3-46 3/4	15408-2-09
1790	17274-0-33 3/4	14082-1-05 3/4
1791	16937-3-43 1/4	16511-0-20 3/4
1792	22970-3-43	17142-2-55
1793	19989-0-01 1/2	16557-1-31 3/4
1794	14767-4-28 1/2	14837-1-13 1/4
1795	14925-4-29	17109-2-00
1796	14920-1-12 3/4	19037-3-36 3/4
1797	14955-1-29 1/4	18562-4-39 1/4

Source: HAG : *CR*, 1648, doc. dated 24 March 1798.

APPENDIX 3

INCOME OF THE *ALFANDEGA DE GOA*, 1806-41

Year	Income (In *xerafins*)
1806	276313-1-00 1/4
1807	233375-0-01 1/2 (?)
1808	210700-3-02 1/2
1809	196910-1-27 1/2
1810	277465-0-13 1/4
1811	290498-3-19
1812	244913-4-25 1/4
1813	118629-1-52
1814	161478-3-25
1815	191199-3-24
1816	217767-3-02
1817	401675-2-30
1820	168545-1-05
1821	178008-3-32 1/2
1822	87708-4-47 3/4
1823	80708-4-45 (?)
1824	87042-4-22 1/2
1825	118377-2-32
1826	73295-1-35
1827	86867-3-01
1828	99066-3-20
1829	99343-2-14 1/4
1830	107635-0-49 1/2
1831	95227-0-01
1832	85230-1-20
1833	71622-2-11 1/2
1834	57129-2-11 1/2
1835	49234-1-06 1/2
1836	43516-3-06 1/4
1837	59529-3-08 3/4
1838	56063-3-57 3/4
1839	75387-1-55
1840	93590-0-58 1/2
1841	74669-2-30
TOTAL	3167481-2-20 3/4

Source: Claudio Lagrange Monteiro de Barbuda (ed.) *IDJ*, Nova Goa, 1841, p. 25.

APPENDIX 4

LISBON SHIPS THAT CALLED AT GOA, 1780-88

Year		Ship
1780	(1)	Polifemo
	(2)	N.S. da Conceição
1781	(1)	Infante D. João e San Pedro de Alcantara
	(2)	Principe do Brazil
	(3)	Rainha de Portugal, N.S. do Rozario e Santo Antonio
1782	(1)	Santo Antonio e Polifemo
	(2)	Princeza de Holstein
	(3)	S. Anna e S. Joaquim
1783	(1)	Jesus, Maria e Joze
	(2)	N.S. da Conceição
	(3)	N.S. da Arrabida
	(4)	S. Joze do Macapa
	(5)	S. de Bomfim e S. Tiago Mayor
1784	(1)	S. Joze Triumfo
	(2)	Mercurio
	(3)	S. Antonio Polifemo
	(4)	Jesus, Maria e Joze
	(5)	N.S. da Piedade e Brio de Mar
1785	(1)	Princeza de Portugal
	(2)	Princeza de Holstein
	(3)	Conde de Atalaya
	(4)	Navio de Viagem
	(5)	N.S. dos Prazeres
	(6)	N.S. da Piedade
	(7)	S. do Bomfim e S. Tiago Mayor
	(8)	N.S. de Oeste Santa Quiteria
	(9)	N.S. do Carmo e S. Antonio
1786	(1)	N.S. do Oeste (?)
	(2)	Santissimo Sacramento
	(3)	N.S. da Coroa
	(4)	Grande Condestavel
1787	(1)	Amavel Donzela
	(2)	Lampadoza
	(3)	N.S. da Vida
	(4)	Bomfim e Santa Maria
	(5)	São Tiago
1788	(1)	Navio de Viagem do Mesquita
	(2)	N.S. da Arrabida
	(3)	Estrela da Azia
	(4)	N.S. do Amparo
	(5)	Navio de Viagem Conceição

Sources: AHU : *MI*, Maço 113, no. 119; Maço 136, no. 129; HAG : *AG*, 6317, fls. 303-303v.

APPENDIX 5

SHIPMENTS OF OPIUM FROM INDIA AND TURKEY TO CHINA, 1800-39

Year	Bengal Opium (In chests)	Malwa Opium (In chests)	Turkish Opium (In chests)	Total (In chests)
1800-01	3224	1346	-	4570
1801-02	1744	2203	-	3447
1802-03	2033	1259	-	3292
1803-04	2116	724	-	2840
1804-05	2322	837	-	3159
1805-06	2131	1705	102	3938
1806-07	2607	1519	180	4306
1807-08	3084	1124	150	4356
1808-09	3233	985	-	4208
1809-10	3074	1487	32	4593
1810-11	3592	1376	-	4968
1811-12	2788	2103	200	5091
1812-13	3328	1638	100	5066
1813-14	3213	1556	-	4769
1814-15	2999	674	-	3673
1815-16	2723	1507	80	4321
1816-17	3376	1242	488	5106
1817-18	2911	781	418	4140
1818-19	2575	977	807	4359
1819-20	1741	2265	180	4186
1820-21	2591	1653	-	4244
1821-22	3298	2278	383	5459
1822-23	3181	3855	-	7773
1823-24	3360	5535	140	9035
1824-25	5960	6663	411	12434
1825-26	3810	5563	-	9373
1826-27	6570	5605	56	12231
1827-28	6650	5504	-	12434
1828-29	4903	7709	1256	13868
1829-30	7443	8099	715	16257
1830-31	5672	12856	1428	18956
1831-32	6815	9333	402	16550
1832-33	7598	14007	380	21989
1833-34	7808	11715	963	20486
1834-35	10207	11678	-	21885
1835-36	14851	15351	-	30202
1836-37	12606	21427	243	34776
1837-38	19600	14773	-	34373
1838-39	18212	21988	-	40200

Source: *Historical Statistical Monographs on Commercial Crops of India. Poppy (Opium)*, Gokhale Institute of Economics and Politics, Pune, 1981, p. 78.

APPENDIX 6

CONSUMPTION OF OPIUM IN CHINA, 1821-34

	Bengal Opium		Malwa Opium	
Period	Number of chests	Total Value (In rupees)	Number of chests	Total Value (In rupees)
1821-22	2910	6038250	1718	2276350
1822-23	1822	2828930	4000	5160000
1823-24	2910	4656000	4172	3859100
1824-25	2655	3119625	6000	4500000
1825-26	3442	3141755	6179	4466450
1826-27	3661	3668565	6308	5941520
1827-28	5114	5105073	4361	5251760
July 1830-December 1830	3082	2738700	7533	4054047
April 1830-March 1831		1790204	12100	7114059
April 1831-June 1831		1312155	1300	900385
July 1833-December 1833	3876	2536470	6533 1/2	4669220
April 1833-March 1834	9535	6089634	11715	7916971

Sources: BA : *RD*, 29/235, 1828, p. 65; 8/336, 1831, pp. 27, 91, 121, 131; 42/586, 1834, pp. 5, 25, 45.

APPENDIX 7

HIGHEST, LOWEST AND AVERAGE PRICES OF BENGAL AND MALWA OPIUM, 1816-31

	Bengal Opium (Price per Chest)				Malwa Opium (Price per Chest)			
Year/Period	Chests produced	Highest $	Lowest $	Average $	Chests produced	Highest $	Lowest $	Average $
1816-17	2610	1320	1080	1200	600	950	800	875
1817-18	2530	1330	1200	1265	1150	800	600	612
1818-19	3050	1200	800	1000	1530	850	600	725
1819-20	2970	1320	1150	1235	1630	1400	950	1175
1820-21	3050	2500	1300	1900	1720	1800	1230	1515
1821-22	2910	2500	1650	2075	1718	1600	1050	1325
1822-23	1822	2550	2080	1552	4000	1500	1080	1290
1823-24	2910	2500	1100	1600	4172	1050	800	925
1824-25	2655	1450	900	1175	6000	950	550	750
1825-26	3442	1150	800	913	6179	850	560	723
1826-27	3661	1250	800	1002	6308	1060	860	942
1827-28	5134	1220	815	998	4401	1420	950	1204
1828-29	5965	1100	880	940	7771	1250	750	968
1829-30	7143	1000	805	860	6857	1030	740	862
1830-31	6660	1050	790	870	12100	760	520	588

Sources: *Historical Statistical Monographs*, pp. 126-127; BA : *RD*, 11/292, (1830), p. 146.

APPENDIX 8

SHIPMENTS OF MALWA OPIUM FROM PORTUGUESE INDIA TO MACAO, 1797-1838

Year	Exported from	Quantity (In chests)	Ship	Remarks
1797	Goa	16	São Luis e Almas Santas	
1798	Goa	3	Nossa Senhora da Luz	
1800	Goa	29		
1802	Goa	10	Esperança	
1803	Goa	14	Bella Julia	
1805	Goa	32		
1807	Goa (?)	13	Nossa Senhora do Rozario	
1810	Goa		Activo	
1812	Goa	53	Angelica	
1813	Goa	11	Angelica	
1814	Goa	4	Angelica	
1815	Goa	3	Angelica	
1816	Goa	114	Angelica	
1817	Goa	249	Angelica	
1818	Goa and Daman	33	Principe Regente	include consignments from Bombay
	Goa	227	Rainha	
1819	Goa	27	Angelica	
	Goa	352 or 57	Carmo	include consignments
	Goa	141	Angelica	from Bombay
	Goa	334 or 390	Caçador	
	Goa and Diu	88 or 49	Socorro Estrela	
1820	Goa and Daman	462	Caçador	
	-do-	471	Santo Antonio	include consignments
	-do-	9	Carmo	from Bombay
	-do-	21	Angelica	
	Goa	9	Viagante	
1821	Goa and Daman	314	Ilustre Almeida	
	Goa and Daman	84	Angelica	include consignments
	Goa and Daman	538	Andromeda	from Bombay
	Goa and Daman	141	Carmo	
	Goa and Daman	147	Santo Antonio	
1822	Goa and Daman	614 (?)	Angelica	
	Goa and Daman	858 (?)	Castro	
	Goa and Daman	79 (?)	Santo Antonio	include consignments
	Goa and Daman	44	Fenix	from Bombay
	Daman	428	Leticia	
	Goa	7	Santa Anna	
1823	Malabar Coast	808	Angelica	
1824	Goa and Daman	85	Santo Antonio	
	Goa and Daman	5	Gentil Indiana	include consignments
	Goa and Daman	204	Caçador	from Bombay
	Daman	126 1/2	Fenix	
1825	Goa and Daman	162	Conde de Rio Parde	
	Goa and Daman	749 3/4	Angelica	include consignments
	Goa and Daman	107	Santo Antonio	from Bombay
	Goa and Daman	984 1/2	Caçador	
	Goa and Daman	63 or 43	Dezempenho	

1826	Goa and Daman	474	Angelica	
	Goa and Daman	329 1/2	Santo Antonio	include consignments
	Goa and Daman	173	Conde	from Bombay
	Goa and Daman	906 3/4	Fenix	
1827	Goa and Daman	412	Angelica	
	Goa and Daman	155	Conde de Rio Parde	include consignments
	Goa and Daman	533 1/2	Santo Antonio	from Bombay
	Goa and Daman	401 1/2	Dezempenho	
	Goa and Daman	412	Caçador	
1828	Goa	2	Eliza	
	Daman	1624 1/2	D.Manoel de Portugal	
	Daman	464 1/2	Leticia	
	Daman	77 1/2	Caçador	include consignments
	Daman	869	Dezempenho	from Bombay
	Daman	427	Dourado	
	Daman	676	S.Sabastião	
	Daman	151	Conde de Rio Pardo	
1829	Goa and Daman	3+138	Conde de Rio Pardo	
	Goa and Daman	(?)	Angelica	
	Goa and Daman	485	Deligente	
	Goa and Daman	1008 1/2 +36 3 sacks	Dezempenho	include consignments from Bombay
	Goa and Daman	581	S.Sabastião	
	Goa and Daman	1084 1/2	Caçador	
	Goa and Daman	294 1/2 + 2 sacks	Eliza	
1831	Goa and Daman	478	Angelica	
	Goa and Daman	733 1/2	Conde de Rio Parde	include consignments
	Goa and Daman	476	S.Francisco de Paula	from Bombay
	Goa and Daman	731 3/4	Caçador	
	Goa and Daman	293 3/4	Esperança	
1832	Daman	554 26/100	Concordia	
	Daman	850 50/100	S.Francisco de Paula	include consignments
	Daman	601 58/100	Caçador	from Bombay
	Daman	480	Camoens	
	Daman	521 23/100	Esperança	
1833	Daman	397	S.Francisco de Paula	
	Daman	493	Santa Anna	
	Daman	382 (?)	Caçador	
	Daman	323	Esperança	
	Goa	1	Feliz Viana	
1834	Goa	10	Feliz Viana	
	Daman	718 20/100	S.Francisco de Paula	
	Daman	331	Azia Feliz	
	Daman	710 30/100	Santa Anna	include consignments
	Daman	549 25/100	Aurelia	from Bombay
	Daman	303	Caçador	
	Daman	326 75/100	Esperança	
1835	Daman	1696 1/4	Suzana	
	Daman	37	Aurelia	include consignments
	Daman	1241	Santa Anna	from Bombay
	Daman	1417 1/4	Caçador	
	Goa	6	Angelica	
1838	Goa	2	Esperança	

Sources: HAG : Compiled from *Macau*, 1296, 1298-1302, 1305-1313, 1315-1320, 1322-1327, 1329-1330, 1332, 1334, 1336, 1338, 1340-1342, 1345.

APPENDIX 9

VOLUME OF SLAVES DESPATCHED FROM MOÇAMBIQUE TO DAMAN AND DIU, 1804-33

Year	Daman (No. of Slaves)	Diu (No. of Slaves)
1804	-	8
1805	-	3
1809	-	30
1817	-	59
1818	-	31
1824	-	26
1825	-	30
1826	-	40
1827	15	-
1828	63	71
1829	37	76
1831-32	43	9
1833	78	-

Sources: HAG : Compiled from *Dio*, 4952, 4953, 4956, 4960, 4963, 4965, 4967, 4969; Compiled from *Damão*, 4839, 4841, 4842, 4846, 4848.

APPENDIX 10

SLAVE CONSIGNMENTS FROM GOA TO MACAO, 1796-1827

Year	Merchant	Number and Type of Slaves
1796	Constantino Golphe	1 young kaffir
1800	Kushta Sinai Dhempe	1 young kaffir
	Fr. Joze Francisco de Figueiredo	1 kaffir
	Fr. Antonio Lobo	1 kaffir
	Vincente Salvador Roiz	1 kaffir
	Joze Alvarez	1 kaffir
	Paulo Antonio de Bragança	1 kaffir
	Lourenço Joze de Almeida	1 kaffir
	Antonio Mathias Lourenço	1 medium-sized kaffir
1812	Manoel de Silva	1 young negress
	Thomas Inacio de Silva	1 young kaffir, 2 negresses
	Antonio Ferreira Balthazar	1 negress
	Manoel Domingos de Viana(?)	1 negress
	Inacio Xavier de Fonseca Unhão	1 negress
	Antonio Fre. de Silva	1 kaffir
	Francisco Soares	1 young negress
	João Tomas de Aquino	3 kaffirs 3 negresses 3 young negresses
	Antonio Joze Gabriel	2 kaffirs
1821	Inacio Loyola da Cruz	1 young negress
	Xavier de Castro	1 young negress
	Bernardo Aleixo de Lemos e Faria	1 young negress
	Joze Maria de Siqueira	1 young kaffir
	Inacio de Loyola de Cruz	1 young negress
1822	João Fellipe de Rozario	1 young negress
	Vitorino T. da Cunha Gurj	2 mulattos
	Antonio da Silva	1 young kaffir
1826		2 kaffirs 5 young kaffirs 2 young negresses
1827	Luciano Antonio Ribeiro	1 young kaffir
	Joze Joaquim de Mesquita	1 young kaffir
	Francisco Antonio de Sa	1 young negress

Sources: HAG : *AG*, 2268, fl. 31v; 6810, fls. 314-315, 318, 323, 325, 340, 344; 6814, fls. 174, 181, 399; 6815, fls. 111, 115; 6816, fl. 741; 8119, fls. 101, 107, 114, 162; 9248, fl. 5; 9254, fl. 605; 9255, fls. 212, 239, 241, 266, 267, 284, 305, 312, 324.

APPENDIX 11

TOTAL VALUE OF IVORY CARGOES SHIPPED TO DAMAN AND DIU FROM MOÇAMBIQUE, 1804-40

Year (In *xerafins*)	Daman (In *xerafins*)	Diu (in *xerafins*)
1804		194099 - 0 -42 1/2
1805		203941 - 1 -17 1/2
1806		266384 -1 1/2-42 3/4
1808		14522 -4 -41 3/4
1809		182597 3/4-4 - 6 3/4
1824		117055 1/2-1 3/4-45
1825		123197 1/4-0 -56 1/2
1826	193697 3/4-0 1/2-53	
1827	32918-0-15	
1828	94251	168782 -3 1/2-37 1/2
1829	33232	44848 -5 -32 1/2
1831-32	114261	60933 -3 -42
1833	15080	
1839	11278-2-30	
1840	5858-2-51 3/4	

Sources: HAG : Compiled from *Damão*, 4839, 4841, 4842, 4846, 4848, 4849; Compiled from *Dio*, 4952, 4953, 4956, 4959, 4960, 4963, 4965, 4969.

APPENDIX 12

TOTAL VALUE OF THE *ESTADO'S* BULLION TRADE WITH MOÇAMBIQUE 1804-39

Year	Goa (In *xerafins*)	Daman (In *xerafins*)	Diu (In *xerafins*)
1804			92114 3/4-4 -04
1805			152378 1/4-1 -07 1/2
1806			158422 -3 -48 1/4
1807			24262 1/2-0 -37 1/2
1808			60874 1/2-0 -22 1/2
1809			128775 1/2-0 -08 3/4
1817			271572 -3 1/2-45
1818			211364 -3 -00
1824	18626-0-00		110070 -0 -00
1825			238271 -0 -00
1826	37067-3-59 1/2		266550 -2 -30
1827		158891-2-30	
1828		149651-3-45	479231 -0 -00
1829		112512-0-00	263252 -0 -00
1831-32		19322-0-00	148204 -2 -30
1832		1440-0-00	
1833	13154-1-37 1/2		
1838	480-0-00		
1839		19-1-00	

Sources: HAG : Compiled from *Dio*, 4952, 4953, 4956, 4959, 4960, 4963, 4967, 4969; Compiled from *Damão*, 4839, 4841, 4842, 4846, 4848, 4849; AG, 9869, fls. 1-4v;, 11318, fls. 2-12.

APPENDIX 13

GOLD CONTRACTORS AT GOA, 1766-69

Year	Gold Contractors	Quantity of gold	Price (per *marco*)	Value of contract (In *xerafins*)
1766	Bulla Naik	5 marcos 4 onças 7 1/2 oitavas	433	2432-1-12
	Bulla Naik	3 marcos 7 onças 5 oitavas	442 1/2	1749-1-11
	Phondu Prabhu	6 marcos 5 onças 7 oitavas	418	2814-4-50
	Phondu Prabhu	4 marcos 6 onças 1 oitava	435	2073-0-13
	Phondu Prabhu	5 marcos 4 onças 1 oitava	418	2305-2-39
	Soirea Prabhu Lawande	3 marcos 6 onças 7 oitavas	432	1670-3-07 1/2
	Bulla Naik	2 marcos 3 onças 1 oitava 18 graons	435	1041-3-06
	Phondu Prabhu	2 marcos 3 onças 1 oitava 6 graons	435	1043-1-36
	Bulla Naik	2 marcos 3 onças 1 oitava 36 graons	437	1048-0-35
	Vitobha Naik	2 marcos 3 onças 1 1/2 oitavas	434	1040-2-35
	Phondu Prabhu Lawande	2 marcos 3 onças 1 1/2 oitavas	437	1048-0-35
	Soirea Prabhu	2 marcos	439	1049-2-25

	Lawande	3 onças 1 oitava		
1766	Soirea Prabhu Lawande	2 marcos 3 onças 1 1/2 oitavas	437	1048-0-00
	Phondu Prabhu Lawande	2 marcos 3 onças 1 1/2 oitavas	450	1079-1-29
	Phondu Prabhu Lawande	2 marcos 3 onças 1 1/2 oitavas	450	1079-1-29
	Soirea Prabhu	2 marcos 3 onças 1 1/2 oitavas	450	1079-1-29
	Phondu Prabhu Lawande	2 marcos 3 onças 1 1/2 oitavas	450 1/2	1080-2-28 1/2
1768	Vithoji Sinai Nerlekar	6 marcos 2 onças 6 oitavas	424	2689-3-45
	Rama Kushta Naik	6 marcos 2 onças 2 1/2 oitavas	413	2597-1-55
	Daquea Naik Karande	6 marcos 2 onças 5 oitavas 12 graons	413	2614-2-57 1/3
	Daquea Naik Karande	6 marcos 2 onças 1 oitava 54 graons	413	2592-2-42 2/3
	Vithoji Naik Coraleiro	6 marcos 2 onças 2 oitavas 48 graons	408	2567-0-00
	Vithoji Naik	6 marcos 2 onças 2 oitavas 12 graons	418	2626-3-15
	Vithoji Naik	6 marcos 2 onças 4 oitavas	418	2638-3-07 1/2
	Vithoji Naik Coraleiro	6 marcos 2 onças 4 1/2 oitavas	415	2622-4-38 2/3
1768	Lakshman Sinai	6 marcos 2 onças 5 1/2 oitavas	416	2635-3-45
	Vithoji Naik Coraleiro	6 marcos 2 onças	420	2657-4-03 4/5

		5 oitavas		
	Phondu Prabhu Lawande	6 marcos 2 onças 2 oitavas	419	2631-4-13
	Phondu Prabhu Lawande	6 marcos 2 onças 4 oitavas 12 graons	416	2630-1-12 1/6
	Phondu Prabhu Lawande	1 marco 3 oitavas 18 graons	421	444-0-07
1769	Phondu Prabhu Lawande	4 marcos 4 onças 2 oitavas	400 1/2	1814-3-49 1/2
	Phondu Prabhu Lawande	5 marcos 7 onças 5 oitavas	401	2387-1-00
	Phondu Prabhu Lawande	5 marcos 7 onças 5 1/2 oitavas	420 1/2	2506-4-07 1/2

Source: AHU : *MI*, Maço 94, no. 92, docs. dated 9 Feb. 1767, 1768-1769.

APPENDIX 14

NATURE OF INDIAN FABRICS, 1770-1840

Calicoes continued to dominate the textile scene of production and distribution in the period under review. *Elefante* or loin cloth was a common and coarser variety of calico. It was made of staple cotton and was the longest of the locally woven varieties. It seems that its standard measurements were 37 yards length and 1 yard breadth. Its length must have provided it its name. Like other varieties of cotton cloth, it was woven in coarse, fine and superfine grades. Markets along the Coromandal coast were important supply centres of long cloth. The coarsest calico was the *dungaree,* a sail cloth of 12 yards length. *Dungarees* were an inferior type of cotton cloth like the *cachchai* or *cacha* cloth. It was used by the common folk as a loin cloth. *Salempores* and parcalles, finer calico varieties were 16 and 18 yards long respectively. While only a few *salempores* and *parcalles* were painted most calicoes were washed and bleached. *Morins* produced at Nellore, Cuddalore and other parts of South India, were also made of staple cotton but were finer and of superior quality. They were much shorter than the long cloth variety, about 10 yards long and 1 yard broad. Of the same texture and weaves as long cloth but woven from cotton thread dyed in bright colours and white stripes and checks, was a type of cloth probably called *negro* or *pano de cafre* much in demand in East Africa and Brazil. *Allegias* were cotton fabrics or cotton interwoven with silk or with gold threads usually worked in two colours, red and white or blue and white. They were known to have been woven near Mausulipatnam. *Beatilha* was a fine linen cloth. This term of Portuguese origin refers to the nun's veil probably indicating that the material was used as a veil by women. *Beatilhas* of superior quality were procured from Cuddalore, Nagora, Arni and other areas on the south-eastern side of India.

Chellas derived from Surat and Jumbasoor in Gujarat and the Coromandal were striped or checkered cotton cloth sometimes with printed heads and borders. The *dupatta* meaning 'two widths' was usually used as a wrap. *Girgaes* acquired from Masulipatnam, Pulicut, Bacaim, Tanna and Bengal were woven in different patterns catering to the different markets in the Archipelago, Siam, Japan and West Asia.

Sucatoons were probably heavy cotton cloth utilized for packing and as blankets. Gune or gunny was specially made for sacking.

Bertangil was a superior quality calico produced in the vicinity of Daman and at Surat usually in blue, black and white colours. *Bafata* refers to another calico of a different quality produced in Gujarat, Bengal and Sind. *Molmol* referred to a fine muslin material manufactured at Gujarat and Bengal. *Cassa* seemed to be a muslin type of cloth. *Rumais* were small cotton or silk handkerchiefs or towels. *Tafetas* were quite costly usually woven in silk with gold or silk threads mainly produced at Bengal and Chaul. *Cutinias*, a product of Bengal and Surat, was a kind of silk or costly handkerchief. *Canequin*, a fine cotton fabric, was produced at Daman and various parts of Gujarat. It was much in demand in Western European countries. *Chita* or spotted cloth was a product of Masulipatnam, Daman, Bassein, Cambay, Surat and Jumbasoor but that produced at Masulipatnam, was much in demand. Designs were applied on it through a complex process of painting. *Anagoas, cadeas, marchas, coromandeis, tiadas, pitamboris, tocas, bancaes, carlanganis, bilaras, sussins, hervas, zuartes, xapurins, tucorins, tofulis, saracas, sanas,* and *naginas* were other varieties of Indian fabrics that *Estado* merchants traded in.

Panos was a generic term used for piece-goods whether linen, cotton, woollen, or silk of different qualities ranging from coarse to superfine, whether spotted, checkered, striped, printed or painted. They bore different designations as *panos sevaigagins, panos de Joris, panos de picotilhos, panos de durgogins, panos de begagis, panos tecidos, panos azuis, panos pretos, panos sadins* and the like.

Sources: HAG : *MR*, 148B, fls. 728-811v; Satya Prakash Sangar, "Indian Fabrics (17th Century)", *Maratha History Seminar*, Kolhapur, May 28-31, 1970; Sinnappah Arasaratnam, *Merchants, Companies and Commerce on the Coromandel Coast, 1650-1740*, Delhi, 1986, pp. 98-102.

APPENDIX 15

WEAVERS, DYERS AND PRINTERS AT DAMAN, 1810-28

		Districts	1810	1811	1812	1814	1817	1820	1822	1823	1824	1827	1828
WEAVERS	MUSLIMS	Damão de Cima	20	20	36	23	23	24	24	24	24	24	26
		Doler	14	9	30	11	11	12	12	13	13	13	13
		Ambavary											
		Chão de Jamporis					4	5	5	5	5	5	5
	no	Damão Pequeno	108	108	100	12	12	13	13	13	13	13	15
		Fora de Jampa			273	65	67	68	67	68	68	68	70
		Carivary	43	43	288	79	83	83	83	82	82	82	82
	–	Varacunda	135	135	279	84	89	92	92	93	93	93	96
	HINDUS	Damão de Cima					2	2	2	2	2	2	2
		Doler											
		Ambavary	8	8	8	3	5	5	5	5	5	5	5
		Chão de Jamporis	12	10	26	8	10	10	10	10	10	10	10
	no	Damão Pequeno	45	45	198	27	29	29	29	28	28	28	28
		Fora de Jampa						2	1	2	2	2	2
		Carivary											
		Varacunda											
	MUSLIMS	Damão de Cima											
		Doler											
		Ambavary											
		Chão de Jamporis											

		Districts	YEAR										
			1810	1811	1812	1814	1817	1820	1822	1823	1824	1827	1828
		Damão Pequeno								1	1	1	1
P	*												
	n	Fora de Jampa											
R	o												
	*	Carivary											
I	-												
B		Varacunda											
N													
		Damão de Cima											
T	H												
	I	Doler											
E	N												
	D	Ambavary											
R	U												
	S	Chão de Jamporis				40	45	45	45	46	46	46	46
S		Damão Pequeno				26	28	28	28	28	28	28	28
	*												
	n	Fora de Jampa					3	3	3	3	3	3	3
	o												
	*	Carivary											
		Varacunda											
		Damão de Sima											
D	H												
	I	Doler											
Y	N												
	D	Ambavary				5	4	3	3	2	2	2	2
E	U												
C	S	Chão de Jamporis				8	10	11	11	11	11	11	11
R		Damão Pequeno				12	14	14	14	15	15	15	15
	*												
S	n	Fora de Jampa					2	3	3	3	3	3	3
	o												
	*	Carivary											
		Varacunda											
	L	Damão de Sima			28	25	29	30	31	32	32	32	34
		Doler			14	11	15	16	17	18	18	18	18
	O	Ambavary			4	6	8	7	7	8	8	8	8
		Chão de Jamporis			18	12	15	16	16	15	15	15	15
D													
	O	Damão Pequeno			99	96	97	98	98	98	98	98	100
	M	Fora de Jampa			91	74	77	82	80	81	81	81	81
	S	Carivary			76	107	114	114	114	115	115	115	118
		Varacunda			92	108	117	120	121	121	121	121	122

	Districts	YEAR										
		1810	1811	1812	1814	1817	1820	1822	1823	1824	1827	1828
	WEAVERS 'A'	385	378	1238	312	335	345	343	345	345	345	354
T												
O	**PRINTERS 'B'**				66	76	76	76	78	78	78	78
T												
A	**DYERS 'C'**				25	30	31	31	31	31	31	31
L	**LOOMS 'D'**			422	439	472	483	484	488	488	488	496

Sources: HAG : *MR*, 190C, fl. 739; 191D, fl. 1188; 192B, fl. 565; 193A, fl. 1334; 195C, fl. 307; 197B, fl. 655, 200B, fl. 139; 202C, fl. 1898, 204B, fl. 681; AHU : *MI*, Maço 188, no. 173, doc. dated 26 Oct. 18101; Maço 192, no. 206, doc. dated 15 Nov. 1811; Maço 193, no. 201, doc. dated 18 Dec. 1812; Maço 198, no. 196, doc. dated 5 Dec. 1814; Maço 201, no. 192, doc. dated 15 dec. 1817; Maço 221, no. 213, doc. dated 20 Dec. 1823; Maço 231, no. 239, doc. dated 1 Jan. 1827;

Note: Figures for 1814-28 relating to weavers and printers refer to textile production houses; prior to this period they refer to textile manufacturing units, while those for the period 1823-28 refer to individuals.

APPENDIX 16

FUNCTIONING OF THE CONTRACT OF BAHIAN TOBACCO LEAF, 1775-1825

Year/ Period	Tobacco Contractors	Price of the contract excluding 1%			Value of Bahian Tobacco	Quantity of tobacco shipped to Goa from Bahia		Quantity of additional tobacco bought in India				Amount spent for additional tobacco bought at India		
		xerafins	*tangas*	*reis*	*reisfortes*	*arrobas*	*arrateis*	*candis*	*quintais*	*arrobas*	*arrateis*	*xerafins*	*tangas*	*reis*
1	2	3	4	5	6	7	8	9	10	11	12	13	14	15
1775-1779	Vithogi Sinai Nerlikar	360570	0	00	6334 $ 119	4659	24							
1777-1779	Govind Sinai Malia	387249	0	45	14436 $ 371	25424	0							
1780-1782	Ramchandra Naik	454500	0	00	11168 $ 909	11415	22	168	3	2				
1783-1785	Ramchandra Naik	456015	0	00	17415 $ 588	11473	20	115	0	0	0	3840	0	12
1786-1788	Ramchandra Naik and Santopa	322089	0	00	16409 $ 889	14991	18	189	3	1	0			
1789-1791	Ramchandra Naik Santopa and Anta Naik	387840	0	00	27168 $ 395	17576	08	05	1	1	12	14497	3	50

(*Contd.*)

Appendix 16 (*Contd.*)

1	2	3	4	5	6	7	8	9	10	11	12	13	14	15
1792-1794	Anta and Pandu Naik	424200	0	00	21281 $ 420	12220	16	150	12378	2	30			
1795-1797	Mukund Sinai Malia	462378	0	00	5953 $ 750	4109	24	544	2	2	14	55145	1	34
1798-1801	Mukund Sinai Malia	424200	0	00	39631 $ 995	18119	0	268	0	2	27	3045	4	46
1802-1804	Anta and Pandu Naik	499950	0	00	11489 $ 265	22199	16	373	0	3	14	1314	3	58
1805-1807	Pandu Naik	475710	0	00	20206	22	18	3	0	24	7	0	52	
1808-1810	Rama Kamat	507828	0	00	12686	14	54	0	3	16	9912	4	0	
1811-1813	Govind Sinai and brothers	565701	0	00	26436 $ 310	28746	22446	183	123	2	04	1852	4	10
1814-1816	Govind Sinai and brothers	540855	0	00	31688	0	34	3	2	17	17540	4	59	
1817-1819	Govind Sinai and brothers	570549	0	00	11772 $ 240	17865	25	176	3	1	04	85608	0	35
1820-1822	Govind Sinai and brothers	575851	2	30	19914	0	185	3	1	07	260181	2	10	
1823-1825	Bardez Municipality	533946	3	00	5971	08	320	3	3	12	24212	3	01	
TOTAL	7949432	1	15	279268	17	3367	0	3	23	969400	1	43		

Source : HAG : *MR*, 202D, fl. 384.

APPENDIX 17

FUNCTIONING OF THE CONTRACT OF LISBON SNUFF, 1675-1824

Year/ Period	Contractor	Period of contract			Price of the contract (In *xerafins*)	Quantity of snuff that arrived at Goa		
		Years	Months	Days		*arrateis*	*quartas*	*onças*
1	2	3	4	5	6	7	8	9
1675						38748		
1678	Vantu Naik & others	1			155208-0-00	76848		
1679-1680	Baxa Babu & Ramaji Sinai	2			389200-0-00	39590	2	
1681	Gaspar Dias, Mathias Pub... and others	1			216333-1-40	35005		
1682	Babuso Gauns & Vantu Naik	1			137550-0-00	15331	3	
1683	Babuso Gauns & Vantu Naik	1			150000-0-00	18635	3	
1684	Gaspar Dias & others	1			154661-1-40	35147		
1685	Apaji Naik & others	1			119000-0-00	39876		
1686	Apaji Naik & others	1			107328-3-20	27227		3
1687	Santu Naik & others	1			121800-0-00	20591		3
1688	Santu Naik & others	1			135000-0-00	14394	3	1 1/2
1689	Malpa Chatim & others	1			142000-0-00	24800		
1690	Malpa Chatim & Vithoji Dalvi & others	1			140500-0-00	13059	2	
1691	Malpa Chatim & Vithoji Dalvi & others	1			112000-0-00	12073	2	

(*Contd.*)

APPENDIX 17 (*Contd.*)

1	2	3	4	5	6	7	8	9
1692	Krishna Naik & others	1			119000-0-00			
1693	same as above & Tandu Naik	1			120000-0-00	5899		
1694	same as above & Rogu Naik	1			118000-0-00	19761	3	
1695	Pedro Soares & others	1			148500-0-00	29145	1	
1697	Krishna Naik & others	1			121000-0-00	18306		
1698	Krishna Naik & others	1			117000-0-00	19777	3	
1699	Pedro Soares & others	1			100000-0-00	22953	2	
1700	Krishna Naik & others	1			78000-0-00	18848	3	
1701-1703	Bassanea Sinai & others	3			364500-0-00	59652	1	
1704-1706	Vithoji Sinai & others	3			304200-0-00	51989	2	
1707	Vithoji Sinai & others	3			336300-0-00	25271		
1710-1712	Santopa Naik & others	3			324300-0-00	59203	2	
1713-1715	Babea Keni & others	3			319800-0-00	73089	2	
1716-1718	Ganesh Kamat & others	3			283200-0-00	27098	1	
1719-1721	same as above & others	3			270300-0-00	45138		
1722-1724	Santopa Naik & others	3			285150-0-00	66438		
1725-1727	Santopa Naik & others	3			285150-0-00	36554		
1728-1730	Surya Pai & others	3			295800-0-00	55171		
1731-1733	Santopa Naik & others	3			300000-0-00	52300		
1734-1736	Santopa Naik & others	3			252000-0-00	12672		
1737-1739	Santopa Naik & others	3			301500-0-00	47739	3	
1740-1742	Fondu Kamat & others	3			315300-0-00	32509		
1743-1745	Zogu Kamat & others	3			315000-0-00	65506		

(*Contd.*)

APPENDIX 17 (*Contd.*)

1	2	3	4	5	6	7	8	9
1746-1748	Surya Naik & others	3			339150-0-00	62038		
1749-1751	Surya Naik & others	3			270300-0-00 (?)	68213	3	
1752-1754	Surya Naik & others	3			433300-0-00 (?)	57003	2	
1755-1757	Govinda Naik & others	3			573300-0-00	92227		
1758-1760	Vithoji Sinai & others	3			559500-0-00	90356	1	
1761-1763	Vithoji Sinai & others	3			601500-0-00	47424	(?)	
1764-1766	Vithoji Sinai & others	3			601500-0-00	78080		
1767-1769	Kushta Kamat & others	3			830100-0-00	70280		
1770-1772	Kushta Naik & others	3			789000-0-00	128616		
1773-1775	Ramachandra Naik & others	3			775500-0-00	117487	3	
1776-1778	Gopal Naik & others	2	11	18	709200-0-00	103526	2	
1779-1781	Gopal Naik & others	3			732600-0-00	98479		
1782-1784	Ramaji Naik & others	3			738000-0-00	76395		
1785-1787	Narayan Sinai & others	3			720600-0-00	103531		
1788-1790	Narayan Sinai & others	3			751500-0-00	92719		
1791-1793	Canaba Sinai & others	3			720300-0-00	103591 (?)		
1794-1797	Canaba Sinai & others	2	6	22	720300-0-00	53461		
1798-1800	Anta Naik & others	2	10	22	693000-0-00	159678		
1801-1803	Gopal Kamat & others	3			642000-0-00	95466		
1804-1806	Narayan Naik & others	3			585000-0-00	56982		
1807-1809	Narayan Naik & others	3			585000-0-00	43258		
1810-1812	Venkatesha Kamat & others	3			451965-0-00	18600		
1813-1815	Venkatesha Kamat & others	2	1	26	436965-0-00	87769		
1816-1818	Venkatesha Kamat & others	3			332786-1-52	47992		
1819-1820	Pundalik Sinai Kenkre	2	5	25	310118-2-50	40096		
1822-1824	Pundalik Sinai Kenkre	2	3	15	310085-0-00	70000		

Source: HAG : *MR*, 202D, fl. 385.

APPENDIX 18

NATURE OF WOOD AT DAMAN

Teak wood (*teca*) abundantly available in the Nagar Haveli area of Daman was considered to be of a superior kind to that of Kanara or Goa. Teak was employed extensively in construction work owing to its inherent ability to resist disintegration. Black wood called *sisso*, used in the making of furniture, was much appreciated in the West. *Kher* was extremely durable. Hence it was employed for all kinds of frame work, for flooring and panelling and as beams to support roofs. *Hedér,* which was white or yellow in colour was used in roofing as rafters. *Sadrá* was used for tanning hides. Available in two varieties, the black type closely resembled *sisso* and was used in the manufacture of furniture. The white variety, found growing along the banks of rivers and in coastal areas was found to be less durable. Another extremely durable wood was *assane*. Even when immersed in water, it had the ability to resist disintegration. Therefore it was used in the making of framework for wells. *Calicanty* was similar in leaf and flower to *kher* but much less durable. *Palasse* of huge dimensions was used to make wooden plates and for roofing. Another tree of great dimensions *sivane*, was used in the making of statues, the butt-end of guns and coach boxes. *Apteira* wood was extremely strong. The tree was one of inferior dimensions but its bark was excellent for producing cords and its leaves for producing local cigarettes called *viris*.

Tanasse was yellow in colour. It was used in framework for carts. Like ebony, *timbri*, of medium dimensions was black in colour. It was used in the making of small agricultural implements. *Jambol* was used in roofing and for wells. *Babul* was of moderate proportions. Its leaves and branches served excellently as fuel in steam engines. *Biá* was a tree of great dimensions, the wood of which was used for timber-work in houses.

Source: A. Lopes Mendes, *A India Portugueza,* vol. 2, Reprint, New Delhi/Madras, 1989, pp. 245-248.

APPENDIX 19

REVENUE INCOME FROM TRADE IN COCONUTS AND COPRA AT GOA, 1787-91

Year	Income from Imports (In *xerafins*)	Income from Exports (In *xerafins*)
1787	14547-2-36	8687-3-43
1788	6047-1-31	4437-2-40
1789	5842-2-46	2630-0-48 1/2
1790	1932-1-02	1870-3-04
1791	3709-3-10	2058-0-02 1/2
Total	32079-1-10	19684-0-18

Source: HAG : *MR*, 173, fl. 284.

APPENDIX 20
GOA CUSTOMS RETURNS, 1500-1814

Year	Amount (In xerafins)
1500	446,666-0-00
1600	226,666-0-00
1610	200,000-0-00
1627	150,000-0-00
1628	125,000-0-00
1629	132,000-0-00
1634	130,000-0-00
1648	98,525-0-00
1649	128,250-0-00
1750	111,007-2-30
1752	132,100-0-00
1753	212,711-3-20
1754	162,100-0-00
1756	214,029-0-50
1757	166,800-0-00
1759	231,653-1-40
1760	233,583-0-00
1762	286,489-1-50
1765	248,889-1-40
1766	250,033-2-40
1769	269,333-1-40
1772	345,240-4-17 1/2
1773	313,964-0-31 1/2
1774	318,237-4-56 1/4
1775	200,313-0-53
1776	272,441-2-21 3/4
1777	189,891-1-23 3/4
1778	188,064-0-34 3/4
1779	284,500-1-27 1/2
1780	271,956-1-21 1/4
1781	274,072-4-00 2/3
1782	380,013-1-07 3/4
1783	478,011-1-12 1/4
1784	500,633-0-56
1785	403,961-4-43 3/4
1786	584,159-0-09 1/4
1787	456,698-4-53 1/4
1806	386,631-1-31 1/6
1807	251,091-2-40 1/2
1809	209,607-2-48 1/2
1810	288,191-0-11 3/4
1811	345,799-3-41 1/4
1812	349,001-4-46 3/4
1813	222,894-2-48 1/2
1814	185,846-0-05 3/4

Sources: HAG : *MR*, 121B, fls. 626-626v; 122B, fls. 421-422; 123B,fls. 614-615; 125B, fls. 632-633v; 126A, fls. 49-50v; 127B, fls. 391-392; 129B, fls. 562-563; 130B, fls. 467-468; 135B, fls. 486-487v; 138D, fls. 996v-1043v; 140B, fls. 569v-609v; 145B, fls. 387v-438v; 161B, fls. 606, 610; 171B, fl. 493; 191B, fls. 1299v-1300; *CR*, 1646, doc. dated 24 March 1798; AHU : *MI*, Maço 200, no. 198, doc. dated 16 Jan. 1815; no. 203, 22 Feb. 1812; Armando Cortesao, (ed.), *The Suma Oriental of Tome Pires*, vol. I, Reprint, Asian Educational Services, New Delhi 1990, p. 58; A. R. Disney, *Twilight of the Pepper Empire Portuguese Trade in South-West India in the Early Seventeenth Century*, Cambridge, 1978, p. 51.

Note: Figures for 1750-1814 exclude revenue income drawn from the Customs Houses of the New Conquest areas and passes/checkposts. In 1806-10 the average revenue collection from the said customs houses was 47665 *xerafins* : Claudio Lagrange Monteiro de Barbuda, *IDJ*, Nova Goa, 1841, p. 25.

BIBLIOGRAPHY

A. MANUSCRIPTS : ARCHIVAL SOURCES

1. Historical Archives of Goa

Monções do Reino
125A-230.

Alfândegas
(1) *Salcete*
5461-5470, 5844-5848, 9309-9311.
(2) *Bardez*
5604-5609, 5913-5917, 9303-9308.
(3) *Nova Goa*
2247, 2668, 5166-5190, 5705-5720, 6315-6425, 6802-6820, 6822-6823, 6826-6827, 8114-8121, 8125-8126, 8130, 9246-9265, 9267, 9269, 9869, 11318.
(4) *Damão*
4839, 4841-4851, 5644-5648, 6020-6070, 8094-8095.
(5) *Dio*
4952-4975, 5665-5671, 5674, 6112-6140.
(6) *Provisões, Régias das Alfandegas*
8042, 8089.

Correspondência para o Reino
1632-1670, 2405-2424, 2567, 2629-2630.

Registos Gerais de Fazenda
2154-2155, 2158, 2216, 2272-2298, 2635, 7709, 7954.

Registos Gerais de Dio
7950

Correspondência de Damão
1055, 1057, 1060-1061, 1063, 1065-1077, 1079, 1081-1082, 1084-1098.

Correspondência de Dio
995-1015.

Correspondência de Moçambique
1443-1448.

Correspondência de Macau
1294-1356, 1359.

Provisões
1584-1588, 1591, 7922, 7924, 7926-7927, 7932-7933.

Petições Despachadas no Conselho da Fazenda
1156-1158.

Processos Judiciaes
1956, 2491-2492, 2546, 2569, 2654, 2664, 2729, 2754-2757, 7808, 7855, 8721-8722, 8784-8787,8792-8793.

Fianças
1850-1851.

Feitorias
7981, 9578-9584, 9701-9702.

Rendas de Arrematação
1940, 2599, 4470, 7849-7851, 7853.

Portarias do Governo
1382-1410.

Cartas, Patentes, Alvarás
628, 700-773.

Ordens Régias
1520-1540, 3085.

Regimentos e Instrucções
1418, 1435-1442.

Estrangeiros
1224-1230, 1651, 1661.

Escravos
2976-2981.

Fábrica de Cumbarjua
1962, 2052-2055.

Conventos
2070, 2082, 2497, 2764, 4484, 4489, 7497, 7500-7504, 7509-7510, 7886-7897, 9452, 9454-9462, 9469-9471, 9478, 9508.

2. Bombay Archives

Miscellaneous Records : Statements and Returns, External and Internal Commerce
vols. 1-25.

Revenue Department
Volumes: 7, 9/9, 10/10, 13/13, 16/40, 18/42, 25/49, 79, 28/80, 29/81, 19/103, 20/104, 9/119, 5/137, 6/138, 3/184, 22/213, 38/234, 29/235, 32/279, 11/292, 5/333, 6/334, 7/335, 8/336, 13/428, 12/429, 42/586, 44/588.

Political Department
Volumes: 22/213, 20/404, 40/507, 92/1088, 89/1190, 90/1191, 91/1192, 12/1289, 75/1290, 69/1396, 103/1525, 104/1526, 105/1527, 84/1617, 85/1618, 86/1619, 87/1620, 98/1982, 99/1983, 100/1984.

Commercial Department
Diaries: 23 (1824), 28 (1825).

General Department
Volumes: 20/23, 9/206, 12/344, 13/345, 14/346.

3. Arquivo Histórico Ultramarino, Lisboa

India (*Papeis Avulsos*)
Maços 52-251.

India (Documentos Organizados)
Maços 16A, 18, 33, 35, 37, 53, 59-60, 62, 64-65.
Seculos VIII e XIX.
Maços 1-2, 4-7, 10-16, 19, 21-26, 28, 28A, 29-31, 34, 36, 38-41, 45-51, 54, 56-58, 66.

Caixas de Moçambique
30-243.

Caixas de Macau
30-45.

Caixas de Timor
3-4.

4. Arquivo Nacional De Torre Do Tombo, Lisboa

Casa da India
MSS 335, 539-540, 557, 559, 567, 576, 578-583, 594, 600, 698, 729, 731-732, 741-742, 750, 769, 782-783, 787, 789-790, 797, 826, 880, 884-890, 911-912, 915-917, 919-920, 928, 930, 937, 939, 987, 990, 995-996, 1005-1007, 1030, 1034, 1039, 1046, 1048, 1052, 1063-1064, 1068, 1081, 1095, 1098, 1107-1108, 1114, 1119, 1122, 1130-1131, 1138-1139, 1202-1213, 1217, 1226, 1228-1229, 1247-1248, 1311-1312, 1314, 1320, 1478-1479, 1483-1486, 1489-1491, 1500-1501, 1510-1516, 1537-1552.

Ministério do Reino
Maços 999-1000.

5. Biblioteca De Palácio De Ajuda, Lisboa

India
46-XIII-24
49-II-82.
49-V-6.
50-V-33.
50-V-37 and 38.
51-VI-54.
51-VIII-42.

51-IX-6.
51-IX-33.
51-XI-19 and 20.
51-XII-6.
51-XIII-25.
54-XIII-15 and 16.
54-XIII-22.

Macau
51-X-35.
54-XIII-48 and 49.

Moçambique
51-V-72.
51-VII-25.
51-VII-31 and 32.
51-VII-34.
54-V-12.
54-XI-2.
54-XIII-3.

6. Biblioteca Nacional De Lisboa

Fundo Geral
MSS 35, 41, 76, 174, 211.
Cod. 34-36, 230-231, 233, 235, 245, 308, 420, 423, 465-466, 598, 600, 607, 637, 655, 675, 748, 853, 2161, 2257, 4179, 4401, 4411, 4530, 7640, 8548, 8529, 8746, 8841, 9451, 9809, 9860-9861, 10633-10635, 10758, 10801 10949, 11026.

Collecção Pombalina
Cod. 171-172, 439, 455, 460, 467, 475, 479, 495, 525, 610, 612, 616, 630, 633, 639-641, 643-644, 649, 653-654, 657, 666, 687, 698, 720, 735, 744.

Alcobacenses
Cod. 132, 139-140.

7. India Office Library, London

Abstracts of Revenue Letters from Bombay
L/E/3/11.

Revenue Letters from Bombay
L/E/3/339-349.

Revenue Despatches to Bombay
L/E/3/782-785.

Bombay Proceedings
P/419/56-59.

Political and Secret Proceedings
L/PS/1/2, 9-11, 13-18.
L/PS/2/1-2.
L/PS/3/1, 3-4.
L/PS/4/7-9.
L/PS/5/302-306, 321-327, 363-371.
L/PS/6/160-161, 163-166, 169-185, 256-259, 638-641.

Home Miscellaneous Series
Home/Misc./762.

Finance : Bombay Letters and Closures Received
L/F/3/598, 600.

Bombay Despatches
E/4/1022, 1034-1036, 1038, 1040-1041, 1044, 1046-1049, 1057-1059, 1061-1062, 1065, 1067-1069.

Portuguese Records
1. *Conselho Ultramarino*
I/3/151-154.
2. Noticias da India
I/3/113, 119.

B. MANUSCRIPTS : PRIVATE PAPERS

1. Xavier Centre of Historical Research, Goa

1. *Mhamai House Papers*
English Papers vols. 1-3.
French Papers vols. 1-9.
Portuguese Loose Papers.

2. *J. N. da Fonseca Papers*
Loose and uncatalogued papers.

2. Bombay University Library

Jamsetjee Jejeebhoy Papers
vols. 348-349, 351, 355, 358, 375.

C. PRINTED WORKS

Abreu, Miguel Vincente de, *Noção de alguns filhos distinctos da India Portugueza*, Nova Goa, 1874.

_____, *O Governo do Vice-Rei Conde de Rio Pardo no Estado da India Portuguesa desde 1816 ate 1821*, Nova Goa, 1869.

Administração das Comunidades das Ilhas de Goa, *O Arroz Cultura, Producção e Consumo em Goa*, Nova Goa, 1909.

Albuquerque, Teresa, *Anjuna - Profile of a Village in Goa*, New Delhi, 1987.

Andrade, Jose Ignacio de, *Cartas Escriptas da India e Da China nos Annos de 1815 A 1835*, vol. I, Lisboa, 1843.

Aragão, A. C. Texeira de, *Descrição geral e histórica das moedas cunhadas em nome dos Reis, Regentes e Governadores de Portugal,* vol. III, 2nd edn., Porto, 1964.

Arasaratnam, Sinnappah, *Merchants, Companies and Commerce on the Coromandel Coast, 1650-1740*, Delhi, 1986.

Arez, Joaquim Jose Fernandes, *Breves Considerações Sobre O Resultado Económico e Financeira do Tratado da India de 26 de Dezembro de 1878*, Lisboa, 1891.

_____, *Relatorio da Gerencia do Commisarindo do Sal, Abkari e Alfandegas da India Portugueza*, Lisboa, 1884.

Barbuda, Claudio Lagrange Monteiro de, (ed.), *Instrucções com que El Rei D. Joze mandou passar ao Estado da India no anno de 1774*, Nova Goa, 1841.

Bordalo, Francisco Maria, *Ensaio Sobre a Estatistica do Estado da India*, Lisboa, 1862.

Borsa, Giorgio, (ed.), *Trade and Politics in the Indian Ocean*, New Delhi, 1990.

Bossa, Jose Silvestre Ferreira, *Communidades de Goa. Principios duma Reforma Agraria*, Goa, 1946.

Bouchon, Geneveive, *Regent of the Sea. Cannanore's Response to Portuguese Expansion, 1507-1528*, Delhi, 1988.

Boxer, C. R., *From Lisbon to Goa, 1500-1750 : Studies in Portuguese Maritime Expansion*, Valorium Reprints, London, 1984.

_____, *Portuguese India in the Mid-Seventeenth Century*, Delhi, 1980.

_____, "The Carreira da India (ships, men, cargoes, voyages)", *Centro de Estudos Históricos Ultramarinos Comemorações Henriquinas*, Lisboa, 1961.

_____, *The Portuguese Seaborne Empire, 1415-1825*, The History of Human Society, (gen. ed.) J. H. Plumb, London, 1977.

Bragança Pereira, A. B. de, *Etnografia da India Portuguesa*, 2 vols., Nova Goa, 1923.

_____, "Os Arabes em Goa no seculo X", *O Oriente Portugues, 1ª serie*, vol. XVI, pp. 31-33.

Campos, J. J. A., *History of the Portuguese in Bengal*, Calcutta, 1919.

Carmo Nazareth, J. M. do, "Alfandegas Portuguezas no Oriente", *O Oriente Portugues*, vol. VI, 1909, pp. 15-22.

_____, "Monopolio do Tabaco na India", *O Oriente Portugues*, vol. III, 1906, pp. 93-99.

Chandra, Satish, (ed.), *Essays in Medieval Indian Economic History*, New Delhi, 1987.

_____, (ed.), *The Indian Ocean. Explorations in History, Commerce and Politics*, New Delhi, 1987.

Chaudhuri, K. N., *The Trading World of Asia and the East India Company, 1660-1760*, Cambridge, 1978.

_____, *Trade and Civilisation in the Indian Ocean. An Economic History from the Rise of Islam to 1750*, New Delhi, 1985.

Chaudhuri, Susil, *Trade and Organisation in Bengal, 1650-1720*, Calcutta, 1975.

Clarence Smith, Gervase, *The Third Portuguese Empire, 1825-1975, A study in Economic Imperialism*, Manchester/Dovey, New Hampshire, 1985.

Coates, Austin, *Macao and the British Prelude to Hong Kong, 1637-1842*, Hong Kong, 1988.

Correa Mendes, *F. C. Cultura do Coqueiro em Goa*, Lisboa, 1907.

Correia-Afonso, John, (ed.), *Indo-Portuguese History, Sources and Problems*, Bombay, 1981.

_____, *Intrepid Itinerant*, Bombay, 1990.

Costa, Antonio Anastasio Bruto da, *As Communidades Agricolas de Goa O que foram, O que são na actualidade*, Margão, 1879.

Costa, Bernadino C. da, *Geografia Fiscica e Politica*, vol. I, Nova Goa, 1923.

Couto, Diogo do, *Negocios da India*, Lisboa, 1942.

Cunha, A. M., *Sir Roger de Faria, Notas Genealógicas e Biográficas*, Nova Goa, 1828.

Cunha, J. J. da, *Nossa Terra Estudos Económicos Financeiros, Sociais e Internacionais*, vol. I, Bastora, 1939.

Curtin, Philip D., *Cross-Cultural Trade in World History*, Cambridge, 1984.

Dames, Mansel Longworth, (ed.), *The Book of Duarte Barboza*, 2 vols., Reprint, New Delhi/Madras, 1989.

Danvers, F. C., *The Portuguese in India*, 2 vols., London, 1894.

Das Gupta, Ashin and Pearson, M. N., (eds.), *India and the Indian Ocean, 1500-1800*, Calcutta, 1987.

_____, *Indian Merchants and the Decline of Surat, 1700-1750*, Wiesbaden, 1979.

_____, *Malabar in Asian Trade, 1740-1800*, Cambridge, 1967.

Datta, K. K., *Economic Condition of the Bengal Subah*, Calcutta, 1984.

Davis, Ralph, *The Rise of the Atlantic Economies*, London, 1975.

Dietmar, Rothermund, *Asian Trade and European Expansion in the Age of Mercantilism*, Delhi, 1981.

Disney, Anthony, "Goa in the Seventeenth Century", *The First Portuguese Colonial Empire*, (ed.) Malyn Newitt, Exeter Studies in History, no. 11, Exeter, 1986, pp. 85-98.

______, "Smugglers and Smuggling in the Western Half of the Estado da India in the Late Sixteenth and Early Seventeenth Centuries", *Indica*, vol. 26, nos. 1 & 2, March-Sept. 1989, pp. 57-75.

_____, *Twilight of the Pepper Empire, Portuguese Trade in South-west India in the Early Seventeenth Century*, Cambridge, 1978.

Documentação Ultramarina Portuguesa, 5 vols. Centro de Estudos Históricos Ultrmarinos, Lisboa, 1960-67.

Drewit, Dawtrey F., *Bombay in the Days of George IV, Memoirs of Sir Edward West*, London, 1907.

Ellert, H., "Indo-Portuguese Imports and Trade Goods in Zimbabwe, (1570-1900)", *Purabhilekh-Puratatva*, July-Dec. 1985. pp.3-14.

Fawcett, Charles, (ed.), *The Travels of Abbe Carré in India and the Near East, 1672-1674*, 3 vols., Reprint, New Delhi/Madras, 1991.

Fernandes, Francisco Xavier Ernesto, *Memória Histórico-Económica das Alfandegas do Estado da India Portuguesa*, Lisboa, 1899.

_____, *Regimen do Sal, Abkary e Alfandegas da India*, Lisboa, 1905.

Fischel, Walter J., "Leading Jews in the Service of Portuguese India", Reprint, *Jewish Quarterly Review*, vol. XLVII, July 1956.

Fonseca, Jose Nicolau da, *An Historical and Archaelogical Sketch of the City of Goa*, Reprint, New Delhi, 1986.

Foster, William, (ed.), *Early Travels in India, 1583-1619*, London, 1921.

Furber, Holden, *Bombay Presidency in the Mid-Eighteenth Century*, Bombay, 1965.

_____, *Rival Empires of Trade in the Orient, 1500-1800*, Minnesota/ Oxford, 1976.

Godinho, Manoel, *Relação do Novo Caminho da India para Portugal*, Lisboa, 1974.

Gokhale, B. G., *Surat in the Seventeenth Century*, London, 1979.

Gracias, J. A. Ismael, *O Imposto e O Regimen Tributario da India Portugueza*, Nova Goa, 1898.

Gracias, J. B. *Amancio, Subsidios para a História Económico-Financeira da India Portugueza*, 1909.

Greenberg, Michael, *British Trade and the Opening of China, 1800-1842*, New York/London, First Pub. in 1951.

Habib, Irfan, *An Atlas of the Mughal Empire*, Delhi, 1982.

Hanson, Carl, *Economy and Society in Baroque Portugal, 1668-1703*, Minnesota, 1981.

Hatalkar, V. G., *Relations Between the French and the Marathas, (1668-1815)*, Bombay, 1958.

Heaton, Herbert, *Economic History of Europe*, Tokyo, 1966.

Jesus, de C., *The Tobacco Monopoly in the Philippines, Bureaucratic Enterprise and Social Change, 1766-1880*, Manila, 1980.

Journal of Abbé Cottineau de Kloguen, Instituto Vasco da Gama, Nova Goa, 1874-75.

Karaka, Dosabhai *Framji, History of Parsees*, 2 vols., London, 1884.

Kumar, J., *Indo-Chinese Trade, 1793-1833*, New Delhi, 1974.

Lach, Donald S., *Asia in the Making of Europe*, Chicago, 1965.

Livermore, H. V., *A New History of Portugal*, London, 1967.

Ljungstedt, Andrew, *An Historical Sketch of the Portuguese Settlements in China*, Boston, 1836.

Lobo, Sertorio, C., *Industrias Posiveis No Momento Atual, 9º Congress Provincial Da India Portuguesa Secção III*, Nova Goa, 1931.

Lopes, Mendes A., *A India Portuguesa*, 2 vols. Reprint, New Delhi/ Madras, 1989.

Macgregor, John, *Commercial Tariffs and Regulations, Resources and Trade*, London, 1847.

Magalhães, Godinho V., *Os Descobrimentos e a Economia Mundial*, 4 vols., Lisbon, 1981-83.

Mannuci, Niccolao, *Storia do Mogor*, (transl.) William Irvine, 4 vols., Reprint, Calcutta, 1966.

Marques, Oliveira de A. H., *História de Portugal*, Lisboa, 1980.

Marshall, P. J., *East India Fortunes : The British in Bengal in the Eighteenth Century*, Oxford, 1976.

_____, "The Moral Swing to the East : British Humanitarianism, India and the West Indies", *East India Company Studies*, (eds.) Kenneth Ballhatchet and John Harrison, Hong Kong, 1986.

Mathew, K. S., *Portuguese and the Sultanate of Gujarat. (1500-1573)*, Delhi, 1986.

_____, *Portuguese Trade with India in the Sixteenth Century*, New Delhi, 1981.

_____, (ed.), *Studies in Maritime History*, Pondicherry, 1990.

Meilink - Roelofsz, *Asian Trade and European Influence in the Indonesian Archipelago Between 1500 and 1630*, The Hague, 1962.

Moniz, A. F.,"A Alfandega de Damão" *O Oriente Portugues*, vol. XI, 1914. pp. 127-134.

_____, "A Feitoria Portuguesa de Surrate", *O Oriente Portugues*, vol. XV, 1ª serie, pp. 5-29.

_____, "As Moedas dabu e sivrai em Damão", *O Oriente Portugues*, vol. XI, pp. 75-79.

_____, A visit to Daman, *The Examiner*, 8 March 1913.

_____, "Commercio do opio em Damão no governo de Prefeito Bernardo Peres da Silva", *O Oriente Portugues*, vol. XI, pp. 225-232.

_____, *Noticias e Documentos para a História de Damão Antiga Provincia do Norte*, 4 vols., Bastorá, 1900/17.

_____, "Um Judeu Director de Feitoria Portugueza de Surrate", *O Oriente Portugues*, vol. II, Nova Goa, 1905, pp. 56-58.

Moreland, W. H., *From Akbar to Aurangzeb. A study in Economic History*, London, 1923.

Morse, Hosea Ballou, *The Chronicles of the East India Company trading to China, 1635-1834*, vols. II-IV Cambridge Havard, 1926.

Mudenge, Gorerazvo, I. S., "Goans in the Zambezi Valley", *Purabhilekh Puratatva*, vol. II, no. 2, July-Dec. 1984, pp. 1-7.

Nambiar, O. K., *The Kunjalis : Admirals of Calicut*, Bombay, 1963.

Nazareth, Casmiro de Sequeira, "Barcos nativos da India", *O Oriente Portuguese,* vol. IX, pp. 227-234.

Nightingale, Pamela, *Trade and Empire in Western India, 1784-1806,* Cambridge, 1970.

Pannikkar, K. M., *Malabar and the Portuguese*, Bombay, 1929.

Pearson, M. N., *Before Colonialism : Theories on Asia-European Relations, 1500-1750*, New Delhi, 1988.

_____, "Brokers in western Indian port cities: Their role in servicing foreign merchants", *Modern Asian Studies*, 22, 3, 1988, pp. 455-472.

_____, *Coastal Western India, Studies from the Portuguese Records,* New Delhi, 1981.

_____, "Indigenous Dominance in a Colonial Economy: The Goa Rendas, 1600-1670", *Mare Luso-Indicum,* Tome II, Geneve Librarie Droz II, rue Massot, 1973, pp. 61-73.

_____, *Merchants and Rulers in Gujarat, The Response to the Portuguese in the Sixteenth Century*, Berkeley/New Delhi, 1976.

_____, "The Portuguese in India", *The New Cambridge History of India,* Cambridge, 1987.

Pinto, Celsa, "At the Dusk of the Second Empire : Goa-Brazil Commercial Links, 1770-1825", *Purabhilekh Puratatva*, vol. VII, no. I, Jan.-June 1990, pp. 41-69.

Pires De Lima, J. A., *Mouros, Judeus e Negros na História de Portugal,* Porto, 1940.

Pissurlencar, Panduranga S. S., *Portuguese Records on Rustamji Manockji, the Parsi Broker at Surat*, Nova Goa, 1933.

Prakash, Om, *The Dutch East India Company and the Economy of Bengal, 1630-1720*, Delhi, 1988.

Pyrad, F. de, *Voyage de Franois Pyrard de Laval contenant sa navigation aux Indes Orientales aux Moluques et ou Brésil,* 2 vols., Paris, 1619.

Rea, William Francis, *The Economics of the Zambezi Misions, 1580-1759,* Roma, 1976.

Rita-Ferreira, A., "Moçambique E Os Naturais Da India Portuguesa", *II Seminário Internacional de História Indo-Portuguesa : ACTAS,* (ed.) Luis de Albuquerque and Inacio Guerreiro, Lisboa, 1985, pp. 615-648.

Rodney, Walter, *How Europe underdeveloped Africa*, Tanzania, 1980.

Sadiq Ali, S., "India and Moçambique : Past and Present", *Purabhilekh Puratatva*, vol. VI, no. 1, Jan.-June 1988, pp. 5-15.

Sahu, A. C., "Genesis and Growth of Indo-Chinese Opium Monopoly under East India Company", *Journal of Indian History*, vol. LVII, 1979.

Saldanha, M. J. Gabriel, *História de Goa*, 2 vols. Bastora', 1925-1926.

Scammell, G. V., "Indigenous Assistance in the Establishment of Portuguese Power in the Indian Ocean", *Indo-Portuguese History: Sources and Problems*, (ed.) John Correia Afonso, Bombay, 1981.

_____, *The World Emcompassed the First European Maritime Empires*, London, 1981.

Selections from the Records of the Bombay Government, no. X and no. XVII, New Series, Bombay 1855.

Sen, S. N., *Indian Travels of Thevenot and Carreri*, New Delhi, 1949.

Sen, S. P., *The French in India*, New Delhi, 1971.

Sharma, Kalpana, "Opium Trade in the Holkar State, 1816-1856", Studies in Maratha History, Proceedings of the Fourth All India Maratha History Seminar, May 1979.

Shastry, B. S., *Studies in Indo-Portuguese History*, Bangalore, 1981.

Shirodkar, P. P., "Slavery in Coastal India", *Purabhilekh-Puratatva*, vol. III, no. 1, Jan.-June 1985, pp. 27-43.

_____, "The Concept of Trade and Commerce during the Portuguese Regime", *Purabhilekh-Puratatva*, vol. II, no. 1, Jan.-June 1984, pp. 25-45.

Siddiqi, Asiya "Some Aspects of Indian Business under the English East India Company", *State and Business in India : A Historical Perspective*, (ed.) Dwijendra Tripathi, New Delhi, 1986, pp. 78-90.

_____, "The Business World of Jamsetjee Jejeebhoy", *IESHR*, vol. XIX, nos. 3 & 4, July-Dec. 1982.

Silva Rego, Antonio da, *O Ultramar Português no Seculo XIX (1834-1910)*, 2ª edição, Lisboa, 1966.

_____, *Portuguese Colonization in the Sixteenth Century : A study of the Royal Ordinances*, Johannesberg, 1959.

Simkin, C. G. F., *Traditional Trade of Asia*, London, 1968.

Singh, O. P., *Surat and its Trade in the Second Half of the 17th Century*, Delhi, 1976.

Souza, George Bryan, *The Survival of Empire. Portuguese Trade and Society in China and South China Seas, 1630-1754*, Cambridge, 1986.

Souza, Teotonio R. de, "A Study on the Indo-Portuguese Coinage and the Working of the Goa Mint", *Indian Numismatics Chronicle*, 1975, pp. 67-72.

_____, *Essays in Goan History*, New Delhi, 1989.

_____, "Glimpses of Hindu Dominance of Goan Economy in the Seventeenth Century", *Indica*, vol. XII, 1975, pp. 27-35.

_____, "Goa-based Seaborne Trade in the Early Seventeenth Century", *IESHR*, vol. XII, 1975, pp. 433-442.

_____, "Goa-Mahe Trade Links (Late 18th - Early 19th Centuries): A new Source Material", *Studies in Maritime History*, (ed.) K. S. Mathew, Pondicherry, 1990, pp. 165-174.

_____, (ed.), *Goa Through the Ages, An Economic History*, vol. II, New Delhi, 1989.

_____, (ed.), *Indo-Portuguese History, Old Issues, New Questions*, New Delhi, 1984.

_____, "Marine Insurance and Indo-Portuguese Trade History : An Aid to Maritime Historiography", *IESHR*, vol. XIV, no. 3, July-Sept. 1977, pp. 377-384.

_____, *Medieval Goa*, New Delhi, 1979.

_____, "Mhamai House Records : Indigenous Source for Indo-Portuguese Historiography", *Instituto de Investigação Cientifica Tropical*, Lisboa, 1985.

_____, "The Afro-Asian Church in the Portuguese Estado da India", *African Church Historiography : An Ecumenical Perspective*, (ed.) Ogbu U. Kalu, Nairobi, 1986.

_____, "Xenddi Tax : A Phase in the History of Luso-Hindu Relations in Goa, (1704-1841)" *Studies in Foreign Relations of India*, (ed.) Q. M. Joshi, Hyderabad, 1975.

Spate O. H. K. and Learmonth, A. T. A., *India and Pakistan : A General and Regional Geography*, Metheun, 1967.

Steensgaard, Niels, *The Asian Trade Revolution of the Seventeenth Century, The East India Companies and the Decline of the Caravan Trade*, Copenhagen, 1975.

Stephens, H. M., *Portugal*, London, 1908.

Strandes, Justus, *The Portuguese Period in East Africa, (transl.)* Jean F. Wallwork, (ed.) J. S. Kirkman, Nairobi, 1971.

Subrahmanyam, Sanjay, *Improvising Empire : Trade and Settlement in the Bay of Bengal, 1500-1700*, Delhi, 1990.

_____, (ed.), *Merchants, Markets and State in the Early Modern India*, Delhi, 1990.

Subramaniam, Lakshmi, "Bombay and the West Coast in the 1740s", *IESHR*, vol. XVIII, no. 2, April-June 1981.

Tabela Estatistíca de Goa, 1849.

Tavernier, *Jean-Baptiste, Travels in India,* (transl.) V. Ball, 2 vols., London, 1925.

Teles, Domingos, "Alguns alemães, holandeses e outros estrangeiros em Goa", *Colloquium,* vol. 2, no. 1, Jan.-June 1979.

The Cambridge Economic History of India, 2 vols., New Delhi, 1982/ 1984.

The Compilation Group, *The Opium War,* for the "History of Modern China Series", Peking, 1976.

The Suma Oriental of Tomé Pires, (ed.) Armando Cortesão, Reprint, New Delhi, 1990.

The Travels of Abbe Carré in India and the Near East, (transl.) Lady Fawcett, (ed.) Sir Francis Fawcett, vol. 1, New Delhi, Reprint, 1990.

The Travels of Pietro Della Valle In India, no. LXXXIV, vol. 1, Letter 1, From Surat March 22, Anno 1622, Works issued by The Hakluyt Society, London.

The Voyage of J. H. Linschoten to the East Indies, 2 vols., London, 1885.

Thomaz, Luis Filipe F. R., "Factions, Interests and Messianism : The Politics of the Portuguese Expansions in the East, 1500-1520", *IESHR* vol. XXVIII, no. 1, Jan.-March 1991, pp. 97-109.

Tori, Michelguglielmo, "In the Deep Blue Sea : Surat and its Merchant Class during the Dyarchic Era, 1759-1800", *IESHR,* vol. 19, nos. 3-4, July-Dec. 1982.

Torie, João Stuart da Fonseca, *Relatorio do Serviço de Saude do Estado da India Portuguesa Relativo ao Anno de 1879,* vol. 1, Nova Goa, 1880.

Tripathi, Amales, *Trade and Finance in Bengal Presidency, 1793-1833,* Calcutta, 1979.

Tripathi, Dwijendra, (ed.), *State and Business in India A Historical Perspective,* New Delhi, 1987.

Viljoen, Stephen, *Economic Systems in World History,* London, 1974.

Wallerstein, Immanuel, "Incorporation of Indian Subcontinent into Capitalist World-Economy" *Economic and Political Weekly,* January 25, 1986.

_____, The Modern World System - I, *Capitalist Agriculture and the Origins of the European World Economy in the Sixteenth Century,* New York, 1974.

_____, *The Modern World System - II, Mercantilism and The Consolidation of the European World Economy, 1600-1750,* New York, 1980.

Weber, Max, *General Economic History* (transl.) Franck H. Knight, New York, 1961.

White, David L., "Parsis in the Commercial World of Western India, 1700-1750", *IESHR*, vol. XXIV, no. 2, April-June 1987, pp. 183-203.

Whiteway, R. S., *The Rise of the Portuguese Power in India, 1497-1550,* London, 1890/1967.

Winius, George D., and Diffie Bailey, *Foundations of the Portuguese empire, 1415-1580*, Minnesota, 1977.

_____, "Jewel-Trading in Portuguese India in the XVI and XVII Centuries", *Indica*, vol. 25, no. 1, pp. 15-34.

_____, *The Fatal History of Portuguese Ceylon, Transition to Dutch Rule*, Cambridge/Masachussetts, 1971.

_____, "The 'Shadow Empire' in the Bay of Bengal", *Itinerario*, vol. VII, no. 2, 1983, pp. 83-101.

Xavier, Carlos "Daman Port and Shipyards (1800-1875)", *Purabhilekh-Puratatva,* vol. III, no. 1, Jan.-June 1985, pp. 7-25.

Xavier, Felippe Nery, *Collecção de Bandos e Outras Differentes Providencias Que Servem de Leis, Regulamentos Para O Governo Económico e Judicial Das Provincias Denominadas das Novas Conquistas,* 2 vols., Pangim, 1840-50.

_____, *O Gabinete Litterario das Fontainhas*, vols. I and II, Nova Goa, 1847.

INDEX